OKLAHOMA TRACKMAKER SERIES

OKLAHOMA TRACKMAKER SERIES

Oklahoma Heritage Association
Trackmaker and Horizons Committee, 1996

ALFRED P. MURRAH

Alfred P. Murrah

OKLAHOMA TRACKMAKER SERIES

AMERICAN JURIST: THE LIFE OF JUDGE ALFRED P. MURRAH

by
Von Russell Creel
Bob Burke
and
Kenny A. Franks

Series Editor: Gini Moore Campbell

Published for the Oklahoma Heritage Association
by Western Heritage Books 1996

Library of Congress Catalog Number: 96-067015

Manufactured in the United States of America for the Oklahoma Heritage Association, Oklahoma City.

ISBN: 0-86546-090-6

DEDICATION

Oklahoma experienced its Day of Infamy on April 19, 1995 when a car bomb destroyed the Alfred P. Murrah Federal Building in Oklahoma City with loss of life in the hundreds. There is a terrible irony that this act of brutality and cruelty, an act the antithesis of the rule of law, should have been directed at a building honoring a man for whom the rule of law was the foundation stone of any just social order. For more than three decades, Murrah devoted his intellect and his spirit to preserving and maintaining the proper balance between liberty and order. The bombing was an assertion that this tension can never be satisfactorily struck. Murrah's life was a ringing affirmation that it can be and that it must be.

Murrah's great heart would have grieved for those who perished. His unbounded sense of compassion would have enveloped all those who mourned. His righteous indignation would have demanded swift, certain, and stern punishment for those duly tried and convicted of a deed which was unalloyed evil.

As Murrah would have been saddened and angered by the senseless violence which in the blinking of an eye changed a peaceful spring day into a day from Hell, he would also have been incredibly proud of how Oklahomans responded to the tragedy. Murrah's sense of community was deep and abiding. He loved Oklahoma City and its people. Particularly after he became chief judge with its attendant administrative responsibilities, it would have been easier to live in Denver, but the Murrahs simply could not bring themselves to leave Oklahoma City. After the bombing, the thousands who flocked to donate blood, the volunteers who spent days in an increasingly heart-breaking task, the senior citizens and the school children who gave the widow's mite, and the allowance to help the victims all evinced that sense of community which was so central to Murrah's being.

April 19, 1995 confronted Oklahomans with a choice. They could succumb to the evil which had been done, or they could overcome evil with good. Unhesitatingly, they chose to overcome. In the days after this crime against the innocents, Oklahomans demonstrated in full measure that they are a courageous, determined, compassionate people, qualities which were abundantly manifest in Murrah's life as well. And anyone who knew Murrah knows that his spirit was with Oklahoma City in those days of trial and grief.

As of October 10, 1995, there were 169 confirmed fatalities, 168 of whom have been identified. This book is dedicated to the memory of all those who perished in the April 19, 1995 bombing of the Alfred P. Murrah Federal Building. *Requiescat in pace.*

Aleman, Lucio
Alexander, Teresa
Allen, Richard Arthur
Allen, Ted Leon
Almon, Baylee
Anderson, Rebecca *
(* Nurse who died during rescue)
Argo, Pamela
Avery, Sandy
Avillanoza, Peter Robert
Battle, Calvin Coolidge
Battle, Peola
Bell, Danielle
Bender-Long, Rheta Ione
Biddy, Oleta Christine
Bland, Shelley DeAnn
Blanton, Andrea Yvette
Bloomer, Olen Burl
Boldon, Renee
Boles, James Everett
Bolte, Mark
Booker, Casandra
Bowers, Carol Louise
Bradley, Peachlyn
Brady, Woodrow
Broxterman, Paul Gregory
Bruce, Gabreon
Burgess, Kimberly
Burkett, David Neil
Burns, Donald Earl
Campbell, Cynthia
Carrillo, Michael
Carr, Karen Gist

Chafey, Rona
Chavez, Zachary
Chestnut (Wood), Sharon L.
Chipman, Robert
Chumard-Reese, Terry
Clark, Kimberly Kay
Clark, Margaret L.
Cooper, Anthony C.
Cooper, Antonio
Cooper, Dana Leanne
Cottingham, Harley
Coverdale, Aaron
Coverdale, Elijah
Coyne, Jaci
Creagan, Kathrine L.
Cummins, Richard L.
Curry, Steven Douglas
Daniels, Brenda
Davis, Benjamin Laranzo
Day, Diane Lynne
DeMaster, Peter L.
Deveroux, Castine (Brooks)
Dillow (Cousins), Kim Robin
Driver, Sheila
Eaves, Taylor
Eckles, Ashley
Ferrell, Susan Jane
Fields, Carol
Finley, Kathy A.
Fisher, Judy JoAnn (Froh)
Florence, Linda Louise
Fritzler, Lee Donald
Fritzler, Mary Anne
Garrett, Tevin
Garrison, Laura
Genzer, Jamie
Gottshall, Kevin Lee
Griffin, Ethel
Guiles, Juretta Colleen
Guzman, Randolph
Haddock, Kayla Marie
Hammon, Cheryl
Harding, Ronald Vernon
Harrison (Goodson), Margaret
Hawthorne, Thomas, Sr.
Higginbottom, Doris Adele
Hightower, Anita
Hodges, Thompson Eugene
Holland (Jenkins), Peggy L.
Hollingsworth (Althouse), Diane
Housley, Linda Coleen
Howard, George Michael
Howell, Wanda
Huff, Robin
Hurlburt, Anna Jean
Hurlburt, Charles
Ice, Paul Douglas
Jenkins, Christy
Johnson, Norma Jean
Johnson, Raymond Lee
Jones, Larry James
Justes, Alvin
Kennedy, Blake Ryan
Khalil, Carole Sue
Koelsch, Valerie
Kreymborg, Carolyn Ann
Lauderdale, Teresa
Leinen, Catherine Mary
Lenz, Carrie Ann
Leonard, Donald Ray
Levy, Lakeshu
London, Dominique
Loudenslager, Michael Lee
Luster, Aurelia
Luster, Robert

Maroney, Mickey B.
Martinez, Gilberto X.
Martin, James Kenneth
McCarthy, James Anthony
McCullough, Kenneth Glenn
McGonnell, Betsy Janice
McKinney, Linda
McKraven, Cartney
Medeans, Claude Arthur
Meek, Claudette
Merrell, Frankie Ann
Miller, Derwin Wade
Mitchell, Eula Leigh
Moss, John Clayton, III
Nix, Patricia Ann
Parker, Jerry Lee
Randolph, Jill Diane
Reeder, Michelle Ann
Rentie, Mary
Reyes, Antonio Castillo
Ridley, Kathryn
Rigney, Trudy
Ritter, Claudine
Rosas, Christine
Sanders, Sonja
Scroggins, Lanny
Seidl, Kathy Lynn
Sells, Leora Lee
Shepherd, Karen
Smith, Chase
Smith, Colton
Sohn, Victoria
Stewart, John Thomas
Stratton, Delores
Tapia, Emilio
Texter, Victoria
Thomas, Charlotte
Thompson, Michael G.
Thompson, Virginia
Tomlin, Rick L.
Treanor, Luther Heartman
Tumer, Larry LaVern
Valdez, Jules
Van Ess, John
Wade, Johnnie Allen
Walker, David Jack
Walker, Robert Nolan
Watkins, Wanda Lee
Weaver, Michael Don
Welch, Julie Marie
Westberry, Robert G.
Whicher, Alan G.
Whittenberg, Jo Ann
Williams, France
Williams, Scott Dwain
Williams, William Stephen
Wilson, Clarence
Woodbridge, Ronota
Worten, Tresia
Youngblood, John

WITH APPRECIATION

Writing a book is an excellent way to incur debts of gratitude. Certainly, this work is no exception. Requests for assistance were met cheerfully, and even with interest. For this, a heartfelt thank you is in order.

Financial assistance: The Kerr Foundation; the Hatton W. Sumners Foundation; Richard E. Coulson; Dallas and Chris Ferguson; J. Hugh Roff, Jr.; and Richard J. Gore.

Research assistance: Kellye Bates; Eric Dabney; Shayna Kirby; Kristin Lynch; Jerry Brown; Lorinda Holloway; and Cindy Wilson.

Manuscript preparation: Gini Campbell; Ann Aldrich; Vickey Cannady; Victoria Martinez; Sandy Cowden; Debbie Smith; and Karen Harris.

Archival materials: Janice Mathews and Todd Kosmerick of the Carl Albert Congressional Research Center of the University of Oklahoma; Dianna Litvak of the Colorado Historical Society; Fran Deathe, Oklahoma City University Law Library; Rosalee Nath, County Treasurer, Grady County, Oklahoma; Pat Gaines, Court Clerk, Seminole County, Oklahoma; Margie Jones, Deputy Court Clerk, Seminole County, Oklahoma; the staffs of the Franklin D. Roosevelt and Lyndon B. Johnson Presidential libraries; the staff of the National Archives; the staff of the Kansas Historical Society; Scott Dowell and Delbert Amen of the newspaper archives division of the Oklahoma Historical Society; Jim Hopper and David Cox of the office of United States Senator David L. Boren; Carol Campbell, Melissa Hayer, Robin Davison, and Mary Phillips, the Oklahoma Publishing Company library.

Computer assistance: Vickey Cannady; Sandy Cowden; Pam Ray; and Sid Terry, Jr.

Special assistance: Senior United States Circuit Judge William J. Holloway, Jr.; Senior United States District Judge Howard C. Bratton; Senior United States District Judge Warren K. Urbom; former United States District Judge Harold Tyler, Jr.; Professor Richard E. Coulson, Oklahoma City University School of Law; Mrs. Betty Pate, secretary to Judges Alfred P. Murrah, Sr., and William J. Holloway, Jr.; Professor Michael Gibson, Oklahoma City University School of Law; Bernard Price, Oklahoma City University School of Law; Peter F. Breitenstein; Robert J. Pickett; Richard F. Pickett; Fred Gipson, Legal Counsel, University of Oklahoma; Charles Baker; and Professor Daniel Gibbens, University of Oklahoma College of Law.

CONTENTS

ILLUSTRATIONS

ALFRED P. MURRAH

1
Heritage: "The Short and Simple Annals of the Poor"[1]

For Judge Alfred Paul Murrah, Sr., "Irishman" was "the highest salutation."[2] Although Murrah's life was lived far from the land of Parnell and Joyce, his Irish lineage was a matter of great pride. When, in the 18th century, his forebears left the old country and crossed the Atlantic for a better life in a new land, journey's end was the Carolinas.

The 1790 decennial census found Charles Murrah, Alfred Paul's great, great grandfather, living in Warren County, North Carolina. The household consisted of Murrah, his wife Margaret, and six children, three sons and three daughters. Murrah owned no slaves.[3] The sons included Charles's namesake, Charles, Jr., who married Avarilla Jones, and, moving to Georgia, continued the Murrah trek westward. Numerous children were born to this union, including William, circa 1820. While William was still an infant, the family moved westward yet again, this time to Alabama, residing at various times in Bibb, Taladega, and Coosa counties.

William and Nancy Ann Bean married in the 1840s. Shortly after the Civil War, William, Nancy Ann, and their five children left Alabama for Texas. Tragedy ended the journey in Mississippi, however, when William and Nancy Ann became ill, probably from yellow fever, and died. Three of the children returned to Alabama, while Mary and her younger brother, George Washington, continued the journey to Texas.

Settling in the vicinity of Granbury, Mary wed J.B.

Waldrup, a rancher. George Washington lived with his sister and brother-in-law until he also married. He and his bride, Lucy Elizabeth James, then crossed the Red River and located in Indian Territory.[4] Their perigrination took them to Earl, a now extinct community, which was located in the Chickasaw Nation[5] three miles north of Mannsville in present-day Johnston County.[6]

Earl was surrounded by such rough and rugged terrain that the area was called Devil's Den. From this inhospitable soil, Murrah attempted to eke a living for his growing family. In time, five children were born to George Washington and Lucy, three of whom lived to adulthood. The birth of their fifth child on July 16, 1901 was followed on August 25, little more than a month later, by the death of Lucy, leaving George Washington with three children to rear, the youngest an infant and the oldest but seven years old.[7]

Murrah's first widowhood ended with his marriage to Lanora M. Simmons. Born March 8, 1874, she was some 10 years younger than her husband. For a time Murrah and his new bride continued to live at Earl, and it was there on October 27, 1904, that Alfred Paul Murrah was born. Shortly after Alfred Paul's birth, the family moved to present-day Grady County. Except for a six-mile-wide strip of land north of the 98th Meridian, Grady County also is located in what was the Chickasaw Nation.[8]

The Murrahs settled near the town of Verden, "one of the richest farming centers of the state."[9] Verden is close to Camp Napoleon where in May 1865 representatives of the Five Civilized Tribes and various Plains Indians met to discuss problems arising from the Civil War. The principal product of the meeting was agreement that "an Indian shall not spill the blood of an Indian."[10]

George Murrah found work on the Half Moon Ranch, a large cattle spread started by W.G. "Caddo Bill" Williams.[11] The 1907 tax roll for Shirley Township lists George Washington Murrah as owning personal property with an equalized value of $110 and paying a tax of $3.30. In 1909 his personal property had increased in assessed value to $352 and his taxes to $8.69, but in 1910 his property had decreased in assessed value to $235 and his taxes to $2.71. In 1912 his property was assessed at $142, and his taxes were $2.88.[12]

Shortly after Alfred Paul's third birthday, the state of Oklahoma was born November 16, 1907, from the union of Oklahoma and Indian territories. Murrah's life during his childhood was what one would expect for a young boy in rural Oklahoma during the first years of statehood. Doing chores and helping around the house as he became older, sporadically attending Tennessee and Gilbert schools, and caring for and playing with younger brothers George and Elmo were the fabric of his daily life, a fabric which was rent February 20, 1912, when Lanora died.[13]

For a time, the family remained in Oklahoma. Willie Mae, George Washington's daughter by his first marriage, cared for the younger children and the home. Then about 1913 or 1914, George Washington returned to Alabama. Alfred Paul and George accompanied him, while Elmo remained with relatives in Grady County.

In Alabama, George Washington purchased a 40-acre dirt scrabble farm and married Callie Cobb Lowery, a widow with three children. One son, Cecil, was born to the marriage. Life was hard on this poor farm, the days filled with hauling logs from a swamp to the mill, chopping cotton, and doing other field work. There was little time for school or recreation. Days, months, and years passed in this fashion until death claimed George Washington Murrah in 1920. An orphan at 15, Alfred Paul found himself with few prospects but the life of a dirt farmer in the rural South of the early 20th century.

However, Murrah was not to spend his life trapped in the poverty common to many Deep South farmers. He attended his father's funeral and then began "riding the rails." In fact, family legend says that his stepmother gave him forty dollars to leave. Whatever the motivation, Murrah traveled through a great part of the southern United States in boxcar accommodations. He supported himself by selling newspapers in Memphis, Tennessee, washing dishes in Miami, Florida, and selling household items door-to-door in Little Rock, Arkansas.

Murrah's days as a knight of the road ended when, stopping in Alabama long enough to take George in tow, he boarded a freight train carrying a piece of farm equipment to Oklahoma. The brothers hid under the machinery, and their journey went smoothly until, in the early hours of a cold fall day, the train arrived in Oklahoma City. In the Santa Fe yards, one of the train's crew discovered the boys and rudely evicted them. Years later when he was successful, affluent, and powerful, Murrah still remembered how "lonely, hopeless, friendless and miserable I felt that night as I limped along, afoot in a strange city, with not a soul in it that I knew or who cared for me."[14]

The brothers made their way to Verden where they visited their mother's grave and were reunited with their sibling and other relations. As had his father before him, Murrah found work at the Half Moon Ranch. Earning 50 cents an hour and room and board, he mowed alfalfa, baled hay, and shocked wheat. By season's end he had managed to save $315 and bought his first pair of long pants.

While working at the Half Moon, Murrah read a biography of Abraham Lincoln and joined the legions of boys who have been inspired by the life of the Great Emancipator. Until then, as Murrah acknowledged, he had been "just a child of fate."[15] However, after reading how

Lincoln attained an education and became an attorney, he decided "that if Lincoln could do that, I could do it too."[16] By way of beginning, Murrah decided to return to school and earn his high school diploma. As a preparatory step, he borrowed school books from the children of Daddy Sparks, foreman of the Half Moon, in an attempt to fill the sizable gaps in his formal education occasioned by his less than stable family life over the past few years.

With the coming of fall and the approach of a new school year, Murrah went to Tuttle, a community in the northeastern part of Grady County, to seek admission to high school. There was an appropriateness in a future lawyer and judge selecting Tuttle as his home, for the town had been conceived in controversy and delivered in litigation.[17]

Located near Silver City, a one-time authentic Old West cow town, and the South Canadian crossing of the famed Chisholm Trail, Tuttle was named for James Harley Tuttle, an early settler of Indian Territory and one of the largest cattle buyers in the Chickasaw Nation at the turn of the century.[18] The third decade of the 20th century saw Tuttle becoming more urbane in its ways. In 1923 the town council adopted ordinances prohibiting the keeping of swine in certain parts of town, making it unlawful for the owner or keeper of ducks, chickens, and guineas to allow their fowl to run at large, and imposing a 9:00 p.m.-to-4:00 a.m. curfew for persons under the age of 18 years. The town marshal was enjoined "each night to ring a bell, which may be heard over the Town of Tuttle, which shall be a warning to all persons under the age of 18 to vacate the streets."[19]

Arriving in Tuttle, Murrah's first task was to find a way to earn a living. He approached a family named MacPhail and told them his ambitions. The MacPhails took Murrah at face value and made his aspirations their

Above: A focal point of community life in Tuttle was the school. Left: Murrah as a high school senior.

own. For milking six cows daily, Murrah received the room and board that were so crucial to his educational hopes. Equally important, the MacPhails gave him the emotional and psychological support he needed to prove himself, for they treated this unknown youngster as if he were kith and kin.

His next task was to gain admission to high school. This was a formidable challenge, for Murrah's nomadic existence had left him short of the necessary credits. Murrah tackled the problem directly, going to S.P. Smith, the principal, and making the case that if given the chance he would succeed. Whether persuaded by Murrah's eloquence or exhausted by his persistence, Smith admitted Murrah, telling him to prove himself. And he did.

In time, Murrah secured additional employment when Virgil Gannaway, owner of the Star Pharmacy, hired him as a soda jerk. Murrah opened the store at 7:00 a.m., swept and dusted, carried water from the town pump for the soda fountain, went to school at 9:00 a.m., returned and worked during the noon hour, came again after school, and worked until 11:00 p.m. Study time was between customers and after working hours. Doing all this, Murrah still managed to make the school debate team.[20] At the end of the first semester, a man in Chickasha offered to adopt Murrah and give him a high school and college education. Smith advised Murrah that the offer was a good one, and Murrah agreed, but stated that he was determined to earn his education.[21]

The pharmacy was a courtroom as well, for Gannaway was justice of the peace. Observing trials from his vantage point behind the counter strengthened Murrah's determination to become a lawyer—maybe even someday a justice of the peace.

Attending school, doing chores, working at the Star Pharmacy, and being part of a loving and caring family, Murrah settled quickly and comfortably into the life of Tuttle. One important aspect of community life was politics, and Murrah's years in Tuttle spanned one of the most turbulent periods of Oklahoma's turbulent political history.

From the earliest days of statehood, Oklahoma had been receptive to movements of the disaffected, disadvantaged, and dispossessed. The period 1907-1914 saw the Socialist Party of America make significant electoral gains in the Sooner State. Beginning with a vote of 9,740

Above and below: The Star Pharmacy, where Murrah worked as a soda jerk and dreamed of being a lawyer and justice of the peace, is still in business in Tuttle.

(3.89%) in the 1907 gubernatorial election,[22] the Socialists increased their vote totals until 1914 when their gubernatorial nominee received 42,703 votes (20.77%) in an election in which the winning candidate garnered only 39.65% of the vote.[23] That same election, Socialists elected one state senator, five state representatives, and scores of county officials. In Roger Mills County the Socialists captured all three seats on the board of county commissioners, the county governing body, and also elected the county judge, county treasurer, county assessor, and county weigher.[24] Then came Sarajevo and the onset of World War I, and the Socialist Party of Oklahoma plunged headfirst into political insignificance. In 1916 the five Socialist representatives lost their bids for second terms,[25] and in 1918 the Socialist count for governor fell to a mere 7,438 ballots (3.83%), fewer in raw votes and smaller in percentage than in 1907.[26] After this the Socialist Party ceased to be a factor in state politics.

Unhappiness with the two major political parties, Democratic and Republican, in Sooner State politics did not perish with the houses of Habsburg, Hohenzollern, and Romanov, however. It merely slumbered. In the years immediately following the Great War, economic adversity and political conflict stirred anew the forces of discontent and dissent, this time in the form of the Farmer-Labor Reconstruction League. As noted Oklahoma historian Angie Debo has written:

> Now in the postwar deflation, Oklahoma was again ready for a radical movement. In the fall of 1921 farmers, laborers, former Socialists, and Non-Partisan adherents met in convention at Shawnee and formed the Farmer-Labor Reconstruction League. They drew up a platform advocating public ownership or regulation of utilities,

Two of Murrah's early benefactors in Tuttle were Mr. and Mrs. Virgil Gannaway. He gave Murrah a job, and she gave him a book authored by Josh Lee. Virgil Gannaway appears in this photograph with Edna L. Cecil, one of his clerks.

mills and grain elevators; a state-owned central bank and reduction of tenantry by credits to farmers and home builders; tax exemption on farm improvements and equipment; labor legislation; and free schoolbooks.[27]

In 1922 John Callaway "Jack" Walton, running with the League's endorsement, easily won the Democratic nomination for governor, and then overwhelmed Republican nominee John Fields in the November general election.[28] Walton's tenure in the governor's office was brief, however, for in his first year he was impeached, convicted, and removed.[29]

The League was a topic of lively interest in Tuttle. The *Tuttle Times* was strongly supportive,[30] while the *Tuttle News* was as strongly opposed.[31] Another organiza-

The backboard and fountain area are the same as when Murrah worked at the pharmacy.

tion, the Ku Klux Klan, also was making its presence felt in Oklahoma during this time. In August and September of 1922 the *Tuttle News* reported that Methodist and Baptist revival services had been visited by Klansmen who made donations and then "silently withdrew."[32]

The years passed quickly, and in May of 1923, 25 seniors graduated from Tuttle High School. The class president and valedictorian was the student who had not been able to attend until he persuaded the principal that he was worthy of admission, Alfred Paul Murrah.[33] In Smith's judgment, Murrah possessed "the keenest and brightest mind of any pupil that ever came to me."[34]

Murrah's residence in Tuttle ended a few months later when he left to attend university. He had lived in Tuttle only a few years, but thereafter he was "from Tuttle." Mrs. MacPhail would always be Mother MacPhail, the mother who scolded him, encouraged him, prayed for

The present owners of the Star Pharmacy, Jim and Ann Arganbright.

him, and counseled him as he struggled to find his way in life. Her photograph would grace his chambers until the day of his death. A quarter of a century after the MacPhails took Murrah into their family, he would write that he could not keep an appointment because Mrs. MacPhail was seriously ill and expressed confidence that "you will appreciate the fact that a seventy-seven year old pioneer who gave an orphan boy a chance when he needed it comes first."[35] The MacPhail family had shaped his "life for future service."[36]

Sharing another's sorrow at the death of a loved one,[37] recommending for the U.S. Naval Academy the son of a teacher "who helped me in many ways,"[38] contributing to the refurbishing of the Christian Church parsonage,[39] and delivering the high school commencement address[40] were a few of the ways Murrah expressed his continuing interest in this small town which had played so large a part in

Murrah did not travel outside the United States until he was in his sixties. Then, typically, he took an around-the-world trip. Not surprisingly, one of the stops was Ireland where he kissed the Blarney Stone.

his life.[41] In Tuttle, Murrah had "acquired the fundamentals of manhood which have sustained me when the chips were down and the stakes were high."[42] Tuttle was a place with traditions, "traditions that have held us close to our churches and standards of decency in a society so prone to abandon them."[43]

2
"Of Campus Beautiful By Day and Night Of Colors Proudly Gleaming Red and White"[1]

Established December 19, 1890, by act of the territorial legislature, the University of Oklahoma is located in Norman, the seat of Cleveland County[2], in central Oklahoma. When classes began in September of 1892, enrollment was simple. Each student met with the president, Dr. David Ross Boyd, to obtain a schedule and then was examined by the faculty of four. The entire listing of courses "was printed on one page."[3] Because none of the first enrollees qualified as degree candidates, the university initially functioned as a college preparatory school. Not until 1907 did baccalaureate candidates outnumber non-degree students.

The political turbulence of the 1920s did not leave the university unscathed. Convinced with a "determination that bordered on madness" that all state agencies were subject to his personal fiat, Governor Walton launched his "first frontal assault" against the University of Oklahoma. He was successful in pressuring President Stratton D. Brooks to resign, but failed in his attempt to replace Brooks with R.L. "Battle Axe" Glover, "a radical agitator from the Rush Springs area."[4]

After a brief interim presidency under James S. Buchanan, who succeeded "in keeping the University on track during two critical years,"[5] the regents, after "many months of public wrangling,"[6] named Dr. William Bennett

Murrah was a member of the University of Oklahoma chapter of Lambda Chi Alpha. He is on the back row, fourth from the left.

Bizzell, president of Texas Agricultural and Mechanical College, as the university's fifth president. Bizzell was the holder of seven earned degrees and "a scholar of the first rank."[7] His presidency would be marked by solid, constructive leadership during many trying times, including the Great Depression.

When Murrah traveled the few miles from Tuttle to Norman, however, his concerns were not academic freedom and institutional responsibility, but how to pay for the education he desperately wanted and sorely needed. Tuition was free for state residents, but room, board, and books were not. Board started at six dollars a week, and rooms began at approximately eight dollars a month.[8] Murrah's solution was his customary one: work.

Selling himself, he persuaded C.T. Land, owner of The Smoker, to hire him as a clerk. The Smoker was a

Murrah represented his fraternity on the Interfraternity Council. He is pictured on the top row, second from right.

cigar and tobacco store located at 127 East Main Street with a diverse patronage—students, politicians, farmers, mechanics, judges, and professional men. Something of a Norman institution, it became a debating society when the customers and clerks gathered around the depot stove in winter or the tables in summer to cuss and discuss the great and not so great issues of the day. Working at The Smoker gave Murrah an opportunity to learn by listening, and to practice and improve his speaking and debating skills.

One of the many people Murrah met at The Smoker was A.C. Bushnell, a division manager for Ligget and Myers Tobacco Company. Bushnell hired Murrah to distribute free Chesterfield cigarettes on campus because of his many acquaintances among students and faculty. Tackling the job with his usual enthusiasm, Murrah even smuggled cigarettes into the women's dormitories.

Murrah also earned money as a clothing salesman. T. Jack Foster, a Norman lawyer and politician, had pur-

Murrah's campus activities included the Jazz Hounds. In this photograph he is seated on the front row on the far left.

chased a tailor shop that was on the brink of financial disaster. Foster hired Murrah to be his salesman. During the academic year the business prospered, and in summer months Murrah put his expertise to good use working for Paul's Clothing Store in Oklahoma City.

Murrah used work as a passport to the classroom and then followed that by work in the classroom. As a student in the college of arts and sciences, Murrah took courses in English, mathematics, Spanish, geology, government, military science, public speaking, art, psychology, history, physical education and economics.[9]

Working and studying took many hours, but there still was time for extracurricular activities. Murrah joined Lambda Chi Alpha fraternity, served on the interfraternity council, was a member of the student congress, and played with the Jazz Hounds, although he did not become head hound, trail hound, or keeper of the bones.[10]

In 1925 a student could enter the college of law after completing two years, or sixty hours, of college work. At the completion of a three-year law curriculum, the student would receive the bachelor of laws degree.[11] Murrah planned to do this as he finished the second semester of the 1924-1925 academic year, but first he had to deal with the ever-present problem of money.

Finding a job selling high school jewelry, he went to Holdenville with a letter introducing him as "My friend and fellow-townsman Fish Murrah. I don't know what he has up his sleeve, but whatever it is, you can be assured that he is honest and trustworthy. I recommend him without reservation or apology." In three weeks, Murrah earned $650 which "meant the difference between going to school that year and staying out and probably never going back."[12]

The law school had admitted its first students in 1909. As dean, the regents had selected Julien C. Monnet, then a faculty member at George Washington University in Washington, D.C. Born in Iowa, Monnet had B.A. and LL.B. degrees from the University of Iowa. After practicing in Iowa and North Dakota for a number of years, he returned to the University of Iowa, earned a master's degree, and then entered the LL.B. program at Harvard Law School, from which he graduated *cum laude* and law review. He taught at George Washington University for one year, and then accepted the deanship of the newly created law school of the University of Oklahoma, a position he would hold until his retirement in 1941.[13] The other full-time faculty members in 1925 were John Begg Cheadle, Victor Henry Kulp, Joseph F. Francis, William Braden Swinford, and Ather H. Huggins.[14]

Monnet had a lasting influence on Murrah's life. Murrah constantly referred to himself as one of the "dean's boys," and he presided at a 1948 dinner honoring Monnet for his many contributions to his adopted state.[15] Monnet was a frequent visitor to Murrah's chambers, and his

Stately Monnet Hall was the home of the University of Oklahoma School of Law during Murrah's student days. A yearly rivalry was the attempt by the engineers to paint the owls on the building green, and the efforts of the law students to prevent such an act of desecration. In 1995, University of Oklahoma President David L. Boren announced that the law school would return to its ancestral seat.

photograph held a place of honor alongside Mrs. MacPhail's. Murrah never tired of quoting Monnet that "No institution can be greater than the traditions that cluster about it."[16] On the dean's death, Murrah wrote, "He symbolized everything that is fine and good—in and out of the law."[17]

In the 1920s most attorneys in Oklahoma with law degrees were graduates of the University of Oklahoma Law School. Consequently, its impact on the bench and bar of the state was far-reaching. Kulp, Monnet, and Cheadle taught at the university until retirement, and in

Murrah was a member of Phi Alpha Delta legal fraternity. In this photograph he is on the back row, fifth from the left.

the process they trained a generation of Oklahoma lawyers and judges. The curriculum was traditional. Murrah took contracts, torts, property, criminal law, legal bibliography, agency and partnership, evidence, mortgages, equity, pleading, bills and notes, wills, sales, damages, corporations, trusts, practice court, constitutional law, conflict of laws, and suretyship. Preparing for practice in Oklahoma, he also took courses in Indian land titles and oil and gas. With the exception of an A in criminal law, his grades were Bs and Cs.[18]

Taking an active part in law school activities, Murrah joined Phi Alpha Delta legal fraternity and the Blackstone Bar. He also served as vice president and president of the League of Young Democrats.[19] Completing his requirements in the spring semester of 1928, he received the Bachelor of Laws degree on June 5.[20]

Murrah's college education had not come easy. He had worked at anything and everything to stay in school and complete his degree. Even then, finances had been tight. One year, taking the traditional trek to Dallas for the O.U.-Texas weekend, he had gone to the game, attended a dance, and then, his finances of five dollars exhausted, "ate some raw turnips at Pauls Valley before I got back to the home base."[21]

Murrah's interest in the well-being of his alma mater never waned. Once when the unexpected resignations of two law school faculty members created a problem of covering classes for the administration, Murrah stepped in and taught Property I. He had to "arise at six in the morning, catch an interurban for an eight to ten class and return to my office in Oklahoma City to carry my load on the court."[22] Learning that Professors Cheadle and Kulp were receiving salaries that were a "disgrace,"[23] Murrah became their advocate. For his "clients," he obtained David Ross Boyd professorships with improved financial compensation.[24]

Murrah's most lasting contribution to the university, however, was his chairmanship of the Law Center Commission. Constituted in January 1969, this was a "blue ribbon" panel, its members including Justice Tom C. Clark and Erwin Griswold, former dean of the Harvard Law School and solicitor general of the United States.[25] Murrah approached the work of the commission with the commitment of a realistic visionary. He challenged his colleagues to grasp the dimensions of the task before them. For Murrah, their charge was no less than to study and define the mission of legal education at the University of Oklahoma well into the 21st century:

> Since our meeting last Monday I have been gravely concerned lest we fail to grasp the conceptual dimensions of the Law Center. As I indicated just as we were leaving, we seem to be more concerned about the preservation of the status quo than the establishment of a Law Center to serve the future needs of this state. The Regents and the

Above: The 1928 graduating class of the University of Oklahoma School of Law. Murrah is on the second row, seventh from the left. Below: The 1928 graduating class of the University of Oklahoma School of Law on its 30th anniversary. Murrah is seated on the first row, third from the left.

Administration have said that our Law Center shall be great, and I am determined to take them at their word. Our 'Whereases' are more negative than they are affirmative. Let's lift our eyes to the hills and meet the challenge.[26]

As a whole, the commission lacked Murrah's breadth of vision, and its accomplishments were circumscribed accordingly. Nevertheless, its work was not without significance. The future of legal education in Oklahoma was the subject of thoughtful and searching scrutiny, the University of Oklahoma Law Center was created and built, and—an important recommendation of the commission which was adopted—the law school was treated as a separate entity distinct from the rest of the university for budgetary purposes.

The ripple effects of a deed sometimes extend far into the future. The commission numbered among its members David L. Boren, a young lawyer and state representative from Seminole. Boren, the son of former Fourth District Congressman Lyle H. Boren, held degrees from Yale, Oxford, and the University of Oklahoma. Boren so impressed Murrah that in 1970 he nominated Boren, then 29, for the presidency of the university. In his letter of nomination, Murrah, as was his wont, put a volume of thought into a minimum of words:

> I presume to suggest the name of David Boren for the presidency of the University of Oklahoma.
>
> Although he has never been a school administrator, that may be in his favor. He is a brilliant young man with both feet solidly on the ground. He has youth—indeed, he may be too young, but God forbid for we need young men to bridge the generation gap without leading us to destruction. I sincerely believe that Boren can do it.[27]

Murrah's support was not sufficient to carry the day, and the appointment went to another. Boren then turned his considerable abilities to other goals. In 1974, after

Murrah and long-time University of Oklahoma law professor Victor H. Kulp. The occasion was the 25th anniversary of the Class of 1928.

starting his campaign with a name recognition of less than two percent, Boren was elected governor, defeating the incumbent as well as a popular and well-known congressman and a state senator from Tulsa. In 1978 he became the first—and to date the only—sitting Oklahoma governor to be elected to the United States Senate. His winning percentages in 1984 (76) and 1990 (83) are Oklahoma records, as is the number of precincts he carried in 1990, 2,352 of 2,354.[28] In April of 1994 he announced his resignation from the senate effective in November 1994 to become—and surely Murrah would have been pleased—president of the University of Oklahoma.[29]

Murrah was an avid fan of Sooner sports, especially football. He was a charter member of the Touchdown Club, and he would hurry home from his frequent meetings "to get back for the game."[30] On his travels he was constantly on the alert for a new running back or defensive lineman for the Big Red. One day he took a "thirty minutes recess from court to talk an East Denver High boy into coming to O.U."[31] Watching one of his "recruits," Charles Baker, score a touchdown, Murrah wrote that it "surely

Left: First dean of the University of Oklahoma School of Law, Julien C. Monnet served in that position for more than 30 years. For Murrah, Monnet "symbolized everything that is fine and good—in and out of the law."

Right: President William Bennett Bizzell, president of the University of Oklahoma during Murrah's student days, and one of the university's greatest leaders.

was gratifying to see my boy sweeping in for pay dirt."[32]

Because of Baker, Murrah was close to the greatest tragedy in the history of the University of Oklahoma. A plane crash took the lives of 23 Naval Reserve Officers Training Corps cadets from O.U.[33] Baker was a NROTC cadet as well, and in the days following the crash he stayed at the Murrah home while attending the funerals. The Murrahs acted as surrogate parents in that sad and difficult time.[34]

On more than one occasion, O.U. took note of Murrah's long list of contributions to the university and the state. He was selected for honorary membership in the university's Phi Beta Kappa and Order of the Coif chapters, and in 1949 he was asked to deliver the commencement address. The Distinguished Service Citation, the university's highest honor, came to him in 1954.

College was a watershed experience for Murrah. But as with high school, it was a mile marker, not the final destination.

3

"I Started to Practice Law in...a Klondike Oil Town."[1]

Admitted to the bar June 5, 1928,[2] the same day he received his law degree, Murrah practiced for a brief time with Gomer Smith, Sr. in Oklahoma City.[3] He then formed a partnership with Leo J. Williams, another young man admitted to the bar in 1928,[4] and opened an office in Seminole, Oklahoma.[5]

There was no better place in 1928 for two novice, struggling lawyers to hang their shingles. Seminole was a country town of fewer than a thousand people in the 1920s. All this changed when, in the waning hours of July 16, 1926, Fixico No. 1, drilled by Robert Garland for the Independent Oil and Gas Company, struck black gold. Soon the well was gushing 5,000 barrels a day, and the Seminole oil field was born.

Overnight the sleepy village became the quintessential boom town. The fewer-than-a-thousand became 35,000. Thirty-first in population of Oklahoma's 77 counties in 1920, Seminole was third in 1930, trailing only Oklahoma and Tulsa counties. Drillers, tool pushers, roughnecks, roustabouts, land men, merchants, gamblers, and women of loose morals came in droves.

New businesses—lumber yards, oil field supply houses, hotels, tourist courts, and hamburger joints—crowded the Seminole landscape. The one block Main Street became six blocks with numerous side streets. None were paved, and with the rains came the mud. Mule trains, wagons, cars, and pedestrians traveled at their peril. In fact, the drowning of a mule team owned by Oklahoma Gas and

Above and below: Murrah's Klondike town of Seminole during the height of the oil boom. Murrah took to the wild and woolly atmosphere of Seminole like a duck to water, defending drunks, ladies of the night, and others who ran afoul of the ubiquitous constable and the greedy justice of the peace.

Electric Company brought Murrah some legal work when the Internal Revenue Service rejected the utility's claim for a deduction. OG&E "had a team of mules pulling some transformers through the center of town, and they fell down, and both of them drowned. So the IRS, as is their custom, didn't believe it, and so we had to get Judge Murrah to make an affidavit about the dead mules."[6]

In the second quarter of 1927 the Seminole post office set a world record for money order sales—$361,308. The Rock Island Railroad station was second in the nation for amount of freight handled—more than a million dollars a month—and oil field payrolls were staggering. In June of 1928 the sum "was over $600,000 a week and was expected to reach the million dollar mark" before year's end.[7]

Sleeping space was a commodity much in demand. Enterprising owners rented the roofs of their buildings to those needing forty winks. Men slept under pool tables while games were in progress, snoring to the click of the balls. Cots were rented, two men to a cot, for eight-hour shifts. Bed bugs and soiled linen were the order of the day.

Bishop's Alley, conveniently located outside the city limits, offered attractions frowned upon by polite society. Beer joints, dance halls, gambling dens, and houses of prostitution flourished. There were some 56 night clubs, including the Blue Heaven, the Palace, and the Skinner. Lucille Sawyer, queen of Bishop's Alley, ran a boarding house with 25 young women as "permanent guests." Queen Lucille, it was said, could out-drink, out-gamble, and out-cuss any man alive.[8]

"The city of Seminole...in its roaring heyday...set a record of a bigger and better hell-on-earth never surpassed in Oklahoma oil history."[9] It was a town made for lawyers.

Seminolians literally lived in the shadow of Black Gold.

Williams and Murrah appear to have handled whatever came through the door—damage suits sounding in negligence,[10] felony cases,[11] suits for injunctive relief,[12] actions for accounting and foreclosure of liens,[13] and motions for provisional relief against interference with property interests.[14] Divorce and separate maintenance actions were staples of the firm's caseload.[15] In what may be the first newspaper story about Murrah as a lawyer, the *Seminole Morning News* reported that he appeared for one James Rodwick charged with car theft:

HELD FOR CAR THEFT

Though Found in Car Man Is Sure of Tale That He Was Passenger

James Rodwick, who is alleged to have stolen a Chrysler car, belonging to J.F. Burney, late Saturday night and to have driven it to Shawnee where he was captured with the car a few hours later was held in $2,500

> bond when he appeared before J.W. Fowler, justice of the peace, yesterday.
>
> Rodwick alleged that he did not steal the car but that he was given a ride to Shawnee by another man.
>
> He said that when they reached Shawnee the other man said that he was going in search of an all night garage and that he would be right back.
>
> He claims that when arrested he was not even sitting under the wheel but was simply sitting in the car and waiting for the man to return. A.P. Murrah local attorney is defending Rodwick.[16]

In time, Rodwick pleaded guilty and received a five-year sentence.[17]

Murrah's usual relationship with the bad guys was that of lawyer and client. Occasionally, it was more threatening:

> One night, coming through an alley, I was held up and robbed of $250. The next day an account of it was in the paper and soon thereafter a noted bandit of the day, whom I had defended, came into my office, threw $250 on the table and said, "Murrah, I'm sorry," and walked out.[18]

For whatever reason, the firm of Williams and Murrah did not last long. On July 4, 1929, Murrah and Luther Bohanon, a graduate of the University of Oklahoma College of Law admitted to the bar in 1927[19] who had practiced in Oklahoma and Texas, met under a shade tree over a few bottles of Choctaw beer purchased at Grace's. The result was the law firm of Murrah and Bohanon which would last until Murrah went on the bench—and a friendship which would be dissolved only by death.

For a time the new partners slept in their office and washed in cold water from the lavatory because rooms were almost impossible to find, and they could not afford them in any event. They handled suits on promissory notes and breach of contract actions,[20] property damage

As far as the eye could see, the Seminole landscape was dominated by oil derricks.

cases,[21] actions on debts,[22] lien and mortgage foreclosures,[23] cases sounding in wrongful detention of property,[24] suits on insurance policies,[25] proceedings to dissolve a corporation,[26] divorce cases,[27] and negligence actions.[28] Murrah's clients included few with "Inc." or "Co." in their name, but many Bear Graceys and Rat Gills.[29]

Not all clients came through the door. Murrah's office was above a justice of the peace court. More than 25 years after his Seminole days, Murrah recalled that when law officers brought in a catch of oil field workers for summary "justice," they began "hollering for me as the deputy sheriffs led them up the alley to the court."[30] Murrah's experiences with justice of the peace justice in Seminole

And we think traffic congestion is bad today.

left a deep and lasting impression. It was "a farce—a vicious thing."[31]

Two areas came to dominate Murrah's practice: negligence cases and workmen's compensation claims. In a negligence case the plaintiff must show that he was injured because of the defendant's failure to exercise due care under the circumstances. Deciding if a defendant has breached the governing standard of care requires close attention to the facts, and the attorney's persuasiveness in presenting the client's version of what happened may carry the day. Murrah's ability to relate to a jury and to present the plaintiff's case in a convincing and forceful manner served him well in this type of litigation. Negligence cases were filed in the state district, superior, and common pleas courts or in federal district court if the adverse parties were of diverse state citizenship, e.g., a plaintiff citizen of New Mexico suing a defendant citizen of Oklahoma, and a certain monetary sum was in controversy.

Workmen's compensation was a statutorily created remedy for employees in enumerated employments who sustained injuries in the course of and arising from their employment. First enacted in Oklahoma by the fifth legislature in 1915, liability was imposed without fault,

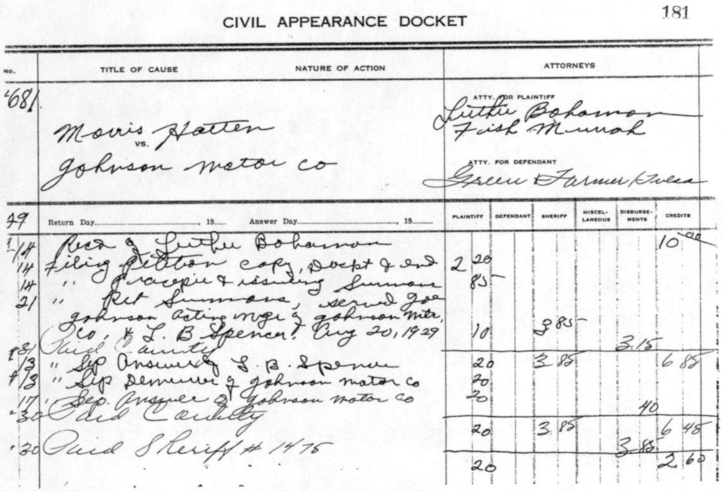
181

CIVIL APPEARANCE DOCKET

NO.	TITLE OF CAUSE	NATURE OF ACTION	ATTORNEYS
4681	Moris Hatten vs. Johnson Motor Co		ATTY. FOR PLAINTIFF Luther Bohanon, Fish Murrah; ATTY. FOR DEFENDANT Green & Farmer

Return Day........ 19.... Answer Day........ 19....

PLAINTIFF | DEFENDANT | SHERIFF | MISCELLANEOUS | DISBURSEMENTS | CREDITS

Docket sheet from Seminole County for one of the first cases filed by the law firm of Murrah & Bohanon. Murrah is identified by his nickname of Fish.

and the traditional common law defenses of contributory negligence, assumption of the risk, and fellow servant doctrine were abrogated. The balance having been struck heavily in favor of the employee, the primary counterbalancing factor was a statutory limitation on the amount of recovery. Additionally, claims for death were not cognizable in workmen's compensation until the state constitution was amended in 1950. This was because article XXIII, section 7 of the constitution provided that damages recoverable for wrongful death could not be limited by statute.[32]

Compensation claims were not tried in the district, superior, or common pleas courts. They were heard by a three-member commission whose members were appointed by the governor for definite terms subject to confirmation by the state senate. Compensation awards were reviewable by the state supreme court in an original proceeding.

Besides practicing law, the partners engaged in various business ventures. Many of these prospered, and Murrah and Bohanon became increasingly affluent. In 1931 they moved their practice to Oklahoma City, although they maintained an office in Seminole for a time. Their business continued to increase, and J.I. Gibson, Leonard Savage, George McElroy, and Joe Fred Gibson joined them in the practice.

Murrah and Bohanon also began to dabble in politics. In 1934 they were active in the campaigns of three men who were running for district judge in Oklahoma and Canadian counties. The three—Clarence Mills, George Giddings, Jr., and Ben Arnold—won their races.[33] Murrah's ventures into politics would prove very successful, and the long-term consequences would extend far beyond having three friends elected state district judges.

As the years passed, Murrah and Bohanon's practice became more diversified. The firm represented more corporations and did more of the staid and sedate aspects of civil practice, e.g., breach of contract cases and corporate work. But workmen's compensation remained the bedrock of the firm's caseload. Indeed, with two exceptions, every Murrah and Bohanon case decided by the state supreme court was a workmen's compensation case.[34] The two exceptions were a bar disciplinary proceeding in which they represented the lawyer,[35] and a suit on an insurance policy as Murrah was leaving the firm.[36]

And that was the way Murrah wanted it. Representing the man injured on Wewoka Avenue between Highland and University streets by the defendant's negligence[37] or the oil field worker whose foot and leg were crushed when they were caught between a swivel and swivel ball on a drilling rig was what the practice of law should be.[38]

For some, handling personal injury litigation and criminal defense work is akin to having a social disease. Not for Murrah. Proudly he wrote that he represented "drill-

This photograph of the Murrahs was taken during their honeymoon.

ing contractors, roughnecks, whores and bootleggers, until they decided to put me on the bench."[39]

Attending a social event at O.U., Murrah met Agnes Milam during a tag dance. Milams (originally Mileham) came to Virginia at least a half century before the War of Independence. Agnes's great-great-great-grandfather Benjamin Milam fought with the colonists, was captured at the Battle of Guilford Courthouse in North Carolina, and died a British prisoner.[40]

Milams went sundry directions from the Old Dominion. Born in Wisconsin May 3, 1907, Agnes and her family moved to Oklahoma City while she was a young child. Almost immediately tragedy struck when her father was killed in an accident. Her mother Maude sup-

Mrs. Murrah was an accomplished golfer. This photograph was taken following her second hole in one in a six-month period. (Published in the Daily Oklahoman *on July 17, 1940. Courtesy Oklahoma Publishing Company.)*

ported Agnes and her older brother and sister by teaching school. Agnes graduated from Central High School, and then earned her baccalaureate degree from the University of Oklahoma in 1927. She too became a teacher. Murrah and Milam dated for some six years. They shared a love of dancing, and she was attracted to the young student and lawyer by his piercing blue eyes and gentlemanly manner.

When they married June 29, 1930, it was over Maude's objection, although she later became reconciled to the match. Only Bohanon and Agnes's sister attended the ceremony at St. Luke's United Methodist Church in Oklahoma City.[41]

Following a honeymoon to Carlsbad Caverns, El Paso, and Juarez, the newlyweds established their first home at 1120 Bedford Drive in the Nichols Hills section of Oklahoma City. Three children were born to the marriage: Ann in 1931, Alfred Paul, Jr. in 1933, and Sue in 1937.

Because Agnes did not like her given name, family members called her Baby as she was the last born in her family. Murrah shortened it to Babe, and the name stuck. She was Babe to one and all. Always busy as wife and mother, Babe was also active in civic affairs and was an accomplished bridge player and golfer. In one six-month period, she had two holes-in-one at the Oklahoma City Golf and Country Club.[42]

For forty-five years the Murrahs would be married. Whenever Murrah spoke of his lovely and gracious bride, it was with infinite love and obvious pride. In happiness and sadness, good health and sickness, trial and triumph, she sustained, supported and loved him. She was, in every sense of the word, a lady.

In choosing a partner in life and a law partner, Murrah was exceptionally fortunate. Perhaps this was because he realized

> that practicing law and being married are alike—you share each others triumphs and trials and tribulations. You must learn to share them together, work together, overlook each others faults, and keep your eye on the doughnut and not on the hole.[43]

4

"I want to be Federal Judge more than anything else in the world."[1]

Completed in 1931 at a cost of $3 million, the Ramsey Tower at 200 North Robinson was a prestigious Oklahoma City professional building.[2] In 1935 Murrah and Bohanon leased a suite of offices for an annual rental of $2,400.[3] From his windows on the 14th floor, Murrah could see the railroad yard where he and George had been tossed from the freight car many years earlier. In physical distance, it was but a stone's throw from the railroad tracks to the Ramsey Tower. In adversity, achievement and accomplishment, it had been many long, hard miles, but the journey was not to end with a successful and lucrative law practice.

When Oklahoma was admitted to the Union, it was divided into two federal judicial districts, the eastern (Indian Territory) and the western (Oklahoma Territory),[4] each authorized one judge.[5] Oklahoma has the distinction of being the only state in the history of the Republic to have more than one federal judicial district when it became a state.[6]

The first judge of the western district was John H. Cotteral,[7] while the eastern district post went to Ralph E. Campbell.[8] Cotteral and Campbell had been Republican nominees for the state supreme court in 1907.[9] Unsuccessful during this period of Oklahoma history when Democrats dominated state-wide elections, they received federal judgeships as consolation prizes. In this instance, the consolation prize was better than first place.

The Ramsey Tower in Oklahoma City where Murrah & Bohanon had offices on the 14th floor when Murrah was appointed to the newly created roving federal district judgeship for the Northern, Eastern, and Western Districts of Oklahoma. The building was constructed in 1931 at a cost of $3 million and was located at 200 North Robinson. (Courtesy Oklahoma Historical Society.)

Campbell served until 1918 when he resigned to return to private practice. Over the strong opposition of organized labor, President Woodrow Wilson appointed retiring Governor Robert Lee Williams to the vacancy. Williams served almost two decades on the eastern district bench. A bachelor, Williams was of irascible temperament, and it is said that lawyers who felt the brunt of his disposition were known to remark that Williams was never married and neither were his parents.

Williams is unquestionably in the first rank of Oklahoma's legal and political leaders. He was a member of the state constitutional convention, first chief justice of the state supreme court, and the state's third governor. The state capitol was built during his administration without a hint of graft or corruption. A major force in the Oklahoma Historical Society for years, he also was a philanthropist of note. The imprints he left on Oklahoma history were deep, lasting, and constructive.[10]

In 1922 a second judgeship was added to the eastern district.[11] The appointment went to Franklin E. Kennamer from Madill in Marshall County.[12] Kennamer was a rarity in the early days of statehood, a Republican from southern Oklahoma. In 1920 he had done his party duty and run for the state supreme court. Benefitting from the Warren G. Harding landslide—and probably to his surprise—he won, as did the three other GOP supreme court candidates.[13] The four were the first Republicans ever elected to Oklahoma's highest civil appellate court.[14]

Having Williams and Kennamer in the same district was like trying to mix oil and water. It does not work. Williams and Kennamer were both natives of Alabama, and both had been justices of the Supreme Court of Oklahoma, but there the similarities ended. One was a yellow-dog Democrat, the other a yellow-dog Republican. Williams "did not welcome Kennamer's appointment,"[15] and matters did not improve with time. The "tension...became so intense...that Congress was persuaded to create a new district for Kennamer."[16] That is how the northern district, carved from 12 counties in the eastern and western districts, came to be.[17] Williams stayed in the eastern district, Kennamer went to the northern district, and civility returned to the federal bench in Oklahoma. Such is the logic of judicial district line drawing.

Tragedy came to Kennamer's life in 1935 when his son Phil was convicted of manslaughter and sentenced to 25 years imprisonment.[18] Paroled for military service in World War II, Phil Kennamer died a paratrooper's death in France in 1944.[19]

After 20 years on the trial bench, Judge Cotteral was

appointed to the circuit court of appeals in 1928.[20] His successor as district judge was Edgar S. Vaught, an eminently successful Oklahoma City attorney and prominent Republican.[21]

This was the composition of the Oklahoma federal bench in 1936 when congress created a fourth judgeship for the state.[22] The new judgeship was unique in Oklahoma's history, because the occupant would be a roving jurist, i.e., he would be commissioned in all three districts, the eastern, the northern, and the western. Never before—or since—has the selection of a federal judge in Oklahoma generated the public attention and media coverage which this one did. Who would be the new federal judge was front page news on an almost daily basis for three months.

Life tenure and the nonreducible annual salary of $10,000 made the new judgeship, as one newspaper aptly described it, the "year's juiciest Democratic plum,"[23] and there was no shortage of putative plum pickers. United States Senator Elmer Thomas told the department of justice in mid-September 1936 that there were "thirty applicants for the place; all members of the Supreme Court save one are in the list."[24] By November the number had grown to 40.[25]

Because at all pertinent times the national administration and the state's federal senators were Democratic, the process by which the 40 would be winnowed to one was straightforward. The senators would submit names to the department of justice for investigation and evaluation. From those deemed qualified, the senators would make a formal recommendation to the attorney general. The attorney general would join the senators in sending that person's name to the president, and, barring the most unusual circumstances, he would be the nominee.

When the judgeship bill became law in June of 1936,

Oklahoma's United States Senators were Thomas P. Gore and Elmer Thomas, both well-established political figures in the state. Gore had been chosen in 1907 as one of the state's first two United States senators.[26] Winning full terms in 1909[27] and 1914,[28] he was defeated in 1920 largely because of his opposition to Wilsonian foreign policy.[29] In 1930 he made a comeback and won the state's other senate seat.[30]

Elmer Thomas had been elected to the first Oklahoma state senate[31] and served as president pro tempore in the 1911 session.[32] Nominated for congress from the sixth district in 1920, Thomas had been defeated in the Harding landslide.[33] He ran again and won in 1922[34] and in 1924.[35] In 1926 he defeated incumbent United States Senator J.W. Harrell,[36] and won a second term in 1932.[37]

No significant steps to fill the new judgeship occurred during the summer of 1936 because Senator Gore was in a hotly contested reelection campaign. Fighting for his political life, Gore knew better than to do something which would make one person happy and a hundred angry. When the dust settled from the July 7th primary, Gore was no longer a factor in selecting the new judge. Finishing fourth, he did not make the second primary.[38]

The July 28th runoff pitted freshman fifth district Congressman Josh Lee against Governor E.W. Marland. Lee trounced Marland,[39] and then easily defeated Republican nominee Herbert K. Hyde in the November general election.[40] The equation had changed from T(homas) + G(ore) = J(udgeship) to T(homas) + L(ee) = J(udgeship).

Yet another Alabamian by birth, Joshua Bryan Lee had added "his own middle name after hearing the Great Commoner."[41] Shortly before statehood, his family moved to southwest Oklahoma. A gifted public speaker, Lee received his bachelor's degree from the University of Oklahoma in 1917, joined the faculty as an instructor in

Murrah with the two men who launched his judicial career in 1937, United States Senators Elmer Thomas (on Murrah's right) and Josh Lee (on Murrah's left), on the day after President Roosevelt sent Murrah's name to the senate. (Published in the Oklahoma City Times *on February 9, 1937. Courtesy Oklahoma Publishing Company.)*

the speech department, and became chairman two years later. In time, he earned a master's degree in political science from Columbia University and a law degree from Cumberland while becoming Oklahoma's "most popular after-dinner speaker."[42] Elected to congress in 1934, his race for the senate two years later was "a dazzling performance. His promises were generous: 'A Farm for Every Farmer, and a home for Every Family.' His practiced wit never deserted him as he glad handed his way across the state, ignoring his opponents and slashing the 'Old Deal' Republicans."[43]

As the state's senior United States Senator—and one in good stead with the Franklin D. Roosevelt administration—Thomas's position warrants close attention. That position may be surprising at first blush, but it made good sense. If Lee had a candidate who was acceptable to labor, agriculture, and the drys, the political constituencies Thomas deemed important, and who was considered qualified by the justice department, then Thomas would "be forced to concede to Senator-elect Lee."[44] The reason for Thomas deferring to Lee lay with the calendar, the political calendar.

Thomas would be a candidate for a third term in 1938, and there was good cause to expect the race would be the most difficult of his senate campaigns. Governor Marland, who had lost to Lee in 1936, likely would be a candidate again, and he would run with the backing of the statehouse machine. Oklahoma City attorney Gomer Smith, Sr., who barely missed edging Marland for a runoff spot in 1936 and who had won a special election in 1937 for the fifth district congressional seat when Congressman R.P. Hill died,[45] also was eyeing the race. Smith was a stem-winding orator and vice president of the Townsend Clubs, "the group that agitated on behalf of Dr. Francis Townsend's scheme of granting every old person $200

Josh Lee on the campaign trail. The brotherly, though sometimes strained, relationship between Lee and Murrah had a profound impact on the political and legal landscape of the Sooner State.

monthly."[46] Smith had also received nationwide publicity in 1936 when he defended Roosevelt against an attack by Gerald L.K. Smith.[47]

Thomas could not have too many friends in 1938, and he read the 1936 election returns to show that the "Lee Organization...represents a vast majority of the democratic citizens of the State."[48] What better way to gain Lee's support—or at least his benevolent neutrality in 1938—than by giving him first choice on the judgeship?

There was none, and that is what Thomas did. As one newspaper reported:

> Senator-elect Josh Lee and Sen. Elmer Thomas will try to agree before the end of this week on a Democratic lawyer for Oklahoma's new federal judgeship—and he will be Lee's man.... Practical politics dictate that Senator Thomas should take such a course.[49]

If—and only if—Lee's choice or choices faltered would Thomas push for the selection of his own candidate. If that occurred, Thomas would advance the claims of Fletcher Riley.[50]

Fletcher Riley was from Comanche County, Thomas's home county. Elected to the state supreme court in 1924 when he was in his early thirties,[51] Riley won second and third terms in 1930[52] and 1936.[53] His career had not been without controversy, including impeachment in 1929.[54] However the articles of impeachment had been dismissed,[55] and his reelection victories in 1930 and 1936 suggested that the voters did not take the matter too seriously.

Riley had an unquenchable thirst for the federal bench. As early as January of 1935, a year and a half before the roving judgeship bill passed, Riley had written Thomas seeking a federal judicial appointment. What Riley really wanted was an appellate judgeship, but he informed Thomas that he was willing to serve a district court "apprenticeship...with the hope that I may...move on after a short duration."[56]

Because of Thomas's approach, the judgeship ball was in Josh Lee's court, and it is pellucidly clear what he wanted. A.P. Murrah was his first choice, and if Murrah fell by the wayside, then Royce Savage was his second choice. As early as November 9, 1936, less than a week after the general election, a United Press story reported, "The No. 1 man on U.S. Sen.-elect Josh Lee's list of probable appointees to the new federal judgeship is A.P.

(Fish) Murrah, youthful Oklahoma City attorney who helped manage his campaign."[57] At this time Senator Thomas wrote, "I know that [Lee] favors some more than others, and among the first is a young lawyer from Oklahoma City, A.P. Murrah, and second is a young attorney from Tulsa, Royce Savage."[58] The young professionals who had supported Lee so ably and enthusiastically in 1936 were known as Rover Boys, and Murrah and Savage, as Rover Boys of the first order, held high title deeds to Lee's friendship and patronage.

While Murrah was living in Tuttle, Mrs. Irma Gannaway, wife of the Star Pharmacy owner, had given him a book of poetry authored by Lee. Murrah was so taken with the work that he memorized the entire volume. Murrah had heard Lee speak in Grady County, and he had taken courses from him at the University of Oklahoma. In the front line of Lee's backers in the 1934 congressional race, Murrah bore primary responsibility for Lee making the "iffy" 1936 senate race. One journalist noted "that Murrah pushed Lee into the senate race against Lee's own best judgement, when the junior senator was not at all certain he wanted to give up a sure house seat for a possible senate position."[59] Having pushed Lee into the contest, Murrah had been unstinting with his advice, time, and money to insure that the campaign was successful.

Murrah initially supported Ben Arnold for the appointment,[60] but Arnold was never a serious contender because he did not have the call on Lee's support that Murrah and Savage did. By the end of 1936 Murrah was for Murrah.[61]

Savage was from Blanco in Pittsburg County. He had debated for Lee at O.U., and had introduced Lee when he announced his senatorial candidacy in a state-wide radio broadcast. Admitted to the bar in 1927, Savage was in practice in Tulsa with Eugene Monnet, a son of Dean

Monnet. His chances were not hurt by the fact that he and a son of Thomas were fraternity brothers.

The 40 names for the appointment quickly became three: Murrah, Savage, and Riley. The judgeship was Murrah's to lose, while Savage's chance depended on Murrah, and Riley's chance on Murrah and Savage, faltering.[62]

Murrah and Savage tried not to be perceived as adversaries. Murrah wrote Lee that he had offered to step aside in favor of Savage but that Savage had insisted that he, Murrah, should receive the appointment.[63] For his part, Savage said he was willing "to withdraw in favor of Murrah."[64] This did not keep friends of Savage from urging his nomination, however. Adding to this drama within a drama was the fact that Leonard Savage, who practiced law with Murrah, was the brother of Royce Savage.

Murrah's strategy was twofold. First, he would convince Thomas that he was the popular choice for federal judge in Oklahoma. Second, he would persuade the justice department that he was qualified to be a federal judge. The first part of the strategy would be accomplished by inundating Thomas with expressions of support.

In December of 1936 the Oklahoma City Trades and Labor Council, representing street car and railroad engineers, post office employees, locomotive firemen and engineers, teachers, printers, retail clerks, sheet and metal workers, typographical employees, office workers, and bakers endorsed Murrah.[65] Additional support came from railway organizations in Pottawatomie County,[66] the McCurtain County Veterans of Industry of America,[67] the Brotherhood of Railroad Trainmen,[68] miners and other labor groups in LeFlore County,[69] Local 293 of the International Brotherhood of Boilermakers, Ironship Builders, Welders and Helpers of America,[70] and Local 180 of the

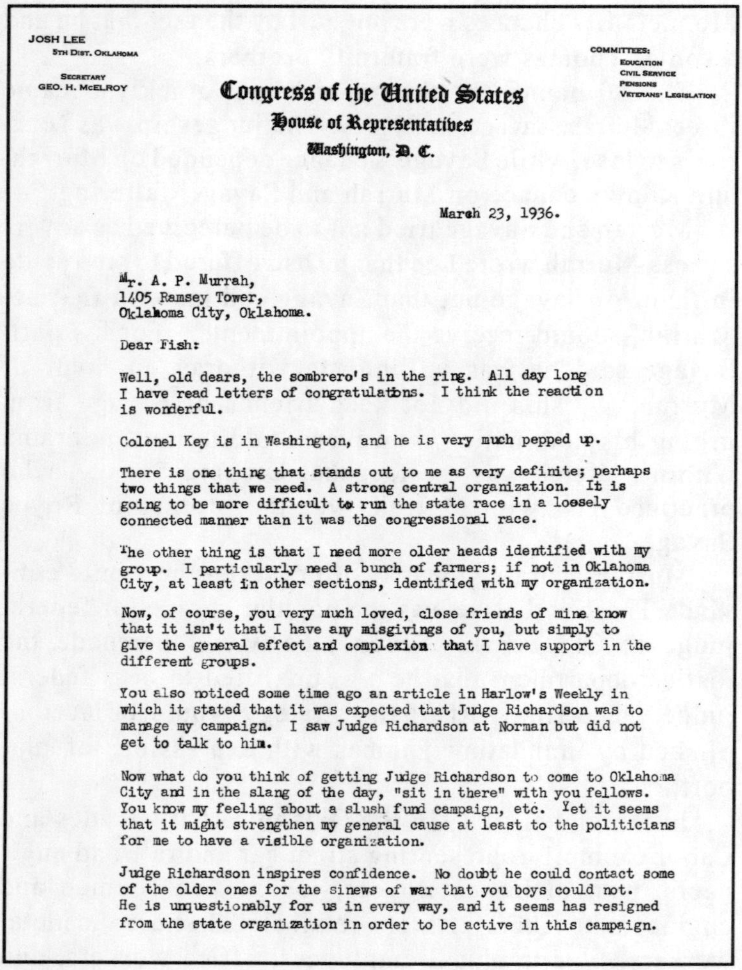

JOSH LEE
5TH DIST. OKLAHOMA

SECRETARY
GEO. H. McELROY

COMMITTEES:
EDUCATION
CIVIL SERVICE
PENSIONS
VETERANS' LEGISLATION

Congress of the United States
House of Representatives
Washington, D. C.

March 23, 1936.

Mr. A. P. Murrah,
1405 Ramsey Tower,
Oklahoma City, Oklahoma.

Dear Fish:

Well, old dears, the sombrero's in the ring. All day long I have read letters of congratulations. I think the reaction is wonderful.

Colonel Key is in Washington, and he is very much pepped up.

There is one thing that stands out to me as very definite; perhaps two things that we need. A strong central organization. It is going to be more difficult to run the state race in a loosely connected manner than it was the congressional race.

The other thing is that I need more older heads identified with my group. I particularly need a bunch of farmers; if not in Oklahoma City, at least in other sections, identified with my organization.

Now, of course, you very much loved, close friends of mine know that it isn't that I have any misgivings of you, but simply to give the general effect and complexion that I have support in the different groups.

You also noticed some time ago an article in Harlow's Weekly in which it stated that it was expected that Judge Richardson was to manage my campaign. I saw Judge Richardson at Norman but did not get to talk to him.

Now what do you think of getting Judge Richardson to come to Oklahoma City and in the slang of the day, "sit in there" with you fellows. You know my feeling about a slush fund campaign, etc. Yet it seems that it might strengthen my general cause at least to the politicians for me to have a visible organization.

Judge Richardson inspires confidence. No doubt he could contact some of the older ones for the sinews of war that you boys could not. He is unquestionably for us in every way, and it seems has resigned from the state organization in order to be active in this campaign.

International Brotherhood of Bookbinders.[71] Oklahoma Farming[72] and the Farmer's Union added agriculture's voice to that of labor.[73]

The temperance movement was a potential weak spot, however. One newspaper story predicted that Murrah's chances might be hurt because of his "alleged moist tinge."[74] These concerns were enough to cause Mrs. Alice

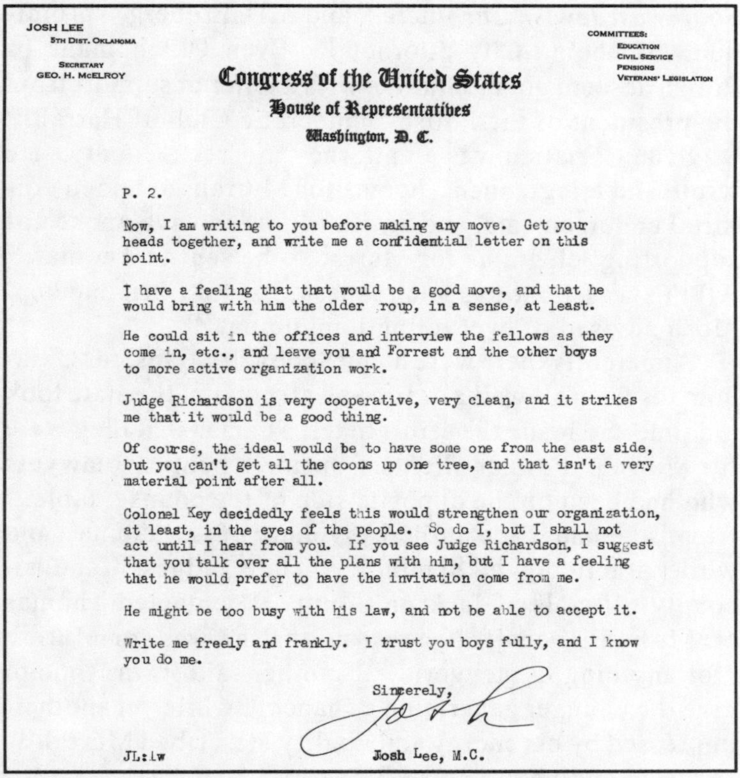

JOSH LEE
5TH DIST. OKLAHOMA

SECRETARY
GEO. H. McELROY

COMMITTEES:
EDUCATION
CIVIL SERVICE
PENSIONS
VETERANS' LEGISLATION

Congress of the United States
House of Representatives
Washington, D. C.

P. 2.

Now, I am writing to you before making any move. Get your heads together, and write me a confidential letter on this point.

I have a feeling that that would be a good move, and that he would bring with him the older roup, in a sense, at least.

He could sit in the offices and interview the fellows as they come in, etc., and leave you and Forrest and the other boys to more active organization work.

Judge Richardson is very cooperative, very clean, and it strikes me that it would be a good thing.

Of course, the ideal would be to have some one from the east side, but you can't get all the coons up one tree, and that isn't a very material point after all.

Colonel Key decidedly feels this would strengthen our organization, at least, in the eyes of the people. So do I, but I shall not act until I hear from you. If you see Judge Richardson, I suggest that you talk over all the plans with him, but I have a feeling that he would prefer to have the invitation come from me.

He might be too busy with his law, and not be able to accept it.

Write me freely and frankly. I trust you boys fully, and I know you do me.

Sincerely,

JL:lw

Josh Lee, M.C.

In this letter to Murrah shortly after announcing his senatorial candidacy (left and above), Lee expresses the need to have some "older heads" identified with the campaign.

M. David, state organizer for the Women's Christian Temperance Union, to withhold her endorsement.[75] This problem, which could have been a serious obstacle to Murrah's success, was met by supporting letters from the executive secretary of the United Drys, Methodist and Baptist pastors, and sundry church members.[76]

The Jewish community expressed its approval of Murrah in letters from Samuel D. Friedman, editor of the

Southwest Jewish Chronicle,[77] and A.D. Erdberg, a prominent Oklahoma City attorney.[78] Even Oklahomans of Polish descent got into the act with a letter of support from the president of the Polish Democratic Club of Harrah.[79]

Sebe Christian was an attorney in Creek County. He wrote and telegraphed Thomas for Murrah, obtained editorial endorsements, and arranged for an "avalanche" of supporting telegrams for Murrah to be sent to Thomas.[80] All this was done "as you requested," and Christian kept "Josh advised of everything I am doing."[81]

Apparently there were many Sebe Christians, for Oklahomans from all walks of life and all parts of the state took the time and made the effort to tell Thomas that they were for Murrah. Former clients,[82] business people,[83] lawyers who had been on the opposite side of the counsel table,[84] friends he had made at the University of Oklahoma[85] and while practicing in Seminole,[86] state judges,[87] and all county officials of Jackson County,[88] contacted Thomas on Murrah's behalf. One wrote that he was for Murrah "for anything in the world,"[89] another said it was time to give the younger generation a chance,[90] while yet another, impressed by his energy and vitality, described Murrah as "a steam engine in pants."[91]

Grady County was not reticent about its favorite adopted son. E.L. Harvey, justice of the peace at Verden, Ben Johnson for whom Murrah had worked at the Half Moon Ranch, and S.P. Smith, Murrah's high school principal, all took pen in hand for the youngster who had asked only a chance to succeed and, when given it, had.[92]

Other supporters were not so general. Some adopted a quid pro quo approach to Thomas—support Murrah now, and we'll show our gratitude in 1938. Ruth Hendricks, national committeewoman of the Young Democrats, assured Thomas that Murrah "has a host of friends...and these friends will appreciate your favor now."[93] W.S.

Rodgers, Lee's Bryan County chair, wrote Thomas that, if he endorsed Murrah, "the many friends of Josh Lee in Bryan County will be deeply indebted to you."[94] And James O. Hood, Cleveland County campaign manager for Lee and mayor of Norman, promised Thomas that if he supported Murrah, Lee Democrats in Cleveland County would "show their appreciation to you in the next campaign."[95]

The letter and telegram campaign worked. Responding to a letter criticizing Murrah's selection, Thomas was candid why he had not exercised a veto:

> Murrah had the endorsement and support of every major organization in the state. By major organizations I refer to organized labor, the railroad brotherhoods, the veterans of industry, the farmers' union and anti-saloon league. In addition, he was endorsed by a number of leading lawyers of our state. In addition, he was endorsed by the state democratic chairman and vice-chairman and by our national committeeman. With such a build-up and such support, it was impossible to hold out against his appointment.[96]

This is not to say that Murrah was a consensus choice. The first major salvo of opposition was fired at a meeting of the State Bar of Oklahoma in late December of 1936. The bar resolved that the "appointment of Federal Judges, who hold office for life, should not be made to pay political debts."[97] *Harlow's Weekly* reported that the resolution "was based on the published reports that Senator Josh Lee was inclined to press the appointment of his personal friend and supporter, A.P. Murrah, an Oklahoma City attorney."[98] Murrah agreed, writing Lee, "Obviously this resolution was directed toward me."[99]

Thomas astutely observed, "If there is anything in a man's past, it certainly comes out when he is suggested for the Federal Judgeship."[100] Such was the case with Murrah.

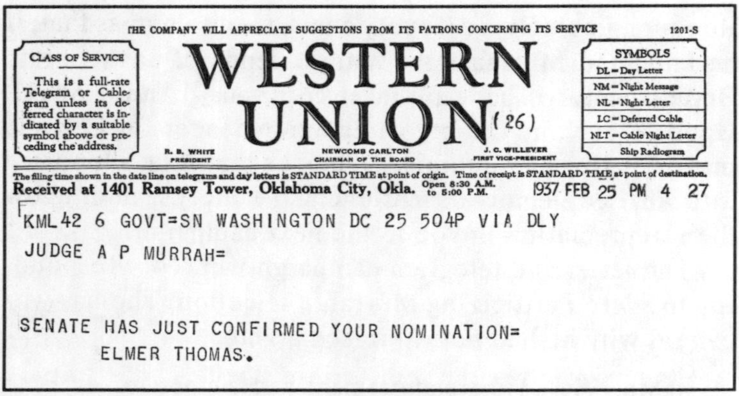
THE COMPANY WILL APPRECIATE SUGGESTIONS FROM ITS PATRONS CONCERNING ITS SERVICE 1201-S

CLASS OF SERVICE
This is a full-rate Telegram or Cablegram unless its deferred character is indicated by a suitable symbol above or preceding the address.

WESTERN UNION (26)

R. B. WHITE PRESIDENT | NEWCOMB CARLTON CHAIRMAN OF THE BOARD | J. C. WILLEVER FIRST VICE-PRESIDENT

SYMBOLS
DL = Day Letter
NM = Night Message
NL = Night Letter
LC = Deferred Cable
NLT = Cable Night Letter
Ship Radiogram

The filing time shown in the date line on telegrams and day letters is STANDARD TIME at point of origin. Time of receipt is STANDARD TIME at point of destination.
Received at 1401 Ramsey Tower, Oklahoma City, Okla. Open 8:30 A.M. to 5:00 P.M. 1937 FEB 25 PM 4 27

KML42 6 GOVT=SN WASHINGTON DC 25 504P VIA DLY
JUDGE A P MURRAH=

SENATE HAS JUST CONFIRMED YOUR NOMINATION=
ELMER THOMAS.

Telegram from Elmer Thomas to Murrah informing him that the senate had confirmed his nomination.

A recurring issue used by his opponents was the state of his health. Thomas wrote Savage that an "objection has been raised to Murrah's appointment because of the fact that his health is not the best."[101] Reports from doctors at the Mayo Clinic and from Murrah's Oklahoma City physician that the problem was one of fatigue, which was responding to rest, dispatched this objection.[102]

Graver objections than being a wet or in ill health were allegations that Murrah had been part of a conspiracy to rig bids in the selling of materials and supplies to the federal government, and that his conduct as attorney for certain receiverships had been improper.[103] After exhaustive investigation, the department of justice found the accusations to be baseless.[104]

Finally, there was the episode of the unsigned letter. Daniel E. McGraf, a special assistant to the attorney general, received a telephone call from a friend, a "responsible and reputable attorney"[105] in Tulsa, regarding Murrah, Savage, and Riley. McGraf invited this friend to send a memorandum addressing their qualifications, "and if he didn't care to sign it, it would be all right."[106] He did not, and McGraf forwarded the memorandum to Matthew McGuire, another justice department official. McGraf wrote that he would divulge the identity of the writer if McGuire requested. Whether McGuire did is not known.

As to Murrah and Riley, the anonymous attorney wrote with a pen dipped in malice leavened with invective. He wrote that Riley was partially deaf, a serious impediment for a trial judge, and that he was woefully lacking in litigation experience. Most damning, the writer said there were rumors that certain lawyers, one in particular, enjoyed improper influence with Riley and that Riley was one who might well abuse power.

This writer continued that Murrah was nothing but a run-of-the-mill workmen's compensation lawyer. He had no federal practice experience, and he was not considered a leader of the bar. One "could scarcely believe him to be of federal court judgeship caliber."[107]

However, Savage, said the anonymous writer, was studious, industrious, affable, and courteous. His appointment would be the start of "a long and distinguished judicial career."[108]

Whether the letter caused any difficulty for Murrah with the justice department is not a matter of record. Obviously, in view of the outcome, it did not produce the result desired by the author. Yet the incident does evidence starkly how high the stakes were and how low the depths to which some people would sink in trying to influence the final decision.

While Murrah's friends were showing support in Oklahoma, Murrah was in Washington, D.C., covering bases with the justice department and the Roosevelt administration. Fletcher Riley was there as well, except for a quick trip to Oklahoma to take his oath for a third term on the state supreme court. Employment for the next six years secured, Riley hurried back to the nation's capitol in quest of even better job tenure.[109]

In early January of 1937 Murrah met with officials of the justice department,[110] and then things slowed as the January 20th inauguration neared. Less than a week after Roosevelt took the oath for a second term, Lee and Murrah met with the president, a meeting which apparently went well. Lee told Roosevelt that Murrah was the man he wanted for the judgeship. Roosevelt inquired if Murrah was liberal enough for the post, and Lee, describing the hardships of Murrah's life, assured FDR that he was.[111]

On the third of February, Joseph Keenan, another justice department official, informed Lee and Thomas that Murrah, Savage, and Riley were acceptable. Keenan made particular reference to Lee's support of Murrah and "added that since Lee was 'so strong for' Murrah his appointment would be satisfactory."[112] Thomas visited with justice department officials on February 6 "to assure himself personally that the department ha[d] no objection" to Murrah's appointment, and then said that he would join Lee in recommending Murrah to Roosevelt.[113]

Murrah's name was sent to the senate on February 8, 1937.[114] A few protests were received, but they covered already traveled ground and posed no impediment to confirmation.[115] The judiciary committee speedily approved the nomination, and Murrah was confirmed by voice vote on February 25, 1937.[116] His commission followed in a few days, and less than nine years after graduating from law school and being admitted to the bar, Alfred Paul Murrah was nominated, confirmed, and commissioned as United States District Judge for the Eastern, Northern, and Western Districts of Oklahoma.

The making of Oklahoma's newest federal judge had begun in earnest immediately after the general election on November 2, 1936, and concluded almost exactly three months later. From a reading of Thomas's correspondence, it is possible to glean why Murrah was chosen to wear the ermine. The reasons are simple. First, Josh Lee was adamant that Murrah be named. In early November of 1936 he said, "I'll give him anything within my power because I consider him first among my supporters," and Lee never wavered from that position.[117] Second, Elmer Thomas refused to thwart Murrah's appointment. Thomas never wavered in his position that if Lee's choice was politically acceptable in Oklahoma and met justice department standards, he would concur in submitting that name to Roosevelt. In dealing with Lee regarding Murrah, Thomas had "to either face a deadlock or finally yield to the man recommended" by Lee.[118]

Murrah clearly was not the person Thomas favored for the judgeship.[119] But Thomas had passed the appointment to Lee, and Lee was unequivocally committed to Murrah. When it became clear that Murrah would be a popular choice in Oklahoma with that patchwork quilt of interests jokingly called the Democratic Party and that he was considered qualified by the department of justice, the deed was done.

Some have interpreted the events of late 1936 and early 1937 differently. When Judge George McDermott, a circuit court of appeals judge from Kansas, died suddenly on January 19, 1937, Judge Williams immediately became a candidate to succeed him. Three days later, January 22, Thomas and Lee endorsed Williams for the post. This sequence of events has led some to suggest that Thomas and Lee struck a deal—Lee would support Williams, and Thomas would support Murrah. As one historian concluded, "While the evidence is far from conclusive, it seems possible that an agreement was reached by which Lee would support Judge Williams for the circuit court and Thomas would endorse Murrah for the position

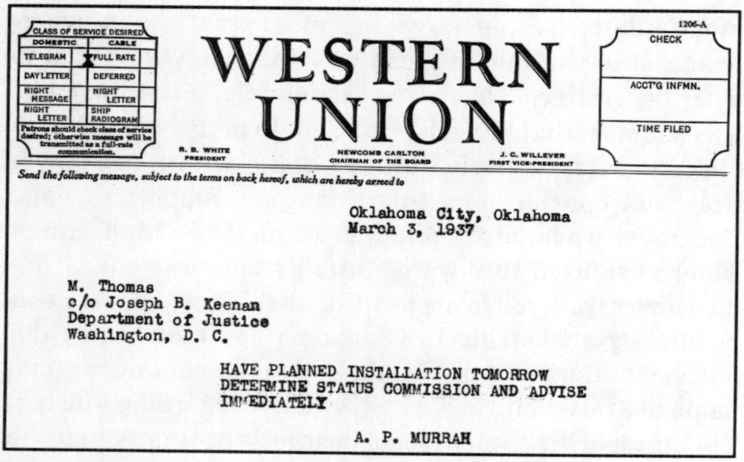

CLASS OF SERVICE DESIRED
DOMESTIC | CABLE
TELEGRAM | FULL RATE
DAY LETTER | DEFERRED
NIGHT MESSAGE | NIGHT LETTER
NIGHT LETTER | SHIP RADIOGRAM
Patrons should check class of service desired; otherwise message will be transmitted as a full-rate communication.

WESTERN UNION

R. B. WHITE, PRESIDENT — NEWCOMB CARLTON, CHAIRMAN OF THE BOARD — J. C. WILLEVER, FIRST VICE-PRESIDENT

1206-A
CHECK
ACCT'G INFMN.
TIME FILED

Send the following message, subject to the terms on back hereof, which are hereby agreed to

Oklahoma City, Oklahoma
March 3, 1937

M. Thomas
c/o Joseph B. Keenan
Department of Justice
Washington, D. C.

HAVE PLANNED INSTALLATION TOMORROW
DETERMINE STATUS COMMISSION AND ADVISE
IMMEDIATELY

A. P. MURRAH

Was Murrah anxious to begin the art of judging?

of roving judge."[120]

This thesis is not implausible, but there are convincing reasons for rejecting it. First, Thomas's hope of having Lee's support in 1938 would not have been served by tying endorsement of Murrah to endorsement of Williams. Thomas needed Lee to be indebted to him. If the debt was paid in 1937, no account would be due and owing in 1938 when Thomas needed to collect.

Second, the "bargain" theory is at odds with the course of conduct Thomas had followed since November 1936 and had reaffirmed as recently as January 11, 1937. On that date he wrote Judge Thomas H. Doyle, "If the Department of Justice finds that Murrah is acceptable then I have no reason for opposing his appointment."[121] For Thomas to abruptly change his position in midstream and become less yielding regarding approval of Murrah would have risked alienating Lee, the last man in Oklahoma Thomas wanted to offend. It would have been dumb politics, and Elmer Thomas was not dumb.

An interesting bit of circumstantial evidence concerning Lee's attitude on the circuit judgeship is a letter from Williams to Thomas.[122] Williams wrote Thomas that he had learned of McDermott's death from Forrest Parrott.[123] Parrott had been close to Lee in the 1936 campaign, and had been early rewarded with a job, state director of the National Emergency Council. Parrott told Williams he was certain Lee would be for him. While not conclusive, such evidence is probative that Lee was favorably disposed to Williams's elevation to the circuit court of appeals from the beginning. It also is worthy of note that the appointment of Williams to the circuit would create another district court vacancy in the state, one which Lee would have a significant voice in filling.

When all the evidence is marshaled and considered, the most persuasive exegesis is that Thomas thought a third senate term was worth a federal district judgeship, and his appraisal of how Lee's supporters would respond to his acquiescence in Murrah's appointment was unerringly accurate. A newspaper story the day after Murrah's nomination said it all:

> **LEE'S FRIENDS TO AID THOMAS IN NEXT RACE**
>
> While the appointment definitely removes Murrah from the political picture so far as any personal activities are concerned his friends feel that approval of the young leader of Josh Lee's campaign by the senior senator, Elmer Thomas, cause them to owe Thomas a debt of gratitude.
>
> It is certain that when Thomas seeks re-election he will have the support of most of the young group who backed Josh Lee. There will be some deflections, of course, but even Monday afternoon Lee's friends here were casting an eye to the next election.[124]

5
"Only conduct is legal tender."[1]

Shortly after his nomination, Murrah ended his long vigil in Washington, D.C., and returned to Oklahoma. Mrs. Murrah, the Luther Bohanons, and Bryan Rakestraw drove to Bristow to meet his train, but the nominee was sound asleep. By the time he was awakened, the train was ready to leave, and there was no room for Mrs. Murrah. The foursome returned to their car and sped to Oklahoma City. Beating the train, they and a host of friends greeted Murrah on his arrival. As a homecoming gift, Mrs. Murrah presented her husband with a scrapbook of newspaper clippings chronicling his rise to the federal bench.

In his final days as a private practitioner, Murrah turned his attention to the myriad of details involved in closing a law practice and purchasing a new residence at 820 Northwest 39th. This would be home until the late 1950s. Murrah also gave his last speech as a private citizen before entering the cloistered precincts of the federal judiciary. Addressing a Democratic party fundraiser in Tulsa, Murrah plighted his political troth: "I'm a democrat, a democrat from Alabama and a Franklin Delano Roosevelt democrat."[2] Roosevelt had won a popular and electoral vote landslide in November, but "sixteen million people are in violent disagreement with his program and are entitled to their views and due the protection of the federal courts because that is the American system."[3] Murrah pledged "to so conduct myself as a federal judge from the bench, in public and private life, that when you see me talking to someone you'll know in your heart and mind that I'm not talking about your lawsuit."[4]

Commissioned March 3, 1937, Murrah took the oath

CONGRATULATIONS, Mr. Murrah,

....upon your appointment as Federal Judge. We are wishing you a continued and greater success in whatever you undertake.

It just naturally gives us all a happier feeling to watch the progress and the accomplishments of a fellow Oklahoman.

More power to you!

Sincerely yours,

of MAY BROTHERS
Apparel for Men
136-138 West Main

SLM:NM

One of the more unusual congratulations Murrah received on his appointment as United States District Judge was this one from Milton and Solomon May, prominent Oklahoma City clothiers.

of office in Oklahoma City on March 12th. Appropriately, Mrs. MacPhail was in the audience. Murrah introduced her as "my mother... There couldn't have been a better. All I ever did to deserve it was to milk her cows."[5] The oath was administered by Judge Williams. Judge Vaught was in attendance, but Judge Kennamer was absent because of illness. A reporter wrote that as the oath was read by Judge Williams, Murrah listened with down-

United States District Judge Robert Lee Williams administers the oath of office as federal district judge to Murrah while United States District Judge Edgar S. Vaught observes. (Published in the Daily Oklahoman *on March 13, 1937. Courtesy Oklahoma Publishing Company.)*

cast eyes, "apparently measuring each word."[6] When Murrah repeated the oath, "He spoke slowly and with emphasis,"[7] and when he came to the final phrase—so help me God—"he lifted his voice, biting off each word."[8]

One of Murrah's first acts reached back to his Tuttle days. He named S.P. Smith, his high school principal and the man who had let him come to school when the rules said he could not, as his bailiff.

J.D. Lydick, a former justice of the state supreme court, undertook to select and furnish the photographs that were to adorn the walls of the courtroom. An unrepentant Democrat, Lydick chose only Democrats, including President Roosevelt, Vice-President John Nance Garner, and Attorney General Homer Cummings, because, "We don't want any person to go into the courtroom and feel that some inferior of his is hanging on the wall when he ought to be hanging from something else."[9]

Murrah had definite ideas about courtroom behavior and attire. Smoking was not permitted, and neither were women in trousers. When Mrs. Naomi Still entered in slacks, her stay was brief. Murrah ordered the bailiff to remove her from the courtroom, intoning, "This is a court of justice and I will not tolerate such conduct. Women must wear dresses and not pants in my court."[10]

As he began his service on the bench, Murrah looked to the life of Louis Dembitz Brandeis as a model for his own tenure as a judge. For Murrah, Brandeis was a "philosopher of law...[and] a crusader for human rights."[11] Speaking before the state convention of African-American lawyers, Murrah said that it was not necessary to hire a white lawyer to secure fair treatment from him "because justice under the law knew no race, creed or color and that would be the pillar from which I would conduct my court."[12]

Books and their study are the vital life force of the law, and Murrah exercised great care and discretion in furnishing his library. He requested the department of justice to provide him with the *Pacific Reporter*, *Pacific Digest*, *Shepard's Pacific Citations*, *Oklahoma Compiled Statutes*, *Northwestern Reporter*, *Montgomery's Manual of Federal Jurisdiction and Procedure*, *Pomeroy on Equity*, *Roberts' Federal Liability of Carriers*, *Thornton on Oil and Gas*, *Clark on Receivers*, *Brannon's Negotiable Instruments*, *Couch on Insurance*, *Cyclopedia of Federal Procedure*, *Johnson on Corporate Reorganization*, and *Gerdes Reorganization*.[13]

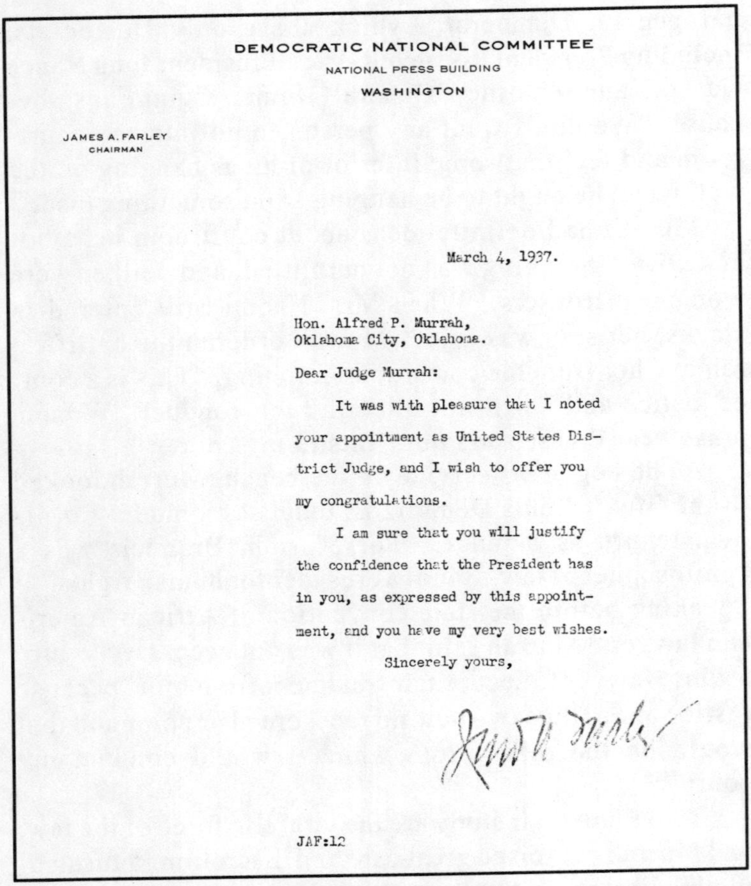

DEMOCRATIC NATIONAL COMMITTEE
NATIONAL PRESS BUILDING
WASHINGTON

JAMES A. FARLEY
CHAIRMAN

March 4, 1937.

Hon. Alfred P. Murrah,
Oklahoma City, Oklahoma.

Dear Judge Murrah:

It was with pleasure that I noted your appointment as United States District Judge, and I wish to offer you my congratulations.

I am sure that you will justify the confidence that the President has in you, as expressed by this appointment, and you have my very best wishes.

Sincerely yours,

JAF:12

This letter of congratulations from James Farley is signed in his famous green ink.

Created by the Judiciary Act of 1789, federal district courts are the principal trial courts of the federal judicial system.[14] Because the federal government is a government of limited powers, federal district courts exercise only the subject matter jurisdiction authorized by the Constitution of the United States and conferred upon them by statute. In 1937 federal district courts heard principally two types of controversies: diversity and federal question cases.

Diversity cases are suits between citizens of different states, e.g., a citizen of Oklahoma suing a citizen of Texas. The year after Murrah went on the trial bench, two major developments in the handling of diversity cases occurred. *Erie Railroad Company v. Tompkins*, 304 U.S. 64, 58 S.Ct. 817, 82 L.Ed. 1188 (1938), was decided, and the *Federal Rules of Civil Procedure* became effective.

Erie held that the normal rule of decision for substantive issues in diversity cases was state law, while the *Federal Rules of Civil Procedure* made the decision of procedural matters independent of state law rules. Whether in a diversity breach of contract case the statute of frauds defeated the plaintiff's claim would be decided by state law, but whether the plaintiff's complaint was sufficient as a matter of pleading would be decided by federal law.

Federal question cases were cases arising under the Constitution, laws, or treaties of the United States, such as a suit for infringement of a patent. Federal question cases did not have the qualitative or quantitative significance in 1937 they now enjoy, for the great proliferation of civil causes of action based on federal law was yet to occur. For example, the first case to imply a private right of action under Section 10b of the Securities Exchange Act of 1934, one of the staples of federal litigation today, was not decided until 1946. *Kardon v. National Gypsum Company*, 69 F.Supp. 512 (E.D. Pa. 1946).

Federal courts also heard prosecutions for violation of federal criminal statutes. In fact, Murrah's first act as a United States District Judge was to accept a plea of guilty in a Dyer Act case (transporting a stolen motor vehicle across a state line knowing the same to have been stolen). He sentenced the defendant to 18 months in prison.[15]

Murrah's docket during the few years he served as a

trial judge was typical of federal district courts in the 1930s. He tried personal injury and wrongful death,[16] conversion of trust assets and breach of fiduciary duties by trustees,[17] rights in an estate,[18] ownership of an insurance policy,[19] rights and liabilities on indemnity bonds, life insurance and automobile liability policies,[20] quiet title,[21] breach of contract,[22] recovery of real and personal property,[23] and patent infringement[24] cases.

1938 witnessed passage of the Fair Labor Standards Act, the last major piece of New Deal legislation.[25] This statute regulated the wages and hours of employees engaged in commerce or the production of goods for commerce. It increased the federal question jurisdiction of the district courts because it gave covered employees a cause of action for back wages, liquidated damages of an equal sum, and provided for court costs and attorney fees.

Murrah had not been on the bench long before he had occasion to interpret and apply the Fair Labor Standards Act. The plaintiffs were employed by the defendant as salesmen. Each plaintiff was assigned a definite territory, and each assigned area was solely within the state of Oklahoma. The plaintiffs supplied their customers with goods manufactured in Illinois and shipped to a warehouse in Tulsa. The goods were not shipped to the warehouse pursuant to a specific order for a particular customer, but rather were based on the volume of sales of a given item over the past four weeks less the number of items presently in stock.

Recognizing the remedial nature of the legislation, Murrah held that the plaintiffs were covered by the act because the shipment of goods from Illinois to the homes of the customers in Oklahoma constituted an uninterrupted flow of commerce. Thus the plaintiffs met the commerce nexus requirement of the statute.

The circuit disagreed. *Williams et al. v. Jewell Tea*

Company, 118 F.2d 202 (10th Cir. 1941). It reasoned that the stream of interstate commerce ceased flowing when the goods came to rest in the warehouse. Commerce did not begin again until the article was taken from the warehouse and delivered to customers, an activity which was totally intrastate. Alternatively, the circuit court of appeals held that the plaintiffs met the definition of "outside salesmen," a category of workers exempted from coverage by the statute.

In part a question of statutory interpretation, *Jewell Tea* was also a question of how one perceived the American economy. For Murrah, it was a national economy, not 48 separate economies. A too-restrictive view of what constituted interstate commerce ignored the realities of the marketplace. Murrah thought the power of congress to regulate interstate commerce plenary, and he gave an expansive reading to statutes enacted pursuant to that power.

When Oklahoma entered the union, it extended the suffrage to male citizens over 21 years of age, excepting felons, paupers and lunatics. Shortly after its admission, however, a constitutional amendment imposing a literacy test for voters was approved. The amendment included a grandfather clause which had the purpose and effect of denying the ballot to African-American voters. Perceiving the purpose and disapproving the effect, the Supreme Court of the United State invalidated both the literacy test and the grandfather clause in *Guinn v. United States* , 238 U.S. 347, 35 S.Ct. 926, 59 L.Ed. 1340 (1915).

The *Guinn* decision came after adjournment of the regular 1915 session of the legislature. Meeting in special session in 1916, the legislators adopted a twofold response. First, they submitted to the electorate a proposed constitutional amendment again imposing a literacy test for the exercise of the franchise and including a grandfather clause even more extreme than the one invalidated in *Guinn*. This silliness was too much for the voters, and they rejected the proposed amendment by a vote of 90,605 to 133,140.[26] Second, the special session passed Oklahoma's first general registration law. In order to vote, one was required to register between April 30, 1916, and May 11, 1916, but anyone who had voted in the 1914 general election remained a qualified elector.[27]

I.W. Lane, an African-American who did not get on the rolls in 1916, tried again in 1934. Unsuccessful, he brought suit in the eastern district claiming that the 1916 registration law denied Negro voters equality of treatment with white voters. Specifically, he grounded his right to a remedy in the Civil Rights Act of 1871 granting an action at law to any person deprived under color of state law of any right, title, privilege or immunity secured by federal law. Substantively, he relied upon the 15th Amendment to the Constitution of the United States prohibiting denial of the right to vote by a state "on account of race, color or previous condition of servitude." Murrah directed a verdict for the defendants, and the tenth circuit affirmed in *Lane v. Wilson*, 98 F.2d 980 (10th Cir. 1938). The circuit court of appeals held that the registration law did not violate the 15th Amendment because it accorded the same treatment to African-Americans and whites who had not voted in 1914.

The supreme court granted certiorari and reversed, per Justice Felix Frankfurter, 307 U.S. 268, 59 S.Ct. 872, 83 L.Ed. 1281 (1939). The purpose of the 15th Amendment was to prevent "contrivances by a state to thwart equality in the enjoyment of the right to vote by citizens of the United States regardless of race or color."[28] The Oklahoma registration law violated this principle of equality because it protected those who had benefitted from the unconstitutional grandfather clause "while subjecting colored citizens to a new burden."[29] In sum, the challenged statute "operated unfairly against the very class in whose behalf the protection of the Constitution was successfully invoked [in *Guinn*]."[30]

The rights, often conflicting, of capital and labor were at issue in *Houston v. North Texas Motor Freight Lines, Inc. v. Local Union No. 886, etc.*, 24 F. Supp. 619 (W.D. Okl. 1938). The complainant, an interstate motor carrier, commenced a suit in equity to enjoin a union local and certain individuals from interfering with the complainant's transportation of freight. The purpose of the interference was to persuade (the union's view) or coerce (the complainant's view) the complainant's employees to join the union.

Legally, the dispositive question was whether the conflict between the parties came within the language of the Norris-LaGuardia Act prohibiting federal courts from issuing "any restraining order or temporary or permanent injunction in a case involving or growing out of a labor dispute." Murrah wrote that the answer lay not in any abstract proposition of law, but in the balancing of "social and economic"[31] factors by congress in the controlling legislation. In deciding how the balance had been struck, Murrah engaged in an extensive historical analysis of legislative responses to capital-labor disputes, and of judicial interpretations of those responses.

Murrah's reading of the cases left him with "grave doubt that the courts have given to that legislation the effect intended by the legislative bodies."[32] Indeed, he quoted as extensively from dissenting opinions, particularly those of Brandeis, as he did from majority opinions, thus laying the predicate for his conclusion "that the Norris-LaGuardia Act was designed to make lawful that which the Courts had construed to be unlawful"[33] by their pre Norris-LaGuardia rulings. Under the rubric of now

Agnes "Babe" Murrah at the time of Murrah's appointment to the federal trial bench. (Published in the Daily Oklahoman *on February 2, 1937. Courtesy Oklahoma Publishing Company.)*

lawful conduct assuredly came peaceful picketing for organizational purposes. Consequently, the complaint was dismissed for want of equity to the extent that it sought to enjoin such protected conduct. However, acts of fraud and violence, as conduct not enjoying immunity from the sanction of the chancellor, were enjoined.

Murrah's appointment to the bench had rested in significant measure on the support of organized labor. But he decided the case as a judge, not as an advocate. The complainant was not guilty of illegal conduct, and thus it stood before the court "an innocent victim."[34] In sum and substance, the case was not about wrongs and fault. It was about economic warfare, congress had legitimatized the union's conduct, and the court's responsibility was to apply the law, not to pass moral judgment.

During Murrah's years as a district judge, federal actions to enjoin the enforcement of state statutes were required to be heard by a three-judge district court, i.e., a district court composed of three judges, at least one of whom had to be a supreme court justice or circuit judge. The typical three-judge court was one circuit judge and two district judges. Though composed of three judges, the court was still a trial court, and appeals from a properly constituted three-judge court lay directly to the supreme court.

In 1938 Murrah served on a three-judge court for the District of New Mexico. The other members were Judge Sam Bratton, circuit court of appeals judge, and Judge Colin Neblett, federal district judge for New Mexico.

Sovereign Camp, *WOW v. Casados*, 21 F. Supp. 989 (D.N.Mex. 1938), was a suit to enjoin enforcement of a New Mexico statute which imposed a privilege tax on fraternal benefit associations, but exempted those which (1) limited their membership either to members of one religious faith or to persons engaged in one or more hazardous occupations in the same or similar lines of business; (2) did not employ paid solicitors or salesmen either on a salary or commission basis for procuring new members; and (3) did not solicit insurance applications from the general public, but limited its solicitation to members in good standing of the society. The gravamen of the complaint was that the differences in treatment visited upon exempt and nonexempt associations was violative of the due process and equal protection clauses of the 14th Amendment.

Murrah first considered the effect of a recently passed act of congress, the Tax Anti-Injunction Act,[35] which interdicted federal injunctions of state taxing statutes if state law provided a plain, speedy, and efficient remedy. Because the act did not apply to suits commenced before its passage, as the litigation before the three-judge court had been, the case could be heard on the merits.

Beginning with the grandfather of the power to tax cases—*McCulloch v. Maryland*, 4 Wheat. 316, 4 L.Ed. 579 (1819)—Murrah traced the case law and concluded that the controlling jurisprudence recognized the power of legislative bodies "to classify for purposes of taxation...if any reasonable or sound basis can be found to sustain it."[36] Examining the New Mexico statute's classification scheme, Murrah concluded that it was rationally related to a legislative purpose of fostering fraternal societies which wrote insurance as a benevolent or incidental part of their business and that such a goal was a legitimate legislative end which "this court is not at liberty to question."[37] Judge Bratton concurred, while Judge Neblett dissented. On appeal, the Supreme Court of the United States affirmed unanimously—305 U.S. 558, 83 L.Ed. 52, 59 S.Ct. 79 (1938).

Hamrick v. Bryan, 21 F.Supp. 392 (N.D. Okla. 1937), heard by Kennamer and Murrah *en banc*, was an equity action for removal of the trustees of a business trust, injunctive relief, and an accounting. The genesis of the suit was a proposal by the trustees to transfer the assets of the trust estate to a corporation of which they were the board of directors and principal officers. The complainants also alleged that they were aggrieved by a decision of the trustees to pay dividends to all classes of stockholders. Previously, only preferred stockholders had been paid earnings on their shares.

Kennamer and Murrah found both grounds for relief meritorious. When the trustees dealt with the corporation of which they were officers and directors, they "were remiss in their duty of loyalty to their cestuis que trustent."[38] The trustees "were the corporation,"[39] and "such a relationship would compel a very material self-interest in the corporation on their part."[40] Relying on Section 70 of the *Restatement of Trusts*, Kennamer and Murrah held that the trustees had violated their fiduciary duties by selling trust property to a corporation in which they had a substantial interest. Their conduct was blatant self-dealing which Kennamer and Murrah, as chancellors exercising the equity powers of a federal court, could not and would not condone.

Concerning the alterations in the rights of the different classes of stock ownership, the trustees based their defense on a state court decree authorizing such changes. Kennamer and Murrah rejected the defense because the order had been made without notice to the stockholders, and "[d]ue process requires that every person shall have the protection of his day in court, and an opportunity to be heard is an essential requisite of due process and judicial proceedings."[41] Finding a notice dimension in 14th Amendment procedural due process, Kennamer and Murrah anticipated the holding of *Mullane v. Central Hanover Bank & Trust Co.*, 339 U.S. 306, 70 S.Ct. 652, 94 L.Ed. 865 (1950), that deprivations of property generally must be preceded by "notice reasonably calculated, under all the circumstances, to apprise interested parties of the pendency of the action and afford them an opportunity to present their objections" 339 U.S. at 314, 70 S.Ct. at 657, 94 L.Ed. 865 at 873.

On appeal, the circuit court of appeals disagreed. *Bryan v. Hamrick*, 106 F.2d 245 (10th Cir. 1939). It did not address the question of self-dealing, holding simply that the assets of the business trust could be transferred to the corporation as long as the corporation's purposes were essentially the same as those of the business trust. Regarding notice, the appellate court ruled it was sufficient the trustee said notice had been given without inquiring whether any effort had been made to individually notify shareholders whose identity was known or reasonably ascertainable. The circuit court of appeals had the last word, but Kennamer and Murrah had the better argument.

The decision in Erie that state law normally supplies the rule of decision in diversity cases left a number of questions unanswered. One was which state's law would be applied when more than one state had a basis for its law being the rule of decision, and the state laws were in conflict. In *Monohan v. New York Life Insurance Company*, 26 F.Supp. 859 (W.D. Okl. 1939), Murrah decided the conflict must be resolved by applying the choice of law rules of the state in which the federal court was sitting. Thus a federal district court in Oklahoma would apply Oklahoma's choice of law provisions. The circuit affirmed, 108 F.2d 841 (10th. Cir. 1939), and subsequently the supreme court read *Erie* the same way. *Klaxon v. Stentor Manufacturing Company*, 313 U.S. 487, 61 S.Ct. 1020, 85 L.Ed. 1447 (1941).

The preponderant part of Murrah's criminal docket flowed from a flourishing cottage industry in Oklahoma, the making of moonshine whiskey. "When I first came to the Federal bench," he recalled, "my jurisdiction included the Cherokee nation, also known as the land of the 'hills and stills.' Law enforcement officers, especially 'revenuers' were quite unwelcome. Many mornings I've come to the bench to look out over a courtroom full of defendants charged with violating the revenue law by making moonshine whiskey."[42]

When it was time to sentence these defendants, Murrah recognized that people "have been making whiskey...in the Kiamichi Mountains all their lives."[43] Imposing a jail term usually meant taking "some old man from his wife and seven or eight children...and turn[ing] them loose as charges on society."[44] Murrah's answer was an agreement. He would agree not to impose a jail sentence, and the defendant would agree to stop making whiskey.[45] The agreement was a solemn compact, and its breach would earn the defendant a quick trip to jail.

Murrah also extended leniency to "farmers with crops yet to be made"[46] and to young people. He continued sentencing for one defendant with 150 acres in cultivation, but warned him to be in court at the next session if he had to "come...on a stretcher."[47] And when a 15-year-old boy appeared before him on a liquor charge, Murrah probably could not escape memories of his own difficult youth. Refusing to send the boy to the penitentiary, Murrah dismissed the charge and told the youth, "Now you have a clean record, so go back to school and make a man of yourself and earn an honest living."[48]

On one occasion, Judge Murrah acted as lawyer Murrah. A defendant charged in a three-count indictment with possession of an illegal still pleaded "non-sufficiency."[49] Treating the plea as not guilty, Murrah offered to act as counsel for the accused. His opening statement denied that the defendant owned the still, or that he had been involved in the use or operation of it in any manner. When the case was submitted to the jury, it acquitted the defendant on two counts and convicted him on one. Murrah commented that he and his client had lost the case but had made a good fight.[50] After consideration of the defendant's record, he sentenced him to two years imprisonment and fined him $500.[51]

Mountain people who were being true to their heritage when they made some white lightning were one thing. Professional bootleggers were another matter. The latter received short shrift from the judge whose rumored "moist tinge"[52] had been a significant threat to his appointment to the bench. When the parole of one bootlegger was revoked for writing hot checks, the government recommended imprisonment for one year. Murrah imposed a three-year sentence and said he "really ought to make it five."[53] Murrah was prone to reject recommendations of the United States attorney's office as too lenient, and five-year terms were not uncommon for bringing whiskey into dry Oklahoma.[54]

Counterfeiters and embezzlers fared no better before Murrah than did bootleggers. Homer Henley's manufacturing, possessing, and passing of counterfeit dimes and half dollars cost him three five-year sentences to be served consecutively. The sentence was said to be "one of the stiffest for such a crime in the history of federal courts."[55] Another defendant received a five-year sentence on a counterfeiting charge even though the prosecutor recommended only one year.[56] And a young banker at Weatherford who pled *nolo contendere* to embezzlement charges received three years in prison. The hardship that would be visited upon his wife and three children could not stay the hand of the law: "If the suffering of the innocent along with the guilty could be produced in a court as a reason why the guilty should not be punished, then there wouldn't be a single bookkeeper convicted. The innocent must suffer along with the guilty."[57]

At the same time, Murrah had great faith in the federal probation system. In less than a year on the bench, he probated the sentences of some 1,500 defendants, and he proudly observed that only five had appeared before him for violating the terms of their probation.[58]

Perhaps the most publicized criminal matter Murrah heard as a district judge was the kidnapping case against Malloy Kuykendall, Dale Stamphill, and W.L. Baker. Described as "young desperadoes,"[59] Kuykendall and Stamphill were serving state sentences for robbery with firearms and Baker for murder when they killed a prison guard during an escape. Apprehended and sentenced to life imprisonment for the homicide, the trio escaped again, abducted a doctor at Leedey, Oklahoma, and crossed the Red River into Texas with their captive.

Apprehended yet again, the three were convicted of violating the federal kidnapping statute. In sentencing Kuykendall, Stamphill, and Baker to life imprisonment, Murrah said that he could "see no hope for you. You have gone so far that society has no choice any longer."[60]

This was not the end of Murrah's relationship with Stamphill and Baker, however. While serving his life sentence, Stamphill wrote Murrah that he intended to file a motion to vacate the judgment of conviction, and he asked Murrah to hear the motion because of his "faith in your intellectual honesty, not to speak of your ability."[61] Murrah was on the appellate bench by this time, and he did not sit. But it speaks volumes about Stamphill's perception of Murrah's fairness and integrity that he wanted Murrah to hear the motion.

Murrah took a deep interest in Stamphill over the years. He discussed Stamphill's situation with his court-appointed attorney many times, and he assisted Stamphill in his effort to obtain relief on his state sentence. Stamphill wrote that if he were successful, "it would be because of this gracious assistance you have given."[62]

When Baker was paroled, he immediately contacted

Murrah and visited with him regarding how to turn his life around. Murrah helped him find a job, kept advised about his post-prison life, and eventually had the happy occasion to prepare an affidavit in support of Baker's successful effort to obtain a presidential pardon. When he learned Baker had received the pardon, Murrah wrote, "No one could be happier than myself."[63]

The presidency was a bully pulpit for Teddy Roosevelt, and the federal bench was the same for Murrah. Sermon topics included political corruption, honky tonks, the state prison system, and constables. When allegations surfaced that some high state officials were levying an "import tax" on liquor illegally brought into Oklahoma to raise campaign funds, Murrah asked "why should one-gallused country boys be brought up here and sent to the penitentiary when they haul the whiskey in here by truck-loads and fancy bottles apparently with the sanction of state officials?"[64] As far as Murrah was concerned, they should not. A "one-gallus" country boy who pled guilty to moonshining had his sentence reduced from one year in the federal prison at Leavenworth to five months in the county jail, and Murrah's only regret was "[t]hat's the best the law will let me do."[65]

A Mann Act case—transporting a female across state lines for prostitution, debauchery, or other immoral purposes—gave Murrah occasion to damn honky-tonks, state penal institutions, and constables in one fell swoop. Honky-tonks were "dens of lawlessness, where prostitutes ply their trade and fee grabbing constables wait for someone to get drunk so they can drag him before a justice of the peace and grab their fee."[66] The prostitute and the constable mutually benefitted from the system: "Three dollars for the constable, three dollars for the prostitute."[67] And state prisons and reformatories were "nothing but breeding places for crime."[68]

Murrah's characterization of constables would not normally be considered approbative, but it almost was compared to what he said during sentencing proceedings for two Seminole County constables convicted of liquor law offenses. "A constable is the most reprehensible creature in Oklahoma."[69] That was only the beginning. Warming to his subject, Murrah continued that being a constable from Seminole County was "evidence on its face that a crime has been committed."[70] And he concluded, "Put a gun on the best citizen in Seminole County, tell him he's a constable, and in six months he isn't worth killing."[71]

Inexplicably, some of the state constabulary took offense at these remarks. W.H. Stephenson from Okmulgee County took Lee to task for the remarks of his "Juvenile Federal Judge,"[72] and informed Lee that the constables of the state had "organized themselves into an officers protective association, for self protection against unwarranted assaults from any source."[73] Lee, recognizing there were constables in every county in the state, wrote Stephenson that constables "represent some of the most influential citizens of every community,"[74] and he implored Murrah to "[p]lease do something about the 'constables.'"[75] Murrah responded that he was sorry for causing Lee any trouble, but he had "no apology to make...and if it is necessary for the constables of the state of Oklahoma to organize a protective association in order to protect themselves against the law and efficient enforcement of the law, then in my opinion an indictment of them is not out of place."[76]

Murrah completed three-years service on the federal bench in March of 1940. Before the end of the year, he would be a circuit judge, there would be two new district judges in the state, and a third would be waiting in the wings, a wait that would be lengthy and that would have

Murrah at the time of his appointment as a federal district judge.

emanations extending into the 1960s. The district court vacancies would result from Murrah's appointment to the circuit, Kennamer's retirement in the northern district, and the creation of an additional judgeship for the western district. The filling of these judgeships was a single ball of thread, and it is necessary to return to 1937 to unravel the skein.

Shortly after Murrah's nomination for the district court, the justice department approved Judge Williams for the circuit. President Franklin Roosevelt nominated him, and the nomination was confirmed. Murrah administered the oath to Williams as Williams had administered the oath to Murrah. For the vacancy in the eastern district, Senator Thomas wanted Bower Broaddus, a state senator from Muskogee County, while Judge William Jones of Pittsburg County was mentioned as the likely choice of Lee. Murrah opposed the appointment of either Broaddus or Jones. He favored Judge Eugene Rice, a state district judge from Stephens County,[77] and the appointment eventually went to Rice.

In 1939 Judge Williams, as he had agreed, retired when he reached 70 years of age. He was succeeded by Walter A. Huxman of Kansas. This meant that Oklahoma had no member of the circuit court of appeals, and it was widely expected, given Oklahoma's status as the largest state in the circuit by population and volume of litigation, that the next vacancy would be filled by an appointment from Oklahoma. And that is what happened, but not before a series of events that strained the Lee-Murrah friendship.

In January of 1940, Orie Phillips and Sam Bratton, two members of the circuit court of appeals, approached Murrah, told him that Judge Robert E. Lewis wanted to retire, and said Lewis wanted Murrah to be his successor. Phillips and Bratton told Murrah that his elevation was satisfactory to them and to Judge Huxman as well. The judges promised endorsement from the bar associations of their states, and Judge Bratton threw in the New Mexico governor and supreme court for good measure.[78]

Murrah withheld a response until he spoke with Lee.

When he broached the subject, he learned that Lee had another candidate in mind if a vacancy occurred—a candidate named Josh Lee. Knowing that the matter was hopeless without senatorial backing, Murrah immediately informed the circuit judges that he was not a candidate.[79]

Two months later, on March 4, 1940, Lee reversed his position and told Murrah that he had the "full, bright green light" to go for the circuit appointment.[80] But the green light quickly turned amber. As early as March 17, Murrah wrote Thomas that "Senator Lee has indicated that he is now interested in the position for himself,"[81] and the next day he cryptically wrote Lee that with "respect to other matters, I have expressed myself permanently frankly and fairly—there is nothing else to be said."[82] By the end of March, Murrah was writing Lee that circumstances "convince me that something is wrong concerning my proposed promotion to the court of appeals."[83] In early April he informed Lee that "Judge Phillips has the impression, gathered from some sources, that you are still inclined to accept the position on the circuit court of appeals."[84] During this same period, newspaper speculation was great that Lee was going to resign his senate seat for a circuit appointment.[85]

Murrah's response to the mounting circumstantial evidence that Senator Lee wanted to be Judge Lee was twofold. Naturally, he would not press his claim in opposition to Lee, but he was adamantly opposed to Lee leaving the senate. Murrah pulled no punches in telling Lee what he thought. Not completing his senate term would be an act of "faithlessness," an act which would destroy the cause for which Lee's supporters had fought so hard:

> In 1936 it was predicted that the Josh Lee Boys would soon fall apart; that petty jealousies and selfish aggrandizement would split them into factions. Three years

later, and through some pretty hard tests, they stand today as united, as loyal, and as devoted as they were on the night when the votes were counted. There seems to be that personal touch, something that is unusual and not often found in organizations of this type. Nothing can destroy it but the faithlessness of their leader. If he fails them they lose faith in humanity because he represents something that is good, true and loyal; something that is not found in the ordinary person.

That night, above mentioned, we talked about the leader, about how he stood by his friends and how some day he would vindicate the principles for which we have worked so hard. I know that it cannot be, I must be in a daze but I want you to tell me, fairly and frankly just what is in your mind. You have never kept anything from us, which we should know, and if you entertain the thought of leaving the "bridge" and the "helm" while the ship is sailing through a quiet sea, you should tell us so that we can justify it in some way in our own hearts.[86]

Nor was Murrah shy in seeking the help of the state's senior senator to keep Lee in the senate. He wrote Thomas,

I repeat, I do not believe Senator Lee should accept a position on the Federal Bench, because he has no right to do so. The people of Oklahoma elected him to the United States Senate and in his campaign speeches he told the people: "If you will fight my battles now, I will fight yours in the United States Senate." I subscribe to that declaration—I hold it to be a solemn pact between the people and Josh Lee and those who had a part in his campaign. I do not believe that any man has the right to break it. Moreover, I am confident that in the event a vacancy occurs in the United States Senate Gomer Smith will eventually succeed to it. This, I abhor as much as anything in the world, not for myself but my friends, which includes you. Therefore, and not for selfish reasons (please believe me), but for the sake of those who

Oklahoma's newest federal judge arrives at his chambers. (Published in the Oklahoma City Times *on March 26, 1937. Courtesy Oklahoma Publishing Company.)*

> have a right to ask, I sincerely hope that something can be done to dissuade Senator Lee from accepting the place on the Circuit Court of Appeals. To this end I pledge my unqualified assistance.[87]

As events developed, it appeared that Murrah's worst fear would materialize. Lewis formally announced his retirement on May 21, 1940, and the Sunday Edition of the *Tulsa World* for May 26 reported that Lee was leaving the senate and named a number of possible successors.[88] Murrah immediately wrote Lloyd Benefield, by then Lee's secretary, that if Lee would complete his term, he, Murrah, would resign whatever judgeship he then held in Lee's favor.[89] The next day, before Lee could have received this letter, Lee announced his support for Murrah.

Murrah's name was submitted to the senate on August 5, 1940.[90] The confirmation process moved smoothly and swiftly. There were the usual expressions of support from lawyers and bar associations, and, as promised, Judge Bratton obtained endorsements for Murrah from the governor and justices of the Supreme Court of New Mexico. Murrah was confirmed on August 29, 1940,[91] his commission was issued, and he took the oath of office on September 9, 1940. A little more than 12 years after graduation from law school and being admitted to the bar, Alfred Paul Murrah was a United States Circuit Judge.

Murrah's appointment may be unique in the history of the tenth circuit. It appears to be the only instance in which the judges of the court actively worked to secure the appointment of a particular person. For Murrah, the efforts of Lewis, Phillips, Bratton, and Huxman to secure his elevation to the circuit court of appeals were "a greater compliment than the appointment."[92]

The story of Murrah's appointment is not quite complete, however, for there is the unanswered question why

The new jurist at work in his chambers. (Published in the Daily Oklahoman *on March 25, 1937. Courtesy Oklahoma Publishing Company.)*

the judgeship went to Murrah and not to Lee. It may be that Lee did not want the judgeship. When he endorsed Murrah, he said, "My whole interest is in continuing to serve the people of Oklahoma in the United States Senate."[93] Be that as it may, it simply does not ring true that Murrah so completely misinterpreted Lee's intentions. Murrah's statement to Thomas that Lee "is now interested in the position for himself" admits of little ambiguity.[94] And the pervading tenor of his correspondence with Lee himself from mid-March until the matter was concluded in mid-May is that Lee wanted the appointment. Murrah's perception may have been mistaken, but it is passingly strange that Lee did not bother to disabuse Murrah of his error.

Or it may be that the administration was not receptive to appointing Lee. This makes some sense. Lee was a strong Roosevelt supporter, and if he resigned from the senate the vacancy would initially be filled by gubernato-

United States Circuit Judge A.P. Murrah administers the oath of office to newly named United States District Judge Royce Savage. Retiring Judge Franklin E. Kennamer is to Murrah's right.

rial appointment. Oklahoma's governor was Leon C. "Red" Phillips, and he was anything but a stalwart New Dealer. Of course, Lee's good standing with the administration also argues in favor of Roosevelt acceding to Lee's wish. The appointment of a strong legislative supporter to the bench was not unprecedented in the annals of the New Deal.[95]

Or it may be that Judge Lewis refused to retire until Lee withdrew from the picture. There were news stories that Lewis did not want to be succeeded by a politician,[96] although what is a federal judge but a lawyer who is on good terms with a United States Senator. Lewis may have decided to thwart Lee's aspirations by not retiring until Lee disavowed interest in going on the bench.

The possibilities are many. What must be admitted

finally is that we have no definitive answer to this, one of the most teasing questions in Oklahoma political history. And probably we never shall, for likely the answer went to the grave with Joshua Bryan Lee.

Soon after Murrah's confirmation, Royce Savage was named for the northern district and Bower Broaddus for the roving position,[97] and their confirmations followed quickly.[98] This gave Lee two appointments, Murrah and Savage, and Thomas one, Broaddus.[99] The count was to be evened by Thomas filling the new judgeship, but that would not happen quickly. Indeed, it would be more than two years before the western district had its second judge.

6
The Old Court, 1940-1949

Second only to the Judiciary Act of 1789 in importance for the federal court system, the Evarts Act of 1891 created circuit courts of appeals for the then nine federal judicial circuits.[1] The principal business of these courts is appellate, i.e., reviewing decisions of the federal district courts. Additionally, the courts of appeals "have jurisdiction to review orders of many administrative agencies, and to issue original writs in appropriate cases."[2]

At statehood, Oklahoma became part of the eighth circuit.[3] Large geographically, this circuit also included the states of Arkansas, Missouri, Iowa, Minnesota, North Dakota, South Dakota, Nebraska, Kansas, Wyoming, Utah, Colorado, and, when it became a state in 1912, New Mexico. In 1929 congress removed Oklahoma, Kansas, Wyoming, Utah, Colorado, and New Mexico from the eighth circuit and created a new four-judge circuit, the tenth, with Denver as its seat.[4]

When Murrah became a circuit judge in 1940, his colleagues were Orie L. Phillips, Sam G. Bratton, and Walter A. Huxman. The salary for circuit judges was $12,500 annually, as it had been since 1926.[5] In 1946 this was raised to $17,500, the first salary increase for circuit judges in 20 years.[6]

Born in 1885 and reared in Illinois, Judge Phillips was a graduate of Knox College and had studied law at the University of Michigan. Because of economics, he was unable to finish at Ann Arbor, and, as was common during that period, qualified for the bar by reading law. After practicing for a brief period in Illinois, Phillips, because of problems with asthma and the possibility of tuberculosis, moved to New Mexico where he built a successful practice and was active in Republican politics.

While serving in the state senate, Phillips was appointed to the federal district bench in 1923, and in 1929 was promoted to the circuit court of appeals.[7] In 1931 he moved to Denver to assist with the administrative aspects of the court. With the retirement of Judge Lewis, Phillips became senior circuit judge, a position he held until 1956.[8]

Sam Gilbert Bratton was born in Texas in 1888. After reading law, he was admitted to the Texas bar in 1909 and practiced in the Lone Star state until he moved to New Mexico in 1915. In 1919, after only four years in the Land of Enchantment, Bratton became a state district judge and then was elected to the Supreme Court of New Mexico in 1922. In 1924 he received the Democratic nomination for United States Senator and won the November general election. Elected to a second term in 1930, Bratton resigned from the senate to accept appointment to the circuit bench in 1933.[9]

Walter A. Huxman was born in Kansas in 1887. He taught school and served as a principal before earning his law degree from the University of Kansas in 1914. Huxman's professional career was varied. He was in private practice, then was an assistant county attorney, city attorney for Hutchinson, Kansas, Democratic nominee for the state supreme court in 1928, and a member of the state tax commission. In the 1936 Roosevelt landslide over Huxman's fellow Kansan Alf Landon, Huxman won the governorship. Running for a second term in 1938 without benefit of Roosevelt's coattails, Huxman was defeated. Shortly after leaving the governor's office, Huxman was appointed to the circuit court of appeals when Judge Williams retired.[10]

When Murrah was appointed, Phillips was 54, Bratton

was 52, and Huxman was 53. Murrah was 35. He was, without question, the "new kid" on the block.

For almost a decade after Murrah became a circuit judge, the size and membership of the tenth circuit remained constant. No period is as famous in the history of the court as the years of Phillips, Bratton, Huxman, and Murrah, one Coolidge-Hoover Republican, the other three New Deal Democrats.

During the 1940s the standard practice was for the court to sit in panels of three judges, although it had the power to order *en banc*, i.e., full court, sittings. *Textile Mills Securities Corporation v. Commissioner of Internal Revenue*, 314 U.S. 326, 62 S.Ct. 272, 86 L.Ed. 249 (1941). *En banc* courts were reserved for only the most important cases presenting issues of extraordinary complexity and difficulty. Indeed, during this time the tenth circuit sat *en banc* but once.[11]

After hearing oral arguments during a session of court, the judges would return to their homes,[12] study the briefs of the cases they had heard, and prepare a lengthy memorandum on each case. In a month or so they would meet again, exchange memoranda, and discuss the case. It would then be assigned for written disposition, the authoring judge usually relying on the memoranda in preparation of his opinion.[13] Of course, there might be concurring and dissenting opinions as well.

For his first opinion as a circuit judge, filed November 18, 1940, Murrah dipped his pen into the inkhorn of administrative law—*Magnolia Petroleum Company v. NLRB*, 115 F.2d 1007 (10th Cir. 1940).[14] A fairly new area of federal litigation, congress first provided for circuit court of appeals review of an administrative agency's decision, in that instance the Federal Trade Commission, in 1914.[15] With the proliferation of the New Deal's alphabet agencies, administrative agency review proceedings came to "account for a significant fraction of the total appellate workload."[16]

Passed in 1935 as part of the "Second New Deal," the National Labor Relations Act guaranteed employees the right to organize and bargain collectively with their employers in industries in interstate commerce or which affected interstate commerce. The statute made it an unfair labor practice for an employer (1) to interfere with the efforts of employees to form, join or assist a labor organization; (2) to dominate a labor organization, thus outlawing the company union; (3) to discriminate in hiring or terms or conditions of employment for union affiliation; (4) to discriminate for filing charges or giving testimony under the act; or (5) to refuse to bargain collectively with a duly designated representative of the employees.

The act was administered by the National Labor Relations Board (NLRB), the members of which were appointed by the president with the advice and consent of the senate. If the board determined that an employer had committed an unfair labor practice, it could enter an appropriate remedial order. Either the agency or employer could obtain judicial review by petitioning the circuit court of appeals to enforce or set aside the order.

In *Magnolia*, the NLRB found that the employer had committed an unfair labor practice by assisting in the formation and domination of a labor organization which claimed to represent Magnolia's employees. It ordered the company to withdraw recognition from the organization, and, when the company refused, commenced proceedings to enforce the order.

After summarizing the proof, Murrah defined the court's role. It was not to review the matter *de novo* and render an independent judgment. The board's findings of facts were to be sustained if supported by substantial evidence, and if more than one inference could be drawn

United States Circuit Judge Alfred P. Murrah in April 1941 after his appointment to the appellate bench in September 1940. The occasion was the sitting of the circuit court of appeals in Oklahoma City. (Published in the Oklahoma City Times *on April 14, 1941. Courtesy Oklahoma Publishing Company.)*

with reason from the facts, it was for the board, not the court, to choose between or among the competing inferences. Concluding that the board's order was supported by the evidence, the order was enforced. Murrah visited the post act company union issue again in *NLRB v. Keystone Freight Lines*, 126 F.2d 414 (10th Cir. 1941), and again found the order supported by the record.

But the rule according deference to the board in finding facts and drawing inferences was not simply a learned response to be recited by rote and leading inexorably to enforcement of the agency's edict. It was a rule founded on reason, and its meaning came from application to the particular facts of the case being decided. Of the six NLRB cases Murrah wrote during these years, he denied enforcement in two, or one-third, of them.[17] New Dealer that he was, Murrah was not the intellectual bond servant of the board.

By prohibiting an employer from interfering with,

restraining, or coercing employees in organizing for collective bargaining purposes, there was an inherent risk the law would impinge on the free speech rights of the employer. Persuading employees not to join a union was permissible; coercing them not to join was not. Deciding when an employer's efforts had ceased being persuasion and become coercion required a discriminating perusal of the alleged unfair labor conduct in the context in which it occurred. In *NLRB v. Continental Oil Company*, 159 F.2d 326 (10th Cir. 1947), there were only 30 employees in the bargaining unit. The statements were uttered by a management person who "undoubtedly had economic power over their jobs, and hence to influence them in the exercise of their industrial freedom." This person was known to be strongly antiunion, and he expressed his views using "violent and profane language."

Considered together, these facts took the conduct "beyond the realm of persuasion. It became coercive"—*ibid.*, 330. But when the employer merely stated that in his opinion it would not be beneficial for the employees to join the union, when there was nothing else from which an inference of coercion could be drawn, then the employer's conduct fell within the realm of legitimate ideological warfare and did not constitute an unfair labor practice. In sum, the task was "to balance the employer's inalienable right of free speech and expression against the right of the employees to freedom of self-organization"—*National Labor Relations Board v. Enid Co-Op Creamery Ass'n.*, 169 F.2d 986 at 988 (10th Cir. 1948).

As mentioned in chapter five, Murrah took a hospitable view of the coverage of the Fair Labor Standards Act (FLSA) as a district judge. This view continued to manifest itself in his circuit court opinions, but, as deference to the board had limits in NLRB cases, not every worker in the United States enjoyed the protection of the FLSA.

In deciding the issue of coverage in a given case, Murrah recognized that the inquiry was fact intensive, that "definitions of coverage, and legal interpretations thereof, do not solve the ultimate problem of applying the particular facts to the legal concepts of the movement of commerce," *New Mexico Public Service Company v. Engel*, 145 F.2d 636 at 639 (10th Cir. 1944), that precedent was "not harmonious and [was] of value only in determining what has been included...and what has been excluded"—*ibid.*

Workers who unloaded equipment, tools, and supplies which had been shipped in interstate commerce and then boxed and crated them for interstate shipment were covered, *Clyde v. Broderick*, 144 F.2d 348 (10th Cir. 1944), as was a plant engineer who operated the machinery at an electrical generating plant which sold some of its power to a railroad, a telephone and telegraph company, and an airport, *New Mexico Public Service Company v. Engel, supra*. But elevator operators in a building with some tenants who were engaged in interstate activities were not covered when the evidence failed to show that any of the persons actually transported in the elevators were engaged, directly or indirectly, in the production of goods for interstate commerce—*Rucker v. First National Bank of Miami, Oklahoma*, 138 F.2d 699 (10th Cir. 1943).

In *Seneca Coal and Coke Company v. Lofton*, 136 F.2d 359 (10th Cir. 1943), Murrah decided that a violation of the statute's provisions, based upon the employer's good faith belief that the law did not apply to its employees, was not a defense to liability for liquidated damages. "Liquidated damages granted by...the Act are mandatory and not discretionary with the courts. It follows that courts are not authorized to exercise judicial discretion based upon good faith violations"—*ibid.*, 363.

A somewhat unusual issue came before Phillips, Bratton, and Murrah in *Walling v. Mid-Continent Pipeline Company*, 143 F.2d 308 (10th Cir. 1944). The administrator of the wage and hour division of the department of labor sued to enjoin the defendant from violating the act. The district court heard the evidence, made findings of fact and conclusions of law, but declined to adjudicate the controversy, and dismissed the action with prejudice.

In reversing the judgment of dismissal, Murrah wrote that the suit "presented an actual controversy which the trial court had the province and the inescapable duty to...decide"—*ibid.*, 310. Canvassing the record, the panel held that the defendant had violated the law, and, because the trial court had not exercised its discretion in granting or refusing injunctive relief, the appellate court deemed "it proper to decide the issue upon the facts as presented by the trial court's findings"—*ibid.*, 311. Balancing the equities, Murrah and his colleagues concluded that the injunction should issue and reversed and remanded for that purpose.

The most significant Fair Labor Standards Act opinion written by Murrah was *Oklahoma Press Publishing Company v. Walling*, 147 F.2d 658 (10th Cir. 1945). Pursuant to the statute, the administrator issued an administrative subpoena to the Oklahoma Press Publishing Company directing it to produce its records concerning the hours worked and the wages paid its employees and concerning the distribution of its papers outside the state of Oklahoma. The company refused to comply, and the administrator instituted enforcement proceedings in the district court. The district court granted the relief sought, and the company appealed.

In the circuit, the company argued that the subpoena could not legally issue until there had been a conclusive determination that its employees were subject to the statute. Otherwise there would be a violation of the 4th

Amendment's prohibition against unreasonable searches and seizures. The administrator argued that the district court's role was purely ministerial, and upon proper application enforcement had to be ordered. Murrah, with Phillips and Bratton concurring, rejected both arguments.

Regarding the administrator's position, the court held that the statute's enforcement provisions "clearly envision[ed] a judicial act"—*ibid.*, 660. The act should not be read to deprive the courts "of the power of discretion in performance of the judicial function expressly committed to them and denied to the Administrator"—*ibid.*, 661.

Equally untenable was the company's argument. One's home could be entered and searched upon authority of a warrant issued by a judicial officer based upon an *ex parte* showing of probable cause, and "[s]urely it is not argued that the right of a person to be secure in his business from an unreasonable investigation under an administrative subpoena is greater or more sound than the right of a person to be secure from an unreasonable search and seizure in the privacy of his home"—*ibid.*, 662. Rather, the proper inquiry was whether the information sought by the subpoena was "pertinent to an inquiry which the Administrator is authorized by law to conduct in order to perform the functions imposed upon him by the Act"—*ibid.*

The powers of the administrator included determining if a particular employer or employee was subject to the statute, and whether the act had been contravened in a given instance. A requirement that coverage be shown conclusively before a subpoena could issue and be enforced would deny the administrator the "very powers deemed necessary in order to effectuate the purposes of the Act." Because the subpoena sought materials pertinent to administration of the act, the district court properly ordered compliance, and its judgment was affirmed. On appeal, the Supreme Court of the United States affirmed unanimously—*Oklahoma Press Publishing Company v. Walling*, 327 U.S. 186, 66 S.Ct. 494, 90 L.Ed. 614, 1945.

The Railway Labor Act did for covered employees in the railroad industry what the National Labor Relations Act did for employees in other industries. Sometimes, however, the law operated to harm, rather than benefit, a given employee. In *Lewellyn v. Fleming*, 154 F.2d 211 (10th Cir. 1946), Murrah held for the court that the statute could abrogate rights under a private contract which concerned matters within the scope of the legislation. Thus an employee who would have enjoyed certain seniority rights by virtue of a private contract lost those rights because of a collective bargaining agreement. The employee had "no constitutional right to insist upon the observance of a private contract, the effect of which is to deny the incidence of a [bargaining agreement] entered into in furtherance of an expressed Congressional policy, which the Congress is free to adopt"—*ibid.*, 214.

With the New Deal came the National Labor Relations Act and the Fair Labor Standards Act. With World War II came the Emergency Price Control Act of 1942. This statute established the Office of Price Administration and gave its administrator broad authority to set maximum prices and rents. Suits to recover damages for past violations of pricing regulations and to enjoin future violations could be brought in federal district court with appeal to the appropriate circuit, but judicial review of the validity of a regulation, as opposed to whether it had been violated, was vested exclusively in two courts, the emergency Court of Appeals and the Supreme Court of the United States. The Emergency Court of Appeals was composed of three or more federal district and circuit judges appointed by the Chief Justice of the United States, and it had "exclusive equity jurisdiction, subject to review by certiorari in the Supreme Court, to determine the validity of regulations, orders, and price schedules issued pursuant to the price control act" (Moore's *Federal Practice*, I, ¶ 0.3[9], 57).

Murrah saw the act as part of the national effort required to win the war, and his opinions interpreting and applying the statute read it accordingly. He wrote opinions rigorously observing the jurisdictional limitations imposed by the legislation on federal district courts and the circuit courts of appeals, *Bowles v. Nu Way Laundry Company*, 144 F.2d 741 (10th Cir. 1944); interpreting expansively the administrator's standing to bring civil suits for violations of pricing regulations, *Bowles v. Madl*, 153 F.2d 21 (10th Cir. 1945); and holding that strict, not substantial, compliance with a regulation was a precondition to the right to charge the regulated price, *Baggett v. Fleming*, 160 F.2d 651 (10th Cir. 1947).

Ruling against a person on the merits regarding violations of a regulation was one thing. Denying the person the opportunity to argue the merits was another matter, one which Murrah would not countenance if he could avoid it.

Initial attacks on the validity of a regulation were to be made before the administrator. If unsuccessful, the aggrieved person could then seek relief from the Emergency Court of Appeals, the decision of which was reviewable by the supreme court on certiorari. Exhaustion of administrative remedies was a usual prerequisite for judicial review. However, a person who was sued in district court by the administrator for violating a regulation could obtain leave from the district court after final judgment to file a complaint in the Emergency Court of Appeals challenging the validity of the regulation without having first complained to the administrator if the challenge was made in good faith and with good and sufficient cause for failure to challenge the regulation's validity before the administrator.

In *MacRae v. Creedon*, 162 F.2d 989 (10th Cir. 1947), a person had protested a regulation, but sent the protest to the incorrect office. She then was sued by the administrator for damages and injunctive relief for violating the contested regulation and sought leave to file a complaint in the Emergency Court of Appeals challenging the regulation's validity. The administrator argued that her failure to protest before him barred her from judicial review. The district court agreed, and denied relief.

Nonsense, wrote Murrah, when the case reached the circuit. Good faith and reasonableness were shown by attempting to lodge a protest and by strenuously arguing the confiscatory character of the regulation throughout the litigation. Through no fault the defendant had been caught in an "administrative phalanx...and now [came] before the bar of this court entangled in a maze of procedural technicalities"—*ibid.*, 994. The judgment was reversed with directions to grant leave to file the appeal, for this was precisely the type of situation to which the ameliorative language of the law applied. The defendant might not—probably would not—win on the merits, but she should be heard.[18]

Not surprisingly, the tenth circuit heard and decided many cases having their genesis in the complicated—and often uneasy—relationship among the Indians of Oklahoma, the federal government, and the state of Oklahoma. These appeals required the court to address difficult questions of statutory construction and interpretation, the constitutionality of federal legislation, and jurisdictional conflicts between state and federal courts. Murrah wrote frequently in the area, and his opinions contributed significantly to the circuit's Indian law jurisprudence.

A 1901 act of congress authorized the secretary of the interior to grant appropriate state officials permission to open and establish highways across lands held in severalty by restricted Indians. The building and maintenance of the highway had to be "in accordance with the laws of the State or Territory in which the lands" were situated (§ 4 of the Act of March 3, 1901, 31 Stat. 1084).

Pursuant to this statute, the secretary of the interior in 1928 granted permission for the construction of a highway crossing land owned by a restricted Kickapoo. Years later, in conformity with state law, Oklahoma authorized a public utility to construct and maintain a rural electric line along the highway where it traversed the restricted Indian's land. The United States, through the secretary of the interior, sued for a judgment declaring its rights, for an injunction requiring removal of the poles, and for money damages, claiming that permission from the secretary was required before the building and maintenance of the lines would be legal.

The district court held for the defendant, and an appeal was taken. Writing for the court, Murrah said the task before it was to determine what congressional policy was regarding the building on lands subject to the exclusive control of the United States "of highways, electric, telephone and telegraph lines necessary and essential to the needs of an advancing and progressive civilization"—*ibid.*, 352. After an exhaustive canvass of the relevant acts, Murrah concluded that congress had evinced no "purpose to restrict the grant of the right-of-way beyond the requirements of state law, in accordance with which the highway was opened and established." Because the building of the rural electric line was in conformity with Oklahoma law, the judgment of the district court was affirmed—*United States v. Oklahoma Gas & Electric Company*, 127 F.2d 349 (10th Cir. 1942). The supreme court granted certiorari and affirmed—*United States v. Oklahoma Gas & Electric Co.*, 318 U.S. 206, 63 S.Ct. 534, 87 L.Ed. 716 (1943).

Take me out to the ball game. The Old Court watches the Oklahoma City Indians play the Shreveport Sports. From the left: Judge Bratton, Murrah, Judge Phillips, and Judge Huxman. Trailing, the Indians tied the game in the 9th inning and won it 9 to 8 in the 10th inning. (Published in the Oklahoma City Times *on May 14, 1948. Courtesy Oklahoma Publishing Company.)*

When Peter Minco, a restricted member of the Five Tribes, died, petitions for letters of administration were filed in the county courts of Okfuskee and Tulsa counties. The Tulsa county matter was removed to the United States District Court for the Northern District of Oklahoma.[19] Before any rulings were made in the removed action, the county court of Okfuskee County held that the decedent had died a resident of that county, that it had jurisdiction to administer his estate, and appointed administrators. Subsequently, the northern district held the actions of the Okfuskee county court void for want of jurisdiction and appointed different administrators. The Okfuskee county administrators moved to vacate the northern district appointments, Judge Savage refused, and an appeal was taken.

The circuit reversed—*Merrell v. United States*, 140 F.2d 602 (10th Cir. 1944). Murrah wrote that once the fact upon which the jurisdiction of the probate court to administer the estate depended, residence of the decedent in the county at the time of his death, was litigated and adjudicated by the state court, the federal court was required to give conclusive effect to that jurisdictional determination and dismiss the proceedings before it.

There may be no more contentious litigation than when the living fight over what the dead have left behind. This was certainly the case with Jackson Barnett's estate. Barnett, a full-blood Creek, died owning an estate with a net value of $1,235,724.72, representing the proceeds of oil and gas produced on his restricted allotment. Quiet title actions were commenced in McIntosh and Muskogee counties, and administration proceedings were commenced in Muskogee County. The ultimate goal of all these proceedings was determination of heirship and distribution of the estate.

The United States removed the suits to the United States District Court for the Eastern District of Oklahoma. Alleging that all Barnett's heirs were restricted Indians, it asked the court to require those claiming an interest in the estate to appear and offer their proofs in the eastern district, determine Barnett's heirs, and distribute the estate accordingly. After a trial of five years, the district court determined the heirs, all of whom were restricted Indians, and distributed the estate to be held by the secretary of the interior for the heirs' use and benefit. The district court's decision was affirmed—*Scott v. Beams*, 122 F.2d 777 (10th Cir. 1941), 132 F.2d 985 (10th Cir. 1942).

Subsequently, attorneys for the successful claimants filed a petition for attorney fees. After notice and hearing, the district court approved a fee of 25 percent of the amount recovered to be paid proportionately from the distributive share of each successful heir.

The United States appealed. Its principal contention on appeal was that, because an Oklahoma court could not award attorney fees to be paid from the funds of a restricted Indian without approval of the secretary of the interior, the federal court on removal had no greater power.

Murrah began by referring to the historic power of a court of equity to award a fee to an attorney who creates a fund for the benefit of her client and others, the fee to be paid by those benefitting from the fund. The district court had relied upon this power in making the award, and the judgment should stand unless the removal character of the action made it inapplicable.

As a general proposition it was correct, Murrah wrote, that the jurisdiction of a federal court on removal is coexistive with the jurisdiction of the court from which the case was removed. But the state actions in this instance had been removed not pursuant to the general removal statute, but under a specific statute providing for removal of state actions concerning the lands of members of the Five Tribes or the proceeds, profits, or rents derived from said lands. Under this statute the removal court had the full plenitude of jurisdiction it would possess if the action had been filed originally in federal court. The United States could have filed suit initially in federal court, and in such an action the federal court would have had traditional equitable jurisdiction, including the power to award attorney fees under the common fund rule. Consequently, Judge Williams had the power to award fees, and because his award was well within his judicial discretion, the judgment was affirmed—*United States v. Anglin & Stevenson*, 145 F.2d 622 (10th Cir. 1944). Subsequently, the court, again Murrah writing, held that the lawyers could not recover interest on the judgment—*Anglin & Stevenson v. United States*, 160 F.2d 670 (10th Cir. 1947).

That most essential attribute of sovereignty, the power to tax, was a frequent subject of tenth circuit decisions. Murrah wrote opinions for the court: (1) sustaining the standing of the United States to sue to recover state taxes illegally assessed against and collected from unrestricted Indians, and holding that a judgment in a prior action against the assignee of the Indians was not binding on the United States—*Bryan County, Oklahoma v. United States*, 123 F.2d 782 (10th Cir. 1941)—and (2) holding that restricted, but taxable, Indian lands could be sold for delinquent ad valorem taxes—*United States v. Hester*, 137 F.2d 145 (10th Cir. 1943). When his colleagues held that Oklahoma could not impose an inheritance tax upon the restricted estates of deceased full blood Indians, Murrah dissented—*United States v. Oklahoma Tax Commission*, 131 F.2d 635 (10th Cir. 1942)—a view which was vindicated when the supreme court granted certiorari, and reversed—*Oklahoma Tax Com'n v. United States*, 319 U.S. 598, 63 S.Ct. 1284, 87 L.Ed. 1612 (1943).[20]

In *United States v. Hellard*, 322 U.S. 363, 64 S.Ct. 985, 88 L.Ed. 1326 (1944), the Supreme Court of the United States held that any state court partition judgment involving restricted Indian lands rendered in proceedings in which the United States was not a party was void. The *Hellard* decision was then overturned by statute—§ 3, Public Law 116, 79th Congress, Chapter 223, 59 Stat. 313.

Whether constitutionally the statute could retroactively validate a partition judgment which fell within the condemnatory language of *Hellard* was considered by

Phillips, Bratton, and Murrah in *Goddard v. Frazier*, 156 F.2d 938 (10th Cir. 1946). The legislation was attacked on the ground that retroactive validation was violative of the due process clause of the 5th Amendment.

Speaking for a unanimous panel, Murrah drew a distinction between jurisdictional defects in a proceeding which could not be cured by retroactive legislative and nonjurisdictional or modal defects which could be cured retroactively. Whether the statute violated due process depended not upon "legalistic formulae, but...upon considerations of fundamental fairness"—*ibid.*, 941. Because congress could have expressly provided that the United States did not have to be a party to partition proceedings, and because jurisdiction failed not because it could not be conferred but because it had been invoked improperly, the curative legislation was "founded upon justice and equity, generated...to right a wrong and...not unconstitutional"—*ibid.*, 943.

Within a six-day period in 1936, congress passed two acts having important consequences for the taxing powers of state and local governments. The Act of June 20, 1936, declared restricted lands purchased from trust or restricted funds to be instrumentalities of the federal government and nontaxable, while the Act of June 26, 1936, gave the secretary of the interior discretionary authority to acquire for Indians "agricultural and grazing lands of good character"—§ 1 Act of June 26, 1936, 49 Stat. 1967. Title was to be taken by the United States in trust for the Indian for whose benefit the lands were acquired, and while the lands were held by the United States they were to be free from taxation.

The constitutionality of both statutes was addressed by the tenth circuit in opinions written by Murrah. In *Board of County Commissioners, etc. v. Seber*, 130 F.2d 663 (10th Cir. 1942), the court held the Act of June 20,

1936, a valid exercise of the power of congress to legislate for its Indian wards. The acquisition of lands for the Indian ward, the restricting the same against alienation without the consent and approval of the secretary of the interior, and the immunizing of the lands from state taxation were constituent parts of that power, and congress could exercise none, some, or all as it chose. Additionally, the circuit held that the United States was not subject to state procedural requirements in suits to recover taxes assessed and collected contra to the statute. The supreme court granted certiorari, and affirmed—*Board of County Com'rs v. Seber*, 318 U.S. 705, 63 S.Ct. 920, 87 L.Ed. 1094 (1943); rehearing denied, 319 U.S. 782, 63 S.Ct. 1162, 87 L.Ed. 1726 (1943).

In *Board of Commissioners of Pawnee County, Oklahoma v. United States*, 139 F.2d 248 (10th Cir. 1943), the circuit court of appeals held that the Oklahoma Indian Welfare Act of June 26, 1936, was not an unconstitutional delegation of legislative authority to the secretary of the interior. The requirement that the lands acquired be "agricultural and grazing lands of good character and quality in proportion to the respective needs of the particular Indian" sufficiently declared congressional policy so that the secretary's discretion to acquire was limited and informed, rather than arbitrary and capricious. It would have been unreasonable to expect congress to choose the particular lands or the particular Indians who were to benefit. Consequently, the vesting of those decisions in the secretary, "the guardian of the Indian ward" —*ibid.*, 252—was reasonable, and in conformity with the power of congress to delegate to the executive "appropriate discretion in the administration and effectuation of declared congressional policy"—*ibid.*, 251.

The sovereignty issues raised by the Indian cases did not exhaust the fund of tax questions reviewed by the circuit. Other Murrah opinions sustained the constitutionality of the capital stock taxes levied by the National Industrial Recovery Act—*Utah Oil Refining Company v. Hinckley*, 121 F.2d 578 (10th Cir. 1941); interpreted an act of congress allowing, as a matter of "legislative grace," the recovery of taxes levied and collected under an unconstitutional statute—*Linder Packing & Provisions Company v. Commissioner of Internal Revenue*, 118 F.2d 656 (10th Cir. 1941); addressed the right of a party to a private contract to recover taxes included in the contract price and paid to the other contracting party, but not paid by that party to the sovereign when the tax was declared unconstitutional—*United States v. American Packing and Provision Company*, 122 F.2d 445 (10th Cir. 1941); and considered the res judicata effect of tax judgments—*Gillespie v. Commissioner of Internal Revenue*, 151 F.2d 903 (10th Cir. 1945).

Whether the income from a family trust was taxable to the grantor under Section 22 of the Internal Revenue Code was a recurrent subject of appellate opinions. Murrah visited the issue in *Jones v. Norris*, 122 F.2d 6 (10th Cir. 1941), and *Hall v. Commissioner of Internal Revenue*, 150 F.2d 304 (10th Cir. 1945), writing that taxability depended ultimately on whether the grantor, after creation of the trust, could still be treated as the owner of the corpus, i.e., whether the grantor could realize economic gain from the trust agreement. The answer to this query required close scrutiny of the facts of the transaction in question, and the issue was one of law.

The power of a state or its political subdivisions to tax came before the court in *Chestnut Securities Company v. Oklahoma Tax Commission*, 125 F.2d 571 (10th Cir. 1942), and *Morton Salt Company v. City of South Hutchison*, 159 F.2d 897 (10th Cir. 1947). *Chestnut* involved the constitutionality of an Oklahoma statute

An avid outdoorsman, Murrah looks at the day's catch.

which taxed the income from intangible securities owned by a Delaware corporation and located without Oklahoma. The basis for subjecting the income to the taxing power of Oklahoma was that the corporation had its principal place of business in Oklahoma. The statute did not violate the due process or equal protection clauses of the 14th Amendment, Murrah wrote, because the taxpayer had benefitted from its affiliation with and relationship to Oklahoma. The state was doing no more than requiring "those who avail themselves of the privileges and protections afforded by the State of Oklahoma to bear the proportionate burden"—125 F.2d 571 at 575.

The procedural posture in which *Morton Salt Company* was decided is important for understanding the case. The complainant owned property having an assessed value of 46 percent of the total assessed value of property within the city. Bonds were to be issued for the construction of a waterworks system, and the complainant was to be assessed for 46 percent of the tax levy made for payment of the bonds even though the system would not supply water to any property owned by the taxpayer.

Pleading due process and equal protection claims, the taxpayer sought to enjoin issuance of the bonds. After a hearing, the district court denied a preliminary injunction, but the circuit granted a stay pending appeal. Because the appeal was from the denial of temporary injunctive relief, the issue was not who would prevail on the merits finally. Rather it was whether the complainant faced the danger of irreparable injury, whether the equities favored or disfavored injunctive relief, and whether the complainant was likely to prevail on the merits. There was no dispute that the taxpayer would be harmed irreparably if the bonds were sold, nor that the city could be protected by requiring the complainant to post security for any loss resulting from issuance of the injunction. What, then, were the taxpayer's chances of winning on the claim that the tax as applied to it was unconstitutional?

Starting from the proposition that state taxing power was subject to few constitutional constraints, Murrah wrote there was no rule of absolute equality or uniformity in taxation, nor was it a valid constitutional attack that the taxpayer was not benefitted directly by the tax or that the taxpayer was benefitted less than others paying the same levy.

Nevertheless, the taxing power did admit of limitations. Fourteenth Amendment due process was violated if there was a flagrant and palpable inequality between the tax imposed and the benefit conferred. Turning to the case at bar, the complainant's allegation that it would have to bear 46 percent of the tax burden for what at most would be indirect benefits from the waterworks project raised "a serious constitutional question...which should be decided first by the trial court after a full hearing" —*ibid.*, 902. Consequently the matter was remanded with directions to grant a preliminary injunction. Judge Phillips concurred, while Judge Huxman dissented.

As a matter of exclusive federal concern and following in the wake of the Great Depression, bankruptcy appeals were a significant part of the circuit's docket. More often than not the appeal focused on the powers of the bankruptcy court.

Writing in *Brinton v. Federal Land Bank of Berkeley*, 129 F.2d 740 (10th Cir. 1942), Murrah held that a final order of dismissal for failure of the debtor to pursue bankruptcy proceedings with due diligence did not bar a subsequent invocation of the bankruptcy court's jurisdiction as to the same property as long as the debtor had a justiciable interest, while *Paradise Land and Livestock v. Federal Land Bank*, 131 F.2d 950 (10th Cir. 1942), sustained the power of the bankruptcy court to vacate, change or modify an order fixing rents in a farmer-debtor proceeding as long as the bankruptcy case had not been terminated. A contrary ruling "would unduly restrict the equitable jurisdiction of the court to effectuate the beneficent and equitable purposes of the Act"—*ibid.*, 952.

The complexities which can characterize bankruptcy litigation at times were well illustrated in *Miller v. Mangus, et al.*, 125 F.2d 507 (10th Cir. 1942). A husband and wife entered into a contract for purchase of land as joint tenants. Encountering financial difficulties, the husband filed for bankruptcy protection while the contract was in default, but before forfeiture. After forfeiture, the wife attempted to join as a petitioning debtor.

Writing for the court, Murrah held that the wife had lost any interest which she had in the contract before attempting to become a party to the bankruptcy proceedings, and, consequently, she had no estate which could be administered in bankruptcy. Because, however, she was an indispensable party to the proceedings, that is one without whom the court could not in equity and good conscience proceed, the husband's interest as joint tenant in the land purchase contract could not be administered in bankruptcy.

The supreme court granted certiorari and reversed—*Mangus v. Miller*, 317 U.S. 178, 63 S.Ct. 182, 87 L.Ed. 169 (1942). Writing per Chief Justice Harlan Fiske Stone, the court held that the language of the statute allowed a single joint tenant to file for bankruptcy protection without some or all of the remaining joint tenants joining. Concerning the difficulties of administering the estate because of lack of clarity of the respective rights of the parties, Stone wrote that those difficulties could be obviated "by affording the interested parties opportunity to assert their rights in the state courts and, when they were ascertained and defined, by administering the debtor's interest as the Act provides, so far as they may be found to be practicable"—317 U.S. at 185; 63 S.Ct. at 185, 87 L.Ed. 169 at 174.

Resolving a great contrariety of opinion, the supreme court in *United States v. Hudson and Goodwin*, 7 Cranch 32 (1812), held that the jurisdiction of the federal courts did not extend to common law crimes. For conduct to be prosecutable in federal court as a crime, it would have to be made criminal by legislative act. The Article I powers most frequently relied upon by congress for this purpose are the powers to lay and collect taxes and to regulate interstate commerce. What conduct congress can make criminal under the interstate commerce clause was the subject of a 1995 supreme court case, *United States v. Lopez*, 115 S. Ct. 1624, 131 L.Ed. 2d 626 (1995), and produced a sharply divided court.

Judgments of conviction for violation of the internal

revenue laws relating to liquor dealers,[21] income tax evasion,[22] mail fraud,[23] transporting a female across a state line for purposes of prostitution or debauchery or other immoral purpose,[24] obstructing and impeding the administration of justice,[25] homicide in Indian country,[26] and that favorite of federal prosecutors, conspiracy,[27] were all scrutinized in Murrah opinions. The issues raised by the appeals usually concerned sufficiency of the evidence to convict, admissibility of evidence, jury instructions, and interpretation and construction of statutory language.

Federal courts in the 1990s daily wrestle with what constitutes an unreasonable search and seizure violative of 4th Amendment. And so it was in the 1940s.

Pursuant to two arrest warrants, federal agents seized George Harris at his apartment. In searching the apartment for two canceled checks, which were relevant to the offenses for which Harris had been arrested, the officers found a number of selective service registration certificates and notice of classification cards. Indicted for illegal possession of the draft materials, Harris sought to suppress them as the fruits of an unlawful search and seizure. The district court denied the suppression motion, admitted the cards and certificates into evidence over the objection of Harris, and convicted him after a bench trial.

The circuit affirmed—*Harris v. United States*, 151 F.2d 837 (10th Cir. 1945). Murrah wrote that a search and seizure conducted without a valid search warrant was usually unreasonable, thus rendering the evidence obtained by it inadmissible and making any conviction based upon such evidence infirm. But the law recognized an exception to the warrant requirement for searches incident to a valid arrest. Then, and without warrant, officers could search for and seize the instrumentalities or fruits of the crime for which the arrest was made. Applying that exception to the record before it, Murrah concluded that the agents had not conducted a prohibited general, exploratory search, but one for the checks which had been used to commit the offenses for which Harris had been arrested. The registration certificates and draft cards had been found and seized in the course of the legitimate search for the contraband checks and thus there was no 4th Amendment violation. The Supreme Court of the United States granted certiorari and affirmed—*Harris v. United States*, 331 U.S. 145, 67 S.Ct. 1098, 91 L.Ed. 1399 (1947); rehearing denied, 331 U.S. 867, 67 S.Ct. 1527, 91 L.Ed. 1871 (1947).

The application of the 4th Amendment to cars was considered in *Hart v. United States*, 162 F.2d 74 (10th Cir. 1947). Convicted of transporting intoxicating liquor into dry Oklahoma, the appellant challenged on constitutional grounds the search of the car, the seizure of the contraband found in it, and its admission into evidence against him. Recognizing that the mobility of cars could justify warrantless searches under certain conditions, Murrah said that a warrantless search was proper only if it was not "reasonably practical to obtain a search warrant"—*ibid.*, 76. If probable cause were the sole test of reasonableness, then the judicial role was limited "to a postmortem examination," and the exceptions would "consume the rule, and render impotent those safeguards which...have been called 'the very essence of constitutional liberty and security'" —*ibid.* Because it would have been possible to obtain a warrant, the search could not be justified by the existence of probable cause standing alone. The search and seizure were unreasonable, the evidence was admitted improperly, and the judgment of conviction was reversed.

Federal criminal convictions are subject to challenge by direct appeal, and federal and state convictions are reviewable by habeas corpus as well. The writ enables a prisoner to challenge the legality of his detention by an

Just sitting and waiting for the coffee to make was good relaxation from the burdens of judging.

original proceeding in federal district court with appellate review in the circuit court of appeals. At one time the writ would test only whether the committing court had jurisdiction to deprive the petitioner of his liberty. Over the years the concept of jurisdiction was given a broader and broader reading until, shortly after Murrah reached the bench, it was held that habeas was available to set aside a conviction whenever it had been obtained in violation of constitutional guarantees.[28]

There is, then, a significant distinction between matters cognizable by direct appeal, and matters cognizable by habeas. Trial errors which are reviewable on direct appeal, e.g., the admission of evidence, are not reviewable by federal habeas unless they implicate constitutional values, e.g., the 5th Amendment protection against compelled self-incrimination. Habeas is not a substitute for appeal; rather it is to guard against deprivations of liberty by constitutionally infirm action.

Murrah took an expansive view of the scope of habeas inquiry. Writing in *Baker v. Hudspeth*, 129 F.2d 779 (10th Cir. 1942), he held that a claim of misconduct by the jury and the United States marshal, if true, "would be wholly obnoxious to the fundamental rules of fairness and justice, as contemplated by the spirit of petitioner's constitutional safeguards"—*ibid.*, 782—and thus a proper habeas claim, as was a claim that the petitioner was insane at the time of his trial, conviction and sentence—*Brewer v. Hunter*, 163 F.2d 341 (10th Cir. 1947).

In applying constitutional guarantees in habeas cases, Murrah sought to give them substance and not mere form. *Johnson v. Zerbst*, 304 U.S. 458, 58 S.Ct. 1019, 82 L.Ed. 1461 (1938), allowed a petitioner to assert denial of the 6th Amendment right to counsel by habeas. In *Willis v. Hunter*, 166 F.2d 721 (10th Cir. 1948), Murrah held "that the right to the effective assistance of counsel contemplates the guiding hand of an able and responsible lawyer, devoted solely to the interest of his client[,] who has ample opportunity to acquaint himself with the law and facts of the case, and is afforded an opportunity to present them to a court or jury in their most favorable light"—*ibid.*, 723. Subsequently, the fifth circuit adopted the Willis standard as the proper test for effectiveness of representation—*Roberts v. Dutton*, 368 F.2d 465 (5th Cir. 1966).

The right to effective assistance of counsel came before Murrah again in *Beets v. Hunter, et al.*, 75 F.Supp. 825 (D. Kan. 1948), another habeas case. This time, however, Murrah was sitting by designation as a district judge.[29]

The petitioner had been convicted by court martial proceeding in which he had been represented by a military JAG lawyer who had not seen the charges until the day before trial. Having no hesitancy in concluding that "this petitioner was entitled to due process of law while in Germany fighting for his country...the same as if he were walking the streets of Kansas City, Kansas"—*ibid.*, 825, 826—Murrah held that the trial was "wholly obnoxious and repulsive" to fundamental fairness, "saturated with tyranny," an "empty and farcical thing"—*ibid.*, 826. The writ issued, and no appeal was taken.

Because federal courts have limited, not general, subject matter jurisdiction, the power to hear and decide a given case or controversy must be established affirmatively. It cannot arise by implication, consent or waiver, and the court has the right, indeed the duty, to satisfy itself that the matter being litigated lies within its adjudicatory authority.

Murrah explored the intricacies of federal subject matter jurisdiction in several opinions. The questions considered included when a case arises under federal law for purposes of federal question jurisdiction, *Viles v. Symes*, 129 F.2d 828 (10th Cir. 1942); when a suit can be maintained against the United States under the Tucker Act, *United States v. Ohio Oil Company*; 163 F.2d 633 (10th Cir. 1947); the significance of the citizenship of unanswering and unknown defendants for determining whether all the plaintiffs have different state citizenship from all the defendants, *Becker v. Angle*, 165 F.2d 140 (10th Cir. 1947); and interpretation and application of the general removal statute, *Updike v. West*, 172 F.2d 663 (10th Cir. 1949).

An exceedingly interesting interplay of jurisdictional and remedial provisions was presented in *Delaney v. Carter Oil Company*, 174 F.2d 314 (10th Cir. 1949). The plaintiff sued three defendants for declaratory relief that a contract between plaintiff and two of the defendants was binding on all the defendants, and determining the respective rights and duties of defendants under the contract.

Jurisdiction was based on diversity, the plaintiff being a citizen of West Virginia, the defendants being citizens of Oklahoma, and requisite amount in controversy.

Two of the defendants then asserted a cross-claim against the remaining defendant. Because all the defendants were citizens of Oklahoma, the power to adjudicate the cross-claim depended on the power to adjudicate the principal claim. Jurisdiction of the principal claim would, under the concept of ancillary jurisdiction, carry the cross-claim as well. The cross-claim defendant argued that because he had admitted he was bound by the contract, the plaintiff had no justiciable controversy with him, and thus there was no jurisdiction over the main claim.

Incorrect, said Murrah. The existence or nonexistence of jurisdiction was to be determined by the allegations of the complaint. While plaintiff did not pray for coercive relief, that is monetary damages or injunctive relief, plaintiff did seek a determination of the respective rights and obligations of the parties to the contract.

The ascertainment of legal rights and duties so that one could order one's conduct accordingly was one "of the highest offices of declaratory procedure"—*ibid.*, 317. Plaintiff's complaint stated a justiciable controversy between adverse parties, the cross-defendant's concession of some of plaintiff's claims constituted "an exercise of jurisdiction and not a denial of it"—*ibid.*, 316—and the district court had jurisdiction to decide the cross-claim. The judgment of dismissal was reversed, and the case remanded for further proceedings.

Murrah came to the bench in 1937, and the Federal Rules of Civil Procedure became effective in 1938. Proceeding from the premise that cases should be decided on the merits, not on technicalities, the rules approached procedural matters from the practicalities and pragmatics of litigation. Murrah's years on the bench would be a consistent effort to make the promise of the rules, and of federal procedural and remedial provisions generally, a reality.

One of the most important provisions of the Federal Rules of Civil Procedure is Rule 56. This authorizes the entry of judgment without trial if there is no genuine issue of material fact. This is deemed proper because if the dispositive facts are not controverted there is nothing for the jury to decide.

Murrah wrote for his court concerning when summary judgment is proper in *Avrick v. Rockmont Envelope Co.*, 155 F.2d 568 (10th Cir. 1946). Summary disposition of cases if the legally operative facts were not in dispute was a rational procedural goal, but it was "not the purpose of the rule to deprive litigants of their right to a full hearing on the merits if any real issue of fact is tendered. The power to pierce the flimsy and transparent veil should be temperately and cautiously used lest abuse reap nullification"—*ibid.*, 571.[30]

Another Federal Rule of Civil Procedure, Rule 59, concerning the grant of new trials, received an interesting application in *Barush v. Beech Aircraft Corporation*, 172 F.2d 445 (10th Cir. 1949). In *Barush*, the matter had been tried to judgment in the district court and an appeal properly perfected to the circuit. The losing party then petitioned the court of appeals to remand the case to the district court for it to rule upon a new trial motion based on newly discovered evidence. Murrah wrote that remand should not be ordered unless it was reasonably apparent, considering the newly proffered evidence, that "the trial court would be disposed to grant a new trial"—*ibid.* Canvassing the record, the panel concluded that the requisite showing had not been met and denied remand.

Murrah considered the declaratory judgment act a

statute to be given a broad reading consonant with its remedial purposes. In *Hargrove v. American Century Insurance Company*, 125 F.2d 225 (10th Cir. 1942), he wrote that whether the 7th Amendment right of jury trial applied in a declaratory judgment action depended on whether the issues were legal or equitable. If legal, there was a right to trial by jury; if equitable, there was not. A declaratory judgment proceeding was not, by definition, legal or equitable.

Is a deposition taken in one action admissible in a subsequent action absent complete identity of parties between the two cases? Relying upon Wigmore's analysis of the question, Murrah answered yes in *Insulated Wool Insulation Corporation v. Home Insulation*, 176 F.2d 502 (10th Cir. 1949), if the party against whom the deposition was offered had been a party to the prior proceeding, the cases involved identical issues, and the objecting party, or one with the same interest as the objecting party, was accorded full opportunity for cross-examination in the earlier case. This view was adopted subsequently in the Federal Rules of Evidence—see Federal Rules of Evidence 804.

The crash of a Western Airlines plane took the life of a husband and father. In a wrongful death action sounding in negligence, the plaintiffs offered the testimony of an aviation mechanic as an expert concerning the cause of the fatal crash. The district court sustained an objection to the testimony on the ground that the witness did not qualify as an expert, the jury returned a verdict for the defendant, and the plaintiff appealed.

The circuit reversed in a Murrah opinion—*Bratt v. Western Airlines*, 155 F.2d 850 (10th Cir. 1946). The trial court had great discretion in the admission or exclusion of evidence, but the discretion had to be exercised within legal bounds. If the trial court applied the incorrect standard in informing its decision to exclude the evidence, then it was subject to corrective action by the appellate court.

The trial court had held the witness not qualified as an expert because (1) he had not been involved in an accident akin to the one in question, and (2) he did not have formal academic training in the area. Neither basis was a proper ground for excluding the testimony.

Expertise grounded on actual experience seldom would exist, Murrah wrote, for "few ever survive to relate their experience"—*ibid.*, 853. Scholastic training to be considered an expert was not, nor should be, the policy of the law, for such a rule would exclude highly probative evidence. Expertise could be found in practical experience as well as in textbooks, and it was for the jury to decide the weight to be given such evidence in a given case.

Of course, not all litigation presents public law questions or jurisdictional and procedural issues. Murrah spoke for the court on a wide variety of private law problems as well.

Questions of proximate cause—*Mandles v. Guardian Life Insurance Company of America*, 115 F.2d 994 (10th Cir. 1940)—predicting whether, under the Uniform Warehouse Receipts Act, New Mexico would place the burden on the warehouseman to show that in the exercise of ordinary care he is unable to deliver the bailed goods—*Denning Warehouse Co. v. Widener, et al.*, 172 F.2d 910 (10th Cir. 1949)—it would, for it "is a salutary rule, based upon experience"—*ibid.*, 913; subsequently, the Supreme Court of New Mexico agreed with the "view adopted by Judge Murrah and the reasoning upon which it is based"—*Cole v. Younger*, 58 N.M. 211, 269 P.2d 1096 at 1097 (N. Mex. 1954); common law fraud in a suit between "ignorant farmers" and their banker [guess who won]—*Lawson v. Haynes*, 170 F.2d 741 (10th Cir. 1948);

interpretation of the double indemnity clauses in life insurance policies—*Mutual Life Insurance Company v. Hassing*, 134 F.2d 714 (10th Cir. 1943); when an insured is entitled to settle a claim without the consent of the insurer and not forfeit his rights under the policy—*Traders and General Insurance Company v. Rudco Oil & Gas Company*, 129 F.2d 621 (10th Cir. 1942); and whether the mother or widow of a deceased serviceman was entitled to the benefits of a national service life insurance policy—*Bradley v. United States*, 143 F.2d 573 (10th Cir. 1944)—all were grist for Murrah's appellate opinion mill.

A fundamental concept of Anglo-American jurisprudence is proximate cause. Murrah's opinion in *Mandles v. Guardian Life Insurance Company of America*, *supra*, was an exhaustive treatment of the subject. A hospitalized mental patient complained of being bothered by voices. Persuaded to go to her bedroom, she went to the window to call for help, cut her arm when she thrust it through a glass window pane, contracted septicemia, and died.

Her life insurance policy provided for double indemnity if death resulted "directly and independently of all other causes from bodily injuries effected solely through external, violent and accidental means..." [and not] "directly or indirectly from bodily or mental infirmity or illness or disease in any form"—115 F.2d 994 at 995. The question was whether death could be traced proximately to the decedent's mental illness, or whether the chain of causation started with thrusting the hand through the window.

Beginning with Lord Bacon, employing the standard canons of construction, and acknowledging that the question "has been the subject of prolific litigation and has resulted in some sharp conflict along the way"—*ibid.*—Murrah, with Phillips and Bratton agreeing, concluded that the chain of causation did not begin with the thrusting but was proximately traceable to the decedent's mental illness. Consequently, recovery could not be had under the double indemnity clause.

Mervyn S. Bennion was captain of the U.S.S. *West Virginia* when Pearl Harbor was attacked on December 7, 1941. Captain Bennion was killed by a fragment of a Japanese bomb, his widow claimed under the double indemnity clause of a life insurance policy, and the insurer denied recovery. The plaintiff prevailed in the district court, and the insurance company appealed—*New York Life Ins. Co. v. Bennion*, 158 F.2d 260 (10th Cir. 1946). The defendant's position was plaintiff could not recover because the policy excluded coverage for death resulting from "war or an act incident thereto"—*ibid.*, 261.

Writing for himself and Judge Broaddus,[31] Murrah held that the dispositive phrase was unambiguous and that the parties had contracted with reference to "any type or kind of war in which the hazard of human life was involved"—*ibid.*, 265. Thus formally declared war was not necessary for the exclusionary language to apply. Judge Huxman dissented, writing that the phrase was ambiguous and thus should be construed most strongly against the insurer to exclude only death resulting from a legal war.

Federal courts heard many cases seeking recovery under World War I war risk insurance policies. The setting was always the same. A policy was issued, the insured at some point ceased paying premiums, died, and the beneficiary sought the policy proceeds. Payment was refused based on the lapse in premiums, but the beneficiary claimed that the insured had been totally and permanently disabled before he ceased paying premiums; thus the policy was continued in full force and effect until his death.

These cases are marvelous vignettes of social history

Judge "Fish" and William O. "Justice Bill" Douglas were in Oklahoma City to keynote a meeting of the local chapter of the Urban League. (Published in the Daily Oklahoman *on November 30, 1960. Courtesy Oklahoma Publishing Company.)*

of the United States in the years following the Great War. Murrah wrote on the subject in *United States v. McCain*, 118 F.2d 479 (10th Cir. 1941); *Dye v. United States*, 123 F.2d 385 (10th Cir. 1941); and *United States v. Protsch*, 137 F.2d 92 (10th Cir. 1943). The Supreme Court of the United States even visited the subject—see *Galloway v. United States*, 319 U.S. 372, 63 S.Ct. 1077, 87 L.Ed. 1584 (1943)—addressing the sufficiency of evidence to establish total and permanent disability.

Murrah sat on a three-judge court with Judges Huxman and Rice which heard a 1st Amendment freedom of press, speech, and assembly challenge to a Kansas labor law—*Stapleton v. Mitchell*, 60 F. Supp. 51 (D. Kan. 1945). There was clearly federal question subject matter jurisdiction, but it was argued that the federal court should decline to hear the case and require the parties to litigate the matter in a state court.

There was in federal jurisprudence, Murrah acknowledged, a doctrine of abstention, i.e., a voluntary refusal by a federal court to exercise power which it possessed by constitution and statute. As Murrah read the law, the doctrine had developed in cases where property rights were at issue, not in cases involving 1st Amendment freedom of expression values. When fundamental human liberties, such as those protected by the 1st Amendment, were the subject of litigation, then federal courts "are a proper forum for the determination of the question whether a state statute trespasses upon an area which the Federal Constitution has set apart as hallowed grounds for expression of democratic ideas"—*ibid.*, 55. Abstention in the case before the bar was not warranted, for "We yet like to believe that wherever the Federal courts sit, human rights under the Federal Constitution are always a proper subject for adjudication, and that we have not the right to decline the exercise of that jurisdiction simply because the rights asserted may be adjudicated in some other forum"—*ibid.*[32]

Proceeding to the merits, the court held certain portions of the statute facially violative of the 1st Amendment and granted injunctive relief. Judge Huxman dissented in part, urging that certain additional provisions of the statute were unconstitutional.

Stapleton considered the propriety of abstention in a case fraught with public law issues. In *Franklin Life Insurance Company v. Johnson*, 157 F.2d 653 (10th Cir. 1946), Murrah pondered when, if ever, in private civil litigation, a district court should decline to hear a diversity case for declaratory relief because of a pending concurrent state court action. Murrah still took a narrow view of when abstention was proper. The district court's discretion not to hear a case properly within its subject matter cognizance was a limited discretion, and its exercise was not warranted merely because another remedy was available. Rather, the controlling question was "whether there is such a plain, adequate and speedy remedy afforded in the pending state court action that a declaratory judgment will serve no useful purpose"—*ibid.*, 657. Finding the standard not met, the circuit reversed the district court's dismissal of the action, and remanded for proceedings on the merits. In yet another abstention case, *Versluis v. Town of Haskell*, 154 F.2d 935 (10th Cir. 1946), Murrah wrote that the difficulty of determining state law when it supplies the rule of decision is not warrant for declining to exercise jurisdiction "squarely conferred" by Article III and statute—154 F.2d at 937.

As recently as its 1994 term, the supreme court revisited the discretion vested in a district court to stay a declaratory judgment action during the pendency of parallel state proceedings. *Wilton v. Seven Falls Co.*, 115 S.Ct. 2137, 132 L.Ed. 2d 214 (1995). The court held that the discretion was of "unique breadth"—115 S. Ct. 2137 at 2143, 132 L.Ed. 2d 214 at 224.

Intellectually, Murrah accepted the doctrine of abstention.[33] Practically, he had great difficulty with a federal court refusing to hear a case when it had jurisdiction of the subject matter and the parties.[34]

Murrah had been on the appellate bench little more than a year when Pearl Harbor was attacked. Geoffrey Perret's title, *Days of Sadness, Years of Triumph*, for his book on the United States during World War II,[35] was poignantly descriptive for Murrah. He watched as his brother Cecil, Babe's brother Martin, and good friends such as Luther Bohanon and Tom Hieronymous answered the call to arms. Fortunately, all returned without harm, but others were not so fortunate.

Alfred Naifeh received his baccalaureate degree from the University of Oklahoma in 1937 and his law degree in 1940. He had strongly supported Murrah for appointment to the district court[36] and in 1940 was hired by Murrah as his law clerk. He served only a short time and then joined the Navy, earning a commission as a lieutenant, junior grade. Naifeh was killed in action during the Battle of the Solomons in 1942. For heroism in aiding survivors of the U.S.S. *Meredith*, he was awarded the purple heart posthumously, and a naval vessel, the U.S.S. *Naifeh*, was commissioned. The University of Oklahoma honored its son by naming Naifeh House, a dormitory, in his memory. More than 30 years after Naifeh's death, Murrah, reading an article about Naifeh, wrote Naifeh's brother that the article "brought back memories of one whom I loved and respected. As you know, he was my law clerk when he volunteered for service. I shan't ever forget our last visit."[37]

Murrah seriously considered entering military service. He wrote Justice William O. Douglas concerning the possibility of a leave of absence from the court, and when Douglas informed him that the administration had a blanket policy against leaves of absence, Murrah determined to resign. Eventually, however, he yielded to strong pressure from his colleagues to remain on the bench.[38]

Murrah and Douglas first met in 1938, and in 1941 they began a correspondence that would extend over the years. Murrah's initial letter to the justice was to invite Douglas to spend part of the summer at a lodge owned by a friend of Murrah's in New Mexico, an invitation which Douglas accepted.[39]

The letters quickly went from "My dear Justice Douglas"[40] and "My dear Judge Murrah"[41] to "Dear Justice Bill"[42] and "My dear Judge Fish."[43] Topics included opinions authored by Douglas,[44] speeches he had given and articles he had written,[45] his travels,[46] his health,[47] and their mutual friend Jimmie Allred.[48] Both shared a love of the outdoors, and fishing figured prominently in their letters. When a Washington, D.C., lawyer challenged Douglas about noodling, Douglas showed the attorney a letter Murrah had written explaining the art, and the lawyer conceded the issue.[49]

Apparently Douglas was interested in virtually anything and everything, including square dancing. On one occasion, Murrah promised to send Douglas "some square dance music and further directions very soon."[50] In the same letter, Murrah expressed the "hope that you will be able to induce Justice Frankfurter to participate as I feel quite sure that he will make a good caller with a little practice."[51]

Murrah was able to persuade Douglas to come to Oklahoma City for a speech, and whenever Murrah was in Washington, D.C., he and Douglas usually saw each other. Once Douglas took Murrah to lunch with his brethren on the supreme court. Thanking Douglas, Murrah observed that "they are inquisitive devils aren't they?"[52]

The Murrah-Douglas friendship was a good one, and Murrah ranked Douglas high in his pantheon of justices. He told Paul:

> Saw Mr. Justice Douglas in Washington the other day. He looked very good and he is as good as he looks. Honestly, Paul, he is a stalwart in the fight for the preservation of human rights. Little do we realize how quickly they can be whittled away or swallowed up in the frenzy and frustrations of public sentiment. We simply cannot seem to keep our balance when threatened by obnoxious ideologies from without. We always seem to destroy ourselves in the process of preservation. Well, it is men like Douglas who stand firm in the face of the mob.[53]

As the United States entered its first full year of global conflict in 1942, Oklahoma had its own version of hostilities—political warfare. Seeking a second term in the United States Senate, Josh Lee encountered significant primary opposition from Orel Busby, a former member of the state supreme court from Pontotoc County. After a heated primary campaign, Lee won renomination by a substantial margin, defeating Busby 188,279 to 96,647.[54]

Things did not go well in November, however. Originally the Republican nominee was W.B. Pine, who had served as United States Senator from 1925 to 1931. Pine died before the general election, and the Republican state central committee substituted E.H. Moore as the nominee. Moore, a Tulsa oil man, had been a Democrat as recently as 1940 when he headed the "Democrats for Wendell Wilkie" organization in Oklahoma. When the ballots were counted, Moore had scored a major upset, defeating Lee by almost 40,000 votes, 204,163 to 166,653.[55]

Sorely disappointed by the election results, Murrah wrote Lee that the "people not only let you down but they let those brave boys in our armed forces down as well, and they will have to pay the price."[56] To his brother Cecil, serving in the Navy, he confided that Lee's defeat "almost broke my heart."[57] More than anyone else, Murrah had been responsible for Lee making the 1936 senate race against a sitting senator, the incumbent governor, and the Oklahoma leader of the Townsend movement. His interest in Lee's career had not waned with the successful outcome of that contest. During Lee's senate years, Murrah corresponded with him concerning every aspect of the Oklahoma political scene—issues, people and patronage.[58] A Murrah draft formed the basis for Lee's 1942 reelection announcement,[59] and Murrah at one point harbored the thought that Lee might be the Democratic presidential nominee in 1940.[60] Murrah even suggested ways that Lee might receive publicity from H.V. Kaltenborn, the Dan Rather of yesteryear.[61]

For Murrah, the relationship with Lee was as close as brothers, and thus he was "prone to criticize as I would a brother."[62] Complimentary, critical, cajoling, one thread permeated Murrah's relationship with Lee—the desire, no, the determination, that Lee succeed politically. When Lee was defeated in 1942, the disappointment was deep and lasting.

Shortly after Lee left the senate in 1943, Roosevelt appointed him to the civil aeronautics board to fill an unexpired term ending that year. Subsequently, in 1943 and 1949, Lee was appointed to full six-year terms. His civil aeronautics board career ended in 1955 when he was unable to secure appointment to a third term. When Lee's term was expiring, Murrah pulled all the strings he could to secure Lee's reappointment.[63]

Murrah and Lee remained close over the years, and Murrah always recalled with pride when he marched "under the Josh Lee Banner."[64] When Lee's portrait was presented to the Oklahoma Historical Society in 1962, Murrah was the principal speaker,[65] and on the occasion of Lee's 75th birthday in 1967, the Rover Boys, "spear-headed by A.P. Murrah," hosted a birthday celebration for their mentor.[66] On that occasion, Lee said his highest contribution to the public good was the "young men and women I recommended to office," naming Murrah, Savage, and former United States Attorney Charles Dierker.[67] Before the end of the year, Joshua Bryan Lee was dead. Murrah was a pallbearer, accompanying his friend and sponsor on his last journey.[68]

For 20 years, from its creation in 1929 until 1949, the tenth circuit had been a four-judge court, and the four were Phillips, Bratton, Huxman, and Murrah. When congress authorized a fifth judge for the circuit in 1949, it presaged the end of an illustrious era in the history of the court.

Josh Lee and Murrah at a celebration of Lee's seventy-fifth birthday organized by the Rover Boys. Lee died before the end of the year. (Published in the Daily Oklahoman *on January 30, 1967. Courtesy Oklahoma Publishing Company.)*

Phillips, Bratton, Huxman, and Murrah were kindred beings. They judged, hunted, and fished together. They fussed and argued a lot. The days of the foursome were good days, days when "the old chief ran the court out of his hip pocket, and we had nothing to worry about but getting out the opinion assigned to us and looking forward to the evening hour when we solved all the affairs of the world in one hour, which we called the 'happy hour,' indeed it was!"[69]

The joys and sorrows of one were the joys and sorrows of all. When the Huxman's only child, a daughter, died, the court was in session, but it adjourned during the time of the service, an act for which Judge and Mrs. Huxman were deeply grateful.[70]

For Murrah, Phillips was "like my father,"[71] and his respect and regard for Phillips was unbounded. Phillips was always the "Old Chief," one who set "a great example for work and dedication. He lived a long and useful life completely dedicated to the cause of justice."[72] When Phillips died, Murrah wrote his sister, "I took the 'Old Chief's' last proposed opinion home with me to read to Babe. It was clear as a bell. Wasn't it wonderful that he could retain mental capacities to the very last."[73]

Judge and Mrs. Phillips had no offspring, and Judge Phillips treated the Murrah children as his own. Phillips gave Paul his first electric razor, and, like his opinions, wrote a detailed letter regarding the cleaning and care of the razor.[74]

As the only Republican on the court, Phillips took a great deal of kidding and ribbing from his Democratic colleagues, but he was more than capable of holding his own. Invited to attend a Democratic fund-raiser for $25, Phillips wrote Huxman there were two explanations for the invitation. Either the sponsors thought "that by your great eloquence and persuasive logic you have beguiled me into becoming a Democrat. God forbid! Or Democrats don't give a damn who comes, so long as he puts up a minimum of $25."[75]

Bratton was the "complete gentleman."[76] Writing an opinion for Bratton when he was ill, Murrah was "quite aware that this case should be written in the 'Brattonian' style and I shall attempt to emulate the jurist in style and content."[77] Bratton's illness on another occasion brought out the poet in Murrah. "We missed you in the morning, We missed you in the evening, And each time we wondered how you were feeling. Without your counsel we floundered around, But have no fear, you'll not be bound."[78]

When Bratton retired, Murrah recognized "no one will ever take the redhead's place. It simply can't be done."[79] And although Murrah worked hard for Bratton's appointment to the supreme court, he admitted it "would break my heart for Judge Bratton to leave the Tenth Circuit Court of

Appeals. I love him with all my heart and I don't know how we would get along without him."[80]

Huxman and Murrah were like siblings, they fought and joked without surcease. Preparing for a radio broadcast on the federal court system, Huxman asked Murrah how old he was. "I could state in my broadcast how old you are from your actions, but if I did everybody would wonder why one so young was on the bench. Or I could state your age from your looks, which would immediately cause a movement to select your successor upon your retirement."[81] Concurring in one of Huxman's opinions, Murrah commented "that you have written a splendid opinion in the Gilbert case. After reading it I could not help but wonder how you can be so wrong in other cases."[82]

Needing money to keep some insurance policies in effect, Murrah borrowed it from Huxman. Until the $3,000 loan was repaid, Murrah addressed Huxman as "Dear Creditor,"[83] while Huxman chortled, "The note as prepared by you meets with my hearty approval and, Oh Boy, will it give me pleasure to invoke the provision for $300.00 attorneys' fees."[84]

The humor between Murrah and Huxman was but the expression of a deep and abiding affection. When Huxman gave Murrah his golf clubs, he meant for them to "constitute a further bond between us."[85] And when he quit judging, Huxman gave Murrah the very personal gift of his robe. Accepting this act of graciousness, Murrah said, "Nothing would please me more than to inherit your robe and you may always know that every time I put it on, I'll remember the many wonderful years we had together, and what you've always meant to me as a Judge, a man, and a friend."[86]

As the judges took senior status—Phillips in 1956, Huxman in 1957, and Bratton in 1961—they saw each other less frequently, but they kept in touch by letter and telephone. And, occasionally, Murrah and his three older brothers in the law would be together again. For that, Huxman "would travel the length of the world."[87] No decent man could forget what men like Phillips, Bratton and Huxman had meant in his life, and Murrah didn't. "I cannot refrain," Murrah wrote, "from harking back to the day when I came on this court under the tutelage of three men who have done more to shape my life than anyone else in the world. I shall always think of you, Phillips and Bratton, as my preceptors and my guiding lights."[88]

Death claimed Judge Bratton first on September 22, 1963, at 75 years of age. Judge Huxman followed in 1972 in his 85th year, and Judge Phillips in 1974, six days shy of his 89th birthday. In less than a year, Murrah died, and the Old Court was adjourned sine die.

7
The New Court, 1949-1959[1]

The legislation creating the fifth judgeship for the tenth circuit became law on August 3, 1949.[2] By September 23, 1949, President Truman had made his choice, nominating John Coleman Pickett of Wyoming to fill the new position.[3] Confirmation speedily followed on October 12, 1949.[4]

Born September 3, 1896, near Ravenna, Nebraska, Pickett graduated in 1922 from the University of Nebraska with a bachelor of laws degree. His university years had begun in 1915, but had been interrupted by military service in World War I and playing semiprofessional baseball. Indeed, Pickett had an opportunity to sign a contract with the Chicago White Sox, but he had declined to pursue his collegiate studies.

Shortly after receiving his law degree, Pickett relocated to Cheyenne, Wyoming where he practiced law, played baseball with the Cheyenne Indians, and was active in Democratic politics. He served three terms as Laramie County attorney in the late 1920s and early 1930s, and in 1935 he was appointed assistant United States attorney for Wyoming. He served in that position until 1949 when he became United States Attorney, only to be appointed to the circuit later that year. Pickett was the first Wyomingite to serve on the tenth circuit.[5]

Murrah and Pickett were not acquainted when Pickett was named to the bench. In fact, his many years as assistant United States attorney notwithstanding, Pickett had never appeared before the court of appeals. In time, however, Murrah and Pickett would become fast friends.[6]

The 1950s witnessed two more changes in the court's

membership. When Judge Phillips took senior status on January 1, 1956, President Dwight D. Eisenhower appointed David T. Lewis of Utah as his successor. Born in Utah in 1912, Lewis held baccalaureate and law degrees from the University of Utah. Prior to his appointment, he had been in private practice, a member of the Utah legislature, and a state district judge.[7]

Judge Huxman was succeeded in 1957 by Jean S. Breitenstein. Born in Iowa in 1900, Breitenstein earned his baccalaureate and law degrees from the University of Colorado. An expert in water law, Breitenstein was United States District Judge at the time of his appointment to the court of appeals. Prior to that, he had been an assistant attorney general, assistant United States attorney, and in private practice.[8]

In 1955, by the Act of March 2, 1955, circuit judge salaries were raised from $17,500 to $25,500. In the late 1950s, the Murrahs purchased a new residence at 2209 Northwest 56th Street.

FLSA cases and NLRB proceedings continued to be plentiful, and Murrah wrote a number of his court's opinions in those areas. As the governing law became more certain, the cases typically required only the application of settled principles to particular facts, usually resulting in affirmance of the district court's judgment, or enforcement of the board's order. See *Tobin v. Traders Compress Co.*, 190 F.2d 677 (10th Cir. 1952) (upholding administrator's definition of "area of production" for exemption purposes under FLSA as neither arbitrary nor capricious); *Mitchell v. Chambers Const. Co.*, 214 F.2d 515 (10th Cir. 1954) (affirming judgment dismissing complaint for injunctive relief against violations of the FLSA when the project had been completed and further work was entirely problematical); *National Labor Relations Board v. Tri-State Casualty Ins. Co.*, 188 F.2d 50

(10th Cir. 1951) (order enforced); *National Labor Relations Board v. Davis Motors, Inc.*, 192 F.2d 782 (10th Cir. 1951) (order enforced); *National Labor Relations Board v. Conover Motor Co.*, 192 F.2d 779 (10th Cir. 1951) (order enforced); *National Labor Relations Board v. Machine Products Co.*, 198 F.2d 313 (10th Cir. 1952) (enforcement denied); *National Labor Relations Board v. Coal Creek Coal Co.*, 204 F.2d 579 (10th Cir. 1953) (order enforced as modified); *National Labor Relations Board v. Construction Specialities Co.*, 208 F.2d 170 (10th Cir. 1953) (order enforced); *National Labor Relations Board v. Stanolind Oil & Gas Co.*, 208 F.2d 239 (10th Cir. 1953) (order enforced); *National Labor Relations Board v. Seamprufe, Inc.*, 222 F.2d 858 (10th Cir. 1955) (enforcement denied); *National Labor Rel. Bd. v. Carpenters Local Union*, 232 F.2d 454 (10th Cir. 1956) (order enforced); and *National Labor Relations Board v. General Drivers, Chauffeurs & Helpers, Etc.*, 264 F.2d 21 (10th Cir. 1959) (order enforced).

Great judicial deference to a state's power to act for the public health, safety, and welfare when First Amendment values were not at issue was the pervading theme of Murrah's constitutional jurisprudence in these years. This broad conception of the police power did not depend on the form in which it was exercised. In *Morton Salt Company v. City of South Hutchinson*, 177 F.2d 889 (10th Cir. 1949), the court of appeals held that it was not violative of 14th Amendment due process or equal protection for a city to tax a business located within the taxing jurisdiction for the construction of a waterworks system which would not serve the taxpayer's plant. Murrah spoke for the court.

When a tax was levied on all property in the taxing jurisdiction for public purposes, the law did not require—and indeed there seldom was—a just relationship between the tax imposed and the benefits received. The benefit need be no more than that which generally followed from living in an organized society. As part of the South Hutchinson community, the taxpayer received benefits "intangible and not susceptible of pecuniary evaluation, but...nevertheless very real in a constitutional sense" in the providing of clean, pure water to the community's school children—*ibid,*, 892. This was benefit enough to warrant imposition of the tax.[9]

By statute, New Mexico provided that a public carrier was liable in the sum of $10,000 for each passenger dying as a result of the negligence of the carrier's employee, but that no cause of action existed against the employee individually. In *Schloss v. Matteucii*, 260 F.2d 16 (10th Cir. 1958), this classification was challenged as a violation of 14th Amendment equal protection.

The challenge availed not. The equal protection standard for legislative classifications was whether they had a rational basis in fact. If they did, then "[p]rotection against unwise and improvident legislation lies in the exercise of the suffrage right, not in the courts"—*ibid.*, 17, 18.

Having mandated a fixed sum recoverable from the employer for wrongful death, it was rational to make that sum the exclusive recovery. Likewise, there was no irrationality in relieving the employee from liability for death, but not for non fatal injuries. "[E]ach facet of liability fits permissively into the symmetry of the legislative scheme, and is not constitutionally infirm"—*ibid.*, 18.

However more, much more, than a rational basis in fact was needed to justify restrictions on freedom of expression. In *Smotherman v. United States*, 186 F.2d 676 (10th Cir. 1950), the dissemination of a statement that a judge was "a tool of big industrialists, unfit to hold...office" resulted in a criminal contempt conviction. The conviction could not stand, Murrah said, unless it posed a "clear and present danger" to the orderly administration of justice—*ibid.*, 679. "Vexatious and irritating" though the comments were, they in no way threatened the integrity of the judicial process, and did not "constitute contempt in law or in fact"—*ibid.*

Beginning with cases such as the prosecution of Al Capone in the early 1930s, the net worth theory of proving income tax evasion became an increasingly employed prosecutorial tool in the 1940s and 1950s. Under this approach, the government attempted to show a beginning net worth at the start of a given year, and then prove increases in that worth for each succeeding year under scrutiny. If the resulting figure for a given year or years was substantially greater than reported income, the government would claim that the excess represented unreported taxable dollars.

Because net worth prosecutions were based on a peculiar type of circumstantial evidence, concerns were expressed in many cases about its possible deleterious impact on the requirement that a defendant's guilt be established beyond a reasonable doubt. Murrah wrote on the subject in *Holland v. United States*, 209 F.2d 516 (10th Cir. 1954), in which the court held that net worth evidence coupled with proper instructions could carry the government's burden of proof. The supreme court granted certiorari and affirmed—*Holland v. United States*, 348 U.S. 121, 75 S.Ct. 127, 99 L.Ed. 150 (1954).

Search and seizure issues continued to be a familiar aspect of criminal appeals. And Murrah continued to write that, probable cause notwithstanding, warrantless searches were reasonable "only as incident to a lawful arrest or under exceptional circumstances making it impractical to secure a search warrant through orderly

The United States Court of Appeals for the Tenth Circuit in 1953 looking judicial. Seated, L to R: Judge Bratton, Judge Phillips, and Judge Huxman. Standing, L to R: Murrah and Judge Pickett.

procedure"—*Steeber v. United States*, 198 F.2d 615 at 617 (10th Cir. 1952).

From a German submarine lying in the chilly waters of the North Atlantic, William C. Colepaugh, clad in civilian clothes and carrying concealed sidearms and forged credentials, secretly landed on the coast of Maine. Apprehended in a matter of months, he was tried and convicted by a military commission convened by order of the president of passing through military and naval lines of the United States for the purpose of committing espionage, sabotage, and other violent acts. Colepaugh, a native of Connecticut, was sentenced to death by hanging.[10]

By habeas corpus, he challenged the jurisdiction of the

military tribunal to try him. The district court denied relief, and Colepaugh perfected an appeal to the circuit. The court of appeals affirmed in an opinion authored by Murrah—*Colepaugh v. Looney*, 235 F.2d 429 (10th Cir. 1956). The trial before a military court did not foreclose the federal courts from determining the validity of the petitioner's restraint, "for to do so would deny the supremacy of the Constitution and the rule of law under it as construed and expounded in the duly constituted courts of the land"—*ibid.*, 431.

Turning to the merits, the president as commander in chief had "constitutional and legislative power"—*ibid.*, 432—to define offenses under the law of war and to establish military commissions with jurisdiction to try persons charged with such offenses. In the exercise of this power, the president had legally defined as an act of unlawful belligerency entering the United States from enemy territory to commit acts of violence and destruction. Colepaugh was charged with precisely such conduct, and it followed that the military commission had jurisdiction to try him.[11]

Murrah's civil procedure opinions during this period continued to reflect his view that the office of procedure was to insure the decision of cases on the merits rather than on technicalities. The federal rules of civil procedure were rules of "simplicity and liberality"—*Vrooman v. Beech Aircraft Corporation*, 183 F.2d 479 at 480 (10th Cir. 1950)—unconcerned "with the nicety of pleaded legal theories"—*Western Machinery Company v. Consolidated Uranium Mines*, 247 F.2d 685 at 686 (10th Cir. 1957)—which applied with equal force to the simple personal injury suit or the complicated antitrust case—*New Home Appliance Center v. Thompson*, 250 F.2d 881 (10th Cir. 1957). The fundamental organizing principle of the rules was that "technical forms of pleading" were no longer permissible—*Blazer v. Black*, 196 F.2d 139 at 144 (10th Cir. 1952). In *Downie v. Powers*, 193 F.2d 760 (10th Cir. 1951), Murrah used the "letter [and] the spirit"—*ibid.*, 767—of the rules to reverse a defendant's judgment in a federal civil rights action brought by Jehovah's Witnesses, "an unpopular minority sect"—*ibid.*, 768—when the district court refused to inform counsel what his instructions would be before jury argument.

It is the usual rule in federal court that an order of a district court granting a new trial is not appealable because the party aggrieved by the order can challenge it on appeal from the subsequent judgment if it is adverse to him. *Kanatser v. Chrysler Corporation*, 199 F.2d 610 (10th Cir. 1952), was an instance in which the rule warranted an exception.

In *Kanatser*, a personal injury action, the district court ordered a new trial after the time in which it could legally act had passed. Additionally, the district judge indicated that he would never allow a jury verdict in excess of a stated sum to stand. This meant, Murrah wrote, that "Other trials of the case resulting in a verdict in excess of fifteen thousand dollars would never reach this court for review...for each case would result in an unappealable order granting a new trial"—*ibid.*, 616.

If this were the case, the district court's great discretion in ruling on motions for new trial would be not merely unappealable, it would be unreviewable as well, and the public interest in an end to litigation would be thwarted: "If a case is to be retried, it should be done with dispatch, lest the error of delay outweigh the error of trial"—*ibid.*, 615. This intolerable result was avoided by the issuance of a common law writ of certiorari bringing the new trial order to the circuit where it was set aside, and the jury verdict reinstated.

Inland Empire Insurance Company v. Freed, 239 F.2d

289 (10th Cir. 1956), gave the tenth circuit occasion to consider the power of a federal court exercising diversity subject matter jurisdiction to appoint a receiver. The genesis of the litigation was the failure of an insurance company doing business in 21 states. Writing for the court, Murrah concluded that the power of a federal court exercising equity jurisdiction to appoint a receiver "cannot be enlarged or diminished" by state law—*ibid.*, 292. Given the large number of states in which the company's assets and liabilities were located, and federal receivership as the only alternative to separate liquidation proceedings in each state, the appointment of the receiver was sustained as a proper exercise of federal equity jurisdiction.

Later, the court considered a dispute between the receiver and a state insurance commissioner over assets located in that one state. The court held that the federal receiver had jurisdiction over the assets, but the appointing court had discretion to relax "its jurisdiction in favor of state court processes for the adjudication of substantive rights to the res"—*Continental Bank and Trust Company v. Apodaca*, 239 F.2d 295 at 299 (10th Cir. 1956). Taken together, the two decisions served both the federal interest in protecting the assets of the failed company, and the interests of the concerned states in the distribution of those assets.

The Federal Tort Claims Act waives the immunity of the United States as a sovereign from suit in certain instances. The statute excepts from waiver claims based upon the performance or failure to perform discretionary acts and claims arising from combatant activities of the armed forces. In *Griggs v. United States*, 178 F.2d 1 (10th Cir. 1949), Murrah held that the United States was subject to suit under the act for the death of a member of the military while performing noncombatant military duties, and allegedly caused by the negligence of government employees acting within the scope of their employment. During the same time, the second and fourth circuits reached the opposite conclusion. The supreme court granted certiorari in the three cases and held that the waiver of immunity did not extend to claims for injuries to military personnel arising from or in the course of activity incident to military service—*Feres v. United States*, 340 U.S. 135, 71 S.Ct. 153, 95 L.Ed. 152 (1950).

Feres rejected Murrah's reading of the statute, but the case has not been without its critics. As recently as 1987, four justices of the supreme court, including such strange ideological bedfellows as William Brennan and Antonin Scalia, wrote that Feres was "wrongly decided and heartily deserves the widespread, almost universal criticism, it has received"—*United States v. Johnson*, 481 U.S. 681 at 700, 107 S.Ct. 2063 at 2074, 95 L.Ed.2d 648 at 665 (1987). Authored by Scalia, the dissent was joined by Marshall and Stevens in addition to Brennan.

Another prevalent issue in Federal Tort Claims Act cases is whether the government's employee who allegedly caused the harm for which redress is sought was acting in the scope of his employment at the critical time. Murrah believed that the resolution of such cases depended upon "the predilections of the court," *United States v. Mraz*, 255 F.2d 115 at 117 (10th Cir. 1958), for there "is doubtless a philosophical divergence in the theory that a master is not liable for the wrongful acts of his servant, unless done in respect to the very transaction out of which the injury arose, and the theory that a master is liable for his servant's negligent acts if done while engaged in the master's business and did not arise from some external, independent and personal motive on his part"—*ibid.*, 117.

Murrah opted for the broad reading of when the conduct of the employee is considered the conduct of the United States. In *Mraz*, he wrote that an officer involved in a traffic accident while traveling from one duty station to another by private automobile and receiving travel reimbursement was acting in the scope of his employment at the time of the collision. This was because the officer "was engaged upon government business in furtherance of the government's interest"—*ibid.* 118. Murrah's analysis was followed by the eighth circuit in *Robbins v. United States*, 722 F.2d 387 (8th Cir. 1983).

Cases under the Securities Act of 1933 and the Securities Exchange Act of 1934 were not staples of litigation in the tenth circuit. Nevertheless, the court of appeals did have its share of such matters. In *Woodward v. Wright*, 266 F.2d 108 (10th Cir. 1959), Murrah considered whether in oil and gas financing, "a strange world of its own"—*ibid.*, 115—the sale of an undivided fractional interest in oil and gas was a sale of securities within the coverage of the Securities Act of 1933. Writing for a unanimous panel, he concluded that it was.

Woodward was described by the fifth circuit recently as "a landmark securities case which remains frequently cited today"—*Adena Exploration, Inc. v. Sylvan*, 860 F.2d 1242 at 1246 (5th Cir. 1988). When that court reached the same result as *Woodward*, it wrote that it "is difficult to improve upon Judge Murrah's reasoning, and we therefore describe it in detail."

As with securities cases, the tenth circuit was not flooded with antitrust litigation, but it was not a Sherman-Clayton Act desert either. A baker selling bread in Santa Rosa, New Mexico raised the ire of a corporate concern selling bread both intrastate and interstate. The corporation responded by instigating a price war in Santa Rosa while maintaining usual price levels in its remaining markets. After being forced to close his business, the baker sued for violation of the Clayton and Robinson-Patman Acts.

The case was tried to a jury which found for the plaintiff, but the court of appeals, Murrah writing, reversed. It reasoned that any consequence of the price cutting on competition "was purely local in its scope and effect and in no way related to or affected interstate commerce"—*Mead's Fine Bread Co. v. Moore*, 208 F.2d 777 at 780 (10th Cir. 1953). The supreme court disagreed, for "If this method of competition were approved, the pattern for the growth of monopoly would be simple. As long as the price warfare was simply intrastate, interstate business could grow and expand with impunity at the expense of local merchants"—*Moore v. Mead's Fine Bread Company*, 348 U.S. 115 at 118, 75 Ct. 148 at 150, 99 L.Ed. 145 at 149 (1954).

Predatory pricing came before the court a second time in *Atlas Building Products Company v. Diamond Block and Gravel Company*, 269 F.2d 950 (10th Cir. 1959). Again asserting Clayton and Robinson-Patman claims, plaintiff alleged that the defendant sold the same product at lower prices in Las Cruces than it did in El Paso, Texas. The defendant argued that no claim was stated under Clayton and Robinson-Patman, unless the price discrimination was between purchasers in direct competition.

Murrah rejected such a restrictive reading of the statutes because "surely there is no more effective means of lessening competition or creating monopolies than the debilitation of a competitor"—*ibid.*, 954. There was no basis in the legislative history for interpreting the phrase "different purchasers" to mean competing purchasers. Consequently, the district court correctly instructed the jury that it could consider price differences in Las Cruces and El Paso "in determining whether the defendant was guilty of actionable price discrimination"—*ibid.*, 955.

Procedurally, Murrah had no difficulty in according antitrust cases the full benefit of notice pleading under the Federal Rules of Civil Procedure. As he observed, no "special form of pleading is indicated or sanctioned in antitrust cases." Rather, "the liberal rules of pleading are as applicable to these cases as any other case"—*New Home Appliance Center v. Thompson*, 250 F. 2d 881 at 883 (10th Cir. 1957).

As mentioned in chapter six, the court of appeals could sit en banc in cases of exceptional importance or difficulty. One such case was *Inter-State Nat'l Bank of Kansas City v. Luther*, 221 F.2d 382 (10th Cir. 1955). The issue was an arcane one, whether when a creditor files a claim in bankruptcy he impliedly consents to the power of the bankruptcy court to summarily adjudicate a voidable preference counterclaim filed by the trustee and seeking affirmative relief. If the filing constituted consent, the bankruptcy court, sitting without a jury, could render decision against the creditor for the amount of the voidable preference and require that he disgorge that sum before he could recover on his claim. The creditor could not merely reduce his claim by the amount of the voidable preference, and he would be considered a general, rather than a secured, creditor.

The case sharply divided the court. Writing for Bratton, Huxman, and himself, Murrah sustained the power of the bankruptcy court to hear the counterclaim, grant affirmative relief, and allow the creditor's claim only as a common claim after payment of the preference. Phillips and Pickett dissented.

The preclusive effect of judgments in tax cases came before the court in *Martin v. Brodrick*, 177 F.2d 886 (10th Cir. 1949), and *Jones v. Trapp*, 186 F.2d 951 (10th Cir. 1950). In *Martin*, the court held that a taxpayer who brought a successful suit for refund of his state taxes was

The United States Court of Appeals for the Tenth Circuit looking decidedly nonjudicial. L to R: Judge Phillips, Judge Bratton, Judge Huxman, Judge Pickett, and Murrah.

not barred from making a later claim for the attorney fees incurred in the refund action. The taxpayer was not guilty of splitting her cause of action because her attorney fee claim "was not in being when the first claim for refund was filed, and the existence of [it] was contingent upon a disposition of that claim"—177 F.2d 886 at 888.

In *Jones*, involving a former governor and first lady of Oklahoma, the taxpayers claimed that they were business partners for the taxable year 1941. In previous litigation it had been decided that they were not business partners for the taxable year 1940. The court, Murrah authoring, held that the 1940 finding was binding as to 1941 because there had been no significant change in the controlling law, and the facts relied upon by the taxpayers to establish a different result for 1941 were mere historical facts which were available at the time of, and could have been presented in, the prior trial.[12]

In addition to the numerous federal law issues the court decided, it also considered an appetizing variety of state law questions. Murrah pondered the extent under Oklahoma law of the liability created by an insurance binder in *Republic Insurance Company v. French*, 180 F.2d 796 (10th Cir. 1950). He ruled if the binder incorporated an agreement as to specific terms of coverage, the insurer could not avoid liability by issuing a policy not covering the risk contemplated by the agreement; the insurer could not "promise one contract and fulfill it with another"—*ibid.*, 798; whether under New Mexico law a workmen's compensation award could be reduced for failure of the claimant to undergo corrective surgery, *Evans v. Stearns-Roger Manufacturing Company*, 253 F.2d 383 (10th Cir. 1958); it could not, for "workmen's compensation statutes should be liberally and fairly construed in the workman's favor"—*ibid.*, 387—and whether New Mexico law recognized a cause of action for unprivileged detention when a police officer arrested plaintiff for violation of a valid ordinance but which did not apply to plaintiff—*Miller v. Stinnett*, 257 F.2d 910 (10th Cir. 1958)—Murrah decided it did when the arrest was "for the purpose of harassment to serve selfish ends"—*ibid.*, 915; whether Oklahoma would adopt the "salutary rule" that a promise to pay additional compensation because of extraordinary and unforeseeable difficulties in the performance of a subsisting contract is enforceable—*Pittsburgh Testing Laboratory v. Farnsworth and Chambers Company*, 251 F.2d 77 (10th Cir. 1958)—it would, Murrah predicted, although the decision rested on a well-established rule of Oklahoma law; whether a claim for refusal to provide hotel accommodations because of race was time barred—*Thomas v. Pick Hotels Corporation*, 224 F.2d 664 (10th Cir. 1955)—it was not; whether under Oklahoma law pain and suffering was a separate compensable item from compensation for wrongful death—*Belt v. St. Louis San Francisco Railway Company*, 195 F.2d 241 (10th Cir. 1952)—it was; decedent had been fishing from a railroad bridge when the first of defendant's trains struck him; "while lying prostrate on the bridge immediately adjacent to the track a second train was moved passed the decedent...over the strenuous objections of relatives and friends, and in disobedience of a call from the [defendant's] dispatcher 'to hold that train until the boy's body was removed from the bridge'"—*ibid.*, 242, 243; and the standard of conduct under Oklahoma law owed by the trustees to an "old simple minded unsuspecting Indian"—*Chisholm v. House*, 183 F.2d 698 (10th Cir. 1950)—the standard was "'stricter than the morals of the marketplace. Not honesty alone, but the punctilio of an honor the most sensitive.'"—*ibid.*, 704.

Being in the minority and penning dissents is not the preferred role of an appellate judge. But it is an almost inevitable aspect of judging as men and women of great intelligence and strong convictions wrestle with issues of life, liberty, and property. It is not surprising, then, that on a fair number of occasions Murrah found himself writing not to marshal the court for a particular result, but to record for history the errors of his colleagues.[13]

The resolution of a fair trial-free press conflict caused Murrah to part company with his brethren in *Marshall v. United States*, 258 F.2d 94 (10th Cir. 1958). Marshall was charged with illegally dispensing certain drugs. During the course of his trial, two newspaper articles were published relating that Marshall had two felony convictions; that while serving a prison sentence for forgery he had testified before a legislative committee that he had practiced medicine, including writing prescriptions for dangerous drugs, with a $25-mail-order diploma; and that his wife had been arrested and convicted on drug charges. It was undisputed that some members of the jury had read the articles. After examining the jurors regarding the stories, the district court denied a mistrial, Marshall was convicted, and the court of appeals affirmed.

Murrah thought the conviction should be reversed. The judiciary's duty was to maintain "the inviolability of jury trials and...to vouchsafe them in the administration of justice"—*ibid.*, 100. In an age when "crime and violence are exploited by news media and jurors are likely to be exposed, and consciously or unconsciously influenced by the emotional impact of the exploitations"—*ibid.*—the integrity of jury trial required wholly disinterested jurors who decided cases based on the evidence provided in open court, not from "extraneous matter disclosed in...newspaper articles"—*ibid.*, 102. However conscientious, a juror could not decide Marshall's guilt or innocence free of the taint of the highly prejudicial material contained in the stories. Only a new trial would accord Marshall a fair trial.

The Supreme Court of the United States agreed. It granted certiorari, and reversed and remanded for a new trial—*Marshall v. United States*, 360 U.S. 310, 79 S.Ct. 1171, 3 L.Ed.2d 1250 (1959).

Maurice E. Travis was a national officer of the International Union of Mine, Mill and Smelter Workers when he executed and filed with the National Labor Relations Board two affidavits that he was not a member of the Communist Party. Convicted for making false statements, he urged on appeal: (1) that because the gravamen of the offense was falsity, the rule in perjury cases requiring the untruthfulness of the statement to be established by the testimony of two independent witnesses or other corroboration applied; and (2) that he was entitled to examine the grand jury testimony of the witnesses against him to determine if there were inconsistencies in their evidence which could be used to impeach them, i.e., to cast doubt on the truthfulness of their testimony. The court rejected both arguments and affirmed over Murrah's vigorous dissent—*Travis v. United States*, 269 F.2d 928 (10th Cir. 1959).[14]

Regarding the perjury rule, Murrah had no doubt that it should apply in false statement cases. The "charge is false swearing, the evidence is indeed indirect and circumstantial"—*ibid.*, 946. It had been argued that a previous decision of the circuit decided this question. If it had, Murrah deemed himself "bound by the pronouncements of my court [but] I cannot refrain from expressing the hope that such is not the law in cases of this kind"—*ibid.*

The panel was correct that a particularized showing for disclosure of grand jury testimony had to be made, and the burden was on the party seeking disclosure. "But if the rule is to have any efficacy, its burden ought not to be insurmountable"—*ibid.* In this case the defendant was in a dilemma. He could not show particularized need without showing inconsistencies between grand jury and trial testimony, and he could not show inconsistencies without the grand jury evidence. Under these circumstances, it was prejudicial error for the district court not "to take a judicial look at the testimony," for otherwise there was no reliable basis for the district court to discharge its ex parte function of deciding "whether the testimony of the witnesses is substantially consistent"—*ibid.*, 946-947.

This case also reached the supreme court on certiorari. The court reversed the judgment on the ground that venue did not lie in the District of Colorado, but in the District of Columbia—*Travis v. United States*, 364 U.S. 631, 81 S.Ct. 358, 5 L.Ed.2d 340 (1961).

While Oklahoma was still dry, some lawyers purchased whiskey to serve clients and prospective clients. They sought to deduct the cost of the liquor as an ordinary and necessary business expense. The government disallowed the deduction, and the taxpayers sued in district court for a refund where they prevailed. On appeal, the government conceded that the price of the whiskey met the statutory definition of a business expense, but it sought to overturn the judgment on a judicially created public policy exception to deductibility. According to this doctrine, the expense was nondeductible if allowing it would result in a severe and immediate frustration of the commonweal's policy.

In *United States v. Winters*, 261 F.2d 675 (10th Cir. 1958), the court of appeals held in favor of the government. It interpreted Oklahoma law to make possession of intoxicating beverages legal only for personal and social use. Because the whiskey was bought to serve business associates, not social guests, the use, though not the purchase, was illegal. The "taxpayer deliberately and knowingly patronized an illegal business. By reason of such patronage there was a severe and immediate frustration of state policy"—*ibid.*, 680.

The flaw in the court's ruling, Murrah responded, is that it was based upon a misunderstanding of Oklahoma prohibitory law. The proposition that one would be prosecuted for serving whiskey to business guests in one's own home was belied by history. "[A]s far as we know," Murrah stated, "no such charge has ever been reported in more than fifty years of prohibition in Oklahoma. It seems only fair to assume, therefore, that at the enforcement level, at least, the prohibition laws have not been construed so severely"—*ibid.*, 681.

In assessing the impact on Oklahoma prohibition of allowing deductibility, it was relevant to examine not merely constitutional, statutory, and case law, but "the mores of the community" as well, for "the people make the law, and by their conduct construe it to reflect the public policy of the state." Would allowing deductibility run afoul of long established and still subsisting values of the community? For Murrah, the answer was clear: "As one living in the state since the very inception of the law, and as one claiming some acquaintance with the mores of the community, I certainly cannot say so"—*ibid.*

The plaintiff in a Federal Employer's Liability Act case in the District of Kansas was represented by lawyers not admitted to practice before that court. Defense counsel objected on ethical grounds to the lawyers being permitted to try the case. A hearing was held at which it developed the attorneys had engaged in the unprofessional obtaining of employment, ambulance chasing, and making improper cash advances to clients. Nevertheless, the district court permitted the lawyers to appear and try the case.

On appeal, the court, although characterizing the attorneys' conduct as "aggravated violations of well recognized ethical and professional standards of long duration and virtually universal observance," affirmed on the reasoning that the trial court had not abused its discretion in the matter—*Atchison, Topeka & Santa Fe Railway Company v. Jackson*, 235 F.2d 390 (10th Cir. 1956).

For Murrah, reversal was required because "public policy of...far-reaching importance is at stake..."—*ibid.*, 394. The issue was not one of discretion, for an "attorney who is guilty of an aggravated violation of recognized professional standards has no standing before the bar, and is not entitled to invoke the discretion of the court whether comity will be extended. In short, the uncontroverted facts leave no room for the exercise of a discretion"—*ibid.*

When a judgment of conviction was reversed because the district court denied a motion for a bill of particulars

Until his schedule made it impossible, hunting was one of Murrah's favorite pastimes.

—*Cefalu v. United States,* 234 F.2d 522 (10th Cir. 1956)—Murrah inveighed against the decision as one which takes "us back to the anachronisms of ancient pleadings"—*ibid.*, 525. As with the Federal Rules of Civil Procedure, the Federal Rules of Criminal Procedure "embraced a new and realistic concept of pleading, one which looks to substance rather than to technical forms"—*ibid.* Because the defendant was in no way prejudiced by the denial of the bill of particulars, the judgment should have been affirmed.

Errors of substance, not form, were another matter. Such an error was accepting a guilty plea from an "emotionally unstable" defendant who was "suffering from a mental infirmity"—*Ruebush v. United States*, 206 F.2d 810 at 812 (10th Cir. 1953). The district court was under duty to insure that the accused fully understood the constitutional protections he enjoyed, and that by pleading guilty he was waiving them. This duty was not discharged by accepting "'yes' and 'no' answers to formal questions"—*ibid.*

In *Wilcoxon v. United States*, 231 F.2d 384 (10th Cir. 1956), two witnesses in a criminal case who did not speak or understand English were administered the oath in English. The defendant was convicted, and Murrah thought he was entitled to a new trial. "An oath without understanding is no oath at all"—*ibid.*, 388—and the defendant did not waive the issue by not objecting, for the oath had been administered to the witnesses en masse. Under the circumstances, there had been no knowing and voluntary relinquishment of a known right, thus it was not "too late to correct the error and I should not hesitate to so order it"—*ibid.*

The United States allowed Arnold Schmidt to enter a military reservation and cut, bale, and remove prairie grass and hay. While so engaged, he found some unexploded bazooka shells. Not knowing their nature and believing them harmless, he took some of them to his home as souvenirs. While his eight children were playing with them, one exploded, killing three and injuring the other five youngsters.

Suit was brought under the Federal Tort Claims Act to recover for the deaths and injuries. The district court dismissed the case, and the court of appeals affirmed—*Schmidt v. United States*, 179 F.2d 724 (10th Cir. 1950). The court assumed negligence on the government's part in failing to remove the shells, but it held that the act of the father taking the shells home could not have been foreseen by the government, and thus the father's conduct, not the government's negligence, was the proximate cause of the injuries and deaths.

Murrah saw the matter differently. It was imminently foreseeable that one finding a shell would take it to his farm or home as a souvenir. And it was quite foreseeable that his "curious and unsuspecting children would be attracted to it"—*ibid.*, 728. Consequently, the father's conduct in no way broke the chain of proximate cause running from the government's negligence to the tragedy.

> If law is experience as recorded by adjudicated cases, it teaches us that the result of leaving this explosive shell in an unguarded place, where it is apt to be picked up by the curious and unsuspecting, is not improbable but commonplace. Things that are commonplace are certainly within the range of apprehension. Whether considered within the range of apprehension or as the proximate cause, I would hold that the complaint states a claim upon which relief can be granted, and accordingly reverse the case—*ibid.*, 729.

Denney v. United States, 185 F.2d 108 (10th Cir. 1950), was an interesting contrast with *Schmidt*. Plaintiff's decedent, a 17-year-old high school junior "above average in intelligence"—*ibid.*, 109—was killed when a shell he found on a government target range exploded. The range was located several miles from town and was enclosed by a fence. A judgment for the United States entered after bench trial was affirmed on appeal by a Murrah opinion. Murrah reasoned that the trier of fact could find the government was not guilty of negligence either in failing to warn of the presence of the shells or in failing to deactivate or destroy them.

The principal difference between the cases is that *Schmidt* was decided as a matter of pleading. Looking at what the plaintiff alleged in his complaint, the district court and the court of appeals thought plaintiff could not make a case of negligence. Murrah thought differently. He believed the jury could find a breach of the duty of due care which proximately caused the harm for which redress was sought, and the plaintiff should have the opportunity to persuade the jury accordingly.

In *Denney*, the plaintiff lost after plenary trial. Plaintiff had the chance to persuade, and he failed. Murrah concluded the appellate court could not say the district court was wrong in deciding the government had done all a reasonable person would do under the circumstances.

People of Colorado ex rel. Watrous v. District Court of United States for District of Colorado, 207 F.2d 50 (10th Cir. 1953), was a suit to compel the state of Colorado to bring proceedings to determine the compensation to which plaintiffs were entitled for the alleged taking of their property. The state sought a writ from the court of appeals prohibiting the district court from granting the relief prayed. The writ issued, the court of appeals reasoning that the affirmative relief sought by the plaintiffs would trench upon the state's sovereign immunity.

Murrah thought not. The sovereign was "amenable to the law and must act within it and an agent of the sovereign cannot act under color of law to invade the rights and properties of a citizen and claim immunity for it as an act of the state"—*ibid.*, 58. Nor was Murrah impressed by the majority's suggestion that the taking could be prohibited until just compensation was paid, even though the state could not be ordered to bring a compensation action. "The procedural distinction between a negative and affirmative decree does not in these circumstances mark the difference between sovereign immunity for the exercise of governmental functions and suability for unconstitutional invasion of property rights"—*ibid.*, 59. The issue was one of power, and the district court clearly had the power to order that which the plaintiffs requested, for "the reach of the Fourteenth Amendment is coextensive with any exercise by a state of power in whatever form asserted. And the federal jurisdiction extends to the deprivation of rights secured to the citizen by the Fourtheenth Amendment against state infringement"—*ibid.*, 60.

Other cases found Murrah dissenting from holdings that a $55,000 liquidated damage clause was a penalty and not enforceable—*National Cooperative Refining Association v. Northern Ordinance*, 238 F.2d 803 (10th Cir. 1956). "Looking at this whole transaction," he wrote, "we have two oil companies involved in a two-million dollar transaction, the amount of damages stipulated was, in view of all the circumstances, not unreasonable or disproportionate to the actual damages sustained"—*ibid.*, 807 and 808; and that the New Mexico common carrier wrongful death statute gave a cause of action against the employer, but not against the negligent employee—*Tilly v. Flippin*, 237 F.2d 364 (10th Cir. 1956). "I can't believe," Murrah explained, "that the New Mexico legislature intended to confine the liability for wrongful death caused by the negligence of a common carrier's employee exclusively to the carrier, and to exempt the employee, who is primarily liable, from any damages whatsoever"—*ibid.*, 369.[15] And in one case, *Employers Liability Assurance Corporation v. Freeman*, 229 F.2d 547 (10th Cir. 1955), he dissented from affirmance of a judgment with which he was "in complete sympathy and accord."—*ibid.*, 552. He felt "constrained to dissent"—*ibid.*—because the trial court had directed a verdict for the plaintiff when the evidence was in dispute.

Dissents do not have to be—and Murrah's usually were not—lengthy. One or two fundamental points, pithily stated, could be highly effective and persuasive. In *D'Hondt v. Hopson*, 269 F.2d 759 (10th Cir. 1959), the court held that the plaintiff-passenger was contributorily negligent when she failed to warn her driver about and remonstrate with him concerning his careless driving. Only two sentences were required for the dissent. "The law of this case undoubtedly makes every passenger in a moving automobile a 'back-seat' driver. I can't believe

Kansas courts ever intended any such result"—*ibid.*, 763.

Close to a dissent, but written as a special concurring opinion because of the way the case was pled and tried, was *Merrill v. Beaute Vues Corporation*, 235 F.2d 893 (10th Cir. 1956). In *Merrill*, Murrah urged that the law should impose a duty on manufacturers to warn allergic or unusually susceptible persons of known dangers in their products. While this duty should not extend to "one isolated individual out of literally millions who use the product without harmful consequences"—*ibid.*, 898—it was sufficient to trigger the duty that a small proportion of those using the product could be injuriously affected by it. It was a grievous "failure of the law to recognize the allergic or unusually susceptible plaintiff as a class of people to whom a manufacturer owns a legal duty to warn of potential dangers"—*ibid.*

In addition to his appellate court duties, Murrah sat frequently on three-judge courts. Some of the cases presented public law issues of great importance.

The 1950s began to witness attacks on Oklahoma's system of segregated public education. G.W. McLaurin, an African-American, sought admission to a Ph.D. program at the University of Oklahoma. The program was not available at any of the all-black schools in the state. In *McLaurin v. Oklahoma State Regents for Higher Education*, 87 F. Supp. 526 (W.D. Okl. 1948), a three-judge court of Murrah, Vaught, and Broaddus held *per curiam* that to deny McLaurin admission to the University of Oklahoma under the attendant circumstances was unconstitutional. The court carefully limited its ruling, however. It was not declaring Oklahoma's segregation laws unconstitutional, but merely "that insofar as they are sought to be enforced in this particular case, they are inoperative"—*ibid.*, 528.

McLaurin was then admitted, but his education was

How easily the judicial dignity is shed! This fishing trip found Judge Pickett, Hugh Woodward, Murrah, Dr. Howard, and Judge Phillips without a thought of habeas corpus, due process, or anything else that did not have fins and gills.

provided on a segregated basis in classroom, library and cafeteria. The same court, again writing *per curiam*, held there was no violation of equal protection—*McLaurin v. Oklahoma State Regents for Higher Education*, 87 F. Supp. 528 (W.D. Okl. 1949).

The supreme court reversed unanimously—*McLaurin v. Oklahoma State Regents*, 339 U.S. 637, 70 S.Ct. 851, 94 L.Ed. 1149 (1950). The education accorded McLaurin was separate but not equal, for the restrictions "impair and inhibit his ability to study, to engage in discussions and exchange views with other students and, in general, to learn his profession"—339 U.S. at 641, 70 S.Ct. at 853; 94 L.Ed. at 1153.[16]

In 1953 the Oklahoma legislature undertook to regulate eye care in the Sooner State. It may well be, as one authority has suggested, that the legislation was "the product of an interest group struggle in the Oklahoma legislature, and represented a victory for the ophthalmologists and optometrists of the state over the opticians."[17] In any event, the opponents of the measure shifted the venue of the dispute from the legislative halls to the courtroom. In *Lee Optical of Oklahoma v. Williamson*, 120 F. Supp. 128 (W.D. Okl. 1954), a three-judge court of Murrah, Vaught, and Wallace held constitutionally infirm under the due process and equal protection clauses of the 14th Amendment the parts of the law prohibiting any person not a licensed ophthalmologist or optometrist from fitting lenses to the face without prescriptive authority from an Oklahoma licensed ophthalmologist or optometrist, applying the statute to optometrists but not the sellers of ready-to-wear glasses, making it unlawful to solicit the sale of frames, mountings, or other optical appliances, and prohibiting retail merchants from renting space to any person doing eye examinations or providing visual care.

"With reluctance and some misgivings"—*ibid.*, 144—which, it would develop, were well warranted, Murrah concurred as to the prescriptive authority holding. The other findings of unconstitutionality, however, were based upon a failure to keep "in mind the extremely limited restrictions that the due process clause of the Fourteenth Amendment places upon the states"—*ibid.*, 147. Policy judgments of state legislative bodies were subject to scrutiny under the Fourteenth Amendment only for "palpable abuse"—*ibid.*—a standard which, regardless of the wisdom of the statute, the challenged legislation did not offend. The court's decision was "an unwarranted interference with the police power of the state over a subject with which the state is fully competent to deal"—*ibid.*

The supreme court agreed. On appeal, it sustained the constitutionality of all the challenged provisions—*Williamson v. Lee Optical of Oklahoma*, 348 U.S. 483, 75 S.Ct. 461, 99 L.Ed. 563 (1955).[18]

The decade 1949-1959 had been full and busy for Murrah. He had carried more than his share of the court's case load, and his opinions had contributed significantly to the court's jurisprudence. The coming decade would find Murrah doing all this and more.

8
Chief Judge[1]

Judge Bratton ceased to be, and Murrah became, chief judge of the circuit on August 6, 1959. His tenure as chief judge lasted more than a decade, and witnessed significant changes in the size and membership of the court.

In 1961 congress authorized a sixth judge for the circuit.[2] The appointment went to Delmas Hill. Born in Wamego, Kansas in 1906, Hill held the LL.B. degree from Washburn University. He had been a private practitioner, county attorney, assistant United States attorney, and general counsel for the state tax commission during Judge Huxman's gubernatorial term. He served as a United States District Judge for Kansas from 1949 until he was elevated to the court of appeals in 1961.[3]

In 1962 Judge Bratton took senior status. He was succeeded by Oliver Seth. Born in Albuquerque, New Mexico in 1915, Seth earned his A.B. at Stanford and his LL.B. at Yale. Seth's legal career had been almost exclusively as a private practitioner. He also had been active in New Mexico civic and cultural affairs.[4]

In 1966 Judge Pickett retired. He was succeeded by John J. Hickey. A native of Wyoming, Hickey was born in 1911. He held an LL.B. from the University of Wyoming and had been a city treasurer, county attorney, and United States Attorney for Wyoming. Elected governor in 1958, he resigned midterm to be appointed to the United States Senate when Senator-elect Keith Thomson died. Defeated in 1962 for election to the unexpired term by the man he ousted from the governor's chair in 1958, Milward Simpson, Hickey practiced law in Wyoming until his appointment to the circuit. He died in 1970 after only four years on the court of appeals.[5]

Murrah and his longtime secretary, Mrs. Odessa James, read congratulatory messages on the occasion of Murrah becoming chief judge succeeding Judge Sam G. Bratton. (Published in the Oklahoma City Times *on August 8, 1956. Courtesy Oklahoma Publishing Company.)*

In 1968 congress created a seventh judgeship for the court.[6] This appointment went to William J. Holloway, Jr. of Oklahoma, the son of William J. Holloway, Oklahoma governor, 1929 to 1931.[7] The younger Holloway earned a B.A. from the University of Oklahoma where he was Phi Beta Kappa, and the LL.B. from Harvard. He was an attorney with the department of justice, practiced with his father and uncle, and was an associate and partner with Crowe & Dunlevy, one of Oklahoma's most prestigious firms, until his appointment to the court of appeals.

During Murrah's years as chief judge, salaries for court of appeals judges were increased to $33,000 in 1964 and to $42,500 in 1969. In the early 1960s, the Murrahs purchased a new home at 1208 Sherwood Lane in the Nichols Hills section of Oklahoma City.

Being chief judge did not, of course, exempt Murrah from opinion writing. It simply added various administrative responsibilities to the primary duty of deciding cases.[8]

In a number of opinions Murrah ruminated on the 4th Amendment "right of the people to be secure in their persons, houses, papers, and effects, against unreasonable searches and seizures." He refused to interpret the statutory authority of game management agents to include probable-cause-based warrantless searches, for such a reading of the statute would not be "consonant with the highly restrictive province of any enforcement officer to appraise the extraordinary circumstances under which a search without a warrant would be justified"—*Aiuppa v. United States*, 338 F.2d 146 at 148 (10th Cir. 1964). But warrantless searches incident to a lawful arrest did not violate Fourth Amendment protections—*Welch v. United States*, 361 F.2d 214 (10th Cir. 1966); *Sumrall v. United States*, 382 F.2d 651 (10th Cir. 1967)—nor did the seizure of evidence of one crime discovered while executing a search warrant for evidence of a different offense because "the officer is not required to close his eyes to the realities of the situation"—*Seymour v. United States*, 369 F.2d 825 at 827 (10th Cir. 1966).

Murrah found the 4th Amendment's touchstone in protection of the right of privacy. Thus standing to complain of a 4th Amendment violation depended on one having been "the victim of an unlawful invasion of his own privacy"—*Sumrall v. United States*, *supra* at 655. For this reason, a driver and one passenger could not complain of the search of another passenger's person.

Standing also was an issue in *Simpson v. United States*, 346 F.2d 291 (10th Cir. 1965), heard *en banc*. The question was whether a defendant convicted of violating the Dyer Act had standing to challenge a search of the car for evidence that it was, in fact, a stolen vehicle. The court held that he did, that the "sole prerequisite to a defendant's raising the Fourth Amendment issue is that he claim a proprietary or possessory interest in the searched or seized property"—*ibid.*, 294. Because the accused's lack of ownership was not established until after the search, his claim of a possessory interest gave him standing.

Pickett, joined by Murrah, dissented. Invasion of the defendant's right of privacy was the predicate for standing to invoke the 4th Amendment. An expectation of privacy could flow from being in rightful possession of the property, but that did not apply in the case at bar for the car was stolen. "Simpson had no right to be in it in the first place, and acquired no better right to get back into it once he left it"—*ibid.*, 300. Nor did the narrow rule allowing standing without a claim of ownership or possession if the very act of possession would be a crime apply, because mere possession of a stolen car was not a federal offense. The holding of the court did no less than allow a thief "to use the very property which he stole as a cloak of immunity"—*ibid.*

Murrah's most important 4th Amendment opinion as chief judge was *United States v. Humphrey*, 409 F.2d 1055 (10th Cir. 1969). The issue was whether searches of persons stopped for routine traffic offenses were constitutionally infirm.

Murrah had no difficulty in concluding that they were. None of the reasons for sustaining warrantless searches—protection of the arresting officer, prevention of escape or seizure of fruits or instrumentalities of the crime—applied in the context of the run-of-the-mill traffic stop. The 4th Amendment condemned "the search of persons and automobiles following routine traffic violations. Such searches can only be justified in exceptional,

The Tenth Circuit in 1962. Judge John C. Pickett of Wyoming is seated to Murrah's right, and Judge David T. Lewis of Utah is seated to Murrah's left. Standing: to Murrah's right is Judge Jean S. Breitenstein of Colorado, and Judge Delmas Hill of Kansas is to Murrah's left. (Published in the Daily Oklahoman *on March 27, 1962. Courtesy Oklahoma Publishing Company.)*

on the spot circumstances which rise to the dignity of probable cause"—*ibid.*, 1058.

Humphrey was well received. The sixth circuit "recognize[d] and approve[d] the rule set forth in *United States v. Humphrey*"—*United States v. Garner*, 451 F.2d 167 at 169 (6th Cir. 1971)—while Judge J. Skelly Wright of the District of Columbia Circuit commended *Humphrey's* "forceful statement of the [Fourth Amendment] principle applicable here."—*United States v. Robinson*, 447 F.2d 1215 at 1232 (D.C. Cir. 1971) (dissenting opinion). Justice James C. Otis of the Supreme Court of Minnesota wrote Murrah that his "excellent opinion fortified me both philosophically and judicially and helped me persuade a majority of my brethren in a very close, difficult fact situation."[9]

The relationship between law and psychiatry, particularly in the criminal law area, was one to which Murrah gave much thought. As part of this intellectual journey, he corresponded for many years with the famous psychiatrist, Dr. Karl A. Menninger. Murrah's attempts to bring law and psychiatry into a somewhat harmonious relationship resulted in several significant opinions.

The law presumes a criminal defendant sane, but the presumption disappears in the face of contrary evidence, and the prosecution then bears the burden of proving beyond a reasonable doubt that the defendant is sane. Murrah wrote that the presumption of sanity would disappear before "any relevant evidence of mental illness before or after the offense"—*Phillips v. United States*, 311 F.2d 204 at 204 (10th Cir. 1962)—and the sufficiency of defendant's evidence to rebut the presumption of sanity was initially a question of law for the court—*Fitts v. United States*, 284 F.2d 108 (10th Cir. 1960). The required showing was minimal, and it was met for example by diagnosis of mental illness and confinement in a mental institution a little more than a month after the commission of the offense at issue. "[C]onfinement in a mental institution upon an adjudication of mental illness is sufficient to generate in the minds of all of us a doubt sufficient to provoke inquiry"—*ibid.*, 113.

Murrah attached such importance to not convicting a defendant lacking the requisite mental capacity that he considered the issue in *Fitts* and *Phillips* even though the defendants did not challenge the sufficiency of the prosecution's evidence to prove sanity. When mental capacity was in question, it was the appellate court's "duty to notice and correct the error"—*ibid.*

Murrah and Judge John J. Hickey of Wyoming, Judge Oliver Seth of New Mexico, Judge David T. Lewis of Utah, Judge William J. Holloway of Oklahoma, Judge John C. Pickett of Wyoming, Judge Jean S. Breitenstein of Colorado, and Judge Marvin Jones of the United States Court of Claims. (Published in the Daily Oklahoman *on November 21, 1968. Courtesy Oklahoma Publishing Company.)*

Neither *Fitts* nor *Phillips* explicitly addressed the standard for determining whether when the accused allegedly committed the act in question he possessed the requisite mental capacity to be held criminally responsible for his conduct. This issue came for decision in *Wion v. United States*, 325 F.2d 420 (10th Cir. 1963), and was deemed of such importance that it was heard by the *en banc* court of Murrah, Pickett, Lewis, Breitenstein, Hill, and Seth. The chief judge assigned the opinion to himself.

Murrah began by affirming that the law, not medical science, must define the proper test of criminal responsibility for one's conduct. When a defendant placed his sanity in issue, he usually did not dispute doing the act, and whether he was convicted, or acquitted by reason of insanity, "the law must in some way protect the community by rehabilitation or isolation"—*ibid.*, 428. Necessarily, then, the law "as an instrument of the social order"—*ibid.*—must decide when responsibility would and when it would not attach. In sum, "the emphasis on psychiatry at the point of criminal responsibility is misplaced"—*ibid.*

This did not mean that science was to be banished from the courtroom. When the question shifted from guilt to sentencing, it "is at this point that the behavioral scientist can be of most help to the Court, and to the offender as well"—*ibid.* Murrah made approving reference to the Model Sentencing Act, promulgated by the Council of Judges of the National Council on Crime and Delinquency, which mandated diagnostic centers as integral elements of the penal system. By classifying offenders according to their potential for rehabilitation, the sentencing court would be able "to formulate a sentence to fit the offender. If found to be dangerous, he may be permanently incapacitated. If found to be rehabitable, either by supervised probation or suitable institutionalization, the sentence may be patterned accordingly"—*ibid.*, 430.

Having delimited the proper jurisdiction of law and science, Murrah turned to articulating the tenth circuit's test for criminal responsibility. It was one which proceeded from "the fundamental premise that moral responsibility and moral sanctions are the warp and woof of the law"—*ibid.*, 427—and which was unwilling "to concede that the law is unconcerned with the morals of one's conduct"—*ibid.* The salient elements of criminal responsibility were cognitive, the capacity to know and appreciate the nature and quality of one's actions, and volition, the capacity to control or conform conduct to society's norms:

> The jury is then to be told that, as applied to their case, the test for criminal responsibility means that before they may return a verdict of guilty, they must be convinced beyond a reasonable doubt that at the time the accused committed the unlawful act, he was mentally capable of knowing what he was doing, was mentally capable of

> knowing that it was wrong, and was mentally capable of controlling his conduct—*ibid.*, 430.

Murrah thought this standard would allow psychiatrists and other behavioral scientists full freedom to put their knowledge, training, and expertise before the jury and "should go far toward bridging the gulf between psychiatry and the law" while giving "the trial judge a definition which he can articulate to the lay jury"—*ibid.*

Murrah wrote for a unanimous court, and approval of *Wion* came from others as well. Judge Irving Kaufman of the second circuit wrote Murrah that "your opinion is superb. It is thoughtful, scholarly and written with such clarity that it makes a very difficult subject come to light."[10] *Wion* remained the law in the tenth circuit until congress legislated an insanity test for the federal courts.[11]

In *Travis v. United States*, 269 F.2d 928 (10th Cir. 1959), the court affirmed judgments of conviction for failure to file the non-Communist affidavit required by Section 9(h) of the Labor-Management Relations Act of 1947 (Taft-Hartley Act). Murrah dissented because he thought the trial court erroneously refused to inspect the grand jury testimony of certain prosecution witnesses to determine if inconsistencies existed between that evidence and their trial testimony.

In *Dennis v. United States*, 302 F.2d 5 (10th Cir. 1962), the defendants were indicted and convicted for conspiracy to file false Section 9(h) affidavits. Murrah wrote for the court reversing and remanding for new trial some of the convictions because of the erroneous admission of prejudicial hearsay testimony, and reversing and remanding as to other convictions because of insufficiency of the evidence. When the defendants appealed again after their convictions on retrial, the judgments were affirmed. Murrah again spoke for the court—*Dennis v. United States*, 346 F.2d 10 (10th Cir. 1965).

Among other issues, Murrah's opinion revisited the *Travis* question of access to grand jury testimony. Availability of materials other than grand jury proceedings which might show testimonial inconsistencies was not ground for denying access if disclosure of grand jury proceedings might disclose further inconsistencies. And the district court had the inherent power and the inescapable duty "to lift the lid of secrecy on grand jury proceedings in aid of the search for truth"—*ibid.*, 17. Direct contradictions were not essential to show inconsistencies. "Omissions of fact or even contrast in emphasis or different order of treatment may be relevant to the process of testing credibility of a witness' trial testimony"—*ibid.*, 18.

Applying these standards, the district court had not erred in refusing to inspect the grand jury proceedings. While that would have been the safer course of action, the "witnesses were thoroughly and competently cross-examined on numerous other relevant judicial and extra-judicial statements without manifest inconsistency"—*ibid.*—being shown. Thus it was "safe to assume that the grand jury proceedings would not have disclosed anything of impeaching significance"—*ibid.*

The tenor of Murrah's opinion in *Dennis* II is less demanding than his *Travis* dissent regarding the duty of the trial court to at least take a look whether any arguable claim of inconsistency has been made. Applying the dissent would almost certainly have resulted in reversal. But *Travis* was the law of the circuit, not Murrah's dissent.

It would have been well if it had been the other way. The supreme court granted certiorari in *Dennis* II and reversed on the disclosure issue—*Dennis et al. v. United States*, 384 U.S. 855, 86 S.Ct. 1840, 16 L.Ed.2d 973 (1966).

Is the statute of limitations in a criminal case a restraint on the power of the government to convict, or is it a personal defense which is lost by failure to timely and properly assert it? In *Waters v. United States*, 328 F.2d. 739 (10th Cir. 1964), a Murrah opinion concluded that it was "plainly a limitation upon the power to prosecute or to punish. It is, therefore, jurisdictional," and noticeable for the first time on appeal—*ibid.*, 743.

Articulating a view which was—and is—clearly a minority position in the circuits, Murrah reasoned that a policy of repose was a fundamental value of society, and was a protection "to be liberally interpreted in favor of the accused"—*ibid.*, 742. Admittedly, the rule was different in civil cases, but in civil cases a party did not face the loss of life or liberty. The great power brought to bear by the state against an individual charged with a crime warranted, indeed mandated, treating limitations law as a bar on that power.

As the government had no business keeping a prospective defendant in doubt whether he would be charged or not, it likewise had no business distorting the process by introducing improper, inflammatory evidence. When a police officer referred on direct examination to the defendants' records, the government admitted that the evidence was improper but argued that it was harmless as well.

The query, Murrah wrote, was "whether the jury was more prone to convict these appellants knowing they had previous records than without such knowledge. In other words, can we say with reasonable certainty that the reference to prior records 'had but very slight effect on the verdict of the jury?'"—*Sumrall v. United States*, 360 F. 2d 311 at 314 (10th Cir. 1966). Because the court could not, the judgment of conviction was reversed "in the face of overwhelming evidence of guilt"—*ibid.*, 314.

Murrah's teaching in *Avrick* (see chapter six) that summary judgment was not to be used to deprive a litigant

Mrs. Murrah visits with Mrs. Helen Breitenstein (on Mrs. Murrah's right) and Mrs. Lura Pickett (on Mrs. Murrah's left) preceding a luncheon and fashion show during the Judicial Conference of the Tenth Circuit held in Oklahoma City. (Published in the Oklahoma City Times *on June 7, 1961. Courtesy Oklahoma Publishing Company.)*

of his day in court led him to scrutinize with particular care summary disposition of civil rights cases. Claims that protected liberty, life, or property interests had been taken under color of sovereign authority warranted plenary consideration unless it was clear beyond peradventure that the case could be decided but one way.

In *Bethea v. Crouse*, 417 F.2d 504 (10th Cir. 1969), a Kansas inmate sued the prison warden asserting cruel and unusual punishment in violation of the 8th and 14th amendments. Specifically, he claimed that he had been beaten and tear-gassed. The district court granted summary judgment for the defendant. Murrah spoke for the court of appeals in reversing.

The case law of the tenth circuit accorded prison administrators wide latitude in running their institutions. The court of appeals did not sit as a super board of corrections supervising and critiquing every exercise of discretion by the warden or his staff, but the court had "never turned a deaf ear to a bona fide claim for relief based upon the deprivation of a constitutional right when asserted by a federal or state prisoner, either in the nature of a mandamus or habeas corpus proceeding or, as here, a claim under the Civil Rights Act"—*ibid.*, 506.

It was conceded that the acts which were the predicate for the complaint had been done under color of law. The dispositive query then was whether they could be found by a jury to constitute cruel and unusual punishment. If reasonable minds could differ whether the beating and gassing were so severe as "to shock the conscience of a reasonable man"—*ibid.*, 509—summary judgment was improper for the parties should win or lose depending on which view the jury took of the evidence.

The tear-gassing "was a purely disciplinary measure"—*ibid.*—and it would not offend the moral sensibilities of a reasonable man. Consequently, summary judgment was proper as to it, but improper as to the remainder of the case because neither the court of appeals nor the district court could say "whom, on sufficient but conflicting proof, the factfinder will believe"—*ibid.* The plaintiff might well lose his case, but he was entitled to lose it before a jury.

Immunity was the defense raised to plaintiff's allegations that the defendants had assaulted, battered, clubbed, choked, or tortured him. The district court ended the plaintiff's case by summary judgment, but the court of appeals, Murrah writing, thought the defendants had woefully failed to show that they were entitled to immunity—*Morgan v. Willingham*, 424 F.2d 200 (10th Cir. 1970).

The law cloaked the defendants in immunity "for acts done within the outer perimeter of line of duty"—*ibid.*, 201. But immunity could not be established by "purely conclusory statements, either in pleading or affidavit form"—*ibid.*, 202. Immunity had to be pleaded and proved, and defendants' assertions that they had acted within the line of duty "were insufficient to satisfy the requirements of Rule 56"—*ibid.*

Murrah's years as chief judge witnessed an ever growing number of federal habeas corpus attacks on state criminal convictions. A state prisoner challenging a judgment of conviction in federal court would predicate his attack on 14th Amendment due process. For a time, the Supreme Court of the United States read due process of law as guaranteeing "those canons of decency and fairness which express the notions of justice of English-speaking peoples even toward those charged with the most heinous offenses"—*Adamson v. California*, 332 U.S. 46 at 67, 67 S.Ct. 1672 at 1683, 91 L.Ed. 1903 at 1917 (1947) (Frankfurter, Justice, concurring). The more specific provisions of the Bill of Rights were not considered part of the 14th Amendment due process, unless the particular provision was deemed "to be implicit in the concept of ordered liberty"—*Palko v. Connecticut*, 302 U.S. 319, 58 S.Ct. 149, 82 L.Ed. 288 (1937) (Cardozo, Justice, holding that 5th Amendment double jeopardy stricture is not part of 14th Amendment due process). Then what has been called a judicial revolution occurred. The view that various parts of the first eight amendments were incorporated in the 14th Amendment and applied to the states as those amendments applied to the federal government gained ascendancy. In a series of decisions, the supreme court applied the 4th Amendment's prohibition against unreasonable searches and seizures—*Wolf v. Colorado*, 338 U.S. 25, 69 S.Ct. 1359, 93 L.Ed 1782 (1949)—the exclusionary rule—*Mapp v. Ohio*, 367 U.S. 643, 81 S.Ct. 1684, 6 L.Ed.2d 1081 (1961)—the 5th Amendment privilege against compelled self-incrimination—*Malloy v. Hogan*, 378 U.S. 1, 84 S.Ct. 1489, 12 L.Ed.2d 653 (1964)—the 6th Amendment right to counsel—*Gideon v. Wainwright*, 372 U.S. 335, 83 S.Ct.

792, 9 L.Ed.2d 799 (1963)—and to confrontation—*Roberts v. Russell*, 392 U.S. 293, 88 S.Ct. 1921, 20 L.Ed.2d 1100 (1968)—to the states through the 14th Amendment. Indeed, *Palko* itself was overruled in *Benton v. Maryland*, 395 U.S. 784, 89 S.Ct. 2056, 23 L.Ed.2d 707 (1969). These cases, coupled with *Fay v. Noia*, 372 U.S. 391, 83 S.Ct. 822, 9 L.Ed.2d 837 (1963), which lowered the barriers to proceedings in federal habeas when the state court for state law reasons refused to address the merits of a federal constitutional claim, contributed significantly to increased numbers of occasions when federal judges had to put on their habeas glasses and determine whether a state prisoner was unconstitutionally deprived of his liberty.

In *Chase v. Page*, 343 F.2d 167 (10th Cir. 1965), Murrah held that the state had denied the petitioner due process of law in dismissing his appeal on procedural grounds without making an adequate determination whether he was indigent and thus entitled to appointed counsel in preparing and urging his appeal. "We hold that the failure of the state courts to hear and determine that critical issue in accordance with constitutional standards of equal protection and due process of law deprived the petitioner of his fundamental rights, and his cause is cognizable in the federal courts"—*ibid.*, 172.

A normal requirement for federal habeas is exhaustion of state remedies, i.e., the state prisoner must attempt to remedy the alleged error by available state processes before repairing to federal court. But as Murrah recognized in *Smith v. Kansas*, 356 F.2d 654 (10th Cir. 1966), the requirement is grounded in policy, and if a case does not implicate the policy, there is no reason to apply the rule. In *Smith* more than a year passed between filing of a state attack on the conviction and its resolution. Within that time petitioner also filed for federal habeas. Under those circumstances, dismissal for failure to exhaust was not required. "The federal courts have the inescapable duty to entertain a solid claim of an unconstitutional restraint by a state under color of its law, and jurisdiction is not defeated by anything which may occur in the state proceedings. [Citations omitted]. Consistently with these inexorable principles we have recognized that inordinate delay in the adjudication of an asserted post-conviction remedy may very well work a denial of due process cognizable in the federal court"—*ibid.*, 656. And in *Way v. Crouse*, 421 F.2d 145 (10th Cir. 1970), Murrah applied the same reasoning to delay in deciding a direct appeal.[12]

A defendant in a criminal case may, by voluntary and intelligent act, waive his federal constitutional rights. In *Humphries v. Oklahoma*, 373 F.2d 200 (10th Cir. 1967), the petitioner claimed denial of right of counsel. The state responded that he had waived counsel. Murrah held that the state court record was not entitled to absolute verity, and that the federal habeas court was obligated to make an independent determination whether or not defendant had waived his right to an attorney.

The reach of federal habeas is well illustrated by *Heryford v. Parker*, 396 F.2d 393 (10th Cir. 1968). In 1946 a child nine years old was committed to a state institution for the feeble minded and epileptic. Some 20 years later, his guardian challenged the confinement on the ground that he was entitled to but did not have counsel in the commitment proceeding. The district court granted the writ, and the circuit affirmed.

Murrah wrote that *In re Gault*, 387 U.S. 1, 87 S.Ct. 1428, 18 L.Ed.2d 527 (1967) (addressing the constitutional protections applicable to an adjudication of juvenile delinquency) applied to an involuntary commitment proceeding. "It is the likelihood of involuntary incarceration—whether for punishment as an adult for a crime, rehabilitation as a juvenile for delinquency, or treatment

A gathering of judges at the 1967 Tenth Circuit Judicial Conference at Estes Park, Colorado. Front row, L to R: Judge Ewing T. Kerr (District of Wyoming), Judge H. Vearle Payne (District of New Mexico), Judge A. Sherman Christensen (District of Utah), Judge Howard Bratton (District of New Mexico), Judge Arthur Stanley (District of Kansas), Murrah, Judge Wesley Brown (District of Kansas), Judge Fred Daugherty (W.D. Oklahoma), Judge William E. Doyle (District of Colorado), and Judge John R. Brown (Fifth Circuit). Standing, L to R: Judge William H. Becker (W.D. Missouri), Judge Frank Murray (D. Massachusetts), Judge Edwin Langley (E.D. Oklahoma), Judge Luther Eubanks (W.D. Oklahoma), Judge Luther Bohanon (N.,W., and E.D. Oklahoma), Justice Byron White, Judge Alfred Arraj (D. Colorado), Judge Oliver Seth (Tenth Circuit), Judge Olin Hatfield Chilson (D. Colorado), Judge Jean S. Breitenstein (Tenth Circuit), Judge Allen Barrow (N.D. Oklahoma), Judge Frank Theis (D. Kansas), Judge George Templar (D. Kansas), Judge Delmas Hill (Tenth Circuit), and Judge John C. Pickett (Tenth Circuit).

and training as a feeble-minded person or mental incompetent which commands observance of the constitutional safeguards of due process. Where, as in both proceedings for juveniles and mentally deficient persons, the state undertakes to act in *parens patriae*, it has the inescapable duty to vouchsafe due process, and this necessarily includes the duty to see that a subject of an involuntary commitment proceedings is afforded the opportunity to the guiding hand of legal counsel at every step of the proceedings, unless effectively waived by one authorized to act in his behalf"—*ibid.*, 396. Finding no waiver, the only remaining question was whether *Gault* applied retroactively, and Murrah concluded that it did. "In our case the fundamental right to counsel is involved and failure to have counsel at every step of the proceedings may result in indefinite and oblivious confinement and work shameful injustice. Indeed, the expressed concern less retroactivity in cases like these result in wholesale release from confinement in mental institutions is a compelling reason for the desirability, if not necessity, for retroactivity in our case"—*ibid.*, 397.

The reach of the privilege accorded federal employees for allegedly defamatory statements made in the line of duty was at issue in *Preble v. Johnson*, 275 F.2d 275 (10th Cir. 1960). The statements, which reflected on plaintiff's job performance, were made to a grievance committee, to civil service commission investigators, and pursuant to statutory mandate.

For the privilege to attach, it was not necessary, Murrah wrote, that the statements be authorized by rule or regulation. It was sufficient if they were "appropriate to the exercise of the utterer's office or station"—*ibid.*, 278. Touching upon work performance in defendants' areas of responsibility, the statements were clearly made in the line of duty.

When the fifth and eighth circuits decided similar cases, they relied on *Preble* as "squarely in point" and "precisely in point"—*West v. Garrett*, 392 F.2d 543 at 544 (5th Cir. 1968); and *Ruderer v. Meyer*, 413 F.2d 175 at 179 (8th Cir. 1969). Then Circuit Judge Harry A. Blackmun wrote in *Ruderer* that we "agree with the conclusions reached by the Tenth Circuit and we hold here, as it did there"—*ibid.*, 180.

By statute, congress made it a crime to violate any rule or regulation promulgated by the attorney general prohibiting the introduction of things into a federal prison without the consent of the warden. Convicted of violating the statute, the defendant argued that it was an unconstitutional delegation of legislative power to the executive branch.

Murrah was not persuaded. Congress could penalize the violation of any rule or regulation which it was empowered to authorize. Certainly, congress had the power to create a federal prison system and entrust its management and direction to the attorney general, including the adoption of needful rules and regulations. Necessarily, then, the statute was constitutional. "The validity of the regulation is unquestioned here—the power of Congress to penalize its violation is unquestionable"—*Carter v. United States*, 333 F.2d 354 at 356 (10th Cir. 1964).

Years later the third circuit was presented with the same issue. It likewise found the argument unavailing on authority of *Carter*. "We accept the holding of [the Tenth Circuit] and the reasoning employed by Chief Judge Murrah"—*United States v. Berrigan*, 482 F.2d 171 at 182 (3d Cir. 1973).

At a trial for possession of a stolen treasury check, the trial court allowed the prosecuting attorney to ask the defendant if he had been adjudicated a juvenile delinquent for a similar offense. The defendant claimed on appeal that admission of the adjudication was error requiring reversal.

Murrah agreed. The question was one of policy, and the sound policy was to exclude adjudications of status to impeach the credibility of a witness. "After all, the appellant has not been convicted of a crime or even prosecuted as a criminal under the juvenile delinquency act. The adjudication of a status rather than the conviction of a crime would seem to fall within the rationale of the rule which generally excludes evidence of arrest or indictment without conviction"—*Cotton v. United States*, 355 F.2d 480 at 482 (10th Cir. 1966). Citing *Cotton* as expressing the "prevailing view," Federal Rules of Evidence 609(d) follows its teaching.

Histories of the 1960s may well identify as a distinguishing feature of that time the sit-in demonstration. Some University of Denver students made the decision to stage such a demonstration in a nonpublic area of the registrar's office, an unfortunate decision because the university had a chancellor and board of trustees with backbone.

Told to leave, the students refused, the police were summoned, the students were arrested, and subsequently they were suspended from the university for one year. They then brought a class action for reinstatement. The *gravamen* of their lawsuit was that the disciplinary procedure had not accorded them due process of law.

The 14th Amendment protects against deprivation of life, liberty, or property without due process of law only if the deprivation is the result of state action. Because the University of Denver was a private institution, the query was whether the state of Colorado had so involved itself in the affairs of an otherwise private entity that it was a joint participant in the disciplinary proceedings.

Counsel for the protesters keyed upon tax exemptions

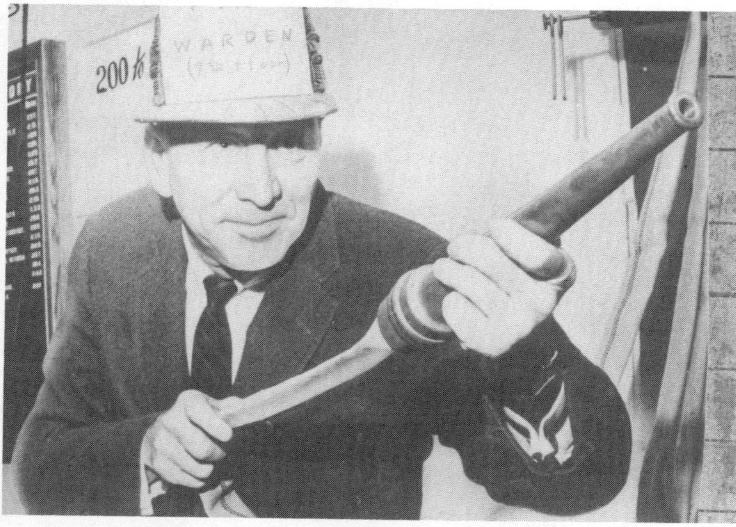

Murrah's responsibilities as chief judge did not keep him from serving as fire warden for the seventh floor of the United States Courthouse in Oklahoma City. (Published in the Oklahoma City Times *on October 8, 1959. Courtesy Oklahoma Publishing Company.)*

enjoyed by the university to establish the requisite state involvement. Murrah judged the argument wholly unpersuasive, for the "benefits conferred, however characterized, have no bearing on the challenged actions beyond the perpetuation of the institution itself. This we hold to be far short of the requisite State involvement"—*Brown v. Mitchell*, 409 F.2d 593 at 596 (10th Cir. 1969).

Nor did the possibility that the university was a forum in which 1st Amendment freedom of expression rights were protected speak to the state action question. While, "[s]uperficially, this line of thought has appeal...it is specious and wholly untenable"—*ibid.* There was nothing in 1st Amendment jurisprudence "to lend credence to the hypothesis that these students have a constitutionally protected right to close the doors of the university in order to enforce their demands, or that the disciplinary action taken against the students for such unauthorized conduct is state action redressable as a violation of the Civil Rights Act"—*ibid.*

For a person to be entitled to social security disability benefits, he must show that he is under disability and unable to engage in substantial gainful activity because of health problems. When the showing has been made, the burden is on the secretary of health, education, and welfare to show the reasonable availability of suitable employment. The court sat *en banc* in 1966 to resolve a "seeming conflict" in its jurisprudence concerning the content of these standards—*Gardner v. Brian*, 369 F.2d. 443 at 444 (10th Cir. 1966). The case produced a three-two division with Murrah writing for the majority.

Acknowledging the power of the secretary of health, education, and welfare to construe and interpret the statutory scheme he was charged with administering, Murrah also accepted the responsibility of the courts to guard against frustration of congressional policy by administrative fiat. Disability was a function of age, education, training, experience, and mental and physical capabilities. Explicitly rejected was the proposition that pain must be endured, that it could not be disabling by itself. Thus the determination of disability had to be made with regard to the individual claimant's situation.

The burden was on the secretary to show the reasonable availability of suitable positions. This did not require the secretary to find a specific job for the claimant, but it did require more than reading a list of the nation's jobs and occupations. Reasonable availability was defined by the labor market in which claimant would normally work. While there was evidence that claimant could perform certain jobs, the evidence was uncontradicted "that claimant would probably have severe difficulty gaining access to any of them in the...area where he lived"—*ibid.*, 447. Consequently, the secretary had failed to show reasonable availability, and the judgment of the district court finding the claimant entitled to benefits was affirmed.

Judge Breitenstein, joined by Judge Lewis, dissented. The thrust of their dissent was that congress did not intend to restrict employment opportunities to those available in the claimant's home community. As the dissenters interpreted the court's reading of the statute, the Social Security Act had been changed to an unemployment compensation act.

Perhaps in no area more than bankruptcy does the law endeavor to reconcile conflicting legitimate interests. During his practice years, Murrah's passion was the case replete with the drama of human existence in all its strengths and weaknesses. Perhaps he found some of this drama in the struggle of debtor and creditor, for he wrote many bankruptcy cases.

Shortly before bankruptcy, a debtor transferred his homestead to satisfy an extant debt. Fraud did not taint the conveyance, and the debtor claimed no exemption for the homestead when he invoked the protection of the bankruptcy court. The trustee in bankruptcy sought to set aside the transfer as a voidable preference. The district court found that the conveyance was not a voidable preference because the homestead was property exempt from the claims of creditors.

The court of appeals affirmed—*Rutledge v. Johansen*, 270 F.2d 881 (10th Cir. 1959). Murrah said it was "textbook law"—*ibid.*, 882—that a conveyance of exempt property by the debtor before bankruptcy was not a voidable preference. The trustee sought to avoid this rule by relying upon statutory language that exemption rights were to be determined as of the date of filing in bankruptcy. Because the debtor claimed no exemption when he filed, the exempt property protection was not applicable.

Murrah thought otherwise. It "seems more in consonance with the spirit and purpose of the exemption laws...to hold these administrative directions applicable only to exempt property of which the bankrupt was seized at the time of the filing of bankruptcy.... Surely, if a bankrupt is entitled to have exempt property of which he is seized at the time of the filing of bankruptcy set apart from the bankruptcy estate, he is entitled to make a valid transfer of it prior to the date of filing. This view accords the bankrupt his full right under the exemption laws, while at the same time preserving to the trustee the right to challenge the exempt character of the transferred property in proceedings like these"—*ibid.*, 882, 883.

A Kansas farmer in bankruptcy sought to exempt his combine from inclusion in the bankruptcy estate. Kansas exemption law had one section which clearly related to farmers: "Two cows, one hundred chickens or other domestic fowls, ten hogs." Under this section, there was a $300 limit on the value of exempted items. Another section exempted items necessary for conducting the work of a "mechanic, miner or other person." The farmer sought to bring the combine under the protective "other person" language, while the creditor invoked the "not exceeding in value $300" language.

Murrah concluded that the Kansas courts would treat the combine as exempt—*Cantrell v. Molz-Frick Implement Co. of Wichita*, Kan. 278 F.2d. 546 (10th Cir. 1960). This would be in accord with the "sensible Kansas policy"—*ibid.*, 547—of giving a liberal construction to exemption provisions. A farmer could not farm without appropriate tools and implements, "including modern machinery such as tractors and combines"—*ibid.*, 547, 548. The absurdity of not including the combine within the exemption language should not be countenanced absent a clear mandate from the Kansas courts.[13]

The jurisdiction of bankruptcy to entertain and decide a counterclaim by the trustee to set aside a voidable preference had been affirmed by the *en banc* court, Murrah authoring, in *Inter-State National Bank of Kansas City v. Luther, Trustee*, 221 F.2d 382 (10th Cir. 1955), certiorari granted, 350 U.S. 810, 76 S.Ct. 77, 100 L.Ed. 726 (1955), certiorari dismissed, 350 U.S. 944, 76 S.Ct. 297, 100 L.Ed. 823 (1956). The issue was considered anew, again *en banc*, in *Katchen v. Landy*, 336 F.2d 535 (10th Cir. 1964), and, Murrah again authoring, the power of bankruptcy to hear a voidable preference counterclaim filed in response to a creditor's claim again sustained.

Judge Phillips, joined by Judges Lewis and Breitenstein, dissented. They reasoned that if the trustee brought an independent action in district court to set aside the preference, the claimant would be entitled to trial by jury. They thought it ran afoul of the 7th Amendment to allow the trustee to assert the preference issue in bankruptcy and avoid jury trial.

As in *Luther*, the Supreme Court of the United States again granted certiorari. Unlike *Luther*, however, the writ was not subsequently dismissed. The case was heard on the merits, and the court, per Justice White, affirmed—*Katchen v. Landy* 382 U.S. 323, 86 S.Ct. 467, 15 L.Ed. 391 (1966).[14]

Parties may contract to have disputes resolved by an arbitrator rather than by a court. However, because arbitration is the product of agreement, courts play a role if the parties disagree concerning what they have agreed.

An employer and a union entered into a collective

bargaining agreement reserving to management all decisions concerning the operations of the company. A conflict arose when the employer subcontracted work which came within job classifications in the collective bargaining agreement. The arbitration clause read upon the proper interpretation and application of the agreement, and the union sought arbitration. The district court held the matter not arbitrable. The court of appeals reversed—*Local 1912, Int. Ass'n of Mach. v. United States Potash Co.*, 270 F.2d. 496 (10th Cir. 1959).

Speaking for a unanimous panel, Murrah said that collective bargaining agreements, as other contracts, are subject to implied covenants of good faith and fair dealing. Neither party was to engage in conduct which would impair or destroy the right of the other party to receive the fruits of their mutual assent.

The controlling canon of construction was to consider a matter arbitrable unless it could be said with positive assurance that it was not. When, as in the collective bargaining agreement under scrutiny, the contract did not specify either the matters included or excluded, it was not to be read "according to its dry words. It is for us to put meat on the skeleton rather than tear the flesh from the bones"—*ibid.*, 498. And it was proper to consider custom and usage in the arbitration world in interpreting the contract.

The employer's reading could injure or destroy the union as an effective bargaining unit. This would contravene national labor policy, a result not to be tolerated. Moreover, the dispute clearly required interpretation of the agreement, the very thing the parties had consensually undertaken to arbitrate. Consequently, the district court had erred in refusing to enforce arbitration, and the case was remanded for that purpose.

Murrah applied the same interpretative doctrine and

reached the same result in *International U., U.A., A., & A.I. Workers v. Cardwell Manufacturing Company*, 304 F.2d 801 (10th Cir. 1962), when the union had been unsuccessful in specifically including as arbitrable the matter in dispute. The parties may have meant not to include the particular grievance, but by including within the arbitrator's jurisdiction any disagreement regarding interpretation or application of the contract, they had agreed to "arbitrate the arbitrability of the grievance"—*ibid.*, at 803.

As noted in chapter five, the Norris-LaGuardia Act deprived federal courts of the power to grant injunctions in cases arising from a labor dispute. Then in 1947, § 301 of the Labor-Management Relations Act of 1947 (Taft-Hartley Act) conferred on the federal courts jurisdiction of suits for violations of collective bargaining agreements. In *Textile Workers Union of America v. Lincoln Mills*, 353 U.S. 448, 77 S.Ct. 912, 1 L.Ed.2d 972 (1957), the supreme court held that § 301 authorized federal courts to grant specific performance of an arbitration agreement.

Unanswered by *Textile Workers* was whether the anti-injunction provision of Norris-LaGuardia survived § 301 of Taft-Hartley when the employer sued to enjoin a strike in violation of a collective bargaining agreement providing for § 301 enforceable binding arbitration. Murrah answered the question for the tenth circuit in *Chauffeurs, Teamsters, etc. v. Yellow Transit Freight Lines*, 282 F.2d 345 (10th Cir. 1960), and the answer was that the federal courts had jurisdiction under Taft-Hartley to grant injunctive relief.

Murrah based his conclusion primarily on *Textile Workers*. He read that case as articulating a broad "concept of jurisdictional authority—one which embrace[s] all violations of labor contracts which [have] been freely arrived at through the collective bargaining process"—*ibid.*, 349. If the federal courts were empowered to enforce arbitration agreements, then assuredly they could enjoin a strike over a grievance which fell within the arbitration language:

> Yet it seems reasonable to say that if the courts are to exercise jurisdiction for the redress of violations of collective bargaining agreements according to notions of federal common law, they are empowered to vouchsafe the integrity of a bargaining contract to the end that neither party shall be deprived of the fruits of their bargain. [citations omitted] And this is so, we think, whether the claimed violation is a refusal to arbitrate according to the terms of the contract, or the violation of an agreement not to strike or tie up the employer's business without first resorting to the grievance procedure prescribed in the contract. It is one thing to utilize an injunctive decree for the negative purpose of interfering with full freedom of association, self-organization, and designation of representatives to negotiate the terms and conditions of employment. It is quite another to utilize the judicial processes to preserve and vouchsafe the fruits of a bargain which the parties have freely arrived at through the exercise of collective bargaining rights—*ibid.*, 349, 350.

The seventh circuit had decided this same question and reached a contra result. The supreme court affirmed the seventh circuit—*Sinclair Refining Company v. Atkinson*, 370 U.S. 195, 82 S.Ct. 1328, 8 L.Ed.2d 440 (1962)—and reversed *Chauffeurs* on authority of that case—*Chauffeurs, Teamsters and Helpers Local Union No. 395 v. Yellow Transit Freight Lines, Inc.*, 370 U.S. 711, 82 S.Ct. 1293, 8 L.Ed.2d 792 (1962).

Not quite a decade later, the supreme court thought about the question again—*The Boys Market, Inc. v. Retail Clerk's Union, Local 770*, 398 U.S. 235, 90 S.Ct. 1583, 26

L.Ed.2d 199 (1970). The new cogitation persuaded the court that *Sinclair* had been erroneously decided, and it was overruled.

Relying on New Mexico decisions, the Internal Revenue Service for a number of years treated taxable transactions of the taxpayer and her husband as involving community property interests. Soon after the husband died, the Supreme Court of New Mexico overruled its prior case law and decided that the interests were separate, not community, property.

The tax treatment of certain transactions after the husband's death depended upon whether the property was community or separate when the husband died. The Internal Revenue Service applied the latest state supreme court decisions, and taxed accordingly.

The taxpayer challenged the power of the commissioner to apply the overruling state decisions retroactively, and argued that the government was estopped by its prior treatment of the interests as community to then treat them as separate. Murrah concluded the arguments were without merit—*Massaglia v. Commissioner of Internal Revenue*, 286 F.2d. 258 (10th Cir. 1961). The controlling principle was that overruling judicial decisions were applied retroactively "unless it can be shown that rights have become vested upon the faith and credit of the prior decision"—*ibid.*, 261. No such disparagement of vested rights would result from treating as always the law that only recently declared to be the law, and New Mexico cases favored giving an overruling decision retroactive as well as prospective effect. Consequently, the commissioner properly treated the taxable events in accord with the most recent case law.

While the very nature of sovereignty counseled great caution in applying estoppel to governmental conduct, the courts would not allow "the government to deal dishonorably or capriciously with its citizens. It must not play an ignoble part or do a shabby thing"—*ibid.*, 262. The present litigation presented no basis for estoppel. In its prior rulings, the Internal Revenue Service had relied upon state law as it was then. Now, it sought only to rely upon state law as it is. "This inconsistency was not brought about by the Commissioner's own doing. He has done no more than follow the vicissitudes of controlling state law in which he had no voice and which he was bound to follow"—*ibid.* The supreme court's current jurisprudence regarding retroactivity of case law in civil litigation is articulated in *Harper v. Virginia Dept. of Taxation*, 113 S.Ct. 2510, 125 L.Ed. 2d 74 (1993).

A recurrent jurisprudential issue is when, if ever, a party should be relieved of the consequences of failure to comply with a rule of procedure. The answer usually lies in a discriminating striking of the balance between the interest in rules being observed, and the interest in cases being decided on the merits, not on technical niceties.

In *Robinson v. Trans America Insurance Company*, 368 F.2d 37 (10th Cir. 1966), the plaintiff failed to answer interrogatories within the prescribed time. At pretrial conference, defendants moved to dismiss the lawsuit. Counsel for plaintiff responded that the delay in answering was due to the pertinent records and documents being located in numerous offices across the United States, and offered to answer the queries immediately. The district court rejected the offer, and dismissed the case.

The court of appeals, per Murrah, reversed. The district court had a broad range of remedies for failure to comply, and the choice of a remedy rested in its discretion. But the discretion was a judicial discretion subject to reversal for abuse.

The office of the various remedies was to secure compliance, not to punish parties. Given the fact that defendants had shown no prejudice, and given plaintiff's readiness and willingness to supply the requested information, no reasonable trial judge would have dismissed the action. Consequently, the trial judge had abused his discretion. "The plaintiff was derelict, but he was contrite. The trial court was obviously impatient, perhaps even injudicious.... We think the spirit and purpose of the rule would have been best served and the expense of this appeal avoided if appellant had been allowed to answer instanter"—*ibid.*, 39). When, however, counsel, having been informed that the dispositive ruling was to be made on a date certain, voluntarily absented himself from the hearing, and then failed to perfect a timely appeal, the district court did not abuse its discretion by refusing to extend the appeal time—*Long v. Emery*, 383 F.2d 392 (10th Cir. 1967). It was the lawyer's responsibility to monitor the course of proceedings, and to advise "himself when the court makes the order he wishes to protest"—*ibid.*, 394. Assuredly, it was not an abuse of discretion to hold that failure to do what one was obligated to do does not warrant a second chance to comply. "To allow counsel to defeat the prescribed period of time for taking an appeal by merely absenting himself from a hearing of which he had notice," Murrah wrote, "would tend to derogate from the spirit of the rules to bring about a just, speedy and inexpensive determination of every action"—*ibid.*, 394, 395.

The 7th Amendment preserves in federal court jury trial for legal issues. Jury impartiality is secured in part by challenges for cause and by peremptory challenges. A challenge for cause tests the qualifications of the prospective juror to sit. Disqualification may result from failure to meet statutory requirements, bias or a particular relationship with a litigant or counsel.

Historically, peremptory challenges have allowed a

party to excuse a potential juror in the unfettered discretion of the litigant. In effect, a peremptory challenge excludes from the jury a person who otherwise is wholly qualified to serve.

In *Photostat Corporation v. Ball*, 338 F.2d 783 (10th Cir. 1964), the defendant suffered an adverse verdict and judgment and sought a new trial on the ground that certain jurors had failed to respond fully to a question on *voir dire*.[15] After hearing, the district court denied the motion.

The court of appeals reversed the judgment in a Murrah opinion. Murrah began by vouchsafing "that the denial or substantial impairment of the statutory right of peremptory challenge is prejudicial to the constitutional right to a fair and impartial jury"—*ibid.*, 786. The litigant who sought to set aside a jury verdict for failure of a juror to fully and truthfully answer *voir dire* questions had to show probable bias of the juror and resultant prejudice to the movant, for courts "act on probabilities, not possibilities"—*ibid.*

Probable bias and prejudice would be shown "if the suppressed information was of sufficient cogency and significance to cause [the court] to believe that counsel was entitled to know of it when he came to exercise his right of peremptory challenge"—*ibid.*, 787). In the case at the bar, a personal injury action arising from an automobile collision, various jurors had failed to disclose that they had been involved in car wrecks with attendant claims. While the information had been withheld inadvertently, it had been withheld through no fault of the defendant; it was information the defendant was entitled to know in exercising his peremptory challenges, and the infirmity in the *voir dire* process was remediable only by a new trial.

Subsequently, the sixth circuit followed the analysis

of *Photostat* in *McCoy v. Goldston*, 652 F.2d 654 (6th Cir. 1981). Later, the tenth circuit applied *Photostat* as the law of the circuit in *Greenwood v. McDonough Power Equipment, Inc.*, 687 F.2d 338 (10th Cir. 1982). However, the supreme court granted certiorari in *McDonough* and reversed—464 U.S. 548, 104 S.Ct. 845, 78 L.Ed.2d 663 (1984). The supreme court held that incomplete *voir dire* answers would be a basis for a new trial only if an honest answer would have warranted a challenge for cause.

Whether the doctrinal underpinnings of *Photostat* survive *McDonough* is a good question. There are reasons for concluding they may. The supreme court severely criticized the court of appeals in *McDonough* for ordering a new trial without giving the district court an opportunity to address the question. In *Photostat*, the court of appeals acted only after initial consideration by the district court.

Moreover, three of the five justices who supplied the votes for the court's opinion in *McDonough* joined in a separate concurring opinion which contains language consistent with the *Photostat* language. And the two justices who joined in the court's judgment in *McDonough*, but not in the court's opinion, cited *McCoy* with apparent approval. Arguably, then, five justices in *McDonough* did not disapprove of *Photostat* and *McCoy*, but did disapprove of the circuit's application of the governing law in *McDonough*. In any event, whatever the supreme court's current view, Murrah considered full and meaningful exercise of peremptory challenges essential to a fair trial, and any significant impairment of that right harmful error warranting reversal.[16]

A majority of Murrah's brethren held that federal officers could conduct a warrantless search of an automobile they had seized. *Sirimarco v. United States*, 315 F.2d 699 (10th Cir. 1963) (*en banc*). Murrah, joined by Hill, dissented.

When the car was searched, it was parked by the courthouse adjacent to the sheriff's office, and the defendant was in jail. No excuse existed for not obtaining a warrant. The exceptions to the warrant requirement, exigent circumstances and search incident to a valid arrest, were to be construed narrowly, and neither had any application to the case under review. The decision of the majority created "a new loophole for stealthy encroachment on the citizen's fundamental right to privacy"—*ibid.*, 703.

Acuna v. Baker, 418 F.2d 639 (10th Cir. 1969), a habeas corpus proceeding, was heard initially by Murrah, Pickett, and Holloway. While a juvenile, Acuna, the petitioner, had been certified to stand trial as an adult. Although indigent, no counsel was appointed for him in the certification proceeding. Once certified, the petitioner entered a plea of guilty while represented by a lawyer. He then sought to vacate the conviction on the ground that denial of counsel rendered the certification void. The district court denied relief, and an appeal was taken.

Murrah and Holloway voted to reverse and set aside the certification and conviction. Pickett thought the writ should be denied because the guilty plea waived any defect in the certification proceeding. And, he said, the court had so held recently in one of his opinions, *Salazar v. Rodriguez*, 371 F.2d 726 (10th Cir. 1967).

The case was then taken *en banc*. The Murrah-Holloway majority quickly became a lonely minority as Pickett, Lewis, Breitenstein, Hill, Seth, and Hickey found that the counseled guilty plea waived any objection to the validity of the certification decision.

Murrah, writing for himself and Holloway, said there was no waiver because the supreme court decision which was the basis for finding a right to assistance of counsel

The Judge.

in certification proceedings—In *re Gault*, 387 U.S. 1, 87 S.Ct. 1428, 18 L.Ed.2d 527 (1967)—had not been decided when Acuna entered his guilty plea. Acuna could not have knowingly and voluntarily relinquished a right which he did not know that he had:

> It is thus clear that counsel for Acuna in the District Court could not have known in the exercise of ordinary professional acumen that Acuna was constitutionally entitled to the assistance of counsel in the Juvenile Court proceedings. Surely it cannot be said that Acuna impliedly waived the right to counsel which he did not know was constitutionally available to him—*ibid.*, 641.

The only remaining question was whether *Gault* should be applied retroactively. As to that issue, Murrah and Holloway entertained no doubt that Acuna was entitled to the full benefits of *Gault*.

The decision of a jury can cost a person wealth, freedom, even life. With consequences of such moment riding on a jury's determination, it is not surprising that the concern with jury impartiality Murrah evinced in *Photostat* obtained in criminal cases as well.

This concern strongly influenced Murrah's view of the fairness of the trial process in *Casias v. United States*, 315 F.2d 614 (10th Cir. 1963) (*en banc*). Before Steve Casias was tried, eight drug cases had been tried, and guilty verdicts returned in each case. Casias was charged with a drug offense as well. The pool from which his jury was selected had 44 people on it. Of that number, 43 had sat on one or more of the previous eight cases. Of the 12 actually selected as jurors in his case, one had served in three of the eight cases, four had served twice, and six had served once. All the jurors except one had heard the testimony of at least two of the prosecution's witnesses against Casias in the previous trials, and ten of the jurors had served together in one or more of the eight cases. Casias unsuccessfully challenged the jury pool in the district court. After trial and conviction, he based his appeal in large measure on the ground that he had been denied his right to an impartial jury, but the judgment was affirmed.

Judges Breitenstein, Lewis, and Pickett acknowledged that if the same transaction gave rise to more than one offense, a juror who had convicted in one case was not competent to sit in another case arising from a common occurrence. They were, however, unwilling to extend this rule to prosecutions arising from separate, distinct, and independent transactions. Bias could not, they thought, be implied from the jurors' actions in the prior cases.

For Murrah, the question was whether this "dope peddler"—*ibid.*, 619—was accorded trial by an impartial jury. The answer was no.

Murrah began with John Marshall's teaching in Aaron Burr's prosecution for treason that the law disqualifies a person from jury service if "it suspects prejudice, because in general persons in a similar situation would feel prejudice"—*ibid.*, 620. If reason to suspect existed, then there was no need to probe for individual cause because that would be a fruitless endeavor. It defied reason to suggest that average men and women "such as these jurors, both collectively and individually, would be capable of searching the state of their minds for evidence of bias"—*ibid.*, 621.

Was there cause for suspecting bias in this case? The defendant was charged with a narcotics offense, a charge with a propensity to generate "a vengeful attitude toward one who is in any way connected with this sordid business, whether we sit in our living room or in the jury box"— *ibid.*—and jurors in this case had already convicted in other drug cases relying upon the testimony of the same prosecution witnesses. Murrah, Hill and Seth could not "conceive of a more aggravated case of compound guilt"—*ibid.* The conviction was affirmed because six judges heard the appeal, and divided evenly. A decision by an evenly divided appellate court results in affirmance.

Murrah's views concerning implied bias did not prevail in the tenth circuit, nor have they carried the day in other federal courts either. But, as has been said, today's dissents may be tomorrow's law. Writing for the first circuit in *United States v. Carranza*, 583 F.2d 25 (1st Cir. 1978), Judge Bownes characterized Murrah's opinion in *Casias* as "trenchant" and expressed surprise that "Despite the caliber of the dissent and its author, this approach has not caught on, at least as yet"—*ibid.*, 28.

Dissenting in *Smith v. United States*, 273 F.2d 462 (10th Cir. 1959) (*en banc*), Murrah wrote that federal appellate courts possessed authority to modify a sentence which was within statutory limits, but which the appellate court considered grossly excessive, or clearly and manifestly cruel and unjust. The district courts had wide discretion to sentence within statutory limits, but that did not "mean that the appellate courts should abnegate a duty imposed by statute when manifest justice requires the exercise of that power"—*ibid.*, 469.

When Murrah dissented in *Smith*, he was in a distinct minority not only in his court, for none of his brethren joined his dissent, but in the other courts of appeals as well. There was an unbreached wall of case authority denying the power which Murrah considered self-evident. But the law changed. Almost all the courts of appeals eventually recognized in dicta that they had the power to review the length of a sentence for manifest abuse of discretion, and this dicta led to some actual holdings to this effect. Wright and Miller—*Federal Practice and Procedure* (Criminal 2d), III, § 533, pp. 173, 174.[17]

The reading of ancient rules of law on the consequences of modern technology produced one of Murrah's most noteworthy dissents as chief judge. *Batten v. United States*, 306 F.2d 580 (10th Cir. 1962), presented "the novel question whether a taking of property, compensable under the Fifth Amendment, occurs when there is no physical invasion of the affected property but the operation and maintenance of military jet aircraft...produce noise, vibration, and smoke which interfere with the use and enjoyment of the property"—*ibid.*, 581. The court answered no. It reasoned that because there was no invasion of plaintiffs' property, the damages they suffered were consequential, not direct, and could not constitute a fifth amendment taking. The majority did suggest that a taking might occur if the homes were rendered uninhabitable.

Murrah read the law differently. Whether a compensable taking had occurred did not stand or fall on physical invasion. The proper query required "an analysis and evaluation of competing interests, i.e., the public versus private, within the framework of our social order—a jurisprudence of interest if you please"—*ibid.*, 586. The plaintiffs were entitled to recover if the government's infringement of a protected interest had been "sufficiently direct, sufficiently peculiar, and of sufficient magnitude to cause us to conclude that fairness and justice, as between the State and the citizen, requires the burden imposed to be borne by the public and not by the individual alone"—*ibid.*, 587. Concerning the majority's suggestion that if the plaintiffs' homes were rendered uninhabitable they could recover, Murrah wondered when the interference would cross the threshold to a taking. "Is it when the window glass rattles, or when it falls out; when the smoke suffocates the inhabitants, or merely makes them cough; when the noise makes family conversation difficult, or when it stifles it entirely?" Canvassing the record, Murrah concluded that infringement by the government had been direct, substantial and peculiar. It followed that the plaintiffs had established a constitutional taking, and were entitled to compensation.

Murrah's dissent has had a good press. As one law review article observed, "The rationale of *Batten* has fared poorly in the marketplace of ideas; Judge Murrah's dissent proved to carry more persuasiveness"—Faden and Berger, 3 Southwestern University Law Review, p. 56 (1971). The Supreme Court of Oregon concluded that "the dissenting view in the *Batten* case presents the better-reasoned analysis of the legal principles involved"—*Thornberg v. The Port of Portland*, 233 Or. 178 at 187, 376 P.2d 100 at 104 (1962). TheSupreme Court of New Hampshire relied upon the dissent in overruling contrary precedent in that state—*Sundell v. Town of New London*, 119 N.H. 839, 409 A.2d 1315 (N.H. 1979)—and the Supreme Court of Tennessee followed the dissent in

Johnson & Johnson v. City of Greeneville, 222 Tenn. 260, 435 S.W.2d 476 (Tenn. 1968).

When the Supreme Court of the United States held that 14th Amendment challenges to state apportionment statutes were cognizable in the federal courts—*Baker v. Carr*, 369 U.S. 186, 82 S.Ct. 691, 7 L.Ed.2d 663 (1962)—and then adopted the one-person-one-vote theory of apportionment, the handwriting was on the wall for Oklahoma's malapportioned legislature. Shortly after *Baker* was decided, a three-judge district court of Murrah, Ross Rizley, and Frederick Daugherty held Oklahoma's legislative apportionment unconstitutional—*Moss v. Burkhart*, 207 F. Supp. 885 (W.D. Okl. 1962); see also *Moss v. Burkhart*, 220 F. Supp. 149 (W.D. Okl. 1963). The battle was then over the remedy. Eventually, the May 1964 primaries held under an Oklahoma state court plan were invalidated, and new elections under court drawn lines were ordered—*Reynolds v. State Election Board*, 233 F. Supp. 323 (W.D. Okl. 1964). The drawing of the district lines was entrusted to Patience Latting, a Phi Beta Kappa graduate of the University of Oklahoma and holder of a master's degree in mathematics and statistics from Columbia University. Working from her kitchen table, Latting redistricted the state in 48 hours and, in the process, wrought major changes in the state's political culture. One of Oklahoma's finest minds, Latting later served one term on the Oklahoma City Council, and three terms as mayor of the capital city.

Not every appeal required constitutional explication or statutory interpretation. Within the constraints of *Erie*, diversity cases afforded the judges the opportunity from time to time to apply their little gray cells to intriguing private law questions.

Hardware Mutual Insurance Company v. Lukken, 372 F.2d 8 (10th Cir. 1967), found Murrah writing about

Murrah and United states District Judges Stephen S. Chandler (on Murrah's right) and Ross Rizley (on Murrah's left). In a few years, Chandler's antics would become a major embarrassment to Murrah and the Tenth Circuit. (Published in the Oklahoma City Times *on June 15, 1960. Courtesy Oklahoma Publishing Company.)*

proximate cause in Oklahoma, "a thorny..., confusing area of Oklahoma tort law"—*ibid.*, 13—while *Cundick v. Broadbent*, 383 F. 2d 157 (10th Cir. 1967), required the court to decide whether a transaction should be undone under Wyoming law for lack of capacity to contract and fraud. And in *American Surety Company v. Gold and Dearmore*, 375 F.2d 523 (10th Cir. 1966), the circuit had to predict whether the Supreme Court of Kansas would deem it contra to public policy to hold an insurer liable for a punitive damages award against its insured. Murrah concluded that it would. When faced with the issue, the supreme court of Kansas reached the same conclusion in

Guardianship of the Person and Estate of Smith, 211 Kan. 397, 507 P.2d 189 (Kan. 1973), relying on Murrah's "well reasoned opinion" in *American Surety Company.*[18]

In the early 1960s Murrah was involved in two judicial appointment controversies, involved far beyond his natural interest in such matters. The Southern District of New York and the Northern, Eastern, and Western districts of Oklahoma were the *loci* of the disputes.

During his years of service as a member of the Advisory Council of Judges of the National Council on Crime and Delinquency, Murrah had become acquainted with—and favorably impressed by—Judge Irving Ben Cooper, a state trial judge in New York. When Cooper was nominated by President John F. Kennedy for the Southern District of New York bench, he encountered the formidable opposition of the American Bar Association and the Association of the Bar of the City of New York.[19] The primary ground for the opposition was that Cooper lacked judicial temperament, although objections also were raised that he was wanting in the experience necessary for a federal district judge. Murrah supported Cooper's confirmation, and wrote a letter on his behalf for submission to the senate judiciary committee. Eventually, after fuss and fury extending over a number of months, Cooper was confirmed by voice vote.

In 1960 Judge William R. Wallace, who had succeeded Bower Broaddus on the latter's death in 1949, was killed in a car accident. The position was not filled before President Dwight D. Eisenhower was succeeded by President Kennedy, and the new administration, following the counsel of the uncrowned king of the senate, Bob Kerr, gave the nod to Murrah's old law partner, Luther Bohanon.

Enter the American Bar Association. The ABA's standing committee on judicial selection looked askance on Bohanon's integrity as well as his ability, and unanimously deemed him unqualified to serve as a federal judge. Murrah was livid. He attributed Bohanon's troubles to "a few well-placed lawyers here in Oklahoma," characterized the opposition as "a gross injustice, generated by envy, malice and vindictiveness," and expressed sadness and dismay that the ABA was "influenced by it."[20]

Murrah left no stone unturned to secure Bohanon's confirmation. He even made a personal appearance, although unsuccessful, before the judicial selection committee in an effort to obtain a favorable rating. Judge Phillips chimed in with a ringing endorsement of the embattled nominee,[21] but the ABA did not change its mind. Neither, however, did the White House, Senator Kerr, or Murrah. Before 1961 had passed, Bohanon was confirmed and took the bench in direct lineal descent from Murrah, occupying the judgeship which Murrah first had filled in 1937.

Then there was the Chandler matter. Quite possibly, this was the most bizarre incident of its kind in the history of the federal judiciary. The genesis of the controversy is traceable at least to 1939. In that year, fresh from a hard-fought reelection campaign, Elmer Thomas decided that Oklahoma City attorney Stephen S. Chandler should be named to the as yet uncreated additional judgeship for the western district .[22] It has been suggested that Chandler was selected because he was the largest contributor to Thomas's 1938 campaign.[23]

Born in Tennessee in 1899, Chandler had moved with his family to Oklahoma City shortly after statehood and graduated from Central High School in 1916. Chandler then attended the University of Tennessee and graduated from the University of Kansas with an LL.B. degree. From 1922 until he went on the federal bench, Chandler engaged in the general practice of law in Oklahoma City.[24]

The president signed the bill creating the new judge-

Murrah welcomes newly commissioned Judge William J. Holloway, Jr., to the Tenth Circuit.

ship on May 24, 1940.[25] With the vacancies created by Murrah's appointment to the circuit and Kennamer's retirement, there were three federal district judgeship appointments to be made in the state.

As discussed in chapter five, two posed little difficulty. Thomas was quite willing for Savage to be named to the northern district, and Lee approved Broaddus for the roving position. Neither Lee nor the justice department was happy with Chandler, however, and they withheld approval. But Thomas could be adamant as well. For a period of time, he insisted on a package deal—Savage, Broaddus, and Chandler, or no one. Finally, after a personal plea from Judge Phillips, Thomas agreed to let the Savage and Broaddus nominations proceed.[26] This left Chandler to stand or fall solely on his own merits.

Not until December of 1942 did Thomas finally persuade the Franklin D. Roosevelt administration to nominate Chandler, and then it was too late in the session for any action to be taken.[27] After he was nominated again in February of 1943, the senate judiciary committee acted favorably on the nomination, but it was opposed on the floor by North Dakota's "Wild Bill" Langer. Langer based his opposition on an incident which resulted in a stenographer accusing Chandler of assault.[28] Chandler paid the woman $3,000, and the matter was dropped. After floor debate and on roll call vote, the nomination was confirmed by the not overwhelming vote of 37 to 28 with 31 senators not voting.[29] Ironically, in light of later events, Murrah administrated the oath to Chandler.

Murrah's involvement in the confirmation battle appears to have been *de minimus*. Thomas wired Murrah in late June or early July of 1940 requesting information regarding the assault. Murrah replied that he had not heard of the matter before Chandler was mentioned for the bench and that he did not attach any importance to it, "because I well know anyone being considered for an appointment to the Federal Bench is the target of base and malignant criticism."[30] He expressed confidence that the investigation being conducted by the justice department "would fully and completely repudiate the charges and exonerate Steve."[31] He also suggested the name of another person who might have relevant information.[32]

For a number of years, the federal judicial waters were calm in Oklahoma, at least on the surface. As late as 1955, Murrah wrote Judge John Biggs of the third circuit, who was then chairman of the committee on court administration of the Judicial Conference of the United States, recommending Chandler for committee service in the area of judicial administration. Chandler was "well qualified in most any administrative field in which you find need of his services."[33]

The calm waters became a seething cauldron, however, shortly after Chandler became chief judge of the western district in 1956.[34] Then, problems relating to the assignment of cases and court personnel became daily concerns in the federal courthouse.

The first public notice of judicial warfare occurred in a bankruptcy reorganization proceeding. One of the litigants, Occidental Petroleum Corporation, sought a writ from the court of appeals disqualifying Chandler from hearing and ruling on any motions directly affecting it. Later it filed an amended petition to disqualify Chandler from the entire case. Initially heard by Murrah, Picket and Breitenstein, the matter was then presented to the court *en banc*. Unanimously, the *en banc* court found that the "proper administration of justice requires that all further proceedings in connection with the Parker bankruptcy be heard and determined by another judge," and directed Murrah, as chief judge, to designate the successor judge—*Occidental Petroleum Corporation v. Chandler*, 303 F.2d 55 at 57 (10th Cir. 1962). Chandler unsuccessfully sought review by the supreme court—372 U.S. 915, 83 S.Ct. 718, 9 L.Ed.2d 722 (1963).

After the decision in Occidental, Murrah washed his hands of the Chandler problem. The responsibility for dealing with the western district situation then came to rest on Judge Pickett's shoulders as next senior circuit judge.

Pickett worked assiduously to effect an amicable resolution of the controversy.[35] He made numerous trips to Oklahoma City for that purpose, and his sense of urgency quickened as he approached his planned retirement date of January 1, 1966, for he did not want to leave the

Chandler dispute unresolved. At one time in 1965 it appeared that he would succeed because Chandler likewise agreed to retire on January 1, 1966, but then he "backed out."[36]

Event piled upon event. The "constant turmoil" in the western district over administrative matters, the collapse of the retirement agreement, and Chandler's increasing notoriety as a litigant and not as a judge transformed the Chandler controversy into the Chandler crisis. In late August of 1965 the Oklahoma County attorney charged Chandler and a former county commissioner with conspiracy to defraud the state by using county materials and equipment to build a road on private property. Subsequently, the information was dismissed, and a grand jury indictment was returned against Chandler and Ed Kessler, the former commissioner. In late November of 1965 the indictment was quashed. On the civil side, a $2.5 million libel suit was filed in state court against Chandler on December 8, 1965. This was eventually resolved in Chandler's favor on the grounds of judicial immunity, but not until 1974—*O'Bryan v. Chandler*, 496 F.2d 403 (10th Cir. 1974).[37] It was in this atmosphere that the famous—or infamous—Order of December 13, 1965, was issued.[38]

An act of congress created a judicial council in each circuit. As the statute read in 1965, the council consisted of the active circuit judges of that circuit. In a sense, when the judges acted as a council, they put aside their judicial robes and donned their administrative hats. The council was empowered to "make all necessary orders for the effective and expeditious administration of the business of the courts within its circuit"—28 U.S.C. § 332.

Acting as a council, the judges found that Chandler had "been a party defendant in both civil and criminal litigation" and that he was "presently unable, or unwilling, to discharge efficiently the duties of his office." The council, citing the judicial council statute as its authority, (1) ordered Chandler to take no further action in any case pending before him; (2) ordered the reassignment of those cases to the other judges of the western district; and (3) ordered that no new cases be assigned to Chandler.

In sum and substance, the council left Chandler with his title, his robe, his chambers, and his salary, but it ousted him of the essence of the judicial position: cases to decide. The council's decision raised the most fundamental questions regarding the role of the judiciary in the American system of government.[39] As an Article III judge, Chandler enjoyed tenure during good behavior. Assuredly, he could be removed through impeachment by the house of representatives and trial and conviction by the senate. But what, if any, disciplinary action short of impeachment could be taken. Had the council usurped the power of impeachment? Did the statute authorize what the council had done? If it did, was the statute constitutional?

The council recognized that it was embarking on unchartered waters. As Judge Pickett stated, "When we signed the December 13th order every one of us had serious doubt as to our statutory authority to do what we did in the manner in which we acted but a majority of us thought the situation warranted the action."[40] Judge Lewis's doubts were so substantial that he declined to sign the order, while Judges Pickett, Breitenstein, Hill, and Seth did. Consistent with his conduct since Occidental, Murrah took no part in the council's action.

Things then moved quickly and slowly. Quickly, Chandler asked the supreme court to stay the order pending the filing of a request for a writ of prohibition and/or mandamus prohibiting the council from enforcing the order and/or requiring it to vacate its order. The stay was denied over the vigorous dissent of Justices Black and

Douglas who considered the council to have acted "completely without legal authority"—*Chandler v. Judicial Council of the Tenth Circuit of the United States*, 382 U.S. 1003 at 1003, 86 S.Ct. 610, at 611, 15 L.Ed.2d 494 at 496 (1966).

In mid-January of 1966 Judge Chandler wrote his western district colleagues that he objected to the reassignment of cases pending before him as of December 28, 1965, but that he concurred in the assignment of cases filed after that date to judges other than himself. The next day the judges of the western district advised the council that all were in agreement as to the assignment of post-December 28, 1965 cases, but that they could not agree as to cases pending before Chandler on December 28, 1965. The council then entered an order on February 4th incorporating the agreement as to new cases and allowing Chandler to keep his old cases. In sum, the February 4 order left Chandler with judicial work to do, i.e., cases to decide.

Slowly, the supreme court did not decide Chandler's attack on the council's orders until mid-1970 when it ruled against the embattled judge—*Chandler v. Judicial Council of the Tenth Circuit of the United States*, 398 U.S. 74, 90 S.Ct. 1648, 26 L.Ed.2d 100 (1970). After discussing serious constitutional and jurisdictional issues produced by the case, the court predicated its ruling on the narrow ground that Chandler's failure "since giving his written acquiescence in the division of business" to seek "relief from either the Council or some other tribunal"—398 U.S. at 87, 90 S.Ct. at 1655, 26 L.Ed. 2d at 109 (1970)—defeated his claim for the extraordinary remedy of mandamus or prohibition. Thus the issue of the council's power to do what it did was not decided, although the court's opinion by Chief Justice Warren Burger contains language favorable to the council's reading of the statute.

Murrah and Mrs. Odessa James on the occasion of her retirement as Murrah's secretary. Mrs. James served as Murrah's secretary for 28 years. When she retired, she was senior in service to every member of the court except Murrah. (Published in the Oklahoma City Times *on August 7, 1969. Courtesy Oklahoma Publishing Company.)*

Justice John Marshall Harlan concurred in the judgment but wrote separately. In his opinion the case was in proper posture for plenary consideration, the council had acted legally, and thus Chandler was not entitled to a writ. Justices Hugo Black and William O. Douglas agreed with Harlan concerning the procedural posture of the case, but, adhering to their dissents when the stay was denied, found the council's order totally lacking in legal warrant and of such an egregious character that it was correctable by extraordinary writ.

If, as Mr. Dooley said, the supreme court reads the election returns, it may be that it reads the calendar as well. The supreme court did not hear oral arguments nor decide the case until some months after Chandler ceased being chief judge of the western district. And when Chandler no longer had the administrative powers of the chief judgeship, "there were no more problems."[41]

This does not mean that Chandler suddenly became the perfect federal district judge. Rather, it means that Chandler's deeds and misdeeds, conduct and misconduct, quirks of temperament, and flaws of character were subsequently addressed on a case-by-case basis as with other district judges in the circuit, rather than on the universal basis reflected by the order of December 13, 1965.[42]

This is the historical record of what happened.[43] Remaining for consideration is what responsibility, if any, Murrah bears for this unseemly occurrence. For the actions of the council, the evidence points unerringly to one conclusion—the decisions of the council were the decisions of the council and no else, least of all Murrah.

The Pickett-Murrah correspondence is candid and frank on the Chandler matter,[44] and it leaves no doubt that Judge Pickett did what his own judgment told him was right. The same must be said for Judges Lewis, Breitenstein, Hill, and Seth. Indeed, as discussed, Judge Lewis refused to sign the December 13 order because of his doubts concerning the council's statutory authority to do what it had done.

Not surprisingly, Pickett and Murrah talked about the western district situation, but there is no evidence to suggest that Murrah tried to influence the council to take any particular course of action. Murrah's bystander role in the council's decisions is well illustrated by the Febru-

The Chief Judge and the First Lady of the Tenth Circuit in 1969. (Published in the Oklahoma City Times *on March 6, 1969. Courtesy Oklahoma Publishing Company.)*

ary 4 order allowing Chandler to keep his pre-December 28, 1965, cases. Murrah entertained serious doubts as to the wisdom of the order. It was "a shame to leave 160 cases at his whim, but he will never try them and that will probably be the end of the matter."[45] What is particularly relevant to the question of Murrah's involvement, however, is that the criticism was expressed after the order was entered and to Judge Pickett who was not, because of taking senior status, a member of the council when the decision to leave Chandler with his old cases was made. Whether, then, history visits praise or condemnation for the orders of December 13 and February 4, the praise or condemnation belongs to the council, not to Murrah.

However, this does not answer the question whether Murrah was accountable for parenting and fostering the situation in the western district which made the council's actions necessary in the first place. Candidly, accountability or non-accountability hinges on credibility. Either one believes or one does not believe Chandler's assertion that for 20-plus years Murrah engaged in a conscious and deliberate campaign to destroy him. One believes or one does not believe that Murrah solicited a $25,000 bribe from Chandler to secure Chandler's appointment to the federal bench, a charge which Chandler did not make public for more than 20 years after the alleged solicitation occurred. One believes or one does not believe that attempts were made to poison Chandler's drinking water in the federal building.

It may be that Murrah did these tawdry, unethical, and illegal things. It may be that Murrah was so consumed by hatred for Chandler, for reasons never given, that he risked his good name, his profession, his judgeship, all he had worked so hard to achieve to destroy another human being. It may be—but the probabilities are overwhelmingly the other way, and Chandler never adduced a scintilla of proof to recast the balance in his favor. If Murrah is to stand convicted before the bar of history for subverting his position of trust to evil personal ends, surely it must be on better evidence than this.

9
The Judge as Benthamite

Probably, given the person he was, Murrah would have been involved deeply in issues of judicial administration whatever the rules of practice and procedure. But there is a certain appropriateness that he and the Federal Rules of Civil Procedure came to the bench at almost the same time. Adopted in 1938, the year after Murrah became a federal judge, these rules charged the courts "to secure the just, speedy, and inexpensive determination of every action"[1] without enlarging, modifying or abridging substantive rights.[2] Murrah took the charge to heart.

Not every rule of civil procedure is implicated by every civil action. If the lawsuit involves only one claim for relief, Rule 18, addressing joinder of claims, does not apply. If there is only one plaintiff and one defendant, Rule 20, addressing permissive joinder of multiple plaintiffs or multiple defendants, does not read on the case. But Murrah thought Rule 16 had significance for every civil case regardless of its simplicity or complexity. Murrah pondered Rule 16, applied Rule 16, and proselytized about Rule 16. In a real sense, he made proper and effective use of Rule 16 his personal responsibility.

The cognizance of Rule 16 is the pretrial conference. Whether or not a pretrial conference is held rests in the unfettered discretion of the trial judge, and if a pretrial conference is held what it accomplishes depends in large measure on the trial judge. Murrah had no doubt what the proper office of the pretrial conference was—it should be a probing scrutiny of the lawsuit in all its dimensions to insure that, if the case was tried, the trial would be as expeditiously handled as was consonant with fairness to the litigants and the integrity of the process.

The pretrial conference was to determine what issues were disputed and the factual predicate for the dispute, thus possibly paving the way for summary judgment motions; learn if there were matters which could be handled by stipulation; resolve evidentiary problems; determine if amendments to the pleadings were necessary; and ascertain if additional parties should be allowed to intervene or be joined. It was proper for the judge to raise concerns about a party's position as long as there was no attempt to coerce a change in that position, as it was proper for the trial court to identify weaknesses in a party's case, thus facilitating the settlement of the litigation. In sum, the pretrial conference was to pare the lawsuit of all undisputed, irrelevant, and extraneous matter, leaving only the core of essential dispute.

Murrah clearly thought the district judge should play an active role in the conference. He was not to be a mere passive observer. It was the trial judge's responsibility to insure that the attorneys understood the pretrial conference was not a meaningless formality, but an important part of the litigation process, and that they came to the conference prepared to simplify issues and facilitate the presenting of evidence so that the trial would be just, speedy, and inexpensive. Murrah conducted pretrials in the courtroom rather than in chambers to convey a sense of the solemnity and significance of the conference.

How Murrah handled pretrials is well-illustrated by a warranty case he tried. Plaintiff sued to recover for breach of warranty on 277 tires. At pretrial the parties indicated their intent to offer opposing expert testimony as to each of the 277 tires. Murrah suggested that the parties submit the names of six persons, three from the plaintiff and three from the defendant, who could examine the tires and submit a report which would be the basis for the court's decision. Murrah examined the six as to their qualifications, bias, and prejudice, and selected one who examined the tires and reported his findings to the court. Murrah then rendered judgment in accord with the report after a two-hour, non-jury trial. If opposing experts had testified and been cross-examined, the trial likely would have taken two to three days.[3]

During his short tenure as a district judge, Murrah made extensive and creative use of the pretrial conference. And his interest in the procedure did not end with his appointment to the court of appeals. He gave pretrial conference demonstrations throughout the United States, organized and chaired meetings on the proper use of the pretrial conference, and wrote and spoke about the many good things which could be accomplished by the pretrial conference.[4] For more than two decades, he corresponded with Harry Nims, a New York lawyer and ardent judicial reformer, about the subject.[5] Nims authored a book on the pretrial conference, calling Murrah "the originator and moving spirit" of the volume.[6] It is not surprising that Murrah came to be considered the "master of the theory and techniques of the pre-trial conference."[7]

In 1944 Murrah was appointed to the committee on pretrial procedure and practices of the Judicial Conference of the United States.[8] He became chairman of the committee in 1948, and served in that position until he took senior status in 1970. Some of Murrah's most significant and meaningful work in the field of judicial administration and reform occurred during his years on the pretrial committee.

It is not uncommon to think of lawsuits in terms of the simple single plaintiff-single defendant model. And there are lawsuits of that character even in the 1990s—and even

Murrah recognized that for many people their only exposure to the judicial system would be in traffic, municipal, or small claims courts. He deemed it exceedingly important that they were left with the impression that they had been treated fairly. Here he sits with Judge James P. Demopolos of the Oklahoma City traffic court. (Published in the Daily Oklahoman *on August 7, 1958. Courtesy Oklahoma Publishing Company.)*

in federal court. But there are also lawsuits in which a plaintiff asserts multiple claims for relief, and the defendant counterclaims (asserts a claim against the plaintiff) and/or cross-claims (asserts a claim against a co-defendant). As lawsuits become more complex in claims, they can also grow in complexity in parties. A defendant may bring in additional parties by impleader, a party may be required to join additional parties, and one not in the lawsuit may intervene and become part of the case even though the original parties object.

The complex case can create many problems in pretrial procedures and in trial of the case. Murrah had no doubt that Rule 16 was quite capable of being applied in a meaningful and useful fashion to the complex as well as the simple case, but the best way to achieve that end required thoughtful consideration.

In 1955 then Chief Justice Earl Warren appointed a group of circuit and district judges to study pretrial procedures and the trial of long and complicated civil and criminal cases in United States district courts. Functioning under the auspices of the pretrial committee and chaired by Murrah, the committee was to report to the judicial conference.

Working with the American Bar Association and leading trial lawyers, the committee labored diligently to fulfill its charge. A particularly effective technique was the conducting of seminars for judges and litigators. The seminars enabled the participants to pool and evaluate ideas, thoughts, and experiences which had been formed and tested on the firing line—the actual pretrial and trial of the complicated and protracted lawsuit.

The product after some five years of effort was the *Handbook Of Recommended Procedures For The Trial Of Protracted Cases*. Adopted by the Judicial Conference of the United States in March of 1960, it has had a long and useful life as the basic textbook for the trial of complicated lawsuits.

Initial thinking regarding the complex case was in the single district context. Not surprisingly, however, the complex case could reach across district lines. The multi-district situation hit the federal courts directly in the early 1960s when a federal grand jury in Philadelphia, Pennsylvania, indicted a number of electrical equipment manufacturers for antitrust violations. The criminal cases were resolved quickly, but in their wake followed more than 1,800 private

In 1953, Murrah participated in a pretrial conference demonstration at the meeting of the American Bar Association. Participants were, seated, Judge James E. Murphy, Superior Court for Fairfield County, Connecticut; Murrah; Judge William T. McCarthy, United States District Judge, District of Massachusetts; Judge Eugene A. Hudson, Superior Court, Massachusetts; and Justice B. Rey Schauer, Supreme Court of California. Standing: Professor James W. Moore, Yale Law School; Richard A. Kaye, an attorney from Boston; W. Arthur Garrity, Jr., an attorney from Boston and later United State District Judge for Massachusetts; and Thomas Burns, an attorney from Boston.

suits for treble damages under the Clayton Act. These civil cases were filed in 35 separate federal districts, and

It seemed apparent that if each were processed in the ordinary manner as an independent lawsuit, their combined impact might seriously disrupt the program of the normal business of the district courts. Moreover, there were only limited possibilities of simplifying the handling of the litigation by such devices as assignment of related cases to the same judge, consolidation or inter-district transfer of the cases.[9]

And this even though a vast number of the cases would involve the same witnesses and the same documents.

The initial response was on an ad hoc basis. The judicial conference created a special subcommittee of the committee on pretrial procedures and practices, the coordinating committee for multidistrict litigation of the United States district courts. Chaired by Murrah,[10] it was charged not merely with pretrial matters in the electrical equipment antitrust suits, but generally with the problems of discovery in multidistrict litigation involving common witnesses and common documentary proof.

Essentially, the coordinating subcommittee's solution was national discovery. This required the agreement and cooperation of the district judges handling the individual cases, and this was obtained. Nationwide interrogatories were drafted and used, nationwide depositions were taken, and nationwide pretrial conferences were held.

The efforts of the coordinating committee and the cooperation of the trial judges and attorneys made manageable what at first blush seemed unmanageable. It was obvious, however, that the electrical equipment antitrust litigation was not unique. The same kind of problems could, almost certainly would, occur again. What if the judges, attorneys, and litigants did not display the same spirit of cooperation and working together that they had in the electrical cases?

The answer was to deal with the problem by rule of law. The coordinating committee proposed, and the judicial conference endorsed, legislation authorizing the transfer of cases pending in different districts, but involving common questions of fact, for coordinated or consolidated pretrial proceedings. Whether cases would be transferred or not would be decided by the Judicial Panel on Multidistrict Litigation. The panel would consist of seven circuit and district judges appointed by the Chief Justice of the United States. The proposal became law in 1968 and is codified as 28 U.S.C. § 1407. Murrah played a key role in the enactment of the proposal, writing and speaking on its behalf, including an appearance before the senate judiciary committee,[11] and he was the first chairman of the panel, indeed he was the only chairman the panel had until his death.

The benefits of Section 1407 are difficult to overstate. The statute has enabled federal courts to deal with a now common discovery problem in a rational and efficient manner, and it has conserved precious judicial resources as well as the resources of litigants.

Another task Murrah undertook for the judicial conference was to head a "task force" of federal judges to relieve docket congestion in the Eastern District of New York. Murrah assembled judges from every part of the United States who descended on the eastern district with the mission of terminating outstanding cases whether by settlement, procedural disposition, or trial on the merits.

Abiding as Murrah's interest in the civil litigation process was, it was not exclusive. From at least his first year on the bench, he evinced a great concern as well in matters penalogical. Addressing the state bar in December of 1937, Murrah asked why as society built more prisons and incarcerated and executed more persons, crime was growing, not shrinking. The primary reason was the way communities responded to those released from prison. Rather than providing them an opportunity to become contributing members of society, to earn their way by lawful, gainful activity, society cast them aside, virtually forcing them to resume their old ways to sustain body and soul. Central to Murrah's criticism of the treatment accorded those who had paid their societal debt for violating the law was his view of human nature. He believed that the overwhelming number of men and women who had served time wanted to be law abiding citizens, but in far too many instances society pushed them to "the edge of law, because that is the only realm of society in which they are permitted to live."[12]

Failure to deal with released offenders humanely and compassionately was part of a larger unwillingness to make prevention the principal response to crime rather than punishment. No more than disease could crime be eliminated, for that would be a world without corruption. But communities could do far more than they were doing to instill in their young people obedience to the law, respect for the rights of others, and tolerance for opposing viewpoints. Particular concern was owing those who did not have the benefit of a strong and loving family life. If these things were done, "we will mend for this country a moral fiber which will withstand the onslaughts of all the isms that you can think of."[13]

From the perspective of punishment, Murrah placed great emphasis on segregation of different types of offenders and on probation. Separating those who were not confirmed criminals, those "for whom there is any hope,"[14] from the professional felon was essential if imprisonment was to be a deterrent to future criminal conduct, rather than a graduate course in felonology. Any rational, reasonable system of penology would diagnose and classify inmates to determine the most appropriate form of incarceration.

Murrah deemed probation "the most forward-looking step ever promulgated in the system of law enforcement and administration of justice."[15] Imprisonment exacted significant societal costs in maintaining and operating prisons, costs which increased if, as happened frequently, the inmate's family became a public charge. A probationary system for those posing no threat to the safety of the community served legitimate interests of both society and the individual.

Likely, many influences formed Murrah's views on crime and punishment. One of the most significant may have been his perception of the direction his life might have taken without the many assists he received during his years at Verden, Tuttle, and Norman. As he candidly and movingly told the bar,

> If you will pardon the personal reference, and I wish to tell you this, because it is the thing that has brought this close to my heart and impressed it upon me throughout my boyhood and my manhood. As an orphan boy who had no one to say "don't," I look back over the rough rocky road and wonder how in the world I ever came to be a citizen of this state without going to some reformatory.[16]

This appreciation of how fortunate he had been in his life and career remained with Murrah the rest of his days as he dealt with the lives and liberties of his fellow citizens.

In the early 1950s this interest in the proper response to the law violator led Murrah to become a member of the Council of Judges of the National Council on Crime and Delinquency.[17] Within a few years, Murrah became chairman of the council, a position he held for almost two decades. Murrah found the council an hospitable forum for giving general concepts and ideas more definite form and expression. During his service the council produced studies on the proper relationship between juvenile courts and the press, procedure in juvenile courts, the handling of narcotics laws violators, and the sentencing process. Of particular interest are the sentencing and narcotics law studies.

The proposed model sentencing act was said to be a "statute conforming to the best concepts of modern penology."[18] Extant sentencing systems were faulted for unwarranted disparities in terms of imprisonment, for failure to protect the public adequately, and for denying sentencing judges flexibility in imposing punishment.

In 1954 Murrah received the first annual Hatton W. Sumners Award of the Southwestern Legal Foundation in recognition of his contributions to the improvement of the administration of justice. The award was presented to Murrah by Gerald C. Mann, vice-president of the foundation, as Hatton W. Sumners observed. Mann served as attorney general of Texas and was a candidate in the 1941 special senate election in Texas in which Lyndon Johnson lost to W. Lee "Pappy" O'Daniel. Sumners was chairman of the house judiciary committee in 1937 when Roosevelt proposed his court-packing plan and was present at the meeting when Roosevelt revealed this plan to the cabinet and congressional leaders. As the legislators left the White House, Sumners is reported to have said, "Boys, here is where I cash in my chips." (Alsop and Catledge, The 168 Days, *New York: Doubleday, Doran, 1937, page 67.)*

The model act proceeded from the premise that the offense was not a useful guide in determining punishment. Rather, the sentence was to be based primarily on the individual characteristics, circumstances, and needs of the particular defendant and the likelihood that he would engage in future wrongful conduct. Only in this way, it was thought, could the community be protected. Sentencing which focused on the offense was not satisfactory "because it does not sufficiently take into account the offender's personality."[19]

The study deemed an in-depth presentencing investigation report critical to an individualized sentencing process which was not tainted by irrational, unwarranted disparities and inequities. The model act mandated such a report for any conviction involving moral turpitude or which could result in incarceration for more than one year, and the trial judge was authorized in her discretion to order a presentence investigation report for lesser offenses. Defendants subject to the most onerous sentencing standards were entitled of right to see the report, and other defendants could examine all or part of it in the discretion of the court.

The act's sentencing provisions drew a bright line distinction between dangerous and non-dangerous offenders. A dangerous offender was one who suffered from a severe personality disorder indicating a propensity to criminal activity, and who committed or attempted to commit a crime threatening serious bodily harm, or which, intentionally or not, seriously endangered the life of another. The definition of dangerous offenders also applied to those convicted of extortion, compulsory prostitution, selling or knowingly and unlawfully transporting narcotics, or participating in racketeering and organized crime.

A defendant could not be sentenced as a dangerous

offender based on propensity until he had been remanded to a diagnostic facility for examination to determine if he had a personality disorder indicating an inclination toward criminal activity, and the sentencing judge determined that he met the standards for treatment as a dangerous offender.

The dangerous offender could be sentenced to a term not exceeding 30 years,[20] but there was no minimum term. The judge could "fix the maximum at any prison term less than thirty years."[21] Thirty years was deemed sufficient "to protect the public and to afford ample opportunity for therapeutic efforts to be made."[22]

For the non-dangerous offender, the options available to judges were many. They could defer entering judgment of conviction and place the defendant on probation. If they fulfilled the probation the judge would then discharge them without adjudication of guilt. The court also could suspend sentence with or without probation, place the defendant on probation, impose a fine with or without probation or commitment, or imprison the defendant for a term not exceeding five years. The five-year limitation was to avoid "the excessive use of long terms, one of the characteristics of American sentences."[23] Parole boards were to have authority to release at any time.[24]

For a person charged with committing an offense during his minority and involving moral turpitude or carrying a possible sentence of commitment for one year or more, the judge could determine to treat the person as a youthful offender. In youthful offender proceedings, the matter was heard by the judge without jury, and the judge had the same sentencing options for youthful offenders as for criminal defendants except any term of imprisonment could not exceed three years. No collateral consequences, such as disqualification for the suffrage or denial of licensure for a profession, was to flow from adjudication as a youthful offender. The adjudication was not a conviction of crime, but it could be used if the person were subsequently convicted of a criminal offense.

Murrah wanted sentencing decisions to protect society without destroying the offender. Until sentences were based on the relevant criteria, irrationality, inequity, and arbitrariness would be the hallmarks of the process. The challenge was to raze the old edifice and replace it with something better.

> Let us hope that the day is not far when the responsibility for the imposition of sentence after the establishment of guilt shall rest upon the broad shoulders of a conscientious judge who approaches the discharge of his inescapable duty with the concept that in the last analysis, rehabilitation, not retribution and revenge, is the prime objective of a sentence; that rehabilitation is seldom achieved by the imposition of punitive punishment; and that no man should be sent to a penal institution until it is definitely determined that he is not a fit subject for probation.[25]

The policy statement regarding narcotics law violations, adopted in 1964, was short in length but abundant in controversial material. In sum and substance, the council urged that possession of narcotics should not be a crime; addiction should be treated solely as a medical problem; doctors should be allowed legally to prescribe narcotic drugs "for relief of conditions incident to addiction";[26] involuntary civil commitment for addiction should be eliminated unless the addict was unable to care for himself despite medication; and narcotics racketeers should be considered dangerous offenders, but other narcotics offenders should not be subject either to mandatory terms or exclusion from eligibility for pardon or parole. While admitting the legitimacy of penal legislation to control drug traffic, the study limited that role to "the criminals at the upper administrative level,"[27] i.e., those who sold for profit only. The majority of narcotics pushers were "primarily users also, whose addiction leads them to sell drugs in order to continue their own supply. These persons are more victims than criminals."[28]

In 1964 the American Bar Association authorized a three-year project on minimum standards for criminal justice. One of the committees for the project, that on pretrial proceedings, was chaired by Murrah. The committee suggested standards relating to pretrial release and discovery and procedure before trial.

The study on pretrial release condemned the extant bail system as "unsatisfactory from either the public's or the defendant's point of view."[29] Bail was set in "a routinely haphazard fashion"[30] which "inevitably discriminates against the poor."[31] The consequences of pretrial detention from inability to make bail were "grave,"[32] and there was good reason to believe "that in a large number of cases defendants safely can be released without bail."[33] The standards addressed these issues in two principal ways.

First, the committee urged that arrest and custody be used only (1) if necessary for legitimate investigative purposes; (2) to protect the accused or others from the threat of immediate harm; or (3) if there was reason to believe the accused would not honor an order to appear.

Otherwise a citation or summons should be issued ordering the accused to appear at a time, date and place certain. The use of the citation or summons in lieu of arrest and custody was to be mandatory for designated minor offenses, and law enforcement officers, magistrates, and judges were vested with discretion to use them for other offenses as well. The use of citations and summons was to be encouraged to the "greatest degree consistent with public safety."[34]

Second, if one was arrested he or she should receive a court hearing without unnecessary delay in which the possibility of pretrial release was considered. If indigent, the accused was to have appointed counsel for the hearing. The controlling inquiry was what the defendant's ties with the community were, the nature and extent of family relationships, his prior criminal record, if any, and all other matters speaking to his proclivity or lack of proclivity for fleeing the jurisdiction. There was a presumption in favor of release pending trial on the accused's own recognizance. Additional conditions were to be imposed only if warranted by the facts of the individual case, and money bail should be required only if no other condition would reasonably insure the defendant's appearance. If money bail was required, a preference was stated for requiring an unsecured personal bond, or cash deposit of ten percent of the bond's face amount. Compensated sureties were to be abolished. Finally, the committee rejected bail as a crime prevention measure. It sought to divorce "measures designed to ensure the defendant's appearance from other measures aimed at curbing crime while awaiting trial."[35]

The discovery standards imposed broad disclosure responsibilities on the prosecution.[36] These included the names, addresses, and written or recorded statements of intended witnesses, including relevant grand jury testimony, the criminal records of prosecution witnesses, statements made by the accused, documents or tangible objects to be offered in evidence or which had been taken from the accused, expert reports, and exculpatory materials. Generally, the accused was required to disclose things not protected by the constitutional prohibition against compelled self-incrimination, e.g., handwriting samples, fingernail clippings, etc. The standards provided for omnibus pretrial hearings to decide procedural matters in advance of trial. Murrah said that the proposals were designed to reduce trial gamesmanship which despite "its obvious entertainment qualities...is generally offensive to the dignity of the court as an institution and destructive of respect for legal processes."[37]

Established in 1967,[38] the Federal Judicial Center is akin to a command and general staff school for the federal judiciary. It is charged by statute with studying the operation of the federal courts, developing plans and programs for improving the administration and management of the courts, conducting seminars and other educational programs for federal judges and support personnel, including court clerks, probation officers, and mediators and arbitrators, providing staff research and planning assistance for the Judicial Conference of the United States, and acting in conjunction and cooperation with the State Justice Institute in establishing and coordinating research and programs concerning the administration of justice.

The center is governed by a board consisting of the chief justice of the United States and the director of the administrative office of the United States courts as permanent members, and two circuit judges, three district judges, and one bankruptcy judge elected by the Judicial Conference of the United States.[39] The elected members serve four-year terms and are not eligible for reelection. The board selects the director and deputy director, who serves at its pleasure, and the director must retire on reaching 70 years of age.

The first director of the center was retired Supreme Court Justice Tom C. Clark. When Clark reached the mandatory retirement age in September of 1969, attention immediately focused on Murrah as his successor. Unquestionably, Murrah was one of the best-known federal judges in the nation. His service as chairman of the pretrial committee of the Judicial Conference of the United

Murrah was equally at home on the bench or behind the lecturn. In 1967, he spoke at an Omaha Bar Association dinner honoring the Nebraska judiciary.

States and as Chairman of the Judicial Panel on Multidistrict Litigation had brought him to the attention of judges in every circuit and district. As with his selection for the trial and appellate benches, however, his selection as center director was not without its difficulties.

In 1969 the members of the board were Warren E. Burger, chief justice of the United States, William E. Foley, acting director of the administrative office of the United States courts, James M. Carter and Wade H. McCree, circuit judges of the ninth and sixth circuits respectively, and Edward J. Devitt, Harold Tyler, Jr., and William A. McRae, Jr., federal district judges from Minnesota, New York, and Florida.

As early as September 29, 1969, Alan Cromley, Washington correspondent for the *Daily Oklahoman*, wrote that Murrah was "angling for an important job in Washington, but his chances are believed jeopardized by his acceptance of ten thousand dollars a year as trustee of an oil man's estate."[40] Murrah denied "angling" for the directorship. He stated that he had been approached, not that

In 1968 the judicial conference committee to implement the criminal justice act met with President Lyndon B. Johnson at the White House. Judge John Hastings of the Seventh Circuit is seated to the immediate left of President Johnson, Judge Harvey Johnsen of the Eighth Circuit is seated next to Judge Hastings, and Judge Wade McCree of the Sixth Circuit is seated next to Murrah. Judge Homer Thornberry of the Fifth Circuit is second from the right on the standing row, and Judge Roszel M. Thomsen of the District of Maryland is fifth from the right on the standing row. The Lyndon B. Johnson Library could identify the other participants, but it could not place them in the photograph.

he had approached anyone, regarding the position.[41]

The trustee issue arose because, unbeknownst to Murrah, an old friend, F.E. Harper, had named him as one of the executors of his estate, and, when the estate was administered, he was to be one of the trustees of a trust for the benefit of Harper's wife and children. The creating instrument contemplated the payment of statutory trustee fees.

Years before the Federal Judicial Center was created, Murrah had asked the committee on professional ethics of the American Bar Association and the department of justice whether it would be ethical and proper to serve as a trustee. Each advised Murrah there was no impropriety in the trusteeship.[42]

Despite the hostile tone of his earlier piece, Cromley on November 7, 1969, wrote that Murrah was "still being considered for the directorship of the federal judicial center."[43] The "consideration" did not take a definitive direction for a time, however. In late January 1970 Judge Walter Gewin of the old fifth circuit wrote Murrah expressing his pleasure "that the present plans call for you to serve as Director of the federal judicial center."[44] Murrah responded that he had been "tempted but we simply couldn't bring ourselves to leave our home and move to Washington at this stage of our lives."[45]

One week later, Judge McRae, a member of the board, wrote Murrah that the nominating committee "composed of Jim Carter, Ed Devitt, and myself, was unanimous in its recommendation of you as the successor to Tom Clark."[46] McRae continued that he was "at a loss to understand the inordinate delay which is taking place."[47] Murrah's response was brief and cryptic: "Dear Bill: Thank you for your nice note. The whole matter is a bit perplexing but that also makes it challenging. We will just wait and see."[48]

Judge Tyler's recollection is "that there was some opposition to the appointment of Judge Murrah from outside our Board. Certainly, there was no objection by any Board member at the time."[49] The objections came from "some judges particularly in the east."[50] He does not, however, "remember the nature of the complaints."[51] In any event, as Judge Tyler comments, "They could not have amounted to much,"[52] for Murrah was named director on March 19, 1970, by unanimous vote of the board.[53] He took senior status on May 1, 1970, and began his duties as director that date.[54]

Murrah brought great strengths and deep experience to his new position, and the appointment was well-received by the federal judiciary in large measure. A federal district judge in Massachusetts wrote, "By general acknowledgment you bring to the Center the unconquerable and seasoned spirit of a pioneer in many of the programs in judicial administration. Certainly, in judicial education you stand as the foremost pioneer. You also enjoy the friendship of all the Federal Judges, and many on the State courts, and, more important for the responsibility you now assume, you have their confidence. These are important assets, and no other could offer them."[55] On the other side of the nation, Judge George Harris of the federal district bench for the Northern District of California, knew "no one of the federal judiciary who has given more of his talents and industry in achieving constructive results than you. Truly, as it was said, you are the father of so many of our trial procedures which we recognize today."[56]

In one sense, Murrah found himself in a unique position as he took over the reins of the center. For the first time since he began the practice of law in 1928, he was an employee. Legally, his employer was the board. Practically, it was the chief justice of the United States, Warren E. Burger.

The Burger-Murrah relationship, involving two men of strong wills and not small egos, had, from the beginning, great potentiality for friction. It was not long in coming. When Murrah became director, the position of education director at the center was vacant. Murrah promptly filled it with the appointment of William Whittaker. Whittaker was well-known to Murrah, having served as law clerk to Judge Phillips and then as clerk for the tenth circuit.

The problem was that Chief Justice Burger viewed the

appointment as the responsibility of the board, and by telegram he immediately directed Murrah to fire Whittaker, which Murrah did. It is not difficult to imagine the humiliation Murrah experienced as a result of this incident. For years he had been the first among equals on his court, a position he no longer enjoyed as director of the center.

Murrah wrote the board a three-page "explanation in mitigation."[57] Not unreasonably, he observed that the statute creating the center empowered the director to "appoint...such additional personnel as the Board may deem necessary."[58] Nevertheless, he acknowledged that his action "was contrary to my avowed intention to stay close to the Board."[59] Judge Devitt wrote Murrah that he had "the statutory authority to do what you did"[60] and expressed regret that he had been required to discharge Whittaker.

A similar occurrence gave 1972 a rocky start. When certain items on the board's February agenda were not reached, Murrah submitted the matters to the members for mail response. Burger wrote that he deemed it "not sound policy...to propose ad hoc programs and submit them to the Board for approval by mail."[61]

Murrah replied that the matters in question had been on the agenda, and thus were not ad hoc, that some of them were "urgent," and expressed his commitment "to involve the Board in all Center affairs" but lamented that "until now our efforts have been unsuccessful."[62]

Burger responded "to keep the record straight."[63] It was immaterial whether the items were on the agenda or not. If they were not reached and decided, "there can be no action."[64] The suggestion regarding involving the board was putting "the cart before the horse."[65] If the board was not involved, no action could be taken lawfully, for the board, not the staff, was "charged with the responsibility and the power."[66]

During a seminar for federal judges on protracted litigation, Murrah met with the Chief Justice of the United States, Earl Warren, and Shelden D. Elliott of New York University.

Perhaps surprisingly, given incidents of this kind, Burger and Murrah in time came to a satisfactory accommodation. Murrah had known Burger since the latter's days as an assistant attorney general. Indeed, Murrah had invited Burger to be a speaker at the tenth circuit's annual judicial conference shortly before Burger was nominated for the chief justiceship. From this acquaintanceship had grown a strong mutual respect, if not affection.

Murrah believed that Burger sincerely was committed to improving the administration of justice in the United States. He thought that Burger was providing "excellent leadership,"[67] that his efforts were "positive and dynamic,"[68] "direct and hard hitting."[69] Reading a biography of John Marshall after he had retired as director, Murrah wrote that it "reminded me of the present Chief

Justice. As a matter of fact, I see his image throughout."[70]

Because the two men shared the same goals for the fair, efficient, and effective dispensation of justice, Murrah could tolerate the demands of a personality as willful as his own. Finally, it appears that Murrah liked Burger. As he left Washington at the end of his service as director, he wrote Burger, "Through the years I have accumulated the personal notes you have written me. I just want you to know that they have a very special place in a book and in my heart."[71]

From Burger's perspective, there was great respect for Murrah as a judicial reformer, as one who could make "the stand patter judge...mend his ways."[72] Even after Murrah relinquished the directorship, even as he almost literally lay dying, Burger sought his advice and counsel.[73] One of Murrah's responses was sent "without signature, only because of my inability to sign my name."[74]

And Burger had great concern for Murrah personally. Official correspondence was supplemented by many hand-written notes, particularly as Murrah's health declined. When Murrah wrote Burger that his letters "had propped me up on the leaning side,"[75] Burger replied that "you have been propping me up not just since 1970 but long before!"[76] On another occasion, Burger issued "an ex parte order to forget all official duties and concentrate on Murrah—something you don't do enough of."[77]

In sum, Burger and Murrah appreciated the strengths and abilities of the other, they liked each other, and they were kindred spirits in the struggle to make the judicial process adequate to the burdens and challenges of the decades to come. Their disagreements were not lasting, and they were disagreements over details, not long-range strategies.

If there was an issue touching upon the proper administration of the courts which the center did not consider during Murrah's tenure as director, it was not for want of trying. A faint flavor of what the center did during the Murrah years is conveyed by a partial listing of projects. Studies were conducted concerning geographic reorganization of the circuits, the working time of circuit judges and their support personnel, support personnel in the courts of appeals, the printing and publication of opinions, comparison of the internal operating procedures of the courts of appeals, the structure and function of appellate courts of the future, transcription of records, juror utilization, district court time use, court management information systems, delay in criminal cases, multidistrict litigation, videotaping of depositions, use of nonprofessional case aids for federal probation officers, sentencing, and state-federal relations.[78]

The significance of the concerns the center addressed is illustrated by the metropolitan districts project. The chief judges of the 22 largest federal district courts, districts accounting for some 54 percent of federal court dockets, met at the center periodically to discuss the particular problems of large urban districts, including speedy trial plans, results of civil and criminal docket studies, utilization of magistrates, local discovery rules, and hearing practices in criminal cases. Beginning on a temporary basis, the project became a permanent part of the center's activities, the center providing research and staff support. Similarly, Murrah organized a meeting of circuit chief judges held in conjunction with the sessions of the Judicial Conference of the United States.[79]

Murrah was a firm believer in seminars as an exceedingly effective way of going to the heart of a problem and finding the most efficient way of solving it. In 1958 Murrah wrote Judge Devitt that he considered seminars for incoming judges "fundamentally sound."[80] He suggested Devitt write the chief justice about it, "but please don't recommend me for the responsibility."[81] Judge Devitt did the former, but not the latter. In 1961 the Judicial Conference of the United States authorized Murrah's pretrial committee to organize and conduct seminars for newly appointed district judges.[82] From that time, Murrah never looked back, and seminars became an integral aspect of continuing education in the federal judicial system.

In 1973 the center conducted 34 seminars, short courses, and conferences for federal judicial personnel. These included sessions for circuit judges, district judges, newly appointed district judges, court executives, magistrates, public defenders, probation officers, court reporters, district court clerks, courtroom deputy clerks, and judicial secretaries. This continuing education reached 1,400 participants, and utilized 400 faculty members.[83] Murrah's parenting and nurturing of judicial seminars led one writer to dub him "school master for the judiciary."[84] It was a title well merited. As Judge E. Barrett Prettyman of the District of Columbia Circuit said, "I wanted very much...to participate again in one of these Murrah seminars. As you probably know, he is the inventor of the judicial seminar, and a greater invention I think you will never see."[85]

The four years at the center were a watershed in Murrah's career. For years he had thought about the failings of the American justice system and how those failings could be corrected. The center was a forum from which he could address nationwide problems from a nationwide perspective. He was "convinced that the responsibility of putting our house in order lies with the judges themselves, working under the aegis of the Judicial Center."[86]

Informing his attitude toward delay and congestion in the courts was the firm conviction that "this laissez faire attitude" on the part of judges to case management was

In 1962, Murrah's good friend and kindred spirit in the field of judicial reform, Judge Irving R. Kaufman of the Second Circuit, was awarded an honorary degree by Oklahoma City University.

totally unacceptable.[87] The decisive issue was "whether the judge will be governor of his calendar or whether he shall leave it to the lawyers to try cases as, if, and when they please."[88] For Murrah, the answer did not admit of dispute.

It was the responsibility of the judge to manage the cases on his docket and move them to final disposition whether by pleading dismissal, dismissal for failure to prosecute, summary judgment, or plenary trial. Murrah was an ardent proponent of the individual calendar system by which a single judge handled a case from filing to final judgment. This, coupled with meaningful use of the pretrial conference, enabled the trial judge, not the lawyers, to control the ebb and flow of litigation. Referring to a comment by a lawyer that everything had changed since judges began taking an active pretrial role in the litigation process, Murrah observed, "That's what we've been striving toward."[89] The ultimate goal was current dockets, every criminal case being tried within 90 days, and every civil case within six months.

As Murrah approached 70 years of age and mandatory retirement, he reflected that the center years "have not all been pleasant, but they have been a rewarding and unforgettable experience."[90] While much remained to be done, great progress had been made in "persuading new and old judges to utilize known and proven methodology for the businesslike conduct of our courts."[91] Laissez faire was on the decline, and more judges were willing to "assume the responsibility for the movement of litigation expeditiously."[92] Murrah could take great pride in his accomplishments as center director. One authority has opined, "In many ways Judge Murrah was the architect of that center, because it was in his tenure that the center gained direction and strength."[93]

The years as director had been, even for Murrah, incredibly busy ones. He simultaneously had worn the hats of administrator, policy maker, speechmaker, advocate, politician, and judge and had given 110 percent to each. Three men on the firing line, three federal district judges, accurately summarized Murrah's career as a judicial reformer. Murrah, Judge Devitt wrote, had "literally trained almost every federal judge on the bench today,"[94] while Judge Bownes concurred with the observation that his "influence on the trial of cases in the Federal District Courts is felt throughout all fifty states."[95] In sum, as Judge Arthur Stanley told Murrah, "You have cut a wide path in your chosen field and, whether you realize it or not, have earned the position secretly desired by all men—the love and respect of your peers."[96]

Murrah's labors in the vineyard of judicial reform earned him numerous honors over the years. In 1954 the Southwest Legal Foundation recognized him as the outstanding lawyer or jurist in Oklahoma, Texas, Arkansas, Louisiana, and New Mexico for his efforts to improve the administration of justice and to preserve democratic and constitutional government. Particular note was taken of his work on the pretrial committee of the judicial conference. Phi Alpha Delta conferred the Order of Achievements Award in 1963 for leadership in the field of jurisprudence, and William Mitchell College of Law and Suffolk University awarded honorary doctor of laws and doctor of juridical science degrees in 1965 and 1968. In 1970 the Oklahoma Bar Association, with United States Supreme Court Justice Byron White as the principal speaker, honored Murrah. Murrah, said White, was "the father of all the true trial procedure we have."[97] Among lawyers and judges, he "was the best known judge of the country."[98] And the exceedingly prestigious Justice Award of the American Judicature Society came to Murrah in 1973.

Murrah's senior status and his incredibly hectic schedule as director did not keep him from the bench. During his years at the center and in retirement, he sat with the second, third, fourth, fifth, sixth, seventh, eighth, ninth, and tenth circuits. His opinions for the court as senior circuit judge addressed a wide variety of issues. The coverage of insurance policies—*Traders State Bank v. Continental Insurance Company*, 448 F.2d 280 (10th Cir. 1971); *State Farm Mutual Automobile Ins. Co. v. Bockhorst*, 453 F.2d 533 (10th Cir. 1972); *Wise v. Westchester Fire Insurance Company*, 463 F.2d 386 (10th Cir. 1972), "Applying these general rules of construction, we think it evident that Mr. and Mrs. Wise would have been befuddled had they attempted to ascertain from a reading of their policy whether they did or did not have the uninsured motorist coverage which they had requested"—*ibid.*, 390; *United Services Auto. Ass'n v. Royal-Globe Ins. Co.*, Col, 511 F.2d 1094 (10th Cir. 1975); the preclusive effect of judgments, *Harrison v. Bloomfield Building Industries, Inc.*, 435 F.2d 1192 (6th Cir. 1970); *Jones v. United States*, 466 F.2d 131 (10th Cir. 1972); interpretation and application of the Sherman Act, *Anderson v. American Automobile Association*, 454 F.2d 1240 (9th Cir. 1972); whether federal question jurisdiction was present, *United States v. Western Casualty & Surety Co.*, 429 F.2d 905 (10th Cir. 1970); interpretation and application of the Fair Labor Standards Act, *Hodgson v. Humphries*, 454 F.2d 1279 (10th Cir. 1972); tax law, *Bear Manufacturing Company v. United States*, 430 F.2d 152 (7th Cir. 1970); *Gar Wood Industries, Inc. v. United States*, 437 F.2d 558 (6th Cir. 1971); appealability of a ruling on class action certification, *Seiffer v. Topsy's International, Inc.*, 520 F.2d 795 (10th Cir. 1975); interpretation and application of the Uniform Commercial Code, *Mitchell v. Shepherd Mall State Bank*, 458 F.2d 700 (10th Cir. 1972); whether there had been a valid gift of certain stock, *Ownes v. Sun Oil Company*, 482 F.2d 564 (10th Cir. 1973); whether the requirements for intervention of right or permissive intervention in school desegregation litigation had been met, *United States v. Board Of Sch. Com'rs, Indianapolis, Ind.*, 466 F.2d 573 (7th Cir. 1972); interpretation and application of the Packers and Stockyards Act of 1921, *Hays Livestock Com'n Co., Inc. v. Maly Livestk. Com'n Co., Inc.*, 498 F.2d 925 (10th Cir. 1974); N.L.R.B. cases, *N.L.R.B. v. Betts Baking Co.*, 428 F.2d 156 (10th Cir. 1970) (order enforced as modified); *N.L.R.B. v. Union Carbide Corporation*, 440 F.2d 54 (4th Cir. 1971) (enforced in part and denied in part; nonstriking employees who refused to cross picket line as matter of principle entitled to reinstatement and back pay, but employee who refused to cross because of fear entitled to neither); *Local 134, Internat'l Bro. Of Electrical Wkrs. v. N.L.R.B.*, 486 F.2d 863 (7th Cir. 1973) (enforcement denied), reversed 419 U.S. 428, 95 S.Ct. 600, 42 L.Ed. 2d 558 (1975). *N.L.R.B. v. Leatherwood Drilling Company*, 513 F.2d 270 (5th Cir. 1975) (orders enforced); interpretation and application of the Securities Exchange Act of 1934, *Naftalin & Co. v. Merrill Lynch, Pierce, Fenner & Smith, Inc.*, 469 F.2d 1166 (8th Cir. 1972); *Vincent v. Moench*, 473 F.2d 430 (10th Cir. 1973); *Resort Car and Rental Sys., Inc. v. Chuck Ruwart Chev., Inc.*, 519 F.2d 317 (10th Cir. 1975); interpretation and application of the Investment Company Act of 1940, *Securities & Exch. Com'n. v. Advance Growth Capital Corp.*, 470 F.2d 40 (7th Cir. 1972) (trial court abused its discretion in not enjoining permanently numerous violations of the statute which were neither inadvertent nor harmless, but it was not an abuse of discretion to refuse to oust the corporation's officers and appoint a receiver for "(e)quitable receiverships are drastic remedies which often fall short of their intended objectives"—*ibid.*, 54); and personal jurisdiction, *George v. Strick Corporation*, 496 F.2d 10 (10th Cir. 1973)—were all subjects to which Murrah turned his pen and mind.[99]

Of particular interest for these years are Murrah opinions for the court speaking to retroactivity of case law, the establishment clause of the First Amendment, and separation of powers. The cases are *Joe v. United States*, 510 F.2d 1038 (10th Cir. 1974); *Anderson v. Salt Lake City Corporation*, 475 F.2d 29 (10th Cir. 1973); and *United States v. Cowan*, 524 F.2d 504 (5th Cir. 1975).

The Major Crimes Act of 1855, 18 U.S.C. Sections 1153, 3242, gives federal jurisdiction over certain enumerated crimes committed by an Indian on an Indian reservation. The listed offenses are to be defined in

Murrah welcomes Grand Justice Harreh Ten Lee of the Republic of China (Taiwan) to the Federal Judicial Center in 1973.

accord with the local law of the state in which the reservation is located. Pursuant to the statute, Joe was convicted in federal district court of rape, one of the enumerated offenses. He requested, and the district court refused, instructions on the lesser, nonenumerated offenses of assault, attempted rape, and battery. On direct appeal, the tenth circuit affirmed—*United States v. Joe*, 452 F.2d 653 (10th Cir. 1972).

After Joe's conviction became final, the supreme court held that, if the evidence warranted, it was error for the district court not to instruct on nonenumerated lesser included offenses as defined by local law—*Keeble v. United States*, 412 U.S. 205, 93 S.Ct. 1993, 36 L.Ed.2d (1973). Joe then filed a Section 2255 motion to vacate his conviction relying on *Keeble.*[100]

The district court denied relief. Murrah wrote for the circuit reversing—*Joe v. United States, supra*. Analysis must begin, Murrah said, with whether *Keeble* was a clear and certain breach with the past. If it was, then retroactivity or non-retroactivity would be decided by: (1) the purpose to be served by the new standard; (2) the extent of reliance by law enforcement authorities on the old standards; and (3) the effect on the administration of justice of retroactive application of the new standard—510 F.2d 1038 at 1041, footnote 2. If Keeble did not speak new doctrine, then "considerations of essential justice"—*ibid.*, 1043—required retroactive application, because Joe's right to have the jury instructed on all offenses warranted by the proof was part and parcel of procedural due process. While "nonretroactivity as a species of stare decisis does indeed have its claims...the doctrine is neither immutable nor sacrosanct. It is based upon the policy of legal stability. And the societal interest in stability must be balanced against essential justice to individuals"—*ibid.*, 1042.

Analyzing the precedents, Murrah quickly concluded that *Keeble* was not a break with the past. It simply "reaffirmed fundamental law," and thus "*Keeble* law should be applied."—*ibid.*, 1043. The judgment was reversed and remanded with directions to vacate the conviction and grant a new trial. The supreme court's current jurisprudence regarding retroactivity of case law in criminal cases is found in *Griffith v. Kentucky*, 479 U.S. 314, 107 S.Ct. 708, 93 L.Ed 2d 649 (1987), for direct appeals, and in *Teague v. Lane*, 489 U.S. 288, 109 S.Ct. 1060, 103 L.Ed.2d 344 (1989), for collateral attacks.

In *Anderson* the Fraternal Order of Eagles was given permission by the state to erect a three-by-five-foot granite monolith on public property. The monolith was inscribed with a version of the Ten Commandments and certain symbols representing the All Seeing Eye of God, the Star of David, the Order of Eagles, letters of the Hebraic alphabet, and Christ or peace. Perceiving a violation of the establishment clause of the 1st Amendment, the plaintiffs sued for injunctive relief, and the district court ruled in their favor. The circuit reversed.

Murrah first said that abstention was not warranted, for the "right asserted here is a basic First Amendment right, of which the federal court has jurisdiction"—*Anderson v. Salt Lake City Corp.*, 475 F.2d 29 at 31. Turning to the establishment clause question, Murrah deigned any purpose of adding "to what has already been so prolifically said elsewhere." Pared to its essentials, the controlling constitutional test was whether the primary effect of the challenged action was to advance or inhibit religion. If it was the former, then there was a constitutional violation.

The Ten Commandments were both religious and secular, the monolith was erected by a fraternal organization, and there was no coercion "unless one considers it coercive to look upon the Ten Commandments"—*ibid.*, 33. These characteristics took the monolith without the pale of constitutional infringement, and the district court had erred in holding otherwise, for it was not "reasonable to require removal of a passive monument, involving no compulsion, because its accepted precepts, as a foundation for law, reflect the religious nature of an ancient era. The wholesome neutrality guaranteed by the Establishment and Free Exercise Clauses does not dictate obliteration of all our religious traditions"—*ibid.*, 34.[101]

Federal Rule of Criminal Procedure 48(a) provides that the government "may by leave of court file a dismissal of an indictment, information or complaint and the prosecution shall thereupon terminate." The issue in *Cowan* was whether the language "by leave of court" fettered the traditionally absolute common law discretion of the prosecutor to end a criminal case.

The controversy was one as to which "history has its claims"—524 F.2d 504 at 509—and because the case implicated separation of powers the court approached its "task with the humility which characterizes the proper exercise of all power"—*ibid.*, 512. Murrah deemed it historically significant that when Rule 48 was adopted, 30 states had limited the prosecutorial power to end a prosecution, and that the American Law Institute's Model Code of Criminal Procedure articulated "a judicial discretion of significant scope"—*ibid.*, 510.

The prevalent practice in the states, coupled with the supreme court's addition of the "by leave of court" phrase, convinced Murrah that Rule 48 "was intended to modify and condition the absolute power of the Executive, consistently with the concept of Separation of Powers, by erecting a check on the abuse of Executive prerogatives"—*ibid.*, 513. The "protection of the defendant" —*ibid.*, 512—while a significant factor informing the district court's exercise of its Rule 48 discretion, was not the only dimension in the "leave of court" calculus. Murrah thought the rule also encompassed "the essential judicial function of protecting the public interest in the evenhanded administration of criminal justice"—*ibid.* This societal concern was separate and distinct from the protection of the defendant.

Even with the public interest factor, the judiciary was not to play the major role in deciding whether or not a prosecution should be ended. Because the rule "was intended as a power to check power" and not to "shift absolute power from the Executive to the Judicial Branch," the prosecutor remained "the first and presumptively the best judge of whether a pending prosecution should be terminated"—*ibid.*, 513. Prosecutorial discretion was not to be "judicially disturbed unless clearly contrary to manifest public interest"—*ibid.*

The supreme court recognized the *Cowan* public interest issue in *Rinaldi v. United States*, 434 U.S. 22, 98 S.Ct. 81, 54 L.Ed.2d 207 (1977), footnote 15, but found it unnecessary to resolve it. The court did, however, quote *Cowan* with apparent approval, and Justices White and William Rehnquist explicitly stated that the "by leave of

Murrah during his tenure as director of the Federal Judicial Center. (Published in the Daily Oklahoman *on April 11, 1971. Courtesy Oklahoma Publishing Company.)*

court phrase" appeared to be "clearly directed toward an independent judicial assessment of the public interest in dismissing the indictment"—434 U.S. 22 at 33; 98 S.Ct. 81 at 87; 54 L.Ed. 2d 207 at 217.

The lower courts, federal and state, have agreed with Murrah's reading of a judicially assessed public interest restraint on the prosecution's power to terminate a prosecution. See, for example, *United States v. Weber*, 721 F.2d 266 at 268 (9th Cir. 1983): "We conclude that in this case the motion for dismissal could not fairly be characterized as 'clearly contrary to manifest public interest'"; *Tennessee v. Landers*, 723 S.W.2d 950 at 952 (Tenn. 1987), "Rule 48(a) [the Tennessee rule] is identical to Federal Rule 48(a) and we adopt the 'manifest public interest' standard usually applied in the federal courts, i.e., whether dismissal of the charge is contrary to the manifest public interest—*United States v. Cowan*, 524 F.2d 504, 513 (5th Cir. 1975)"; *Connecticut v. Lloyd*, 185 Conn. 199 at 204, 440 A.2d 867 at 870 (Conn. 1981), "the proper test is whether there has been a manifest abuse of prosecutorial discretion. The court must accept the entry of the nolle prosequi for the record unless it is persuaded that the prosecutor's exercise of discretion is clearly contrary to manifest public interest. See *United States v. Cowan*, 524 F.2d 504, 513 (5th Cir. 1975)."

Cowan was the last time that Alfred Paul Murrah, Sr., Article III judge for 38-plus years, applied the rule of law to speak the rights and duties of contending litigants. Indeed, the opinion was not filed until after Murrah's death.

It is fitting that Murrah's last effort to "administer justice without respect to persons, and do equal right to the poor and to the rich"[102] was a case presenting public law issues of great consequence and moment. By any proper standard, *Cowan* was a "great opinion by a great judge."[103]

10
Family and Community

For many years, beginning with his father's death, Murrah's ties with his blood kin were fragile at best. In Tuttle he acquired an education which prepared him for college and law school—and a second family as well. With the MacPhails he had the strongest bonds of affection, bonds which were sundered only by death. But as he finished his formal schooling and began his professional life, he also became part of his father's and mother's families again. Over the coming decades he would share the hopes and disappointments, the trials and tribulations of sundry aunts, uncles, nieces, nephews, and cousins.

In the early 1940s Murrah and Judge Williams traveled to Alabama. Murrah became reacquainted with his Deep South relatives and visited his father's grave for which he purchased a headstone.[1] Later, he had a marble slab placed on the grave and a concrete foundation built for it.

Murrah made special efforts to stay close with his brothers, George and Elmo, and his half-brother, Cecil. For a time, Cecil lived with the Murrahs. Murrah advised him regarding military service and helped him enlist in the Navy. During World War II he wrote Cecil countless letters of support and encouragement, paid insurance premiums for him, and even purchased him a subscription to *The New Republic*.[2] Murrah's letters looked beyond the war, advising Cecil to save his money in order to return to school when hostilities ended. Cecil apparently valued his older brother's counsel, for he wrote, "I regard your

The Murrahs purchased this residence at 820 N.W. 39th in 1937. It would be home for some 15 years.

judgment as the authority on any and all matters, and your advice and counsel is always appreciated to the utmost."[3]

Elmo was a source of great pride to Murrah. Although physically disabled, he had a law degree and was a member of the bar. For many years he worked for the Internal Revenue Service.

George farmed and ranched near Lexington, Oklahoma. He helped when Murrah turned to cattle raising for a time both as a form of relaxation and to improve his financial condition. The Alfred-George relationship was not without its stresses and strains, however. Murrah did not hesitate to exercise his older brother prerogatives as when he took George to task for not visiting Elmo in the hospital. More than once he wrote George wondering why

In the mid-1950s the Murrahs moved to 2209 N.W. 56th.

"you are mad at me."[4] On one occasion he asserted that George must be holding him responsible for the drought,[5] although he "positively did not know why."[6] There was never a note of finality in these letters, however. Rather, they would end with an entreaty such as, "now goddamit, come to see me!"[7]

In March of 1965 Murrah received a letter from Calvin Brock which began what would be almost a decade of correspondence. Brock, whom Murrah had never met, was the son of his half-sister, Willie Mae, the half-sister who had cared for Murrah, George, and Elmo when their mother died.

When Brock first wrote his uncle, he was in prison in Arizona serving a sentence of life imprisonment for first degree murder. From that spring until shortly before his death, Murrah counseled, admonished, and encouraged this relative who had run afoul of the law. He insisted that

Lawyer Murrah and his bride with their firstborn, Ann, in front of their home at 1120 Bedford Drive in Nichols Hills.

Brock take responsibility for his actions, that he attempt to make the best of his situation, that he undertake schooling to develop what Murrah considered a fine mind, and, above all, that he not succumb to bitterness. "Meanwhile,

Murrah with Ann and Paul, Jr.

I hope you will not become bitter because I cannot agree nor can I be of any help unless you are able to appreciate the realities of your condition and situation."[8] Unhesitating as he was in demanding that Brock accept reality, Murrah was equally quick to praise Brock when he took steps toward putting his life in order.

Murrah's assistance to Brock extended beyond giving

advice. He also secured the services of John P. Frank and his law firm as cocounsel for Brock's appeal, services Frank rendered because of his high regard for Murrah.[9]

In time the Supreme Court of Arizona reversed Brock's murder conviction—*State of Arizona v. Brock*, 101 Ariz. 168, 416 P.2d 601 (Ariz. 1966). On remand, Brock pleaded guilty to voluntary manslaughter and received a sentence of seven to ten years. Murrah paid the $300 which was necessary to obtain a psychiatric evaluation of Brock for sentencing purposes.[10]

For Murrah the Brock matter was personal and private. He did what he did because one of his own was in need of help. As he wrote Brock's sister, "It would be appreciated if you would refrain from telling Calvin that he is indebted to me in any form whatever for he is not and I did not intend to tell you so. What I did for Calvin, I would do for most anyone else, especially a member of my family. Certainly, all he owes me is the duty to be a good citizen."[11]

In one regard, Murrah would have been perfectly at home in the 18th century, for he was an inveterate letter writer. He even answered Christmas cards, and he included his children and grandchildren in his correspondence. From these letters emerges a marvelous portrait of Murrah family life, a portrait which includes a father who, notwithstanding his myriad of judicial and professional activities, was intensely involved in that life, in the everyday occasions as well as the landmark occurrences.

Murrah's letters to his progeny covered an astonishing variety of subjects. He wrote regarding clothes, "Mother is going down today to find some orange ribbon for your sash,"[12] and "I intend to suggest that you buy the suit you had in mind instead of the sport coat"[13]; merit badges; writing one's mother while away, "You should never get

The Murrahs, Paul, Sue, Ann, Babe, and the Judge at home. His myriad of activities and responsibilities notwithstanding, Murrah considered his family life very important.

too busy...to write your mother"[14]; driving lessons; the advisability of saving money; train reservations; plane schedules; filing income tax returns; and registering for the draft. Epistles of congratulation and encouragement were many. And humor had its place, as when Murrah wrote a friend that his daughter was "in love and needs a guardian,"[15] or when he advised Paul to beware "of women, apples and serpents—they were all found in the same Garden."[16]

Education was the foundation stone of Murrah's success in life, and he hoped that it would be for his children and grandchildren as well. He counseled them regarding their choice of colleges, helped them with admission, and was constantly inquiring what courses they were taking and sending them materials for their classes. He strongly urged them to fit as much English and foreign languages into their schedules as possible. "We Americans are the only people on earth who never learn to speak more than one language, and that not very well."[17] When they were having difficulties, as when Sue thought she would not make the honor roll, or Paul was struggling with physics, he encouraged and supported them—and then applauded when the final grades were honor roll quality and a 98 in physics.[18]

Not surprisingly, Murrah was particularly interested in Paul's choice of law as a profession, but he wanted it to be Paul's choice.[19] He suggested that Paul think about teaching as a career, admonishing him that only "those who love the law for the law's sake have ever made a success of it."[20]

Once it was clear that Paul meant to go to law school after he concluded his military service, Murrah sent him various books to read while on active duty to help prepare him for legal studies. When Paul decided on the Univer-

The women in Murrah's life: Sue, Ann, and Babe.

sity of Oklahoma College of Law, Murrah, somewhat gratuitously, reminded Paul that he, Murrah, was well known at OU, and "if you go to OU you will be expected to make good grades."[21]

Murrah's interest continued as his children's professional careers began. He advised regarding job offers, professing his "willingness to do anything I can to help."[22] When a state judge wrote Murrah a letter complimentary of Paul's handling of a case, he saw, unbeknownst to Paul, that the senior partners in his son's firm received copies of the letter.

Murrah and Babe. Mrs. Murrah possessed the unique quality of being able to take her energetic husband very much in stride, never being overwhelmed by him.

During a great part of the time Ann, Sue and Paul were in college, Murrah's salary was $17,500 per year. Near the end of their college years, congress increased his pay to $25,500 yearly. And Murrah's salary was virtually the entire income of the family. Occasionally, there would be supplements—as when Murrah earned $850 for teaching oil and gas law at the University of Colorado in the summer of 1951,[23] or there would be a small profit (or deductible loss) from his cattle business. But in large measure, his salary was all he had.[24] And at times this was not enough to send three children to college and to meet the normal expenses of everyday life. Thus these years saw Murrah frequently borrowing from banks and from personal friends to make ends meet. Before his salary was raised to $25,500 in 1955, he seriously considered leaving the bench for financial reasons.[25]

The children helped with jobs during summers and holiday periods, and for his last three years at Yale University Paul was on a Naval Reserve Office Training Corps scholarship. Even then, finances were an ever-present concern. As Murrah saw it, his salary belonged "to the whole family. My only task is to make an equitable distribution of it."[26]

No discussion of the Murrah family would be complete without reference to Alonzo Jernigan. Jernigan was an African-American who went to work for the Murrahs as chauffeur and handyman in 1938. A few years later he became law librarian for the judge. His main responsibility was "to keep lawyers from stealing books."[27] In truth, Jernigan was more than an employee. He was a member of the family. He helped rear the children, including running off boyfriends of whom the judge did not approve, and he cared for Murrah in his last illness. When Murrah was in the cattle business, Jernigan was his right-hand helper.

In the days of racial segregation when Jernigan and Murrah would take a trip, Murrah would not eat until they found a place they could eat together. Murrah would say,

The Murrahs enjoying a moment of relaxation on a fall day.

"We're going to eat together," and Jernigan's first 20 years working for Murrah were "spent looking for these places to eat."[28]

A day or two before he died, Murrah wanted some watermelon, and Jernigan found one even though it was late October. For Jernigan, Murrah "lived a Christian life during the week,"[29] not just on Sundays. At Murrah's funeral, Jernigan was seated, as he should have been, with the rest of the family.

Murrah family life was good, not perfect. On one occasion, Murrah wrote Paul suggesting "a peace conference at your convenience,"[30] and on another he complained to Sue, "I never find out anything without cross-examining you, and that makes me mad."[31] But the disagreements and frustrations were far outweighed by the good times.

Nothing better happened to Murrah than his marriage.

He once said that all the Murrah men "outmarried themselves."[32] And his family was "the nearest thing to my heart and soul."[33] Reflecting on his many achievements and accomplishments in life, he thought, "Of all my efforts and meager achievements, the only one that really matters is my family. Whatever happens to me I can always point to them as irrefutable evidence of a successful life."[34]

Ann remembers a father who "really helped me when I needed someone. Everything he did was done with style, integrity and all of himself."[35] In 1947 the family took a trip to New Mexico in their "new Plymouth."[36] They pulled a trailer, and Murrah had it "painted the same color as the car so that it would look nice on the highway."[37] He loved to walk, "fast of course."[38] He was a person who "put people on just a little higher ground."[39] One of his favorite expressions was, "I'm pleased to be associated with you."[40]

For Sue, the essence of her dad is *Proverbs* 22:1: "A good name is more desirable than great riches; to be esteemed is better than silver or gold." The accompanying lesson concludes, "A good name is better than riches. When one dies, one will leave one's possessions behind, but our names and our characters will go with us through eternity." In this teaching, Sue Murrah found her "father's legacy to me, and I feel so very proud!"[41]

After a visit with his father in 1971, Paul wrote,

> Whatever I am, I owe to you and Mom. Thinking back through the years, your guidance and companionship have had a greater impact upon my life than anything else. My respect for your goodness, your success, your enthusiasm for life, your energetic productiveness, has and always will serve as my prime inspiration.
>
> Your contribution to law and justice will endure forever. But, I will always be even more grateful to you for

The Murrahs shared 45 Christmases together as husband and wife.

your contributions to me as a father. Perhaps as it should be, we are now busy in our separate worlds, but the bonds between us remain tied with my deep love and respect for you.[42]

The meaning and value of family which Murrah first found with the MacPhails in Tuttle never left him.

Murrah believed "that a judge's duty goes beyond the prosaic task of deciding lawsuits. He ought to be a citizen and I try to be one."[43] This belief he practiced on a daily basis. If there was good work afoot in the community, Murrah was part of it. For a decade he was a commissioner of the Last Frontier Council of the Boy Scouts of America. Answering "what seemed to be a call to duty,"[44] he chaired the National Committee for Traffic Safety, and spoke frequently on "Christianity in Traffic Safety."[45]

For four years Murrah chaired the Red Cross fund-raising drive in Oklahoma City, for three years he headed

Straw hats are the attire for Judge and Mrs. Murrah on Memorial Day 1953. This photograph was taken in front of their residence at 820 N.W. 39th.

the Red Cross-United Fund drive, and he was active in fund raising for the YWCA. During one United Fund Campaign, he had three luncheons and two breakfasts in one week.[46] Serving as a member of the Rhodes Scholarship selection committee for the Oklahoma region, giving numerous commencement speeches, serving as a trustee of Southern Methodist University and the Hatton W. Sumners Foundation, and chairing a clinic on world affairs sponsored by the Oklahoma City Committee for the United Nations were other ways he contributed to the well-being of his city and state.

Service seemed to run in the Murrah family. Mrs.

The proud grandfather with grandson Standley Milam Murrah.

Murrah was a commissioner of the Girl Scouts, was active in the Red Cross, and cochaired fund-raising for the Oklahoma Arts Center.

Murrah believed that activities of this kind were important not only for the people they helped, but also because they instilled and nurtured a sense of community. They brought together "Nazarenes, Presbyterians, Carmelites, Baptists, Methodists, Catholics and Jews, in a common cause, America at its finest."[47] An unvarying piece of advice he gave young lawyers as they began their practices was to "identify yourself with every good thing in the community. One cannot expect to live off of a community without putting something in it anymore than we can reap from the good earth without putting something back."[48]

E.K. Gaylord, president of the Oklahoma Publishing Company, said Murrah's civic activity "was an exhibition of unselfish devotion to the needs of your fellow man."[49]

Alonzo Jernigan and the Judge in the library of the Tenth Circuit in the Oklahoma City federal courthouse. Jernigan was very much a part of the Murrah family.

Rabbi Israel Chodos of Emanuel Synagogue thought Murrah "one of God's great noble men."[50]

For Murrah personally, his involvement with Crown Heights United Methodist Church may have been the most significant of his community services. Chartered in 1929 as Central Park Methodist, the church moved to Crown Heights in the early 1930s. Murrah became a member on his move to Oklahoma City from Seminole. The church history records that as a member of the building committee "Brother A.P. Murrah was a bloodhound for money."[51]

Murrah's most lasting contribution at Crown Heights was neither money nor buildings, however. It was the Sunday School class he taught for 34 years. The Homebuilders Class began as one for young married couples, and was still going strong when most of the members were grandparents. The class was both faith and works. When a small Methodist church at White Bead, Oklahoma needed funds to sponsor an oratorical contest on world peace, Murrah persuaded the class to furnish the money, because it "will be something really worthwhile."[52]

While at Yale, Paul wrote his father about a fellow student who had no faith in a divine power. Murrah told his Sunday school class about the letter, and then wrote Paul about his own beliefs: "I never debate with anyone about my faith in the divinity of Jesus Christ," he explained. "As a matter of fact, I never stop to debate it with myself, for those things that are taken on faith are not debatable. I sincerely believe that faith is an essential part of one's life. There are just some things that are taken on faith, else we spend our whole lives in doubt."[53] In a similar vein, he wrote his grandson:

> One word about religion. In this country of ours, we may believe as one pleases, or not believe at all, but I have always felt kind of sorry for those who didn't believe at all. My faith is simple, as I said. I do not argue with anyone about it, but I find it a source of great strength as I grapple with the problems of life. And, by whatever forms one professes it or practices it, I think it is essential to a balanced life. But you may not find it so, and that is entirely up to you. I am proud of you for who you are and what you are and always shall be.[54]

From 1938 to 1972 Murrah taught the Homebuilders Class. Finally, the long periods of absence from Oklahoma City occasioned by the directorship of the center led him to resign. In accepting the resignation the class president wrote that the class was better known as "Judge Murrah's class," and "that the sands of time will not dim the trail you have blazed."[55]

Murrah loved his class at Crown Heights. He wrote

One of Murrah's passions was teaching the Homebuilders' Class at Crown Heights United Methodist Church. This photograph was taken in 1953.

one of his daughters that he had not been able to visit her over the weekend because of "the desirability of teaching my Sunday School class,"[56] and he told former governor Johnston Murray that "teaching a Sunday school class is the most important thing I've done in my life."[57] In complimenting a mother on a professional achievement of her lawyer son, he observed, "But most of all, I know that you are proud to see him teach a Sunday school class. That is about the finest thing one can do."[58]

The community took note of Murrah's services in various ways. In 1960 he was selected as king of the 15th annual Beaux Arts Ball. Oklahoma City University honored him with the honorary degree of Doctor of Laws in 1954, and in 1959 he was inducted into the Oklahoma Hall of Fame. The Oklahoma City Chapter of the National

In 1954, Oklahoma City University conferred the honorary degree of Doctor of Laws on Murrah. Dean Roger Stephens of the School of Law hoods Murrah while President Cluster Q. Smith hands Murrah his diploma.

Conference of Christians and Jews conferred upon him its Brotherhood Award in 1957 "because of his outstanding ability, his distinguished service and his spirit which have strengthened our fundamental institutions and created the

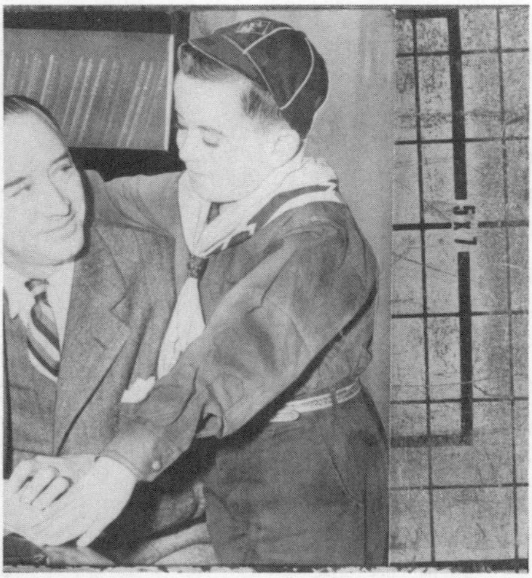

For many years Murrah was very active in the Boy Scouts of America. In 1954 the Denver Area Council named its Eagle Scout class the Judge Alfred P. Murrah Class of Eagle Scouts. (Published in the Daily Oklahoman *on January 20, 1946. Courtesy Oklahoma Publishing Company.)*

spirit of understanding, co-operation and unity."[59] Presenting the award, Dr. Sterling W. Brown, Executive Vice President of the NCCJ, said that "in brotherhood and service, Judge Murrah has been a true exemplar of brotherhood."[60] Accepting the award, Murrah responded, "It never occurred to me that anything this fine and noble could come to me," concluding, "I covet this recognition more than anything that could be bestowed on me by this community."[61]

Murrah's commitment to good works was not an instance of loving humanity and despising people. Simply put, Murrah was a people person. He liked people from all walks and stations of life, and he was concerned for their well-being. "The important thing in life is to live outside of and beyond one's self, and to learn to make your life a part of others."[62]

This interest manifested itself in many ways. It could be something as simple as writing a note of appreciation for the person who cleaned his chambers,[63] or telling a railroad steward's supervisor that when he boarded the

Mrs. Murrah shared her husband's interest in civic and community affairs. Here she appears in her Red Cross volunteer uniform. (Published in the Daily Oklahoman *on March 7, 1954. Courtesy Oklahoma Publishing Company.)*

train he was "weary, irritable, and mean," but the steward "was so pleasant, kind and courteous to me that before I had finished my meal, I felt much better."[64] It could be more serious as urging reinstatement of a 58-year-old woman who had been fired,[65] or giving words of encouragement to a young woman in a juvenile detention center.[66]

How many cleaning people and stewards Murrah helped is not knowable, but his beneficiaries knew, and they reciprocated. A man who believed his life had been changed for the better by Murrah told the judge that one of the things he remembered most about him was "the love the elevator person and doorman at the Hay-Adams have for you, with many, many more in between."[67]

If Murrah could not help directly, he was not above

Mrs. Murrah and Mrs. Nan Sheets, director of the Oklahoma Art Center, and Mrs. Alfred D. Hill, president of the Coterie Club, admire one of the exhibits at the center. (Published in the Oklahoma City Times *on March 23, 1961. Courtesy Oklahoma Publishing Company.)*

using surrogates. Many a former law clerk found himself called upon to be Murrah's instrument for this or that good deed or act. And Murrah's pride on such occasions was as great, if not greater, than if the clerk had won a major lawsuit.[68]

Many are the instances of Murrah's efforts to exemplify the Good Samaritan in his own life. Consider Guglielmo Provenzano, Mary Jean Parsons, and Frank Hunt.

Guglielmo Provenzano had operated a shoe store in Oklahoma City for more than 20 years but had not become a citizen when war with Italy came, and the naturalization process was stayed. Murrah took pen in hand on his behalf, and Provenzano's letter of thanks is a masterpiece

Murrah, Lee B. Thompson (on Murrah's right), and B.D. Eddie (on Murrah's left) celebrate exceeding the goal of the 1952 Oklahoma City United Fund and Red Cross campaign. (Published in the Daily Oklahoman *on December 16, 1952. Courtesy Oklahoma Publishing Company.)*

of expression, if not of style. "Dear Sir: Please except this Little present for the kindness you have shown me. Which I shall never forget."[69] Reluctantly, Murrah accepted the gift. "There is nothing improper concerning it," but the "compensation I received in being able to assist you cannot be measured by any material tokens."[70]

Mary Jean Parsons was unknown to Murrah when, 22 years of age and married less than two months, she shot and killed her Air Force officer husband in El Paso, Texas. Because a good friend of Murrah's was a close friend of the young bride's family, he became interested in her case, particularly making suggestions regarding

Mrs. Murrah, Mrs. J. Knox Byrum (on Mrs. Murrah's right), and Mrs. Hardin W. Masters (on Mrs. Murrah's left) attend a function at the Oklahoma Heritage Association. Mrs. Byrum's husband was a highly regarded district judge for many years in Pottawatomie and Lincoln counties. (Published in the Daily Oklahoman *on May 21, 1976. Courtesy Oklahoma Publishing Company.)*

legal counsel. When Parsons was convicted of murder and sentenced to 10 years imprisonment,[71] he tried to sustain her during her incarceration. And he was instrumental in obtaining her release on parole.

Following her release, Parsons wrote Murrah to thank him for what he had done "for a total stranger,"[72] commenting that it was people like Murrah who "keep an inmate thinking in the right direction instead of carrying 'a chip on their shoulders.'"[73] For Murrah, "Your fine letter is all the compensation anyone could ever want for trying to be useful."[74]

Murrah and Ann Connolly reign as King and Queen of the Beaux Arts Ball.

And then there was Frank Hunt. Hunt was a lawyer Murrah had known from Seminole days. In 1930 Hunt and Paul Cole were charged with the murder of Earnest Irby, a Wewoka druggist. Cole was tried, convicted, and sentenced to death by electrocution. Hunt pleaded guilty and

Being a civic leader may require one to play many different roles. Here Murrah and James Norick babysit while their wives solicit contributions for the Red Cross. Norick, then an Oklahoma City councilman, later served two terms as mayor of Oklahoma City. The boy with the pillow on Murrah's left is Norick's son, Ron, who also would be a mayor of Oklahoma City; it was he who helped lead Oklahoma City through the nightmare of the bombing of the Alfred P. Murrah Federal Building on April 19, 1995. (Published in the Oklahoma City Times *on March 12, 1952. Courtesy Oklahoma Publishing Company.)*

received a life term. In time, Cole was executed, and Hunt was paroled and then pardoned.

Murrah never broke his friendship with Hunt. He spoke to Hunt whenever he saw him, assisted him financially, and always encouraged Hunt to look to the future and build a new life for himself. Hunt did precisely that. Moving to California, he became a successful businessman and took a prominent role in civic activities. He was particularly supportive of the National Council on Crime and Delinquency.

Hunt never forgot Murrah's friendship and support. A letter he wrote Murrah regarding a meeting they had soon after his release from prison paints in bold strokes Murrah's humanity:

> I shall always remember how you looked out of your north window at the sleet being driven almost through the pane by the bitter cold north wind. How you turned to me with a five dollar bill, which I am returning herewith, and said, "Remember to come to me before you do anything to cause your return to McAlester." And every time you met me in the streets, regardless of those who were with you, you always shouted a hearty "hello Frank." It meant so much to me and I still appreciate it more than you will ever know.[75]

The response was quintessentially Murrahian:

> Doubtless you will not believe it, but I am not surprised at your success. You convinced me that you were determined to be decent and respectable against all odds, and you have thoroughly vindicated my faith. I am proud of you from the bottom of my heart. Let me say again, don't let anything deter you, you have gone too far to turn back.
>
> The $5, represented by your money order doesn't belong to me, it belongs to someone whose name I do not

> know, but he will come along and he will need it just like you did when you received it from me. Whether the new beneficiary vindicates my faith or not, I have already been repaid a thousand fold. It regenerates my faith in humanity—a faith I must not lose.[76]

As scores of people can attest, he never did.

11
"To everything there is a season, a time to die"[1]

In 1953 a newspaper reporter interviewed Murrah for a story asking, "Is Life Worth Living?"[2] Murrah's answer was an emphatic yes, a yes that did not change with the passage of time. When an old friend wrote, "We are getting too old to raise hell,"[3] Murrah replied, "We may be a little too old to raise Hell with fire and brimstone, but that doesn't mean we can't still cook on the embers."[4]

The meaning of life was in the "quest...and not in its conquest."[5] Adversity was not to be shunned and a crisis was not to be feared, for adversity was "a great teacher,"[6] and "All history is a record of one crisis after another. There has never been a time when we were not facing a great crisis and we are at our best when we are in the midst of one."[7] In a commencement address, he told the graduates, "There is no room for indifference in this dynamic world of ours, and there is no exit except the future for persons or institutions."[8]

Life and challenge were synonymous, and every task should be approached with the resolve to do the very best one could do, and a little better. In a 1944 letter to the editor about paper boys, Murrah recognized that it was "tough to roll out of a warm bed at 3:00 a.m."[9] But the experience gained far outweighed the hardship, for the paper boys were "learning a lesson in life as important as any course of study in school—that is the courage and confidence to win."[10] When delivering their papers, the delivery boys should become acquainted with their customers, and take the extra time needed on rainy days to put the paper inside the door. Such conduct would "pay dividends, not only on the paper route, but down life's pathway, because you have learned to do the task before you just a little better than the other fellow, and that is what it takes to play in the big leagues."[11]

Two of Murrah's favorite books, books which affirm that the meaning of life is in striving to excel at whatever one does and that life should be approached without fear, were *I Dare You* by William H. Danforth,[12] and *The Conquest Of Fear* by Basil King. Murrah gave copies of the King book to Paul and to one of his close friends.[13]

No one associated with Murrah would have found this sentiment surprising. His zest for life, his determination to do any job a little better than anyone else were part of everything that he did—being a husband and father, writing opinions, making speeches, teaching a Sunday School class. It even extended to how he went to work. A family of five, the Murrahs never owned more than one car. Murrah would say, with more truth than exaggeration, that he could stand on any street corner in Oklahoma City and have a ride in five minutes. At some point his clerks began driving him to chambers. The clerk would come to the Murrah home every morning, and Mrs. Murrah would prepare breakfast for the three of them. Driving the Judge meant that the clerk would get to use his reserved parking space, and Murrah contributed to the cost of gas and oil for the clerk's car. But the inestimable value of chauffeuring Murrah was the opportunity to talk about life. The experience, one of them later wrote,

> gave the Judge and his clerk, both of whom were particularly busy, short of time, a regular period nearly every day in which they could converse about those things which were nearest and dearest to them, whether it be the benefits of church participation and Sunday School teaching, or the benefits of sex, love and marriage, or beauties of people seen along the way to work, or the beauty of the

> sky itself which deserved to be noticed from time to time; things of this life to be shared and to be enjoyed among people who find themselves working together.
>
> These trips to and from the office were indeed a very special time. I think they reflect the Judge's awareness of the need to utilize fully the limited time we are allocated in this life, and his awareness that it was not really the system with which he was engaged in his work, but it was people, and the law clerk of course was one of these people who had the good fortune to have this daily experience.[14]

Nowhere was Murrah's love of life more manifest than in his dying. Murrah's health had been an issue when he was being considered for the district court.[15] He had experienced medical problems in 1936, but they had not been sufficiently severe to prevent his nomination and confirmation. After he went on the bench, he enjoyed excellent health for more than three decades. As he remarked in a speech, "You can just take a man half dead and give him a life-time job and he lives forever."[16]

Prior to 1969 his medical problems had been limited to an occasional cold or bout with the flu. That year he had prostate surgery. The surgery revealed no malignancy, and Murrah's recovery was speedy and uneventful.

But the good news did not last. In late November of 1973, doctors in Washington, D.C., diagnosed Murrah as suffering from a virulent strain of cancer in his kidneys and back. He immediately began undergoing radiation treatments—"cobalt cocktails" he called them. Except for a period of hospitalization for about a week in the winter, he was able to continue with his myriad of duties and responsibilities.[17]

His last year at the center—1974—was a trying one, however. He had 71 radiation treatments that year, and a trip to M.D. Anderson in Houston, Texas was unsuccessful. His health continued to deteriorate in 1975, but not his spirits. When a good friend wrote, "We've got to go some day,"[18] Murrah agreed but asked, "Why leave now?"[19] As previously mentioned, he continued to assist the chief justice with various matters almost until he drew his last breath, and, as he entered the hospital again in September of 1975, he wrote Chief Judge Lewis asking him to "favor me with some *per curiams*."[20]

Shortly before his death, chemotherapy was tried. When it was clear that there was no hope for recovery, he asked the doctors to remove the tubes. When they refused, he did it himself. Three days after his 71st birthday, October 30, 1975, Alfred Paul Murrah, Sr., died in University Hospital, Oklahoma City.

Citing his "integrity, intellect, and independence," his life "of service to his fellow men," Governor David L. Boren declared an official period of mourning, and ordered flags flown at half mast.[21] Services were held in St. Luke's United Methodist Church in Oklahoma City to accommodate the many mourners.

Those attending included Governor David L. Boren, Oklahoma City Mayor Patience Latting, and a host of Oklahoma's most prominent citizens. Twenty-seven federal judges, led by retired Supreme Court Justice Tom C. Clark, were in attendance to honor their colleague. The service was conducted by the Reverend De Hinckley, Pastor of Crown Heights United Methodist Church. He was assisted by the Reverend Irving Smith of St. Luke's, Rabbi Joseph Levenson of Temple B'nai Israel, and Father Ernest Flusche of Christ the King Catholic Church.

Hinckley said the service was to commemorate not a tragedy, but a tender hour. Quoting Henry Wordsworth, "She is in her grave, and, oh, the difference to me,"[22] Hinckley recalled Murrah's contributions as a husband, father, judge, and community servant and reflected on the void his death left in the many lives, known and unknown

Mrs. Murrah and Paul Murrah speak with Father Ernest Flusche following the funeral service for Murrah. (Published in the Daily Oklahoman *on November 4, 1975. Courtesy Oklahoma Publishing Company.)*

to him, he had touched. Murrah, Hinckley said in conclusion, was "a man of the book. He was a man of faith. This world and the next are richer because our friend and loved one, Fish Murrah, lived, worked and shared faith with us."[23]

The casket was escorted from the church by Hinckley, Smith, Levenson, and Flusche to the stirring strains of

"The Battle Hymn of the Republic." Murrah's judicial brethren, clad in their robes, followed. Burial was in Fair Lawn Cemetery.

How far Murrah had traveled and yet how close he had stayed to his roots was shown by the presence of stories on his death in the *New York Times*[24] and the *Tuttle Times*.[25] The Tuttle paper remembered in detail Murrah's ties with that town and his love for the community, and it praised his "honesty, integrity and strict interpretation of the law."[26]

Oklahoma and the nation honored Murrah in various ways following his death. The board of directors of the Federal Judicial Center passed a resolution commending his service to the center and his unceasing efforts to improve the justice system in the United States. A meeting room at the Dolly Madison House was designated the Alfred P. Murrah Conference Room. The Alfred P. Murrah Federal Building in Oklahoma City was dedicated in 1977, and the nursing library at University Hospital was named in his honor as well. The Alfred P. Murrah Professorship in the College of Law of the University of Oklahoma was the first endowed professorship for the law school, and when the Law Center at the University of Oklahoma was dedicated in 1976, the ceremonies were conducted in Murrah's honor. And Murrah's court appropriately held in memoriam proceedings in his honor.[27]

Alfred P. Murrah, Sr., left many legacies to his state and nation when he died. Each of those legacies endures to this day. There is the personal one of husband and father. His experiences as boy and teen-ager instilled in him a firm belief in the importance of family, a belief which shaped his relationships with Babe, Ann, Paul, and Sue.

His judicial legacy is found in the volumes of the *Federal Reporter*, Second Series. Murrah once remarked that it was easy to affirm or reverse a good district judge because it was always clear what the judge did and why he did it. The same could be said of Murrah's opinions. They were always highly literate, incisive, and to the point. Whether he was writing for the court, concurring, or dissenting, there was no doubt what Murrah thought about the case and why he thought it. His contributions to the Republic's jurisprudence are found across the whole fabric of the law, civil and criminal, substantive and procedural. Murrah's opinions insisting upon the most circumscribed judicial review of state exercises of the taxing and police powers, recognizing warrantless searches as valid only under exceptional circumstances, and addressing the standards for holding one criminally accountable for his conduct place him in the front rank of 20th century American jurists.

Murrah's jurisprudence was founded on the concept that "order is God's first law and without order we can't have civilization."[28] Yet order must be tempered by liberty, for the meaning of the rule of law was ordered liberty. "It is the right to dissent," he wrote, "not the duty to conform, which gives men dignity and individuality. The carpenter's son from Nazareth was put to death as a revolutionary. We need the good sense to discern the line between liberty and license, between freedom and anarchy."[29] The rule of law was not, by any means, antithetical to change. But change was to be wrought "in the courts and at the ballot box."[30]

Of all societal forces, law was the most pervasive. And lawyers and judges could not be faithful to the law as an institution unless they thought on that truth. On the occasion of his death, an editorial in the *Daily Oklahoman* caught the essence of his jurisprudential thinking:

> Murrah will be remembered as an outstanding federal judge, but even longer as the great philosopher of the law of his times. Many a young lawyer has found himself

> more deeply concerned with the far-reaching implications of his work after a few sessions with Judge Murrah. Murrah's concern was broader, though, than the mere letter of the law. His studies of religious and historical bases for our legal system, and for our notions of what constitutes justice, led him to become one of the most articulate advocates of American constitutional government, and of the economic system which permits each of us the greatest possible opportunity for personal fulfillment.[31]

In the *Eulogy of Judges*, Piero Calamandrei defined the office of the judge. Murrah's judicial career reads compatibly with that definition: "I know of no office which requires of him who holds it a stronger sense of dignity than that of the judge—a sense which compels one to look into his own conscience rather than to the commands of others for the justification of his actions and to assume responsibility for them openly and fully."

Murrah believed, intensely and without reservation, that rules of conduct conceived in rationality, tested by experience, and applied with equity constitute the foundation stones of every civilized order. For Murrah, the greatness of a society was measured not by its capacity for physical force, but rather by the ability of its legal system to accomodate society's need for stability and change, for liberty and order. Believing that the American legal system accomplished these goals as well as any system devised by human intellect and administered by fallible beings, Murrah served the law with fidelity and courage, thus honoring the master by the acts of the servant.

His legacy as a judicial reformer has no equal. Untiring apostle for the effective use of the pretrial conference, chairman of the Judicial Panel on Multi-District Litigation, director of the Federal Judicial Center, chairman of the Council of Judges of the National Council on Crime and Delinquency, chairman of various American Bar As-

Mrs. Murrah and Paul Murrah cut the ribbon for the dedication of the Alfred P. Murrah, Sr., Library at University Hospital. (Published in the Daily Oklahoman *on March 9, 1978. Courtesy Oklahoma Publishing Company.)*

sociation committees and sections, Murrah was unrelenting in his efforts to improve the administration of justice. The praises of his colleagues for his efforts and accomplishments would make a lengthy chapter. Judge Theodore Roosevelt Dalton, United States District Judge for the Western District of Virginia, spoke for them very well:

> Dear Chief of all Chiefs:
>
> Daniel Webster said, "justice is the highest mission of man on earth."
>
> I remarked to a fellow judge at The Greenbrier last week that you had fulfilled this mission to the bench and bar greater than any person—past, present or in the future. I am overwhelmed when I consider all the work that you have done and that you are still doing, covering nearly two generations of service.[32]

Murrah's judicial reform efforts were not limited to

The Alfred P. Murrah Federal Building in Oklahoma City. The building was destroyed by a terrorist bomb on April 19, 1995, with great loss of life.

federal courts. Over the years, he worked closely with the National Center for State Courts, and his death was felt by his state brethren as well. Paul Reardon, a justice of the Supreme Judicial Court of Massachusetts, and first president of the center, was thankful for "the assistance which he provided so willingly in the early days of the center. Without his kindness and wise advice the great work the center is now engaged in 50 states would not have proceeded as rapidly as it has." In Murrah, "Oklahoma gave a great gift to the country. A state that can produce such a man stands high indeed."[33]

In the 50-plus years of life Murrah had remaining when he was booted from the freight train in Oklahoma City, he made many tracks in the sands of history. Responding to the question what advice he would give young people who wanted their lives to matter, he captured the essence of his own life: "Get a good education," he recommended, then "decide what you want to do. What you like best is what you're best fitted for. Put your finger on a map, close your eyes and pick a place. Then go there and be diligent and decent. You won't have too much competition, and you'll get ahead."[34]

Appendix A
Pickett-Murrah Correspondence Covering the Chandler Matter

UNITED STATES COURT OF APPEALS
TENTH CIRCUIT

JOHN C. PICKETT
JUDGE — Nov. 23

Dear Chief—

On my way home and after arrival I have continued to think about our parting conversation about Judge Chandler and I have concluded that I should explain at least briefly my approach to the matter.

For those of us who have been confronted with the continuing difficulties of the Western District of Okl. it is difficult to generate much sympathy for its chief even though his predicament would be devastating to most people. I have however, done my best to approach the situation with compassion and with a desire to help him salvage something from his long service as a Federal Judge. I fully recognize the degrading reflection that his activities have cast over the Federal Judiciary, particularly in Okl. but I am convinced that the strength of our system and the standing of its judges is such that it cannot be undermined by unfortunate conduct of one. As far as I am concerned I shall try to work it out uninfluenced by aggressive, and sometimes ruthless press or any other pressures.

I have been about quite a spell very little of which has been without problems, many of the sleepless night variety and I learned long ago that the better solutions usually follow the exercise of a little patience and a complete understanding of the result of your actions on the life of someone else. My time and efforts with the Judge may well be wasted. But even if it is we will have the satisfaction in our own minds of knowing that we treated him fairly and with the consideration that we would like to have in time of trouble. We will know too that if misfortune follows him in the future that we gave him the opportunity to cooperate in a manner which we are certain would result to his benefit.

So I say, my good friend, that I am who I am & no one can change that. You are stuck with that unfortunate circumstance and will just have to bear with me.

John

Oklahoma City, Oklahoma
November 29, 1965

Honorable John C. Pickett
United States Circuit Judge
Cheyenne, Wyoming

Dear Calhoun:[1]

I read your letter with a little lump in my throat. It was very much appreciated but wholly unnecessary for, contrary to what you may think, I have never doubted the wisdom of the course you are taking, nor have I undertaken to influence it.

And, I was not aware of any ruthless pressures. If I have been impatient it has been generated over a period of years. This is only the culmination of it. We all know that. But even so, I certainly would not have advocated any action at all while the state charges were pending. My immediate concern was that he should not have been permitted to transact official business while under the cloud. This caused criticism everywhere.

From the enclosed you will see that final disposition has been made of the state charges. You will recall that in the very beginning I told the Council what, in my judgment, had prompted them. It was most unfortunate for everyone.

Just let me say that I am proud indeed to be stuck with you as long as we live, and I will never be able to tell you by word or deed how much I appreciate your friendship.

Sincerely,

Friday February 4

Dear Judge—

Just talked to Sam Rhodes of Tulsa and he told me how cold it was in Okl. and as I sit here with only shorts to cover me up I thought of you. The weather has been cool over most of Mexico but not in Acapulco.

I just received a letter from Jean[2] and he briefed me on the Chandler Matter. It's taken a lot more time and effort than its worth—I had some newspaper stories which indicated that he had submitted some kind of a letter of retirement but apparently it was not out and out but had some condition attached. Jean didn't say what kind of a hearing the council expected to hold in Okl. City on Febr. 10— It occurred to me that some kind of modification of our Dec. 13 order might be worked out to cut the ground out from under his Sup. Ct. action. For the first time I feel badly about the situation. I got the council into it and then eliminated myself from the responsibility—anyway its nice here with no worries—

There have been no developments in a choice for my successor and my guess is that there won't be before the March term. So I guess that I'll be there. I'll have Vivian make the usual reservations. We may have to stop in Denver on the way home as we plan to stay here until about March 1st.

If you haven't time to keep me advised as to happenings let Odessa[3] do it. She looks after me better than you do anyway.

Just met a young lawyer from Okl. City who was honeymooning with Sandy Adams daughter named Crabtree—

Give Babe our best regards—

John—

Jimmy Harden is here— The hotel is doing the best in years. Jimmy will probably want to keep it. I think he likes it here—

Oklahoma City, Oklahoma
February 8, 1966

Honorable John C. Pickett
Hotel Palacio Tropical
Acapulco, Mexico

Dear Calhoun:

Miss Odessa has been sending the newspaper accounts of the running battle to your office. It now seems, in the words of Alonzo[4] "the Council is being pushed back." Of course I do not know what considerations prompted the Council to recede from its original order. It may be that they were well advised to do so. If that is the case, it may be necessary in order to preserve the prospective effect of its order. Now, as you will see from the enclosed articles, it seems that the Court of Appeals is the villain and Judge Chandler is the white knight in shining armor. In any event we may end up before a Congressional committee.

Be that as it may, we can always know that you had the courage to do what is right in the circumstances after exhausting every other available resource. If Congress wants to investigate, we can only say that every judgment or order of the Court or Council—every act, public or private, of its judges are open to inquiry by any one at any time.

Please be not disconsolate over having left the field after starting the battle. I am sure no one feels that way about it. As for your old roommate, I shall always be proud of the stand you took.

I am glad to know that you will be with us in March— I thought you would.

Kindest regards and love to Miss Lura.

Sincerely,

Friday—February 11

Dear Chief—

Thanks for your letter and the clippings. In the same mail I got a letter from Jean enclosing a copy of the council order. I could tell from the tone of what you said that you were not exactly pleased with what happened. You must remember that they were up on the firing line which is a one sided affair. The judiciary is seldom in a position to publicly defend itself and as indicated by some congressional, one from our own circuit, this thing could get out of hand. Our only concern was to rectify a bad situation in Okl—not to establish a principle. When we signed the Dec. 13 order everyone of us had serious doubt as to our statutory authority to do what we did in the manner which we acted but a majority of us thought the situation warranted the action. It will take a little more time but it would appear to me that an end of the trouble is in sight. The order should end the supreme court action and I can see no grounds for any further similar action.

After the February 4th order was entered and before I learned of it I had written to Jean suggesting that almost the identical action as a means of terminating this very unpleasant and time consuming matter. As I stated to Jean that this was (termination) was particularly desirable in view of the fact that the District Judges of the Western Dist. of Okl. did not see fit to back up the council—

I am sitting on our porch with only my pajama pants on—Lura just came out and said to tell you to keep calm, cool and collected. Good advice. This is, I think, the greatest winter spot on earth—I think even you could relax for a few days—why don't you try it? We plan to stay for another 2 weeks—then start for home— In the mean time don't get yourself in a dither— Whatever that is— Have Odessa continue to write to me.

John

Oklahoma City, Oklahoma
February 15, 1966

Honorable John C. Pickett
Palacio Tropical Hotel
Acapulco, Mexico

Dear Calhoun:

Babe and I have just returned from a fast trip to New Orleans where I had two committee meetings and came back by way of Austin.

Of course the Chandler matter is one of the most irritating experiences I have ever had there does not seem to be any end to it. In all the circumstances, I am sure that the Council took the proper action and I am not critical of it at all.

It is a shame to leave 160 cases at his whim, but he will never try them and that will probably be the end of the matter. But it now seems that Congress intends to take a hand in it. As the matter now stands, Chandler is the victim of a sinister conspiracy.

Well, we will just have to ride out the storm and see what happens. Surely everyone will eventually understand the true situation.

Continue to enjoy yourself and we look forward to having you back.

Sincerely,

Appendix B

Murrah would not give a speech unless asked, and he was asked many times. His usual speech, Murrah said, was two hours and 16 minutes long, and he left the audience pleading for more. Four of Murrah's many speeches are reprinted in this appendix. They are a high school commencement address and speeches on the art of judging, the art of advocacy, and the role of the supreme court in American life.

WHAT NOW?[5]

Examinations are over, and for more than a week you have been wearing the cap and gown as symbols of your intellectual achievement. Friends and relatives have been generous. Your proud parents are both relieved and concerned—relieved that you are about to pass another milestone, and concerned with ways and means of providing for your future pursuits into the realm of higher learning, or whatever course you may choose to pursue.

You have been congratulated and complimented. You have been preached to, both at home and in church. All this has made for zestful excitement and some parental anxiety.

You are now restless to make the grand march across the stage, receive written evidence of your learning, put it all behind you and rush out to meet the challenge which lies ahead. But before you say farewell, tradition has it that you shall hear an oracle, and it is my happy privilege to bring it to you in behalf of proud parents, a hopeful faculty, and a grateful community.

Upon being reminded of my engagement with you this evening by Miss Pipkin, I immediately began to think about what would be appropriate to say on this occasion. After casual inquiry among the people with whom I've talked, I have found that few remember who delivered their commencement address, and practically none of them could recall the subject or much of what he said. Most of them remarked rather apologetically that they thought the speech was too long, and one sincere soul confessed that he dozed through it. Perhaps you've heard of the new method of instruction whereby one is made to learn through his subconscious mind, even while he sleeps. Could it be that this is your only familiar means of learning? In any event, it is my hope that what is said here will find lodgment in your subconscious mind.

Tradition dictates that you be reminded that this is not graduation, but commencement—an initiation into a new way of life and service, if you please. You are to be reminded that you have now reached adulthood, and that you are supposed to put away childish ways. Tradition bids me admonish you that acquisition of more knowledge should be your goal.

You are what we commonly refer to as "war babies." You were cradled in the time of great stress and emotional strain. Never before has man's physical environment been so radically changed and rapidly modified as in the short and dynamic space of your lifetime. In comparison with your world today, man fifty years ago was deaf, dumb, blind and earthbound. In 1900 the age old dream of flying through the air was entirely remote. But only three years later, man took wings. Only 32 years ago a non-stop flight from New York to Paris gave America a new hero. Now, however, pilotless planes and guided missiles cut through our atmosphere 5,000 miles per hour, and we may reach the moon before you finish college.

Nuclear physicists and engineers have turned the key that unlocks the incalculable energies confined in the atom. Though born in war and baptized in destruction, these energies have been harnessed to man's constructive purposes. Hardly have we gotten over the shock of one discovery until we are staggered by another still more awesome one. Small wonder, therefore, that we have been a little bewildered and a little frightened.

The terrific acceleration of life has subjected us to immense strains. The ravages of two world wars nipped the flower of two generations. It uprooted the youth who fought and survived, and brought grief and perplexities to millions. The inability of man as a social and economic creature to keep step with science and knowledge has resulted in social stress and frustration.

We have become rich in mechanisms, but poor in purpose. We move about the earth with unprecedented speed, but we do not know and have not thought of where we are going. We stand on the brink of self-destruction, and to what does man turn for his salvation? It is paradoxical that these strains and frustrations have inevitably resulted from man's inability to make the social adjustments to scientific and technological advances he has wrought; yet, it is more science and more knowledge that we now seek to deliver us from this suicidal nightmare. One great American has recently said that "force is no more the therapy for our social ills than it is for the sickness and maladjustment of an individual." He has proclaimed that our problems ahead are primarily problems in human relations, social, economic, technological and psychological.

On the threshold of the atomic age, Einstein spoke to Americans in a practical sort of way. He said that if mankind is to survive and move to higher levels, a new kind of thinking must pervade our lives; that we must remember that if the animal part of human nature is our foe, the thinking part is our friend; and that we can and must use it now. He went on to say that, "When we are clear in heart and mind, only then shall we find courage to surmount the fear that haunts the world."

With the advancement of scientific means for the mass destruction of human life has come an utter lack of respect for it. We are bewildered by the remorseless youth offender with a high I.Q. We literally grope for the answer to the causes for increase in crime and delinquency among those whose knowledge teaches them the plain difference between right and wrong.

Recently a group of experts from various branches of learning assembled to discuss the appalling problem of the apparent increase in crime and delinquency. Each one found the major factors of the cause and cure within his own particular area of specialization. The sociologist found the explanation in "broken homes" and "social disorganization." The anthropologist found it in the clash between immigrant groups. The psychiatrist found it in the mental strains and frustrations of modern living. The doctor found it in an imbalance between human needs and conditions of urban civilization. The minister found it in the decay of morals and the decline of religion and its importance in everyday living. Each one had a plausible case. Each one could give facts, figures, and statistics. In a sense, each was right in his own diagnosis, so far as it went; but, the meeting ended where it began. Each one stayed essentially within his own area of learning. No one related what he knew to what others knew. Each one listened with scholarly respect to what the other said, and then returned, convinced in his own mind that his field was the most important one to combat the problem. True, they were educated men.

They were intelligent and they were knowledgeable. But they had failed. And, in their failure, they proved one undeniable fact, i.e., knowledge alone is not the cure to our human ills.

The cure is found in what scholars have chosen to call wisdom. But for our purposes, we may call it: Firstly, a proper perspective of life; secondly, a courage to live it; and thirdly, an abiding faith in it. "Knowledge is proud that he has learned so much, and wisdom is humble that he knows no more."

The true test of a proper perspective is to be found most of all in the way we relate ourselves to others. The foolish are not concerned to see the ways of other men. They do not understand that the whole of society embraces themselves—those in their own social circle as well as those outside of it—and that we all must live together in this shrunken world, or die by suicide. Only the foolish find themselves a part of the mob, inflamed by hate and consumed by fear. We can only hope that reason and justice will prevail; and it will, only if you have the courage to espouse its cause.

Of all the qualities of mankind, courage is perhaps the most universally admired. Regardless of the changes of fashion in human conduct, courage is never outmoded. Its appeal is timeless, changeless and universal. It has blossomed in every season of man's history. It is the monopoly of no race, the heritage of no tribe. But courage is never to be confused with recklessness, which is lacking prudent caution.

Courage is required in every decision. "Nothing ventured, nothing gained." "There is no crown without its cross." "There is no prize without a struggle, no victory without a contest." True courage is anchored in reason. It is educated fear.

This graduating class has an abundance of intellect and energy. You need only enthusiastic devotion to the pursuit of a purpose. There are unlimited resources of knowledge at man's disposal for his own welfare and happiness, if he would but have faith in his highest aspirations.

Yes, knowledge alone is dangerous. Our greatest need is to utilize our knowledge to acquire a proper perspective, courage and faith. We are thus brought to the crossroads of civilization, and we grope for the way ahead. This is the world, that uncertain world, into which you are about to launch. Your parents fought the war, you must preserve the peace. And, if the span of life which stretches out before you seems uncertain and even bewildering, let me remind you that never in the history of mankind's struggle to survive has visibility ahead been clear, or the course straight and smooth. Let us not forget that after all, life itself is a dangerous experiment, and that we would have it no other way; that by struggle itself, we are made strong to endure. This is no time for cynical bewilderment: as never before, it is a time for faith in our ideals; faith in ourselves and in each other, to make them work for the good of all mankind. With this faith, courage, and the high resolve to labor diligently, we will preserve the heritage that is ours.

You Must Learn To Be A Judge[6]

Your purpose in being in Charlottesville these next three weeks is to learn more about the business of judging, or, to say it more accurately, the art of judging. Believe me, it is an art. Judges are made, not born. We must learn to be a judge. Retired Chief Judge J. E. Murdock, who served on the United States Tax Court for 35 years says: "Far too many have the false impression that any lawyer who has enjoyed a successful practice could mount the bench and be an immediate success there."

A judgeship is not a sinecure or a form of retirement. As you have already found, or soon will, things are completely different from the other side of the bench. It takes time and study—and hard work—to learn how to be a judge.

Although many of your present concerns about your office may encompass trial procedures, instructions to juries, the sentencing of convicted persons, and other similar matters there will come a time when you will be wondering about the more personal things in connection with your judicial status. How do I act now that I am a judge? Do I still keep the same friends and go to the same places of recreation? Does my relationship with people in general, and lawyers in particular, change?

And, of course, the single answer to all of them is to act in all respects the same as you did before—just be yourself. A judgeship may change your office hours, or the nature of your work, or your compassion, but surely it shouldn't change the man.

The courts are manned by judges with feet of clay. Behind the black robe is a human being, striving always but never quite reaching beyond the realm of human frailties. There never has been, and there never will be, a judge worthy of his salt who can be classified as a cold and clammy thinking machine. No judge, however he may try, can, in his decisions, completely and effectively divorce himself from what he has seen, has heard, has experienced and has been. Hamlet said, "A man becomes no less a man when he dons the black robe. The more of a man he remains, the better he is as a judge." Sometimes we are stubborn, dense, arbitrary and even capricious, depending upon which side of the lawsuit you happen to look at the judge.

BE YOURSELF

But this business of adjusting yourself personally is not always as easy as would be implied by the suggested answer to "just be yourself."

The transition from bar to bench is a big one and making the change with equilibrium is not always the easiest task. We must keep our heads about us. Senior Circuit Judge Harold R. Medina observes:

> After all is said and done, we cannot deny the fact that a judge is almost of necessity surrounded by people who keep telling him what a wonderful fellow he is. And if he once begins to believe it, he is a lost soul.

A Mississippi judge once said, in suggesting to his fellow judges to be cautious so they did not usurp authority which was not lodged in the judiciary, that "Judges at least are but men encompassed by error, seasoned with sin, and fettered by fallibility." Perhaps we judges would not be too ready to admit that we are seasoned with sin, but that most judges are encompassed by error and fettered by fallibility seems only too evident when we read the divergent opinions of judges on the trial and appellate courts.

A Chicago lawyer is wont to observe, when capsulizing his displeasure with defects in the judicial personality, that the cowl doesn't make the monk and the robe doesn't make the judge.

We should remember that a certificate from the President, a polished gavel from the Bar Association, and a cushioned seat on an elevated dais are only the apparent indicators of the judicial officer.

But daily association with the external trappings may mislead us to an inflated appraisal of our own importance and so a practical application of the virtue of humility counsels that we must be on our guard.

The greatest deterrent to taking yourself too seriously in any respect is a wise and observing wife who periodically will remark: "Don't get so judgey."

A JUDGE AND HIS DIGNITY

But, notwithstanding these needful reins on our assumed importance, a judge does need to have dignity—it goes with the office. I don't mean that we must go around with nose on high putting on airs; or that, upon assumption of office, you should change your whole manner of life and circle of friends; or that with monk-like subjection, you withdraw from the world. I only mean that we must possess an appreciation of the great prestige of the judicial office and of the respect which is accorded it and its occupant by the American public.

"To the people of his jurisdiction, the judge is the personal embodiment of our American ideal of justice," according to Arch M. Cantrell, former Chief Counsel of the Internal Revenue Service writing in the *American Bar Journal*. He goes on to state:

> People generally, and lawyers as well, want to look up to

their judges. They want to admire and respect him for his ability as a judge and for the way he runs his court. The ideal of justice seems to be innate in every American, and part of his nature is to want to look up to, and respect his court and his judge.

Daniel Webster is quoted as saying that "...There is no character on earth more elevated and pure than that of a learned and upright judge and...he exerts an influence like the dews of heaven falling without observation."

So long as he knows his public's regard for the judicial office, the conscientious judge will conduct himself fittingly.

LAWYERS ARE OUR BEST JUDGES

Our success as judges will be measured in large degree by our success in relations with the attorneys who practice before us. There is no one better qualified to appraise the competence of a judge.

We owe a duty to the lawyers to treat them courteously, to hear them patiently, to study their argument conscientiously, and to decide their cases promptly.

It seems to me that, particularly to the lawyer, patience is the virtue most to be admired in the judicial personality.

The Grand Seignior of the Federal Bench in Minnesota, Judge Gunnar H. Nordbye, says there are three fundamental requisites for a good judge—first, he should have patience; second, he should have patience; and third, he should have patience.

COMMON SENSE — OUR BEST TOOL

It may be that in the first blush of assuming the duties of a military judge you will be so engrossed with conflicting statutes, inconsistent decisions, and all kinds of government rules and regulations, that you will forget all about using one of the principal tools of a good judge, and that is common sense. Really, there is no substitute for it. And it has been said that "the law is common sense modified by the Legislature."

"A judge will never go far wrong," wrote the now deceased Chief Justice Udall of the Arizona Supreme Court, "if he applies this test: Does my proposed action square with good common sense?"

Common sense should tell us many things about the law. For instance, it tells us that only under exceptional circumstances, and after a most forceful showing, should a judge sign an ex parte order. Common sense tells us, too, that while summary judgment looks like an expeditious device for speedy disposition of cases, it is really a special tool for limited application to relatively few cases, and should be granted only on an unmistakable showing of a complete absence of any fact controversy. It is likely that more trial judges have been reversed more often for the improper granting of summary judgment than for any other single judicial act.

As trial judges in the federal system, you and I have a special and important place in the scheme of things. Our close proximity to the lawyers and to the litigants gives us a burden of public responsibility much greater than we may appreciate offhand. May I tell a story?

A certain Bishop, known throughout Europe for his great learning and humility, came to the conclusion that he was unworthy of his high place in the Church and successfully petitioned the Pope for reassignment to service as a simple parish priest. The legend is regrettably vague as to whether this happened in the twelfth century or the thirteenth, or where the diocese of our bishop was, but it is perfectly clear as to what came of the reassignment. After less than a year of parish work, the former Bishop was back in Rome with another petition, this one praying for his restoration to episcopal status, and for good and sufficient reason. "If I am unworthy to be a bishop," he said, "how much more unworthy am I to be priest of a parish. As bishop, I was remote from men and women of lowly station, my shortcomings and weaknesses concealed from them by distance and ecclesiastical dignity. But as parish priest, I move intimately each day among the members of my flock, endeavoring by comfort, counsel and admonition to make their hard lot on earth seem better than it is. I am the Church to them; when my faith flags or my wisdom fails or my patience wears thin, it is the Church that has failed them. Demote me, Your Holiness, and make me bishop again, for I have learned how much easier it is to be a saintly Bishop than to be a Godly priest." The trial judge is the parish priest of our legal order.

What makes a good judge? Former Lord Chief Justice Goddard of England tells us in his interesting manner what the appointing authority in Britain looks for. He says:

> The qualities to be looked for in a judge are first that he should be a lawyer of reasonable capacity. A judge of first instance need not necessarily be a consummate lawyer. He should be a man of even temper and one who can be trusted to display and continue to display courtesy to the litigants and bar; in short, if I may use a much abused expression, he should be a gentleman. A sense of humor is always an asset, but a constant joker is anathema. Another quality devoutly to be wished for is the ability to keep reasonably silent while trying a case. A garrulous judge is a misfortune; he maddens the bar and slows up proceedings, but, unhappily, it does happen that a somewhat taciturn barrister becomes surprisingly talkative once he is seated on the bench.

The Seven Lamps of Advocacy[7]

In searching for material to base my remarks upon, I was led unerringly to a cherished little book in my library entitled "The Seven Lamps of Advocacy" written by an old English judge. He first talked about English judges whom he had known and he reminded me of some of the judges I have known in my 28 years on the bench.

When I went to the court of appeals, I succeeded what everyone seems to agree was the meanest judge that ever graced the federal bench. His name was Robert Lee Williams, and he had been a federal district judge in the Eastern District of Oklahoma for almost twenty years before he became an appellate judge. Judge Williams came to the Indian Territory as a circuit riding Methodist preacher. He raised chickens and while he was out on circuit a spring flood came and drowned all the chickens. When he returned and viewed the havoc, I've heard him say that he right then and there quit preaching. He told the Lord, "If you won't look after my flock while I'm gone, I'll be damned if I'm going to look after yours." So he quit preaching and became a lawyer. He was so cantankerous on the bench that he used to say that when he died every lawyer in his district would come to his funeral and walk by his bier and look, not to pay their respects, but just to be sure he was dead.

This little book of which I speak told of the seven lamps of advocacy, the first of which was

(1) *THE LAMP OF HONESTY*: From the earliest days the advocate is forbidden to maintain or defend wrong or falsehood.

Boswell asked Dr. Johnson whether he did not think "that the practice of law in some degree hurt the nice feeling of honesty?" To which the Doctor replied: "Why no, Sir, if you act properly. You are not to deceive your clients with false representations of your opinion: you are not to tell lies to a judge."

But, said Boswell: "What do you think of supporting a cause which you know to be bad?" To which Johnson replied: "Sir, you do not know it to be good or bad till the judge determines it. I have said that you are to state facts fairly; so that your thinking, or what you call knowing, a cause to be bad must be from reasoning, must be from your supposing your arguments to be weak and inconclusive. But, Sir, that is not enough. An argument which does not convince yourself, may convince the judge to whom you urge it; and if it does convince him, why then, Sir, you are wrong, and he is right. It is his business to judge; and you are not to be confident in your own opinion that a cause is bad, but to say all you can for your client, and then hear the judge's opinion."

Boswell answered: "But, Sir, does not affecting a warmth when you have no warmth, and appearing to be clearly of one opinion when you are in reality of another opinion, does not such dissimulation impair one's honesty? Is there not some danger that a lawyer may put on the same mask in common life, in the intercourse with his friends?" To which Johnson answered: "Why no, Sir, everybody knows you are paid for affecting warmth for your client; and it is, therefore, properly no dissimulation: the moment you come from the bar you resume your usual behavior."

To all of this Boswell was reminded of the Irishman in the dock who, when asked to state whether he was guilty or not guilty, replied: "Why, how can I tell until I hear the evidence?"

A classical example of honesty before the bar is the story of Lincoln's first appearance before the Supreme Court of Illinois. He opened his remarks by stating that this was the first time he had ever been before the court; that he had examined his case with great care; that the only question in the case was one of law and that he had been unable to find any authorities to sustain his side but had found several cases directly in point on the other side. He proceeded to give the authorities to the court and submitted the case. Our conduct as lawyers, as advocates, should never give anyone reason to recall the old saying, "An advocate but not a thief, A thing well nigh beyond belief."

(2) *THE LAMP OF COURAGE*: In 1792 when the great Lord Erskine was defending Tom Paine for publishing the *Rights of Man*, he was roundly criticized for defending one who at that time was a traitor in the public eye. The great Erskine said: "I will forever, at all hazards, assert the dignity, independence and integrity of the English bar; without which, impartial justice, the most valuable part of the English Constitution, can have no existence. From the moment that any advocate can be permitted to say that he will or will not stand between the Crown and the subject arraigned in the court where he daily sits to practice—from that moment the liberties of England are at an end."

If I forget every oral argument I have heard but one, I have no doubt which one that shall be. My Court had been in session for two weeks. The last case was a habeas corpus in which we had appointed a fine young lawyer who was serving without compensation. With typical helpfulness, Chief Judge Phillips explained to the young lawyer that we had looked at his case and that we understood the points and indicated that he should be able to present them very quickly. The young lawyer proceeded to state the facts in detail and to argue with zeal the Constitutional point in the lawsuit. The Court was a bit impatient both because the point was a constantly recurring one with which we were quite familiar and because we were weary from a long two weeks and a long day. Chief Judge Phillips indicated two or three times that we had the point. Each question from the Court was an invitation to the young lawyer to conclude his remarks.

Finally the young lawyer looked up at the Court and with a voice cracking with fear exclaimed, "If it please Your Honors, you apparently don't think much of my client's cause, but you appointed me to represent him and after briefing the law very carefully, I am convinced that my client is unlawfully incarcerated in Leavenworth, Kansas; and unless Your Honors require me to be seated, I should like to present it as I think justice requires." Whereupon, Chief Judge Phillips apologetically replied, "Why, of course counsel, proceed as you wish," and this young lawyer proceeded to take his full 45 minutes. It has always been the custom to express the Court's appreciation for the willingness of appointed counsel to undertake the case. On this day, the appreciation was more than formal. Chief Judge Phillips addressed counsel: "Counsel, I have been a lawyer for more than half a century and a Federal Judge for a long time. I have always been proud of my profession and the members of the bar. But today you have made me prouder to be a lawyer than all the days of my professional life. You have represented your client with zeal, skill and courage and with full credit to the profession. You have the gratitude of this court." That young lawyer was not wanting in courage, and if our profession is to remain true to its high ideals, we must not be either.

(3) *THE LAMP OF INDUSTRY*: Someone has said that it is better to wear out than to rust out. It has been my policy through the years when young lawyers come to me asking advice about where to go in order to carve out their niche in the law to tell them that my only sure admonition is to be diligent and decent, and if they will, they will surely find great rewards in the law.

(4) *THE LAMP OF WIT*: From the earliest times wit has been a light to lighten the darkness of advocacy. It has been the means for putting many young lawyers at ease or turning aside what might otherwise have been a great insult. Wit, properly placed, is subtly effective, but improperly applied in court it is often misunderstood and prejudicial. Wit and courtesy should never be divorced.

An example of wit properly used is the classical answer of the lawyer to the judge when he was asked, "Where do you draw the line in your case?" The lawyer replied, "I don't know, and I don't care, your Honor. It is enough for me that my client is on the right side of it."

Good advocacy displays the highest form of wit.

(5) *THE LAMP OF ELOQUENCE*: This lamp reminds me of an incident about an old judge of the West, with flowing locks, a little black string tie, and a dickey shirt. He was hearing a motion docket in the Courthouse on the square. It was spring and an old lawyer of the same vintage was arguing a demurrer. While walking to and fro in front of the bench, he argued long and loud; his stentorian voice reached out across the square to attract the attention of those who loafed under the trees. He talked about motherhood, he quoted scripture and read poetry, and quoted from the Preamble of the Constitution. What he said had little to do with the law of the case, but the old judge was deeply moved by the force of his oratorical eloquence. When he finally sat down, the judge spontaneously remarked, "That sounds like the law to me." Whereupon, the other old lawyer, knowing the judge's emotional propensity, sprang to his feet and pointing his finger upward exclaimed, "Hold on there, your honor, hold on! If you are going to decide this lawsuit on noise, I want to make some."

The aim of eloquence is persuasion. But, one absolute essential is sincerity—or at least an appearance of sincerity. Someone has said that the modern world has certainly lost its taste for sweet and honeyed sentences, and sets a truer value on fine phrases and the fopperies of the tongue; but there will always be a high place in the profession for the man who speaks good English with smooth elocution, and whose speeches fall within Pope's description:

> Fit words attended on his weighty sense,
> and mild persuasion flow'd in eloquence.

One time a West Virginia lawyer appeared in our Court on a lawsuit which the Court was quick to grasp. The lawyer was tall and lean with a deep voice; and it was soon apparent that he intended to rely more on sound than cases. He opened his argument by reading the mottos around the ceiling of the courtroom, such as "Reason is the Soul of All Law" and other like axioms. The presiding judge quietly and respectfully reminded him that the Judges had read those mottos many times and were quite familiar with them. But the lawyer insisted on reading all of them with positive and dramatic gestures. The presiding judge brought him to the point more than once explaining that as the Court understood the lawsuit, there was only one point involved, and invited the lawyer to come to it. But the West Virginia lawyer went merrily on his oratorical way without ever coming to the only point in the lawsuit. Finally, Chief Judge Phillips reminded him that his time was exhausted without getting to the point of his lawsuit and that the Court would give hin a few minutes to make his point. Whereupon the old lawyer looked to the Court with wild eyes and with one emphatic gesture exclaimed, "Your Honors, you just wait until I get to that and I will tear it up like new ground." Chief Judge Phillips replied with a whimsical smile, "You'll have to do your plowing in West Virginia. Your time is up."

(6) *THE LAMP OF JUDGMENT*: A client is entitled to the independent judgment of the advocate. Whether his judgment is right or wrong, it is the duty of the advocate to place it at the disposal of his client.

But, judgment involves strategy. It involves a psychological approach. One great lawyer has said: "Remember to put forward your best points first, for the weak ones are very likely to prejudice the good ones if they take the lead."

(7) ***THE LAMP OF FELLOWSHIP***: The patron saint of the legal profession, St. Ives, was known as the advocate of the poor. Recently, in a commencement address President Johnson said that "This is a new time in our land—a time young in spirit, a time of renewal, a time of resurgence for those forces which fashion a finer and fairer society." We live in a dynamic, pulsating world—a world of change—a world where the new is obsolete while it is yet on the drawing board. The law must keep pace or something else will surely take its place. Justice is the greatest interest of man on earth—it is the most precious heritage of a free society. We are its trustees with the inescapable duty to administer it—to preserve it and to perpetrate it.

We know that life itself is a dangerous experiment, and we would have it no other way; that by struggle itself, we are made strong to endure. This is no time for cynical bewilderment. As never before, it is a time for faith in our ideals; faith in ourselves and in each other to make them work for the good of all mankind. With this faith, courage and the high resolve to labor diligently, we will preserve the heritage that is ours.

The Supreme Court and Our Liberties[8]

In the last five years, the Supreme Court has rendered more decisions directly affecting the constitutional rights of the individual against state action than in any other era in the history of this country. The cases which have generated such great public interest and alarm, even resentment and rebellion, have covered the whole spectrum of the citizen's relationship to his local government. From public prayer to contraceptives—from search and seizure to self-incrimination—the right of confrontation to sit-ins and televised trials—from apportionment to segregation, the Court has, in the words of one critic, ruthlessly, heedlessly and needlessly swept aside deep rooted constitutional concepts which have traditionally governed the relationship of the individual to his state and social order. The last five years have brought forth an almost constant stream of cases, most of which have the effect of reversing state and lower federal courts in the field of criminal law. During the 1962 term, on a single Monday, the Court announced six decisions concerning constitutional limitations on state procedure. On one day, the Court, by per curiam orders, reversed thirty-one decisions from eight state courts on the authority of one decision, Gideon v. Wainright.

In the last decade, the Supreme Court has overruled itself ten or twelve times, and in most of the cases by a sharply divided court. To name a few of the most noteworthy: Brown v. Board of Education, overruling Plessy v. Ferguson, relating to school segregation; Fay v. Noia, overruling Darr v. Buford, expanding the scope of federal habeas corpus to test the legality of state restraints and closely related to that case is Townsend v. Sain; Gideon v. Wainright, overruled Betts v. Brady, bringing the absolute right to counsel under the 6th Amendment within the due process clause of the 14th Amendment; Mapp v. Ohio, overruling Wolf v. Colorado, making the search and seizure safeguards of the 4th Amendment applicable to state action; Malloy v. Hogan, overruled Twining v. New Jersey, holding that the state, no more than the United States, can compel incriminatory testimony. In this case, Mr. Justice Black's dissent in Twining finally prevailed after seventeen years; Murphy v. New York Waterfront Commission overruled United States v. Murdock, also on the subject of incrimination. The recent reports abound in cases which have the effect of revitalizing constitutional guaranties of the individual.

It causes us to pause and ponder whether we have grown lax and indifferent to fundamental guaranties, or whether the Supreme Court is possessed of an overweening zeal for those charged with criminal conduct, either in the state or federal sphere. Of course the federal courts have taken our spankings with more restraint because we have less difficulty adjusting ourselves to the commands of the higher tribunal. But on matters of federalism, it is more difficult because of the duality of our system of government. Then too, we are prone to forget that while we speak of coequal and coordinate governments, we know that the federal Constitution is the supreme law of the land and the supreme power to interpret and expound that Constitution is vested in one Supreme Court.

More importantly is the public outcry against this decisional trend based upon various forms of communication, most of which reflect the prejudiced or partisan point of view, without regard to the basic or fundamental questions involved. Dean Logan,[9] writing for his local paper, expressed grave concern with the current attack on the courts, which, in his words "indirectly attack our entire system of justice." He went on to say that nearly every day, through the Dean's office, he receives material criticizing the courts, examples of which were segregationalist propaganda which came in an envelope stamped in bold red letters "Mailed in Occupied Mississippi." Another pamphlet reaching the Dean contained a cartoon depicting the members of the United States Supreme Court as an evil looking group opening a cage full of rats labeled "Communist" to allow them to run wild through the country. Then he mentioned the billboards along highways beseeching citizens to impeach the Chief Justice of the United States—a man who had served as Attorney General and longtime Governor of his state and who was the Republican nominee for Vice President. He also called attention to most of the newspaper headlines, such an "Prayer Banned in the Public Schools", "Integrated Schools Required by Supreme Court Decisions", "Courts Assert Jurisdiction to Apportion State Legislatures."

The citizen who reads these headlines does not realize that in the first place, the Supreme Court has no power or authority to decide any question except one which is presented to them as a case or controversy, and when petitioned to do so, they have no alternative. Then too, it is probably worth noting that few people except those in the deep South who are rooted in customs and traditions will today question the rightness and justice of the Brown case. Adjustments are being made, and it seems fair to predict that in a few years the utter fallacy of the doctrine of "separate but equal" is manifest.[10] Whatever may be said of the power of the Supreme Court to read the Due Process and Equal Protection clause of the 14th Amendment into the subject of state legislative representation, it seems now to be fairly well accepted.

Coming more directly to the field of criminal law, let us examine just briefly the Gideon v. Wainright case overruling Betts v. Brady, and guaranteeing to every accused person the right to effective assistance of counsel at every stage of the proceedings against him whether he be charged by the state or federal sovereignty. A great newspaper man has written a book called "Gideon's Trumpet" based upon this case.[11] It ought to be required reading, for surely no one can read it without a wholesome respect for the decision. Gideon was a prisoner in a Florida penitentiary, a second but not dangerous offender. He was charged with the crime of breaking and entering. He had been convicted in a Florida court without counsel which he had requested and which had been denied on the grounds that under the laws of the State of Florida, the court could appoint counsel only in a capital case. While in the penitentiary, he penciled a letter to the Supreme Court in which he swore he was a poor person, that he had been convicted in a Florida court and had been denied his right to counsel. The Supreme Court took note of this inartistically drafted petition in the petitioner's handwriting, appointed Washington counsel who is now the most junior member of that Court.[12] It is to the great credit of our profession that this lawyer undertook the representation of his client whom he had never seen with the same zeal and acumen which he displayed in representing large interests and well-paying clients. The Court simply said that the right of one charged with a crime to counsel may not be deemed essential and fundamental to fair trial in some countries, but it is in ours. One of the justices, specially concurring, announced what now seems to be the prevailing view "that rights protected against state invasion by the due process clause of the 14th Amendment are not watered-down versions of what the Bill of Rights guarantees."

The criticism today by the dissenting justices and others is that the court has in fact incorporated the first eight amendments into the protections of the 14th Amendment. Whatever may be said of these decisions as encroachments upon state action, one cannot read them carefully without pride in the knowledge and conviction that if the court has erred, it has done so on the side of personal liberties. It has upheld the hand of the accused against his government. And, so long an we err on the side of liberty, we need have no fear of tyranny.

Some of the dissenters on the Court and others have criticized the shift in the law as contrary to the traditions of stare decisis. Others answer that constitutional law more than any other area of the law must be subject to judicial change and that the Constitution and especially the Bill of Rights is an organic guarantee which ought to be responsive to the enlightened needs of our social order. Then, there is that sane, sober and somewhat rare thought expressed in an editorial of one of the metropolitan papers this August: "To be sure the recent revolution in criminal justice has made things tougher for the police and for the lower courts. It is not a question of whether the Supreme Court is ahead of the public, however, but whether it is finally enforcing the command of the 14th Amendment that no state 'shall deprive any person of life, liberty or property without due process of the law.'" And then in one short sentence it says, "Due process in that context hardly depends on state boundaries."

Finally we come to the point of history. From the very beginning the Supreme Court has been the subject of bitter and vituperous attacks from those who at the moment are adversely affected by its decisions or who disagree with their ideological dogma. In times like these we need to remember that the Marshall Court was more maligned than the Warren Court, chiefly because Marshall's political philosophy ran contrary to his fellow Virginian who sat in the President's chair. Both men, honest and courageous in their beliefs, left their mark for history to judge, and history has judged well, for it concedes the danger that either of them would have prevailed.

It is difficult to imagine what the history of our country would have been if there had been no Marbury v. Madison, Cohens v. Virginia, Dartmouth College Case, no McCulloch v. Maryland, Gibbons v. Ogden, Brown v. Maryland or Original Package Cases, no Craig v. Missouri or Charles River Bridge Case, and later no Slaughterhouse Cases, all of which served to cement this country together in the most enduring sinews to form a united and imperishable nation.

When President Jefferson charged Aaron Burr with treason and brought Bollman and other aides from Louisiana to Washington for military trial, and Marshall issued a writ of habeas corpus to require a civil trial, the Senate passed a resolution suspending the writ. When

Burr was acquitted in Marshall's court, the Jeffersonian partisans called Marshall a traitor and a champion of treason.

Judges have never been subservient to the appointing power. Jefferson's first appointment to the Supreme Court was young Judge William Johnson, an ardent state's righter from South Carolina. Soon after his appointment, the Gilchrist case involving Jefferson's embargo act reached the Supreme Court. Judge Johnson wrote the unanimous opinion of the Court granting mandamus, and holding that Jefferson's instructions to his collector were illegal and void, and unwarranted by statute. Needless to say, Judge Johnson was a disappointment to his benefactor and accused as a traitor to his party.

As you know, Madison appointed Story, who rendered the opinion of the Court in Martin v. Hunter's Lessee, which has ever since been the keystone of the whole arc of federal judicial power. During all of these formative years, the courts were pillared and vilified by the champions of political, sectional and self interest.

While the dark clouds of the Civil War were hanging overhead, Milligan was convicted of disloyalty by a court martial and sentenced to be hanged. But, the Supreme Court, presided over by Lincoln appointees, stayed the hand of the hangman and released him because he had been denied a trial by jury, guaranteed him by the Constitution.

And, there was the Debs case, the great socialist, who arrogated unto himself the power to obstruct the free flow of commerce by stopping the trains engaged in interstate commerce. Upholding the injunctive power of the Court, Mr. Justice Brever, spearing for the Supreme Court, said that "if the emergency arises, the army of the nation and all its military are at the service of the nation to compel obedience to its laws."

Theodore Roosevelt appointed Holmes, and Holmes promptly disappointed him by his vote in the important Northern Securities case. Coolidge appointed Stone, who became President Hoover's "medicine ball partner", but whose dissent from the conservative majority in the agricultural adjustment act case became the lodestone for the so-called new deal philosophy. Said Stone, "The courts are concerned only with the power to enact statutes not with their wisdom." When Stone uttered these words, he was being talked for the presidency—his biographer comments that no further words were heard after these utterances.[13]

When Mr. Justice Field resigned, he wrote, "As I look back over the more than a third of a century that I have sat on this bench, I am more and more impressed with the immeasurable importance of this court. Now and then we hear it spoken of an aristocratic feature of a republican government. But, it is the most democratic of all. Senators represent their states, and representatives their constituents; but this court stands for the whole country, and as such it is truly 'of the people, by the people and for the people.' It has, indeed, no power to legislate. It cannot appropriate a dollar of money. It carries neither the purse nor the sword. But it possesses the power of declaring the law, and in that is found the safeguard which keeps the whole mighty fabric of government from rushing to destruction. This negative power, the power of resistance, is the only safety of a popular government." Many years afterward, Attorney General Wickersham wrote: "Mistakes have been made by the judiciary. Cases have been wrongly decided and the extension of legal principles to meet new conditions and judicial interpretation of the Constitution has often been slower than impatient reformers desirous of immediate results would wish. Yet no candid critic can say that on the whole the history of the American judiciary does not furnish as high, if not higher, example of adequate results than that of any other branch of the government. They have no patronage with which to reward their followers, and no partisans to sustain them right or wrong; they have no interest except in common with their countrymen, and no ambition except to leave behind them an honored name. Of all note in this World, they have the least temptations to do wrong and the greatest incentive to do right. They are not infallible, and they make their mistakes, but they make fewer mistakes than other men; and so long as they can guard the Constitution of this Republic, it will protect the lives, the liberty and the property of the American people."

Yes, we have a glorious history, but we cannot live on our inheritance. History bids us keep pace or lose our place. It is only by the diligent and efficient application of our learning and professional skill that we can hope to merit the place in the public estimation which we claim, and to render to the public the services which they are entitled to expect from us. We live in a dynamic, pulsating world—a world of change, if you please—in a world where the new is obsolete while it is yet on the drawing board. The law must keep pace or something else will surely take its place. Justice is the greatest interest of man on earth—it is the most precious heritage of a free society. We are its trustees with the inescapable duty to administer it — to preserve it and to perpetuate it. Certainly, we can best perform our task by the skillful use of the tools at hand. By diligent and continuous application of our industry, our intellects, and our integrity, we will strengthen and perpetuate the temples of justice so that when the winds of destruction beat upon their pillars, they will stand like the Rock of Ages.

Appendix C Opinions For The Courts Of Appeals By Murrah, Circuit Judge

Holt v. Thompson, 115 F.2d 1013 (10th Cir. 1940)
Magnolia Petroleum Co. v. N.L.R.B., 115 F.2d 1007 (10th Cir. 1940)
Mandles v. Guardian Life Ins. Co. Of America, 115 F.2d 994 (10th Cir. 1940)
City of Wewoka, Okla. v. Banker, 117 F.2d 839 (10th Cir. 1941)
Brigham Young University v. Lillywhite, 118 F.2d 836 (10th Cir. 1941)
Lidner Packing & P. Co. v. Commissioner of Int. Rev., 118 F.2d 656 (10th Cir. 1941)
United States v. McCain, 118 F.2d 479 (10th Cir. 1941)
United States v. One 1939 Model De Soto Coupe, Etc., 119 F.2d 516 (10th Cir. 1941)
Solintakis v. Orfanos, 119 F.2d 571 (10th Cir. 1941)
Adams v. Hudspeth, 121 F.2d 270 (10th Cir. 1941)
Oliver v. United States, 121 F.2d 245 (10th Cir. 1941)
Oklahoma Natural Gas Co. v. McKee, 121 F.2d 583 (10th Cir. 1941)
Utah Oil Refining Co. v. Hinckley, 121 F.2d 578 (10th Cir. 1941)
Subas v. Hudspeth, 122 F.2d 85 (10th Cir. 1941)
Jones v. Norris, 122 F.2d 6 (10th Cir. 1941)
United States v. American Packing & Provision Co., 122 F.2d 445 (10th Cir. 1941)
Dye v. United States, 123 F.2d 385 (10th Cir. 1941)
United States v. Wallace, 123 F.2d 484 (10th Cir. 1941)
Landman v. Commissioner of Internal Revenue, 123 F.2d 787 (10th Cir. 1941)
Schultz v. Hudspeth, 123 F.2d 729 (10th Cir. 1941)
Bryan County, Okl. v. United States, 123 F.2d 782 (10th Cir. 1941)
Commissioner of Internal Rev. v. I.A. O'Shaughnessy, Inc., 124 F.2d 33 (10th Cir. 1941)
N.L.R.B. v. Keystone Freight Lines, 126 F.2d 414 (10th Cir. 1941)
Gray v. City of Santa Fe, N.M., 135 F.2d 374 (10th Cir. 1941)
Huntley v. Schilder, 125 F.2d 250 (10th Cir. 1942)
Miller v. Mangus, 125 F.2d 507 (10th Cir. 1942)
MacDonald v. Hudspeth, 125 F.2d 465 (10th Cir. 1942)
Chestnut Securities Co. v. Oklahoma Tax Commission, 125 F.2d 571 (10th Cir. 1942)
Hargrove v. American Cent. Ins. Co., 125 F.2d 225 (10th Cir. 1942)

Lunsford v. Hudspeth, 126 F.2d 653 (10th Cir. 1942)
Bozel v. Hudspeth, 126 F.2d 585 (10th Cir. 1942)
Mitchell v. United States, 126 F.2d 550 (10th Cir. 1942)
Purcell v. City of Carlsbad, 126 F.2d 748 (10th Cir. 1942)
Oklahoma Gas & Electric Co., 127 F.2d 349 (10th Cir. 1942)
Levine v. Hudspeth, 127 F.2d 982 (10th Cir. 1942)
Anheuser-Busch v. Grovier-Starr Produce Co., 128 F.2d 146 (10th Cir. 1942)
Cox v. Pabst Brewing Co., 128 F.2d 468 (10th Cir. 1942)
Pandolfa v. United States, 128 F.2d 917 (10th Cir. 1942)
Traders & General Ins. Co. v. Rudco Oil & Gas Co., 129 F.2d 621 (10th Cir. 1942)
Brinton v. Federal Land Bank of Berkeley, 129 F.2d 740 (10th Cir. 1942)
Baker v. Hudspeth, 129 F.2d 779 (10th Cir. 1942)
Rogers v. United States, 129 F.2d 843 (10th Cir. 1942)
Viles v. Symes, 129 F.2d 828 (10th Cir. 1942)
Board of County Commissioners, Etc. v. Seber, 130 F.2d 663 (10th Cir. 1942)
Employers Mut. Cas. Co. v. American Automobile Ins. Co., 131 F.2d 802 (10th Cir. 1942)
Rosenhan v. United States, 131 F.2d 932 (10th Cir. 1942)
Hines v. United States, 131 F.2d 971 (10th Cir. 1942)
Amrine v. Tines, 131 F.2d 827 (10th Cir. 1942)
United States v. First Nat. Bank, 131 F.2d 985 (10th Cir. 1942)
Paradise Land & Livestock Co. v. Federal Land Bank, 131 F.2d 950 (10th Cir. 1942)
Meyer v. City of Eufaula, Okl., 132 F.2d 648 (10th Cir. 1942)
Patsy Oil & Gas Co. v. Roberts, 132 F.2d 826 (10th Cir. 1943)
Muskogee County v. United States, 133 F.2d 61 (10th Cir. 1943)
Hawley v. United States, 133 F.2d 966 (10th Cir. 1943)
Zumwalt v. Goodwin, 133 F.2d 984 (10th Cir. 1943)
Miller v. Miller, 134 F.2d 583 (10th Cir. 1943)
Galbreath v. Metropolitan Trust Co., 134 F.2d 569 (10th Cir. 1943)
Mutual Life Ins. Co. v. Hassing, 134 F.2d 714 (10th Cir. 1943)
Ohio Casualty Ins. Co. v. Callaway, 134 F.2d 788 (10th Cir. 1943)
Ohio Oil Co. v. Sharp, 135 F.2d 303 (10th Cir. 1943)
Perry v. United States, 136 F.2d 109 (10th Cir. 1943)
Seneca Coal & Coke Co. v. Lofton, 136 F.2d 359 (10th Cir. 1943)
National Life & Accident Ins. Co. v. Parkinson, 136 F.2d 506 (10th Cir. 1943)
United States v. Protsch, 137 F.2d 92 (10th Cir. 1943)
United States v. Hester, 137 F.2d 145 (10th Cir. 1943)
Tooisgah v. United States, 137 F.2d 713 (10th Cir. 1943)
Dejordan v. Hudspeth, 137 F.2d 943 (10th Cir. 1943)
Rucker v. First Nat. Bank of Miami, Ok., 138 F.2d 699 (10th Cir.

1943)
Brever v. Goff, 138 F.2d 710 (10th Cir. 1943)
Board of Com'rs of Pawnee County, Okl. v. United States, 139 F.2d 248 (10th Cir. 1943)
Joseph v. Ray, 139 F.2d 409 (10th Cir. 1943)
Roberts v. Hunter, 140 F.2d 38 (10th Cir. 1943)
Estep v. United States, 140 F.2d 40 (10th Cir. 1943)
Merrell v. United States, 140 F.2d 602 (10th Cir. 1944)
Affiliated Enterprises v. Com'r of Internal Revenue, 140 F.2d 647 (10th Cir. 1944)
Boeing Airplane Co. v. N.L.R.B., 140 F.2d 423 (10th Cir. 1944)
National Un. Fire Ins. Co. v. Anderson-Prichard Oil Corp., 141 F.2d 443 (10th Cir. 1944)
Head v. Hunter, 141 F.2d 449 (10th Cir. 1944)
Franklin v. Skelly Oil Co., 141 F.2d 568 (10th Cir. 1944)
Garbutt v. Blanding Mines Co., 141 F.2d 679 (10th Cir. 1944)
Baker v. Hunter, 142 F.2d 615 (10th Cir. 1944)
Mitchell v. United States, 142 F.2d 480 (10th Cir. 1944)
Cochran v. Order of United Commercial Travelers, 143 F.2d 82 (10th Cir. 1944)
Walling v. Mid-Continent Pipe Line Co., 143 F.2d 308 (10th Cir. 1944)
Bradley v. United States, 143 F.2d 573 (10th Cir. 1944)
Mosher v. Hunter, 143 F.2d 745 (10th Cir. 1944)
Farris v. Hunter, 144 F.2d 63 (10th Cir. 1944)
Jones v. Kemp, 144 F.2d 478 (10th Cir. 1944)
Townsend v. Bucyrus-Erie Co., 144 F.2d 106 (10th Cir. 1944)
Clyde v. Broderick, 144 F.2d 348 (10th Cir. 1944)
United States v. McCarty, 144 F.2d 341 (10th Cir. 1944)
Bowles v. Nu Way Laundry Co., 144 F.2d 741 (10th Cir. 1944)
United States v. Anglin & Stevenson, 145 F.2d 622 (10th Cir. 1944)
Scott v. United States, 145 F.2d 405 (10th Cir. 1944)
Smith v. United States, 145 F.2d 643 (10th Cir. 1944)
Taylor v. United States, 145 F.2d 641 (10th Cir. 1944)
New Mexico Public Service Co. v. Engel, 145 F.2d 636 (10th Cir. 1944)
Sonken-Galamba Corporation v. Union Pac. R. Co., 145 F.2d 808 (10th Cir. 1944)
United States v. 1851 Cartons, Etc., 146 F.2d 760 (10th Cir. 1945)
McCallum v. Anderson, 147 F.2d 811 (10th Cir. 1945)
Oklahoma Press Pub. Co. v. Walling, 147 F.2d 658 (10th Cir. 1945)
Jones v. Dawson, 148 F.2d 87 (10th Cir. 1945)
Hopkins v. McClure, 148 F.2d 67 (10th Cir. 1945)
T. & M. Transp. Co. v. S.W. Shattuck Chemical Co., 148 F.2d 777 (10th Cir. 1945)
Cities Service Oil Co. v. Harvey, 148 F.2d 780 (10th Cir. 1945)

White Thunder v. Hunter, 149 F.2d 578 (10th Cir. 1945)
Broadbent v. United States, 149 F.2d 580 (10th Cir. 1945)
Hickok v. Hunter, 150 F.2d 635 (10th Cir. 1945)
Blood v. Hunter, 150 F.2d 640 (10th Cir. 1945)
Wichita Transp. Corporation v. Braly, 150 F.2d 315 (10th Cir. 1945)
Hall v. Commissioner of Internal Revenue, 150 F.2d 304 (10th Cir. 1945)
Crum v. Hunter, 151 F.2d 359 (10th Cir. 1945)
Interstate Securities Co. v. United States, 151 F.2d 224 (10th Cir. 1945)
Harris v. United States, 151 F.2d 837 (10th Cir. 1945)
Gillespie v. Commissioner of Internal Revenue, 151 F.2d 903 (10th Cir. 1945)
Levers v. Berkshire, 151 F.2d 935 (10th Cir. 1945)
Maryland Casualty Co. v. Morrison, 151 F.2d 772 (10th Cir. 1945)
Garbutt v. Blanding Mines Co., 151 F.2d 764 (10th Cir. 1945)
Continental Supply Co. v. Marshall, 152 F.2d 300 (10th Cir. 1945)
Bowles v. Madl, 153 F.2d 21 (10th Cir. 1945)
Mitchell v. Hunter, 152 F.2d 959 (10th Cir. 1946)
Lewellyn v. Fleming, 154 F.2d 211 (10th Cir. 1946)
Thomas v. United States, 154 F.2d 365 (10th Cir. 1946)
Versluis v. Town of Haskell Okl., 154 F.2d 935 (10th Cir. 1946)
Shinn v. Buton, 154 F.2d 629 (10th Cir. 1946)
Meyer v. City of Eufaula Okl., 154 F.2d 943 (10th Cir. 1946)
Porter v. McRae, 155 F.2d 213 (10th Cir. 1946)
Cities Service Gas Co. v. Federal Power Com'n., 155 F.2d 694 (10th Cir. 1946)
Bratt v. Western Air Lines, 155 F.2d 850 (10th Cir. 1946)
Beech Aircraft Corporation v. Ross, 155 F.2d 615 (10th Cir. 1946)
Avrick v. Rockmont Envelope Co., 155 F.2d 568 (10th Cir. 1946)
Anthony's Estate v. Commissioner of Internal Rev., 155 F.2d 980 (10th Cir. 1946)
Barlow v. Federal Land Bank of Berkeley, 156 F.2d 360 (10th Cir. 1946)
American Eagle Fire Ins. Co. v. Peoples Compress Co., 156 F.2d 663 (10th Cir. 1946)
Edmonston v. Sisk, 156 F.2d 300 (10th Cir. 1946)
Goddard v. Frazier, 156 F.2d 938 (10th Cir. 1946)
Oliver v. City of Shattuck, 157 F.2d 150 (10th Cir. 1946)
Franklin Life Ins. Co. v. Johnson, 157 F.2d 653 (10th Cir. 1946)
New York Life Ins. Co. v. Bennion, 158 F.2d 260 (10th Cir. 1946)
One 1941 Buick Sedan v. United States, 158 F.2d 445 (10th Cir. 1947)
Pepper v. Truitt, 158 F.2d 246 (10th Cir. 1947)
Birtch v. Hunter, 158 F.2d 134 (10th Cir. 1947)
United States v. Chapman, 158 F.2d 417 (10th Cir. 1947)
Basler v. Warren, 159 F.2d 41 (10th Cir. 1947)

N.L.R.B. v. Continental Oil Co., 159 F.2d 326 (10th Cir. 1947)
Levers v. Berkshire, 159 F.2d 689 (10th Cir. 1947)
Atchison, T. & S.F. Ry. Co. v. Jarboe Livestock Com'n., 159 F.2d 527 (10th Cir. 1947)
Morton Salt Co. v. City of South Hutchinson, 159 F.2d 897 (10th Cir. 1947)
Baggett v. Fleming, 160 F.2d 651 (10th Cir. 1947)
Long v. United States, 160 F.2d 706 (10th Cir. 1947)
Anglin & Stevenson v. United States, 160 F.2d 670 (10th Cir. 1947)
Morrison v. Hunter, 161 F.2d 723 (10th Cir. 1947)
Edminston v. Hunter, 161 F.2d 691 (10th Cir. 1947)
Christakos v. Hunter, 161 F.2d 692 (10th Cir. 1947)
Leyerly v. United States, 162 F.2d 79 (10th Cir. 1947)
Hart v. United States, 162 F.2d 74 (10th Cir. 1947)
Aviation Club of Utah v. Commissioner of Internal Rev., 162 F.2d 984 (10th Cir. 1947)
McRae v. Creedon, 162 F.2d 989 (10th Cir. 1947)
Taylor v. Brindley, 164 F.2d 235 (10th Cir. 1947)
Brewer v. Hunter, 163 F.2d 341 (10th Cir. 1947)
United States v. Ohio Oil Co., 163 F.2d 633 (10th Cir. 1947)
Shepherd v. Hunter, 163 F.2d 872 (10th Cir. 1947)
Rabon v. Putnam, 164 F.2d 80 (10th Cir. 1947)
Bradshaw v. Superior Oil Co., 164 F.2d 165 (10th Cir. 1947)
Comparet v. United States, 164 F.2d 452 (10th Cir. 1947)
Becker v. Angle, 165 F.2d 140 (10th Cir. 1948)
Williams v. Hunter, 165 F.2d 924 (10th Cir. 1948)
Consolidated Goldacres Co. v. Commissioner of Int. Rev., 165 F.2d 542 (10th Cir. 1948)
Dearing v. United States, 167 F.2d 310 (10th Cir. 1948)
New York Life Ins. Co. v. Durham, 166 F.2d 874 (10th Cir. 1948)
Willis v. Hunter, 166 F.2d 721 (10th Cir. 1948)
Hughes v. Samedan Oil Corporation, 166 F.2d 871 (10th Cir. 1948)
Fleming v. Kellett, 167 F.2d 265 (10th Cir. 1948)
Moss v. Hunter, 167 F.2d 683 (10th Cir. 1948)
Cobb v. Hunter, 167 F.2d 888 (10th Cir. 1948)
Young v. United States, 168 F.2d 242 (10th Cir. 1948)
City of Tulsa v. Midland Valley R. Co., 168 F.2d 252 (10th Cir 1948)
N.L.R.B. v. Fairmont Creamery Co., 169 F.2d 169 (10th Cir. 1948)
Carter v. United States, 168 F.2d 310 (10th Cir. 1948)
Beeler v. Chicago, R.I. & P. Ry. Co., 169 F.2d 557 (10th Cir. 1948)
Chaffee County Fluorspar Corporation v. Athan, 169 F.2d 448 (10th Cir. 1948)
King v. Southwestern Greyhound Lines, 169 F.2d 497 (10th Cir. 1948)
City and County of Denver v. Warner, 169 F.2d 508 (10th Cir. 1948)
Chapman v. United States, 169 F.2d 641 (10th Cir. 1948)

N.L.R.B. v. Enid Co Op Creamery Ass'n., 169 F.2d 986 (10th Cir. 1948)
Merritt v. Hunter, 170 F.2d 739 (10th Cir. 1948)
Bottone v. Lindsley, 179 F.2d 705 (10th Cir. 1948)
Lawson v. Haynes, 170 F.2d 741 (10th Cir. 1948)
Grote v. Brown, 170 F.2d 747 (10th Cir. 1948)
Graber v. Commissioner of Internal Revenue, 171 F.2d 32 (10th Cir. 1949)
Murry v. Rio Grande Motorway, 171 F.2d 82 (10th Cir. 1949)
Ryles v. United States, 172 F.2d 72 (10th Cir. 1949)
Maragakis v. United States, 172 F.2d 393 (10th Cir. 1949)
Neal v. Hunter, 172 F.2d 660 (10th Cir. 1949)
Baruch v. Beech Aircraft Corporation, 172 F.2d 445 (10th Cir. 1949)
Denning Warehouse Co. v. Widener, 172 F.2d 910 (10th Cir. 1949)
Updike v. West, 172 F.2d 663 (10th Cir. 1949)
Bruskas v. Railway Express Agency, 172 F.2d 915 (10th Cir. 1949)
Haigler v. United States, 172 F.2d 986 (10th Cir. 1949)
Bowersock Mills & Power Co. v. Commissioner of Internal Rev., 172 F.2d 904 (10th Cir. 1949)
Gault v. Burford, 173 F.2d 813 (10th Cir. 1949)
Bradburn v. Shell Oil Co., 173 F.2d 815 (10th Cir. 1949)
Delaney v. Carter Oil Co., 174 F.2d 314 (10th Cir. 1949)
United States v. Runner, 174 F.2d 651 (10th Cir. 1949)
Karnowski v. Skelly Oil Co., 174 F.2d 770 (10th Cir. 1949)
Ferguson v. Ringsby Truck Line, 174 F.2d 744 (10th Cir. 1949)
Baruch v. Beech Aircraft Corporation, 175 F.2d 1 (10th Cir. 1949)
Insul-Wool Insulation Corp. v. Home Insulation, 176 F.2d 502 (10th Cir. 1949)
Commissioner of Internal Rev. v. Texas-Empire Pipe Line Co., 176 F.2d 523 (10th Cir. 1949)
Cohen v. Commissioner of Internal Revenue, 176 F.2d 394 (10th Cir. 1949)
Briggs v. United States, 176 F.2d 317 (10th Cir. 1949)
Phillips Petroleum v. Jones, 176 F.2d 737 (10th Cir. 1949)
Holt v. Warren, 176 F.2d 479 (10th Cir. 1949)
Owens v. United States, 177 F.2d 692 (10th Cir. 1949)
Heald v. United States, 177 F.2d 781 (10th Cir. 1949)
Martin v. Brodrick, 177 F.2d 886 (10th Cir. 1949)
Sullivan v. Jones Distributing Co., 177 F.2d 735 (10th Cir. 1949)
Morton Salt Co. v. City of South Hutchinson, 177 F.2d 889 (10th Cir. 1949)
Griggs v. United States, 178 F.2d 1 (10th Cir. 1950)
Oman v. United States, 179 F.2d 738 (10th Cir. 1950)
Steinway v. Majestic Amusement Co., 179 F.2d 681 (10th Cir. 1950)
American Fidelity and Cas. Co. v. All American Bus Lines, 179 F.2d 7 (10th Cir. 1950)

Story v. Burford, 178 F.2d 911 (10th Cir. 1950)
United States v. 716 Cases, Etc., 179 F.2d 174 (10th Cir. 1950)
Oldland v. Gray, 179 F.2d 408 (1950)
Gillette Motor Tr. v. N. Oklahoma Butane Co., 179 F.2d 711 (10th Cir. 1950)
Dastrup v. Smuin, 179 F.2d 860 (10th Cir. 1950)
Hurst v. United States, 180 F.2d 835 (10th Cir. 1950)
Cardenas v. Wilson & Co., Inc., 180 F.2d 828 (10th Cir. 1950)
Republic Insurance Co. v. French, 180 F.2d 796 (10th Cir. 1950)
Oklahoma City-Ada-Atoka Ry. Co. v. City of Ada, 182 F.2d 293 (10th Cir. 1950)
Godish v. United States, 182 F.2d 342 (10th Cir. 1950)
Eckhard v. Commissioner of Internal Revenue, 182 F.2d 547 (10th Cir. 1950)
Hollywood-Maxwell Co. v. Street's of Tulsa, 183 F.2d 261 (10th Cir. 1950)
Vrooman v. Beech Aircraft Corp., 183 F.2d 479 (10th Cir. 1950)
Chisholm v. House, 183 F.2d 698 (10th Cir. 1950)
Acme Distributing Co. v. Rorie, 183 F.2d 694 (10th Cir. 1950)
Shaffer v. Armer, 184 F.2d 303 (10th Cir. 1950)
Kansas City Life Ins. Co. v. Hayes, 184 F.2d 327 (10th Cir. 1950)
Parker v. United States, 184 F.2d 960 (10th Cir. 1950)
Bankers Indemnity Ins. Co. v. Bryant, 184 F.2d 1018 (10th Cir. 1950)
Denney v. United States, 185 F.2d 108 (10th Cir. 1951)
Quincy v. Texas Co., 185 F.2d 139 (10th Cir. 1951)
Donnelly v. United States, 185 F.2d 559 (10th Cir. 1951)
Tooisgah v. United States, 186 F.2d 93 (10th Cir. 1951)
Smotherman v. United States, 186 F.2d 676 (10th Cir. 1951)
Jones v. Trapp, 186 F.2d 951 (10th Cir. 1951)
United States v. Kemp, 186 F.2d 808 (10th Cir. 1951)
Brown v. Stufflebean, 187 F.2d 347 (10th Cir. 1951)
Utah Poultry & Farmers Coop. v. Utah Ice and Stor. Co., 187 F.2d 652 (10th Cir. 1951)
Phillips Petroleum Co. v. Oldland, 187 F.2d 780 (10th Cir. 1951)
N.L.R.B. v. Tri-State Casualty Ins. Co., 188 F.2d 50 (10th Cir. 1951)
Willoughby v. Sinclair Oil & Gas Co., 188 F.2d 902 (10th Cir. 1951)
Simon v. Schaetzel, 189 F.2d 597 (10th Cir. 1951)
Jones v. Baker, 189 F.2d 842 (10th Cir. 1951)
M. W. Kellogg Co. v. Standard Steel Fabricating Co., 189 F.2d 629 (10th Cir. 1951)
United States v. Jaramillo, 190 F.2d 300 (10th Cir. 1951)
United States v. Cox, 190 F.2d 293 (10th Cir. 1951)
Handler v. Thrasher, 191 F.2d 120 (10th Cir. 1951)
Denver & Rio Grande Western R. Co. v. Himonas, 190 F.2d 1012 (10th Cir. 1951)
St. Paul-Mercury Indemnity Co. v. Martin, 190 F.2d 455 (10th Cir.

1951)
Aetna Finance Co. v. United States, 191 F.2d 63 (10th Cir. 1951)
Graves v. United States, 191 F.2d 579 (10th Cir. 1951)
Dille v. Carter Oil Co., 192 F.2d 791 (10th Cir. 1951)
Trust Co. of Chicago v. Samedan Oil Corp., 192 F.2d 282 (10th Cir. 1951)
N.L.R.B. v. Davis Motors, 192 F.2d 782 (10th Cir. 1951)
National Labor Relations Bd. v. Conover Motor Co., 192 F.2d 779 (10th Cir. 1951)
Downie v. Powers, 193 F.2d 760 (10th Cir. 1952)
West Edmond Hunton Lime Unit v. Stanolind Oil & Gas Co., 193 F.2d 818 (10th Cir. 1952)
United States v. Blair, 193 F.2d 557 (10th Cir. 1952)
Atchison, T. & S.F.R. Co. v. Wottle, 193 F.2d 628 (10th Cir. 1952)
Meyer v. Rowen, 195 F.2d 263 (10th Cir. 1952)
Belt v. St. Louis-San Fran Ry. Co., 195 F.2d 241 (10th Cir. 1952)
Reconstruction Finance Corp. v. Service Pipe Line Co., 198 F.2d 775 (10th Cir. 1952)
C. D. Stimson Co. v. Porter, 195 F.2d 410 (10th Cir. 1952)
Oman v. United States, 195 F.2d 710 (10th Cir. 1952)
Mauldin v. Commissioner of Internal Revenue, 195 F.2d 714 (10th Cir. 1952)
Blazer v. Black, 196 F.2d 139 (10th Cir. 1952)
Migliaccio v. Continental Mining & Milling Co., 196 F.2d 398 (10th Cir. 1952)
Calderon v. United States, 196 F.2d 554 (10th Cir. 1952)
Vanhuss v. United States, 197 F.2d 120 (10th Cir. 1952)
Woodruff v. New State Ice Co., 197 F.2d 36 (10th Cir. 1952)
Republic Natural Gas Co. v. Baker, 197 F.2d 647 (10th Cir. 1952)
Baer Bros. Land & Cattle Co. v. Reed, 197 F.2d 569 (10th Cir. 1952)
Atkinson v. Atchison, Topeka & Santa Fe Ry. Co., 197 F.2d 244 (10th Cir. 1952)
Utah State Farm Bureau v. Nat'l Form. United States Corp., 198 F.2d 20 (10th Cir. 1952)
N. L. R. B. v. Machine Products Co., 198 F.2d 313 (10th Cir. 1952)
Steeber v. United States, 198 F.2d 615 (10th Cir. 1952)
Kanatser v. Chrysler Corp., 199 F.2d 610 (10th Cir. 1952)
Tobin v. Traders Compress Co., 199 F.2d 8 (10th Cir. 1952)
Stirk v. Mutual Life Ins. Co. of New York, 199 F.2d 874 (10th Cir. 1952)
Word v. United States, 199 F.2d 625 (10th Cir. 1952)
Standard Roofing & Material Co. v. United States, 199 F.2d 607 (10th Cir. 1952)
Myers v. Hunter, 199 F.2d 662 (10th Cir. 1952)
American Eagle Fire Ins. Co. v. Burdine, 200 F.2d 26 (10th Cir. 1953)
United States v. W. H. Kistler Stationery Co., 200 F.2d 805 (10th Cir.

1953)
Greer v. Stanolind Oil & Gas Co., 200 F.2d 920 (10th Cir. 1953)
Jackson v. Sims, 201 F.2d 259 (10th Cir. 1953)
Garrett v. McRee, 201 F.2d 250 (10th Cir. 1953)
Brink v. United States, 202 F.2d 4 (10th Cir. 1953)
Gordon v. United States, 203 F.2d 248 (10th Cir. 1953)
N.L.R.B. v. Coal Creek Coal Co., 204 F.2d 579 (10th Cir. 1953)
Kahl v. United States, 204 F.2d 864 (10th Cir. 1953)
State Street Trust Co. v. Muskogee Electric Tr. Co., 204 F.2d 920 (10th Cir. 1953)
Harris v. United States, 205 F.2d 765 (10th Cir. 1953)
Reconstruction Finance Corp. v. Service Pipe Line Co., 206 F.2d 814 (10th Cir. 1953)
Moss v. Gillioz Const. Co., 206 F.2d 819 (10th Cir. 1953)
Knox v. First Security Bank of Utah, 206 F.2d 823 (10th Cir. 1953)
Vitale v. Hunter, 206 F.2d 826 (10th Cir. 1953)
Ruby v. Bishop, 207 F.2d 84 (10th Cir. 1953)
Mofrad v. New York Life Ins. Co., 206 F.2d 491 (10th Cir. 1953)
Jackson v. Commissioner of Internal Revenue, 207 F.2d 857 (10th Cir. 1953)
Underwood v. United States, 207 F.2d 862 (10th Cir. 1953)
Roberson v. United States, 208 F.2d 166 (10th Cir. 1953)
Lujan v. United States, 209 F.2d 190 (10th Cir. 1953)
N.L.R.B. v. Construction Specialties Co., 208 F.2d 170 (10th Cir. 1954)
N.L.R.B. v. Stanolind Oil & Gas Co., 208 F.2d 239 (10th Cir. 1954)
Mead's Fine Bread Co. v. Moore, 208 F.2d 777 (10th Cir. 1954)
Switchmen's Union v. Ogden Union Ry & Depot Co., 209 F.2d 419 (10th Cir. 1954)
Hamill v. Maryland Cas. Co., 209 F.2d 338 (10th Cir. 1954)
United States v. Independent School Dist. No. 1., 209 F.2d 578 (10th Cir. 1954)
Holland v. United States, 209 F.2d 516 (10th Cir. 1954)
Phillips Petroleum Co. v. McCormick, 211 F.2d 361 (10th Cir. 1954)
Nelson v. Looney, 211 F.2d 89 (10th Cir. 1954)
Dayvault v. Baruch Oil Corp., 211 F.2d 335 (10th Cir. 1954)
Commissioner of Internal Revenue v. Evans, 211 F.2d 378 (10th Cir. 1954)
United States v. Arizona Canning Co., 212 F.2d 532 (10th Cir. 1954)
Eddy v. Travelers Ins. Co., Hartford, Conn., 212 F.2d 518 (10th Cir. 1954)
Fuller v. Commissioner of Internal Revenue, 213 F.2d 102 (10th Cir. 1954)
Wright v. Looney, 212 F.2d 186 (10th Cir. 1954)
Blue Bell Co. v. Frontier Refining Co., 213 F.2d 354 (10th Cir. 1954)
W. F. Sebel Co. v. Hessee, 213 F.2d 459 (10th Cir. 1954)

United States v. Dougan, 214 F.2d 511 (10th Cir. 1954)
Mitchell v. Chambers Const. Co., 214 F.2d 515 (10th Cir. 1954)
Independent-Eastern Torpedo Co. v. Ackerman, 214 F.2d 775 (10th Cir. 1954)
Peak Drilling Co. v. Halliburton Oil Well Cement Co., 215 F.2d 368 (10th Cir. 1954)
Bantel v. McGrath, 215 F.2d 297 (10th Cir. 1954)
State Finance Company v. Morrow, 216 F.2d 676 (10th Cir. 1954)
Marteney v. United States, 216 F.2d 760 (10th Cir. 1954)
Erwin v. Barrow, 217 F.2d 522 (10th Cir. 1954)
United States v. Interstate Securities Company, 218 F.2d 243 (10th Cir. 1954)
Magnolia Petroleum Company v. Carter Oil Company, 218 F.2d 1 (10th Cir. 1955)
Appleman v. Kansas-Nebraska Natural Gas Company, 217 F.2d 843 (10th Cir. 1955)
Beacham v. United States, 218 F.2d 528 (10th Cir. 1955)
Singleton v. Looney, 218 F.2d 526 (10th Cir. 1955)
Jones v. Koma, 218 F.2d 530 (10th Cir. 1955)
Pacific Employers Ins. Co. v. Gilt Edge Dairy, 218 F.2d 724 (10th Cir. 1955)
Webber v. Commissioner of Internal Revenue, 219 F.2d 834 (10th Cir. 1955)
Union Pacific Railroad Co. v. Snyder, 220 F.2d 388 (10th Cir. 1955)
Kansas Transport Company v. Browning, 219 F.2d 890 (10th Cir. 1955)
Hill Lines, Inc. v. Pittsburg Plate Glass Company, 222 F.2d 854 (10th Cir. 1955)
Inter-State Nat'l Bank of Kansas City v. Luther, 221 F.2d 382 (10th Cir. 1955)
National Labor Relations Board v. Seamprufe, Inc., 222 F.2d 858 (10th Cir. 1955)
Johnson v. First National Bank in Wichita, Kansas, 223 F.2d 31 (10th Cir. 1955)
Knowles v. United States, 224 F.2d 168 (10th Cir. 1955)
Seminole Nation v. White, 224 F.2d 173 (10th Cir. 1955)
Fidelity and Casualty Co. of New York v. Reece, 223 F.2d 114 (10th Cir. 1955)
Deschenes v. United States, 224 F.2d 688 (10th Cir. 1955)
Thomas v. Pick Hotels Corporation, 224 F.2d 664 (10th Cir. 1955)
Pulliam v. Looney, 224 F.2d 913 (10th Cir. 1955)
Loveless v. Universal Carloading & Distributing Co., 225 F.2d 637 (10th Cir. 1955)
Bristol v. Colorado Oil and Gas Corporation, 225 F.2d 894 (10th Cir. 1955)
Thomas v. Continental Casualty Company, 225 F.2d 798 (10th Cir.

1955)
Miller v. Irby, 227 F.2d 942 (10th Cir. 1955)
Hand v. United States, 227 F.2d 794 (10th Cir. 1955)
McDonough v. United States, 227 F.2d 402 (10th Cir. 1955)
Phillips Petroleum Company v. Federal Power Com'n, 227 F.2d 470 (10th Cir. 1955)
Foree v. Tri-County Electric Ass'n, 227 F.2d 945 (10th Cir. 1955)
United States v. Jones, 229 F.2d 84 (10th Cir. 1956)
Murray v. Denver & Rio Grande W. Railroad Co., 229 F.2d 644 (10th Cir. 1956)
Aetna Ins. Co. v. Chicago, R.I. & Pac. R. Co., 229 F.2d 584 (10th Cir. 1956)
Union Pacific Railroad Company v. Ward, 230 F.2d 287 (10th Cir. 1956)
Dayvault v. Baruch Oil Corporation, 231 F.2d 413 (10th Cir. 1956)
National Labor Rel. Bd. v. Carpenters Local Union, 232 F.2d 454 (10th Cir. 1956)
McLeod v. Cities Service Gas Company, 233 F.2d 242 (10th Cir. 1956)
People v. Ohio Casualty Insurance Company, 232 F.2d 474 (10th Cir. 1956)
Attaway v. Stanolind Oil & Gas Company, 232 F.2d 790 (10th Cir. 1956)
Amen v. Black, 234 F.2d 12 (10th Cir. 1956)
Cimarron Insurance Company v. Pomeroy, 234 F.2d 262 (10th Cir. 1956)
Davis v. Mann, 234 F.2d 553 (10th Cir. 1956)
Heltcel v. Skaggs, 234 F.2d 66 (10th Cir. 1956)
Church v. Ingersoll, 234 F.2d 176 (10th Cir. 1956)
Colepaugh v. Looney, 235 F.2d 429 (10th Cir. 1956)
Smith v. Minneapolis-Honeywell Regulator Co., 236 F.2d 573 (10th Cir. 1956)
Sawyer v. Mid-Continent Petroleum Corporation, 236 F.2d 518 (10th Cir. 1956)
Blish, Mize & Silliman Hdwe. Co. v. Time Saver Tools, 236 F.2d 913 (10th Cir. 1956)
Hansen v. Vidal, 237 F.2d 453 (10th Cir. 1956)
Iverson v. Frandsen, 237 F.2d 898 (10th Cir. 1956)
Philips Chemical Company v. United States, 238 F.2d 414 (10th Cir. 1956)
Continental Bank and Trust Company v. Apodaca, 239 F.2d 295 (10th Cir. 1956)
Inland Empire Ins. Co., v. Freed, 239 F.2d 289 (10th Cir. 1956)
Moore v. Dunham, 240 F.2d 198 (10th Cir. 1957)
San Juan Uranium Corporation v. Wolfe, 241 F.2d 121 (10th Cir. 1957)

United States v. Public Service Company of Oklahoma, 241 F.2d 18 (10th Cir. 1957)
Ben Hur Coal Company v. Wells, 242 F.2d 481 (10th Cir. 1957)
Jessen v. United States, 242 F.2d 213 (10th Cir. 1957)
Ditrich v. United States, 243 F.2d 729 (10th Cir. 1957)
Oklahoma State Fair Exposition v. Lippert Bros., 243 F.2d 290 (10th Cir. 1957)
Mark v. Union Pacific Railroad Co., 244 F.2d 268 (10th Cir. 1957)
United States v. Nickel, 243 F.2d 924 (10th Cir. 1957)
Old Colony Ins. Co. v. Anderson, 246 F.2d 102 (10th Cir. 1957)
Utex Exploration Company v. Garwood, 246 F.2d 547 (10th Cir. 1957)
Equity Oil Co. v. National Fire Ins. Co., 247 F.2d 393 (10th Cir. 1957)
American Automobile Ins. Co. v. Fidelity & Casualty Co., 247 F.2d 185 (10th Cir. 1957)
Western Machinery Company v. Consolidated Uranium Mines, 247 F.2d 685 (10th Cir. 1957)
Rogers v. Saiger, 247 F.2d 758 (10th Cir. 1957)
North Drive-in Theatre Corp. v. Park-in Theatres, 248 F.2d 232 (10th Cir. 1957)
Ardison v. Villa, 248 F.2d 226 (10th Cir. 1957)
Madrid v. Spears, 250 F.2d 51 (10th Cir. 1957)
New Home Appliance Center v. Thompson, 250 F.2d 881 (10th Cir. 1957)
Dairy Queen of Oklahoma v. Commissioner of Int. Rev., 250 F.2d 503 (10th Cir. 1957)
Hutchinson Water Co. v. United States Fidelity & G. Co., 250 F.2d 892 (10th Cir. 1957)
Rader v. Boyd, 252 F.2d 585 (10th Cir. 1958)
Pittsburgh Testing Lab. v. Farnsworth & Chambers Co., 251 F.2d 77 (10th Cir. 1958)
Chicago & N.W. Ry. Co. v. Continental Oil Co., 253 F.2d 468 (10th Cir. 1958)
Nelson v. Brames, 253 F.2d 381 (10th Cir. 1958)
Smith v. Gibraltar Oil Company, 254 F.2d 518 (10th Cir. 1958)
City of Wilburton v. Swafford, 253 F.2d 479 (10th Cir. 1958)
Evans v. Stearns-Roger Manuf. Co., 253 F.2d 383 (10th Cir. 1958)
United States v. Mraz, 255 F.2d 115 (10th Cir. 1958)
Harbold v. United States, 255 F.2d 202 (10th Cir. 1958)
Mason v. United States, 257 F.2d 359 (10th Cir. 1958)
Coleman v. Mountain Mesa Uranium Corporation, 257 F.2d 382 (10th Cir. 1958)
Henderson v. National Fidelity Life Insurance Co., 257 F.2d 917 (10th Cir. 1958)
Miller v. Stinnett, 257 F.2d 910 (10th Cir. 1958)
Bernstein v. United States, 256 F.2d 697 (10th Cir. 1958)

Trinity Universal Insurance Company v. Gould, 258 F.2d 883 (10th Cir. 1958)
Erekson v. United States Steel Corporation, 260 F.2d 423 (10th Cir. 1958)
Windom v. United States, 260 F.2d 384 (10th Cir. 1958)
Schloss v. Matteucci, 260 F.2d 16 (10th Cir. 1958)
Kerr-McGee Oil Industries v. Federal Power Com'n., 260 F.2d 602 (10th Cir. 1958)
Lynch v. Call, 261 F.2d 130 (10th Cir. 1958)
Commercial Ins. Co. of Newark, N.J. v. Watson, 261 F.2d 143 (10th Cir. 1958)
Padgett v. Buxton-Smith Mercantile Company, 262 F.2d 39 (10th Cir. 1958)
Gibbons v. Pan American Petroleum Corporation, 262 F.2d 852 (10th Cir. 1958)
Buffalo Insurance Company v. Amyx, 262 F.2d 898 (10th Cir. 1958)
Pryor v. Lee C. Moore, Corporation, 262 F.2d 673 (10th Cir. 1959)
N.L.R.B. v. General Drivers, Chauffeurs & Helpers, Etc., 264 F.2d 21 (10th Cir. 1959)
United States v. One 1957 Ford Ranchero Pickup Truck, 265 F.2d 21 (10th Cir. 1959)
United States v. One 1957 Ford Custom Tudor, 264 F.2d 682 (10th Cir. 1959)
Woodward v. Wright, 266 F.2d 108 (10th Cir. 1959)
Keene v. United States, 266 F.2d 378 (10th Cir. 1959)
Burk v. Cities Service Oil Company of Delaware, 266 F.2d 433 (10th Cir. 1959)
Bennett v. Davis, 267 F.2d 15 (10th Cir. 1959)
Doran Coffee Roasting Co. v. Wyott Manuf. Co., 267 F.2d 200 (10th Cir. 1959)
United States v. Martin, 267 F.2d 764 (10th Cir. 1959)
Structural Steel and Forge Co. v. Union Pacific R. Co., 269 F.2d 714 (10th Cir. 1959)
Atlas Building Prod. Co. v. Diamond Block & Gravel Co., 269 F.2d 950 (10th Cir. 1959)
Local 1912, Int. Ass'n of Mach. v. United States Potash Co., 270 F.2d 496 (10th Cir. 1959)
Rutledge v. Johansen, 270 F.2d 881 (10th Cir. 1959)
Hicks v. Simmons, 271 F.2d 875 (10th Cir. 1959)
Town of Maysville, Okl. v. Magnolia Petroleum Co., 272 F.2d 806 (10th Cir. 1959)
Allen v. W.H.O. Alfalfa Milling Co., 272 F.2d 98 (10th Cir. 1959)
United Steelworkers v. New Park Mining Co., 273 F.2d 352 (10th Cir. 1959)
N.L.R.B. v. Int'l Union of United Brewery, Etc., 272 F.2d 817 (10th Cir. 1959)

Woodmont, Inc. v. Daniels, 274 F.2d 132 (10th Cir. 1960)
Philip Sitton Septic Tank Company v. Honer, 274 F.2d 811 (10th Cir. 1959)
Burns v. Taylor, 274 F.2d 141 (10th Cir. 1959)
Tyler v. Dowell, Inc., 274 F.2d 890 (10th Cir. 1960)
Preble v. Johnson, 275 F.2d 275 (10th Cir. 1960)
Taylor v. Reo Motors, Inc., 275 F.2d 699 (10th Cir. 1960)
Rigby v. Rasmussen, 275 F.2d 861 (10th Cir. 1960)
Hoffmann v. United States, 276 F.2d 199 (10th Cir. 1960)
Kansas Turnpike Authority v. Abramson, 275 F.2d 711 (10th Cir. 1960)
Lopez v. Denver & Rio Grande Western Railroad Co., 277 F.2d 830 (10th Cir. 1960)
Abraham v. H. V. Middleton, Inc., 279 F.2d 107 (10th Cir. 1960)
Cantrell v. Molz-Frick Implement Co. of Wichita, 278 F.2d 546 (10th Cir. 1960)
Ordner v. Reimold, 278 F.2d 532 (10th Cir. 1960)
Winslett v. Rozan, 279 F.2d 654 (10th Cir. 1960)
Appleby v. Kewanee Oil Company, 279 F.2d 334 (10th Cir. 1960)
Clark v. United States, 281 F.2d 230 (10th Cir. 1960)
Steinbrugge v. Haddock, 281 F.2d 871 (10th Cir. 1960)
Foster v. United States, 282 F.2d 222 (10th Cir. 1960)
Chauffeurs, Teamsters, Etc. v. Yellow Trans. Frgt. Lines, 282 F.2d 345 (10th Cir. 1960)
Watts v. Roberts, 282 F.2d 565 (10th Cir. 1960)
Creed v. United States, 283 F.2d 646 (10th Cir. 1960)
Fitts v. United States, 284 F.2d 108 (10th Cir. 1960)
Maurer v. United States, 284 F.2d 122 (10th Cir. 1960)
Taylor v. Godwin, 284 F.2d 116 (10th Cir. 1960)
Bostian v. Miller, 285 F.2d 498 (10th Cir. 1960)
N.L.R.B. v. Central Oklahoma Milk Producers Ass'n., 285 F.2d 495 (10th Cir. 1960)
Midwest Plastics Corp. v. Protective Closures Co., 285 F.2d 747 (10th Cir. 1960)
Martin v. United States, 285 F.2d 150 (10th Cir. 1960)
Early v. Tinsley, 286 F.2d 1 (10th Cir. 1960)
G. E. Co. v. Beehive Telecasting Corp., 284 F.2d 507 (10th Cir. 1960)
McCollar v. Euler, 286 F.2d 327 (10th Cir. 1960)
Thomas v. Farnsworth Chambers Co., 286 F.2d 270 (10th Cir. 1960)
Massaglia v. C.I.R., 286 F.2d 258 (10th Cir. 1961)
State of Utah v. United States, 286 F.2d 30 (10th Cir. 1961)
Day v. Wilson, 286 F.2d 274 (10th Cir. 1961)
N.L.R.B. v. Brown-Dunkin Company, 287 F.2d 17 (10th Cir. 1961)
Devine v. Hand, 287 F.2d 687 (10th Cir. 1961)
Robbins v. United States, 290 F.2d 281 (10th Cir. 1961)
Berger v. State Farm Mutual Automobile Ins. Co., 291 F.2d 666 (10th

Cir. 1961)
Sutherland v. Fitzgerald, 291 F.2d 846 (10th Cir. 1961)
Owens v. Chicago, R. I. & P. R. Co., 292 F.2d 696 (10th Cir. 1961)
Denver & R. G. W. R. Co. v. Conley, 293 F.2d 612 (10th Cir. 1961)
United States v. Allen, 293 F.2d 916 (10th Cir. 1961)
Haynes v. Eagle-Picher Co., 295 F.2d 761 (10th Cir. 1961)
Fireman's Fund Ins. Co. v. Town of Grants, N. M., 295 F.2d 760 (10th Cir. 1961)
Freeling v. Sebring, 296 F.2d 244 (10th Cir. 1961)
T.F. Scholes, Inc. v. United States, 297 F.2d 337 (10th Cir. 1961)
Larson v. United States, 296 F.2d 80 (10th Cir. 1961)
Garcia v. Turner, 297 F.2d 881 (10th Cir. 1961)
Mesmer v. Raines, 298 F.2d 718 (10th Cir. 1961)
Union Carbide Corp. v. Nisley, 300 F.2d 561 (10th Cir. 1961)
Tidewater Oil Co. v. Waller, 302 F.2d 638 (10th Cir. 1962)
United States v. Gregory, 300 F.2d 11 (10th Cir. 1962)
Dennis v. United States, 302 F.2d 5 (10th Cir. 1962)
Whetstone v. Orion Ins. Co., 302 F.2d 15 (10th Cir. 1962)
Lewis v. United States, 301 F.2d 787 (10th Cir. 1962)
Black v. United States, 301 F.2d 418 (10th Cir. 1962)
AFL-CIO v. Cardwell Mfg. Co., 304 F.2d 801 (10th Cir. 1962)
Golden West Const. Co. v. United States, 304 F.2d 753 (10th Cir. 1962)
N.L.R.B. v. McFarland, 306 F.2d 219 (10th Cir. 1962)
Powers v. United States, 305 F.2d 157 (10th Cir. 1962)
Sears, Roebuck & Co. v. Jones, 308 F.2d 705 (10th Cir. 1962)
In re Holmes, 309 F.2d 748 (10th Cir. 1962)
Bradbury v. Dennis, 310 F.2d 73 (10th Cir. 1962)
Plavec v. Burch, 310 F.2d 337 (10th Cir. 1962)
Phillips v. United States, 311 F.2d 204 (10th Cir. 1962)
Wiles v. United States, 312 F.2d 574 (10th Cir. 1962)
N.L.R.B. v. Bear Brand Roofing, Inc., 312 F.2d 616 (10th Cir. 1962)
Beaver v. Fidelity Life Ass'n, 313 F.2d 111 (10th Cir. 1963)
Scarponi v. United States, 313 F.2d 950 (10th Cir. 1963)
Garcia v. Mountain States Tel. & Tel. Co., 315 F.2d 166 (10th Cir. 1963)
Century Refining Co. v. Hall, 316 F.2d 15 (10th Cir. 1963)
White v. North Am. Acc. Ins. Co., 316 F.2d 5 (10th Cir. 1963)
Heyser v. Frankfort Oil Co., 316 F.2d 411 (10th Cir. 1963)
N.L.R.B. v. Southwestern Porcelain Steel Corp., 317 F.2d 527 (10th Cir. 1963)
United States v. Mappes, 318 F.2d 508 (10th Cir. 1963)
Tidewater Oil Co. v. Jackson, 320 F.2d 157 (10th Cir. 1963)
Garfield v. Strain, 320 F.2d 116 (10th Cir. 1963)
Prairie Band of Pottawatomie Tribe v. Puckkee, 321 F.2d 767 (10th Cir. 1963)

Boeing Airplane Co. v. Perry, 322 F.2d 589 (10th Cir. 1963)
Tyler v. United States 323 F.2d 711 (10th Cir. 1963)
Britton v. Green, 325 F.2d 377 (10th Cir. 1963)
Wion v. United States, 325 F.2d 420 (10th Cir. 1963)
Moore v. United States Fidelity & Guaranty Co., 325 F.2d 972 (10th Cir. 1963)
Stewart v. United States, 327 F.2d 201 (10th Cir. 1964)
City of Aurora, Colo. v. Trinity Universal Ins., 326 F.2d 905 (10th Cir. 1964)
N.L.R.B. v. Bechtel Corp., 328 F.2d 28 (10th Cir. 1964)
Waters v. United States, 328 F.2d 739 (10th Cir. 1964)
Straight v. James Talcott, Inc., 329 F.2d 1 (10th Cir. 1964)
Patterson v. Wynkoop, 329 F.2d 59 (10th Cir. 1964)
N.L.R.B. v. Ideal Laundry & Dry Cleaning Co., 330 F.2d 712 (10th Cir. 1964)
Home Stake Production Co. v. Trustees of Iowa College, 331 F.2d 919 (10th Cir. 1964)
Atlas Life Ins. Co. v. United States, 333 F.2d 389 (10th Cir. 1964)
Union, Local 5-283 v. Arkansas Louisiana Gas Co., 332 F.2d 64 (10th Cir. 1964)
Mims v. United States, 332 F.2d 944 (10th Cir. 1964)
Auto Transports, Inc. v. Hinman, 332 F.2d 553 (10th Cir. 1964)
Citizens Bank v. National Bank of Commerce, 334 F.2d 257 (10th Cir. 1964)
Johnson v. United States, 333 F.2d 371 (10th Cir. 1964)
Carter v. United States, 333 F.2d 354 (10th Cir. 1964)
Byers Transp. Co. v. 4th Nat. Bank & Trust Co., 333 F.2d 822 (10th Cir. 1964)
Midwestern Developments, Inc. v. City of Tulsa, 333 F.2d 1009 (10th Cir. 1964)
United States v. Martinez, 334 F.2d 728 (10th Cir. 1964)
First Nat. Bank of Dodge City v. Perschbacher, 335 F.2d 442 (10th Cir. 1964)
Katchen v. Landy, 336 F.2d 535 (10th Cir. 1964)
Cities Service Gas Co. v. Federal Power Comm'n., 337 F.2d 97 (10th Cir. 1964)
Peoples v. United States, 337 F.2d 91 (10th Cir. 1964)
Casias v. United States, 337 F.2d 354 (10th Cir. 1964)
McKee v. Hassebrook, 337 F.2d 310 (10th Cir. 1964)
Aiuppa v. United States, 338 F.2d 146 (10th Cir. 1964)
Photostat Corp. v. Ball, 338 F.2d 783 (10th Cir. 1964)
Lake v. United States, 338 F.2d 787 (10th Cir. 1964)
Otney v. United States, 340 F.2d 696 (10th Cir. 1965)
Ryder Truck Rental, Inc. v. Central Packing Co., 341 F.2d 321 (10th Cir. 1965)
A. C. McKoy, Inc. v. Schonwald, 341 F.2d 737 (10th Cir. 1965)

Hannigan v. United States, 341 F.2d 587 (10th Cir. 1965)
United States v. Hess, 341 F.2d 444 (10th Cir. 1965)
Line Drivers Local No. 961 v. W. J. Digby, [illegible] 341 F.2d 1016 (10th Cir. 1965)
Sill Corp. v. United States, 343 F.2d 411 (10th Cir. 1965)
J. A. Tobin Const. Co. v. United States, 343 F.2d 422 (10th Cir. 1965)
Chase v. Page, 343 F.2d 167 (10th Cir. 1965)
Dennis v. United States, 346 F.2d 10 (10th Cir. 1965)
Patterson v. United States, 344 F.2d 693 (10th Cir. 1965)
Jordan v. United States, 345 F.2d 302 (10th Cir. 1965)
Todd v. United States, 345 F.2d 299 (10th Cir. 1965)
LaFaver v. Turner, 345 F.2d 519 (10th Cir. 1965)
Hillyer v. Pan Am. Petroleum Corp., 348 F.2d 613 (10th Cir. 1965)
Letellier v. Taylor, 348 F.2d 893 (10th Cir [illegible]
Spiess v. United Services Life Ins. Co., 348 [illegible]5 (10th Cir. 1965)
Ottinger v. Siegfried, 349 F.2d 647 (10th Cir., 1965)
J.F. White Engineering Corp. v. General Ins. Co., 351 F.2d 231 (10th Cir. 1965)
Ellis v. Page, 351 F.2d 250 (10th Cir. 1965)
Newman v. Nelson, 350 F.2d 602 (10th Cir. 1965)
Wallace v. Willingham, 351 F.2d 299 (10th Cir. 1965)
United States v. Southwest Potash Corp., 352 F.2d 113 (10th Cir. 1965)
Case v. Abrams, 352 F.2d 193 (10th Cir. 1965)
Denton v. Fireman's Fund Indem. Co., 352 F.2d 95 (10th Cir. 1965)
Ace Const. Co. v. W. H. Nichols & Co., 353 F.2d 110 (10th Cir. 1965)
Great Falls Transfer & Storage Co. v. Pan Am. Petroleum, 353 F.2d 348 (10th Cir. 1965)
Young v. United States, 354 F.2d 449 (10th Cir. 1965)
Bartlett & Co., Grain v. United States, 353 F.2d 338 (10th Cir. 1965)
United States v. Allan Drug Corp., 357 F.2d 713 (10th Cir. 1965)
Cotton v. United States, 355 F.2d 480 (10th Cir. 1966)
Patterson v. Hampton, 335 F.2d 470 (10th Cir. 1966)
System Inv. Corp. v. Montview Acceptance Corp., 355 F.2d 463 (10th Cir. 1966)
Haier v. United States, 357 F.2d 336 (10th Cir. 1966)
Slater v. C. I. R., 356 F.2d 668 (10th Cir. 1966)
Smith v. State of Kan., 356 F.2d 654 (10th Cir. 1966)
Doe v. C. A. B., 356 F.2d 699 (10th Cir. 1966)
Specht v. Patterson, 357 F.2d 325 (10th Cir. 1966)
Sanchez v. Cox, 357 F.2d 260 (10th Cir. 1966)
High Voltage Engineering Corp. v. Pierce, 359 F.2d 33 (10th Cir. 1966)
Maxfield v. United States, 360 F.2d 97 (10th Cir. 1966)
Norton v. Campbell, 359 F.2d 608 (10th Cir. 1966)
Sumrall v. United States, 360 F.2d 311 (10th Cir. 1966)

Marquardt Corp. v. Weber County, Utah, 360 F.2d 168 (10th Cir. 1966)
Hardesty v. State Farm Mut. Auto. Ins. Co., 361 F.2d 176 (10th Cir. 1966)
Welch v. United States, 361 F.2d 214 (10th Cir. 1966)
Choctaw & Chickasaw Nations v. Love County, 361 F.2d 932 (10th Cir. 1966)
Steele v. United States, 362 F.2d 536 (10th Cir. 1966)
Chavez v. Kelly, 364 F.2d 113 (10th Cir. 1966)
Elbel v. United States, 364 F.2d 127 (10th Cir. 1966)
Miller v. State of Okl., 363 F.2d 843 (10th Cir 1966)
Leighton v. Cox, 365 F.2d 122 (10th Cir. 1966)
Nez v. United States, 365 F.2d 286 (10th Cir. 1966)
Aimonetto v. National Union Fire Ins. Co., 365 F.2d 599 (10th Cir. 1966)
Titan Steel Corp. v. Walton, 365 F.2d 542 (10th Cir. 1966)
Burroughs v. United States, 365 F.2d 431 (10th Cir. 1966)
Bayless v. United States, 365 F.2d 694 (10th Cir. 1966)
Brundage v. United States, 365 F.2d 616 (10th Cir. 1966)
Wirtz v. Lieb, 366 F.2d 412 (10th Cir. 1966)
Clifton v. Mangum, 366 F.2d 250 (10th Cir. 1966)
American Sur. Co. of N. Y. v. Gold, 375 F.2d 523 (10th Cir. 1966)
Stafos v. Missouri Pac. R. Co., 367 F.2d 314 (10th Cir. 1966)
Robison v. Transamerica Ins. Co., 368 F.2d 37 (10th Cir. 1966)
Bank of Utah v. Commercial Sec. Bank, 369 F.2d 19 (10th Cir. 1966)
Gardner v. Brian, 369 F.2d 443 (10th Cir. 1966)
Demarest v. T. C. Bateson Const. Co., 370 F.2d 281 (10th Cir. 1966)
Seymour v. United States, 369 F.2d 825 (10th Cir. 1966)
Hidden Splendor Min. Co. v. General Ins. Co., 370 F.2d 515 (10th Cir. 1966)
Hardware Mut. Ins. Co. v. Lukken, 372 F.2d 8 (10th Cir. 1967)
Burrup v. United States, 371 F.2d 556 (10th Cir. 1967)
Homestake-Sapin Partners v. United States, 375 F.2d 507 (10th Cir. 1967)
N. L. R. B. v. Groendyke Transport, Inc., 372 F.2d 137 (10th Cir. 1967)
N. L. R. B. v. Ideal Laundry & Dry Cleaning Co., 372 F.2d 307 (10th Cir. 1967)
Phleps v. United States, 373 F.2d 194 (10th Cir. 1967)
Humphries v. State of Okl., 373 F.2d 200 (10th Cir. 1967)
Amaya v. United States, 373 F.2d 197 (10th Cir. 1967)
Furr's, Inc. v. N. L. R. B., 381 F.2d 562 (10th Cir. 1967)
Bartlett-Collins Co. v. Surinam Nav. Co., 381 F.2d 546 (10th Cir. 1967)
Garcia v. United States, 373 F.2d 806 (10th Cir. 1967)
Midwestern Developments, Inc. v. City of Tulsa, 374 F.2d 683 (10th

Cir. 1967)
Naugle v. State of Okl., 375 F.2d 424 (10th Cir. 1967)
Benscoter v. United States, 376 F.2d 49 (10th Cir. 1967)
Kennedy v. Commandant, Fort Leavenworth, 377 F.2d 339 (10th Cir. 1967)
Burke v. Ford, 377 F.2d 901 (10th Cir. 1967)
Reed v. United States, 377 F.2d 891 (10th Cir. 1967)
Kienlen v. United States, 379 F.2d 20 (10th Cir. 1967)
Betts Baking Co. v. N. L. R. B., 380 F.2d 199 (10th Cir. 1967)
N. L. R. B. v. Jordon Bus Co., 380 F.2d 219 (10th Cir. 1967)
Ryder Truck Rental, Inc. v. National Packing Co., 380 F.2d 328 (10th Cir. 1967)
Coyote v. United States, 380 F.2d 305 (10th Cir. 1967)
Foster v. Colorado Radio Corp., 381 F.2d 222 (10th Cir. 1967)
Steenberg Const. Co. v. Prepakt Concrete Co., 381 F.2d 768 (10th Cir. 1967)
N. L. R. B. v. United Nuclear Corp., 381 F.2d 972 (10th Cir. 1967)
J. C. Penney Co. v. N. L. R. B., 384 F.2d 479 (10th Cir. 1967)
Sumrall v. United States, 382 F.2d 651 (10th Cir. 1967)
Cundick v. Broadbent, 383 F.2d 157 (10th Cir. 1967)
Wheeler v. United States, 382 F.2d 998 (10th Cir. 1967)
Long v. Emery, 383 F.2d 392 (10th Cir. 1967)
Colorado Elevator Co. v. Chicago, R.I. & P. R., 382 F.2d 834 (10th Cir. 1967)
Baca v. United States, 383 F.2d 154 (10th Cir. 1967)
Morgan v. Willingham, 383 F.2d 139 (10th Cir. 1967)
W. S. Ranch Co. v. Kaiser Steel Corp., 388 F.2d 257 (10th Cir. 1967)
Food Basket, Inc. v. Albertson's Inc., 383 F.2d 785 (10th Cir. 1967)
McMillin v. Gardner, 384 F.2d 596 (10th Cir. 1967)
Ninio v. Hight, 385 F.2d 350 (10th Cir. 1967)
Jones v. United States, 387 F.2d 1004 (10th Cir. 1967)
Cave Const., Inc. v. United States, 387 F.2d 760 (10th Cir. 1967)
Gardner v. Travis, 387 F.2d 508 (10th Cir. 1967)
Kuykendall v. United States, 387 F.2d 594 (10th Cir. 1968)
N. L. R. B. v. Midwestern Mfg. Co., 388 F.2d 251 (10th Cir. 1968)
Lunow v. Fairchance Lumber Co., 389 F.2d 212 (10th Cir. 1968)
Branch v. Steph, 389 F.2d 233 (10th Cir. 1968)
Schenfeld v. Norton Co., 391 F.2d 420 (10th Cir. 1968)
Director of Revenue, State of Colo. v. United States, 392 F.2d 307 (10th Cir. 1968)
Conley Electronics Corp. v. F. C. C., 394 F.2d 620 (10th Cir. 1968)
Aiuppa v. United States, 393 F.2d 597 (10th Cir. 1968)
Texaco, Inc. v. Pruitt, 396 F.2d 237 (10th Cir. 1968)
Smith v. McNamara, 395 F.2d 896 (10th Cir. 1968)
Heryford v. Parker, 396 F.2d 393 (10th Cir. 1968)
Owens v. United States, 396 F.2d 540 (10th Cir. 1968)

Garvey v. Freeman, 397 F.2d 600 (10th Cir. 1968)
Christian v. United States, 398 F.2d 517 (10th Cir. 1968)
United States v. Wehrli, 400 F.2d 686 (10th Cir. 1968)
M.F. Patterson Dental Supply Co. v. Wadley, 401 F.2d 167 (10th Cir. 1968)
Chicago, R.I. & P. Ry. Co. v. Howell, 401 F.2d 752 (10th Cir. 1968)
Lumbermens Mut. Cas. Co. v. Rhodes, 403 F.2d 2 (10th Cir. 1968)
Derr v. Safeway Stores, Inc., 404 F.2d 634 (10th Cir. 1968)
C. H. Codding & Sons v. Armour & Co., 404 F.2d 1 (10th Cir. 1968)
King v. United States, 402 F.2d 289 (10th Cir. 1968)
Davis v. Berzak, 405 F.2d 642 (10th Cir. 1969)
Hall v. United States, 404 F.2d 1368 (10th Cir. 1969)
Hall v. United States, 404 F.2d 1367 (10th Cir. 1969)
Hall v. United States, 404 F.2d 1365 (10th Cir. 1969)
Douglas-Guardian Warehouse Corp. v. Jones, 405 F.2d 427 (10th Cir. 1969)
Browns v. Mitchell, 409 F.2d 593 (10th Cir. 1969)
Earnest v. Willingham, 406 F.2d 681 (10th Cir. 1969)
Murphy v. Dyer, 409 F.2d 747 (10th Cir. 1969)
Wolcott v. United States, 407 F.2d 1149 (10th Cir. 1969)
United States v. Humphrey, 409 F.2d 1055 (10th Cir. 1969)
Cotton v. United States, 409 F.2d 1049 (10th Cir. 1969)
Rogers v. United States, 411 F.2d 228 (10th Cir. 1969)
United States v. Winn, 411 F.2d 415 (10th Cir. 1969)
Robertson v. Roy L. Morgan Production Co., 411 F.2d 1041 (10th Cir. 1969)
B'therhood of Locomotive Engineers v. Denver Ry, 411 F.2d 1115 (10th Cir. 1969)
United States v. Wainwright, 413 F.2d 796 (10th Cir. 1969)
Bethea v. Crouse, 417 F.2d 504 (10th Cir. 1969)
United States v. Chadwick, 415 F.2d 167 (10th Cir. 1969)
United States v. Kienlen, 415 F.2d 557 (10th Cir. 1969)
United States v. Wynn, 415 F.2d 135 (10th Cir. 1969)
Peckham v. Metropolitan Life Ins. Co., 415 F.2d 312 (10th Cir. 1969)
N. L. R. B. v. Groendyke Transport, Inc., 417 F.2d 33 (10th Cir. 1969)
N. L. R. B. v. King Radio Corp., 416 F.2d 569 (10th Cir. 1969)
Jones v. Finch, 416 F.2d 89 (10th Cir. 1969)
United States v. Williams, 417 F.2d 630 (10th Cir. 1969)
N. L. R. B. v. Gold Spot Dairy, Inc., 417 F.2d 761 (10th Cir. 1969)
Nolan v. United States, 423 F.2d 1031 (10th Cir. 1969)
Fischer Const. Co. v. Fireman's Fund Ins. Co., 420 F.2d 271 (10th Cir. 1969)
John Long Trucking, Inc. v. Greear, 421 F.2d 125 (10th Cir. 1970)
Adair v. Finch, 421 F.2d 652 (10th Cir. 1970)
Way v. Crouse, 421 F.2d 145 (10th Cir. 1970)
Boatright v. Sclivia, 421 F.2d 949 (10th Cir. 1970)

Burran v. Dambold, 422 F.2d 133 (10th Cir. 1970)
Parsons v. Amerada Hess Corp., 422 F.2d 610 (10th Cir. 1970)
Lewis v. State of N. M., 423 F.2d 1048 (10th Cir. 1970)
Concrete Specalities v. H. C. Smith Const. Co., 423 F.2d 670 (10th Cir. 1970)
Kiner v. Northcutt, 424 F.2d 222 (10th Cir. 1970)
United States v. Keine, 424 F.2d 39 (10th Cir. 1970)
Morgan v. Willingham, 424 F.2d 200 (10th Cir. 1970)
Ketchum v. Nall, 425 F.2d 242 (10th Cir. 1970)
In re Midwest Engineering Co., 425 F.2d 820 (10th Cir. 1970)
N. L. R. B. v. Betts Baking Co., 428 F.2d 156 (10th Cir. 1970)
United States v. Western Cas. & Sur. Co., 429 F.2d 905 (10th Cir. 1970)
Bear Mfg. Co. v. United States, 430 F.2d 152 (7th Cir. 1970)
Charles v. Blount, 430 F.2d 665 (7th Cir. 1970)
Moomey v. Massey Ferguson, Inc., 429 F.2d 1184 (10th Cir. 1970)
Angle v. Laird, 429 F.2d 892 (10th Cir. 1970)
Young v. United States, 433 F.2d 626 (10th Cir. 1970)
Harrison v. Bloomfield Bldg. Industries, Inc., 435 F.2d 1192 (6th Cir. 1970)
N. L. R. B. v. Union Carbide Corp., 440 F.2d 54 (4th Cir. 1971)
Gar Wood Industries, Inc. v. United States, 437 F.2d 558 (6th Cir. 1971)
Garren v. City of Winston-Salem, N.C., 439 F.2d 140 (4th Cir. 1971)
Locks v. Laird, 441 F.2d 479 (9th Cir. 1971)
United States v. Butler, 446 F.2d 975 (10th Cir. 1971)
United States Fidelity & Guaranty Co. v. Bolding, 447 F.2d 462 (10th Cir. 1971)
Traders State Bank v. Continental Ins. Co., 448 F.2d 280 (10th Cir. 1971)
Friedberg v. Resor, 453 F.2d 935 (2nd Cir. 1971)
Anderson v. American Automobile Ass'n., 454 F.2d 1240 (9th Cir. 1972)
State Farm Mutual Automobile Ins. Co. v. Bockhorst, 453 F.2d 533 (10th Cir. 1972)
Hodgson v. Humphries, 454 F.2d 1279 (10th Cir. 1972)
United States v. Kennedy, 457 F.2d 63 (10th Cir. 1972)
Mitchell v. Shepherd Mall State Bank, 458 F.2d 700 (10th Cir. 1972)
In Re United Network, Inc., 459 F.2d 556 (2nd Cir. 1972)
Hensel Phelps Construction Co. v. General Signal Corp., 460 F.2d 109 (10th Cir. 1972)
Wise v. Westchester Fire Ins. Co., 463 F.2d 386 (10th Cir. 1972)
Garren v. City of Winston-Salem, N.C., 463 F.2d 54 (4th Cir. 1972)
United States v. Board of Sch. Com'Rs, Indianapolis, Ind., 466 F.2d 573 (7th Cir. 1972)
Bergenthal v. Cady, 466 F.2d 635 (7th Cir. 1972)

Jones v. United States, 466 F.2d 131 (10th Cir. 1972)
Bohn v. United States, 467 F.2d 1278 (8th Cir. 1972)
S.E.C. v. Advance Growth Capital Corp., 470 F.2d 40 (7th Cir. 1972)
Naftalin & Co. v. Merrill Lynch, Inc., 469 F.2d 1166 (8th Cir. 1972)
Dubois v. Packard Bell Corporation, 470 F.2d 973 (10th Cir. 1972)
Vincent v. Moench, 473 F.2d 430 (10th Cir. 1973)
United States v. Wagner, 475 F.2d 121 (10th Cir. 1973)
Anderson v. Salt Lake City Corporation, 475 F.2d 29 (10th Cir. 1973)
Anderson v. Reynolds, 476 F.2d 665 (10th Cir. 1973)
Barelli v. Levin, 480 F.2d 1207 (7th Cir. 1973)
Owens v. Sun Oil Company, 482 F.2d 564 (10th Cir. 1973)
Baker v. Gold Seal Liquors, Inc., 484 F.2d 950 (7th Cir. 1973)
Int'l Bro. of Electrical Wkrs. v. N. L. R. B., 486 F.2d 863 (7th Cir. 1973)
United States v. Home Indem. Co., 489 F.2d 1004 (7th Cir. 1973)
United States v. Roby, 499 F.2d 151 (10th Cir. 1974)
United States v. Johnson, 495 F.2d 242 (10th Cir. 1974)
George v. Strick Corp., 496 F.2d 10 (10th Cir. 1974)
Hays Livestock Comm. v. Maly Livestock Comm., Co., 498 F.2d 925 (10th Cir. 1974)
Joe v. United States, 510 F.2d 1038 (10th Cir. 1974)
United States v. Kramer, 521 F.2d 1073 (10th Cir. 1975)
United States v. White, 510 F.2d 448 (10th Cir. 1975)
Roddy v. United States, 509 F.2d 1145 (10th Cir. 1975)
Spence v. Latting, 512 F.2d 93 (10th Cir. 1975)
United Services Auto. Ass'n v. Royal-Globe Ins., 511 F.2d 1094 (10th Cir. 1975)
Gregory v. Wyse, 512 F.2d 378 (10th Cir. 1975)
Bishop v. Wainwright, 511 F.2d 664 (9th Cir. 1975)
Meis v. Sanitas Service Corp., 511 F.2d 655 (5th Cir. 1975)
United States v. Huff, 512 F.2d 66 (5th Cir. 1975)
United States v. Hightower, 512 F.2d 60 (5th Cir. 1975)
N. L. R. B. v. Leatherwood Drilling Co., 512 F.2d 270 (5th Cir. 1975)
Resort Car Rental System v. Chuck Ruwart Chevy, 519 F.2d 317 (10th Cir. 1975)
Seiffer v. Topsy's Intern., Inc., 520 F.2d 795 (10th Cir. 1975)
United States v. Ford, 525 F.2d 1308 (10th Cir. 1975)
United States v. Cowan, 524 F.2d 504 (5th Cir. 1975)

Appendix D

Dissenting Opinions In The Courts Of Appeals By Murrah, Circuit Judge

Jones v. Better Business Bureau of Oklahoma City, 123 F.2d 767 (10th Cir. 1941)
United States v. Oklahoma Tax Commission, 131 F.2d 635 (10th Cir. 1942)
Green v. Commissioner of Intemal Rev., 133 F.2d 76 (10th Cir. 1943)
Johnson v. Yellow Cab Transit Co., 137 F.2d 274 (10th Cir. 1943)
Equity Mut. Ins. Co. v. General Casualty Co., 139 F.2d 723 (10th Cir. 1943)
Jackson v. Vance, 179 F.2d 154 (10th Cir. 1950)
Schmidt v. United States, 179 F.2d 724 (10th Cir. 1950)
Inland Freight Lines v. United States, 191 F.2d 313 (10th Cir. 1951)
Tobin v. Pennington-Winter Const. Co., 198 F.2d 334 (10th Cir. 1952)
Carter Oil Co. v. Crude Oil Co., 201 F.2d 547 (10th Cir. 1953)
Ruebush v. United States, 206 F.2d 810 (10th Cir. 1953)
People of Colorado v. District Court, 207 F.2d 50 (10th Cir. 1953)
First Nat. Bank & Trust Co. of Tulsa v. Ingerton, 207 F.2d 793 (10th Cir. 1953)
Cole v. Hughes Tool Company, 215 F.2d 924 (10th Cir. 1954)
Kennecott Copper Corp. v. Graham, 219 F.2d 593 (I0th Cir. 1955)
Employers Liability Assurance Corp. v. Freeman, 229 F.2d 547 (10th Cir. 1955)
Wilcoxon v. United States, 231 F.2d 384 (10th Cir. 1956)
Cefalu v. United States, 234 F.2d 522 (10th Cir. 1956)
Atchison, Topeka and Santa Fe Railway Co. v. Jackson, 235 F.2d 390 (10th Cir. 1956)
Tilly v. Flippin, 237 F.2d 364 (10th Cir. 1956)
National Coop. Refinery Ass'n v. Northern Ordnance, 238 F.2d 803 (10th Cir. 1956)

Thomas v. United States, 239 F.2d 7 (10th Cir. 1956)
K & F Theatres Company v. Bradley, 246 F.2d 456 (10th Cir. 1957)
Likens v. John Hancock Mutual Life Ins. Co., 246 F.2d 897 (10th Cir. 1957)
Lee Way Motor Freight v. Yellow Transit, 251 F.2d 97 (10th Cir. 1957)
Sanders v. Fox, 253 F.2d 855 (10th Cir. 1958)
Marshall v. United States, 258 F.2d 94 (10th Cir. 1958)
United States v. Winters, 261 F.2d 675 (10th Cir. 1958)
Travis v. United States, 269 F.2d 928 (10th Cir. 1959)
D'Hondt v. Hopson, 269 F.2d 759 (10th Cir. 1959)
Smith v. United States, 273 F.2d 462 (10th Cir. 1959)
Richards v. United States, 285 F.2d 521 (10th Cir. 1960)
Copeland v. St. Louis-San Francisco Ry. Co., 291 F.2d 119 (10th Cir. 1961)
Batten v. United States, 306 F. 2d 580 (10th Cir. 1962)
Sirimarco v. United States, 315 F.2d 699 (10th Cir. 4963)
N.L.R.B. v. Brown, 319 F.2d 7 (10th Cir. 1963)
Loehrer v. Harclerode, 367 F.2d 883 (10th Cir. 1966)
Gray v. Johnson, 395 F.2d 533 (10th Cir. 1968)
Tri-State Generation & Transmission Ass'n v. Public Service Commission of Wyoming, 412
F. 2d 115 (10th Cir. 1969)
Acuna v. Baker, 418 F.2d 639 (10th Cir. 1969)
United States v. Marshall, 451 F.2d 372 (9th Cir. 1971)
Upper Pecos Association v. Stans, 452 F.2d 1233 (10th Cir. 1971)
United States v. Davis, 456 F.2d 1192 (10th Cir. 1972)
Colorado Pump & Supply Co. v. Febco, 472 F.2d 637 (10th Cir. 1973)

Appendix E

Opinions For The Courts Of Appeals By Murrah, District Judge

Oklahoma Natural Gas Corp. v. Municipal Gas Co., 113 F.2d 308 (10th Cir. 1940)
Citizens State Bank of Barstow, Tex. v. Vidal, 114 F.2d 380 (10th Cir. 1940)

A.R. Jones Oil & O. Co. v. Commissioner of Internal Rev., 114 F.2d 642 (10th Cir. 1940)

Appendix F

Concurring Opinions In The Courts Of Appeals By Murrah, Circuit Judge

Merrill v. Beaute Vues Corporation, 235 F.2d 853 (10th Cir. 1956)
United States v. Preston, 463 F.2d 544 (7th Cir. 1972)
Young v. Taylor, 466 F.2d 1329 (10th Cir. 1972)
Stafos v. Jarvis, 477 F.2d 369 (10th Cir. 1973)

NOTES

Chapter 1:

[1]Thomas Gray, *An Elegy Written in a Country Church-Yard*. (New York: Charles E. Merrill Co., 1909).

[2]Alfred P. Murrah to Judge John F. Kilkenny, March 5, 1970, Murrah Papers. Murrah hereafter cited as APM.

[3]1790 Federal Decennial Census, North Carolina, 78. Murrah's notable ancestors included Pendleton Murrah, Civil War governor of Texas, and Bishop W.B. Murrah, founder and president of Millsaps College.

[4]Indian Territory refers to the lands allotted to the Five Tribes (the Chickasaws, Cherokees, Creeks, Seminoles and Choctaws) on their removal from the eastern United States. As originally created, the area was coextensive with the present state of Oklahoma (except the Panhandle). Following the Civil War it was reduced by half on an east-west division, the tribes receiving the eastern half. Danney Goble, *Progressive Oklahoma: The Making of a New Kind of State*, (Norman: University of Oklahoma Press, 1980), 45.

Indian Territory was not established by legislative sanction. As McReynolds, Marriott, and Faulconer note in *Oklahoma: The Story of its Past and Present* (Norman: University of Oklahoma Press, 1961), p. 216: "We could almost say that Indian Territory was a territory in name only, for it was not organized under the territorial Organization Act at all. It had no appointed governor, no elected legislature, and no territorial supreme court." Congress did, however, legislate for Indian Territory from time to time. See, for example, Act of March 3, 1885, 23 Stat. 482, limiting the jurisdiction of Indian courts. Oklahoma Territory was a formally organized entity, created by the Organic Act of May 2, 1890.

[5]When the Chickasaws moved to the Indian Territory, they occupied lands in the Choctaw Nation designated the Chickasaw District. In 1855 the Chickasaw District became a separate entity, the Chickasaw Nation. Muriel H. Wright, "The Five Civilized Tribes In The Indian Territory," *Oklahoma Almanac, Golden Anniversary Edition* (Oklahoma City: State Election Board, 1957), 111, 118.

[6]The county was named for Douglas Johnston, many times governor of the Chickasaw Nation. *Directory of Oklahoma—1989-1990* (Oklahoma City: State Election Board, 1990), 443.

[7]Lucy Murrah is buried in the Earl or Blevins Cemetery.

[8]Wright, "The Five Civilized Tribes In The Indian Territory," 118. Grady County was named for Henry Grady, the famed editor of the Atlanta Constitution. *Directory of Oklahoma 1989-1990*, 425.

[9]Mary Hewett Bailey, "A History of Grady County, Oklahoma," (Unpublished MA Thesis, University of Oklahoma, 1937), 21.

[10]Kent Ruth, *The Oklahoma Travel Handbook* (Norman: University of Oklahoma Press, 1974), 234.

[11]*Chickasha Daily Express*, September 8, 1937, Section A, 3.

[12]Tax Roll 1907, Shirley Township, Grady County, Office of the County Treasurer, Chickasha, Oklahoma, 3; Tax Roll 1909, 116; Tax Roll 1910, 63; Tax Roll 1912, 88.

[13]The death of Lanora Murrah is reported in the *Verden News*, February 23, 1912, 5. She was buried in the Verden Cemetery.

[14]*Kansas City Star* (Missouri), February 28, 1937, 1C.

[15]*Ibid.*

[16]*Ibid.*

[17]The litigation concerned the power of the Secretary of the Interior to cancel an allotment after the issuance of the certificate and reserve the subject land for a townsite. See *Wheatland Grain & Lumber Co. et al. v. Dowden*, 26 Okl. 441, 110 Pac. 898 (Okl. 1910); *Appleby et al. v. Dowden*, 35 Okl. 707, 132 Pac. 349 (Okl. 1913); *United States v. Dowden et al.*, 220 F. 277 (8th Cir. 1915), appeal dismissed, 242 U.S. 661, 37 S.Ct. 114, 61 L.Ed. 550 (1916).

[18]Allen Ross, "The Story of Tuttle" (1969), reprinted in the *Chickasha Daily Express*, August 4, 1993, 1.

[19]Ordinance Number 17; Ordinance Number 10; Ordinance Number 35, *Tuttle News*, March 8, 1923, 6.

[20]*Tuttle News*, January 4, 1923, 1: "The final tryout for the debating team was last Wednesday morning and the team selected to represent Tuttle High School for the following year are: Alfred Murrah; Moreen Chenoweth, Stella Davis, Ralph Stephens as substitute." This may be the first time Murrah's name appeared in a newspaper story.

[21]S.P. Smith to Elmer Thomas, December 4, 1936, Elmer Thomas Papers, Box 2, Folder 50, Carl Albert Congressional Research Center, University of Oklahoma.

[22]*Directory of Oklahoma, 1973* (Oklahoma City: State Election Board, 1973), 309.

[23]*Ibid.* 322.

[24]Socialist Party of America Papers, William R. Perkins Library, Duke University, Durham, North Carolina. See also Von Creel, "Socialists in the House: The Oklahoma Experience," Part 1, *The Chronicles of Oklahoma*, LXX (Summer), 144.

[25]Creel, "Socialists in the House: The Oklahoma Experience," Part 2, *The Chronicles of Oklahoma*, LXX (Autumn), 258.

[26]*Directory of Oklahoma 1973*, State Election Board, 330.

[27]Angie Debo, *Oklahoma Foot-Loose and Fancy-Free* (Norman: University of Oklahoma Press, 1949), 47.

[28]*Directory of Oklahoma 1973*, 335, 339.

[29]For one interpretation of these events, see William D. McBee, *The Oklahoma Revolution* (Modern Publishers, Inc., 1956). McBee was Speaker of the House in the special session which voted articles of impeachment against Walton.

[30]*Tuttle Times*, March 17, 1922, 2; March 24, 1922, 2; November 11, 1922, 1.

[31]*Tuttle News*, July 6, 1922, 1; July 27, 1922, 1; November 6, 1922, 1.

[32]*Tuttle News*, August 17, 1922, 1; September 14, 1922, 1.

[33]Rick Banta, principal of Tuttle High School, to Von Russell Creel, March 12, 1993. Murrah's graduation made the paper (*Tuttle News*, May 3, 1923, 4):

McPhail's Entertain Tuttle's Senior High

Mr. & Mrs. J.R. McPhail entertained the Senior Class of T.H.S. Wednesday evening in honor of Alfred Murrah.

Progressive Rook was played at seven tables. Mrs. J.W. Morgan made high score, winning the favor.

To add to the enjoyment of the party Joyce Clark played lively music and the Boys' Quartet sang.

Refreshments were served carrying out the Senior colors of Black and Gold.

There were 27 in all present at the party.

[34]S.P. Smith to Elmer Thomas, December 4, 1936, Elmer Thomas Papers, Box 2, Folder 50.

[35]APM to T.R. Benedum, May 1, 1945, Murrah Papers.

[36]APM to Mrs. Joe Hartin, April 9, 1954, Murrah Papers.

[37]APM to Mrs. J.F. Renegar, November 7, 1970, Murrah Papers.

[38]APM to Josh Lee, January 21, 1942, Murrah Papers.

[39]APM to Stevie Chenoweth, April 15, 1946, Murrah Papers.

[40]APM to Jim H. George, February 25, 1954, Murrah Papers.

[41]Reading the *Tuttle Times* was a weekly ritual in chambers for Murrah, and he corresponded for many years with Holmes Tuttle, the grandson of James Harley Tuttle. Murrah kept Tuttle apprised of community happenings, as when he wrote "Tuttle beat the hell out of Crescent in football" (APM to Holmes Tuttle, November 26, 1974, Murrah Papers). Holmes Tuttle was a highly successful businessman in California, and was active in Republican politics, especially the gubernatorial and presidential campaigns of Ronald Reagan. When Tuttle was honored for a 50-year association with Ford Motor Company, the principal speakers were then California Governor Ronald Reagan and Murrah. In the last year of his life, Murrah found the strength to be the moving force behind Tuttle's selection for the Oklahoma Hall of Fame. Sadly, he did not live to see Tuttle inducted. Tuttle's presenter on that occasion was Ronald Reagan.

[42]APM to Stevie Chenoweth, op. cit., Murrah Papers.

[43]APM to Mrs. Joe Hartin, May 1, 1972, Murrah Papers.

Chapter 2:

[1]From the University of Oklahoma Chant.

[2]Cleveland County is named for President Grover Cleveland. *Directory of Oklahoma—1989-1990*, 401.

[3]Long and Hart, *The Sooner Story: Ninety Years at the University of Oklahoma 1890-1980*, (Norman: The University of Oklahoma Foundation, Inc., 1980), 7-8.

[4]James R. Scales and Danney Goble, *Oklahoma Politics: A History*, (Norman: University of Oklahoma Press, 1982), 121.

[5]Long and Hart, *The Sooner Story*, 46.

[6]Scales and Goble, *Oklahoma Politics*, 121.

[7]Long and Hart, *The Sooner Story*, 48.

[8]*University of Oklahoma Bulletin* (1923), 12-13.

[9]Transcript for Alfred Paul Murrah, Registrar's Office, University of Oklahoma.

[10] *1928 Sooner*, 120.

[11] *University of Oklahoma Bulletin* (1925-1926), 14-15.

[12] Quoted in letter from APM to Tom Phillips, August 23, 1948, Murrah Papers. While attending school in Tuttle, the sun struck Murrah's sandy hair in such a way that a fellow student called him Goldfish. In time, the nickname was shortened to Fish and stayed with him the remainder of his days. *The Sooner Yearbook*, note 15, lists Murrah as Fish Murrah.

[13] 5 *Oklahoma Law Review* 115 (May 1952).

[14] *University of Oklahoma Bulletin* (1925-1926), 239.

[15] Julien C. Monnet to APM, December 15, 1948, Murrah Papers; APM to Julien C. Monnet, December 20, 1948, Murrah Papers; *The Sunday Oklahoman*, December 12, 1948, 24A.

[16] APM to Judge Theodore Roosevelt Dalton, April 30, 1974, Murrah Papers.

[17] APM to Eugene Monnet, April 9, 1951, Murrah Papers.

[18] Transcript for Alfred Paul Murrah.

[19] *1928 Sooner*, 120.

[20] Transcript for Alfred Paul Murrah.

[21] APM to Paul Murrah, December 1, 1952, Murrah Papers. Shortly after taking the bench, Murrah told an audience at O.U. that "he was entitled to no honor, because he had worked his way through school. The disadvantaged were 'the boys who were born with silver spoons in their mouths, because the working boys had a realization of the hardships of life.'" *Norman Transcript*, May 13, 1937, 1.

[22] APM to Josh Lee, September 29, 1945, Murrah Papers.

[23] APM to William M. Taylor, August 20, 1945, Murrah Papers.

[24] Victor Henry Kulp to APM, August 24, 1945, Murrah Papers; George Cross to APM, December 14, 1945, Murrah Papers; APM to George Cross, December 18, 1945, Murrah Papers; Albert G. Kulp to APM, December 28, 1945, Murrah Papers; APM to Albert Kulp, January 5, 1946, Murrah Papers.

[25] 40 *Oklahoma Bar Association Journal* 2288.

[26] Quoted in the *In Memoriam Proceedings for Judge Alfred P. Murrah*, 574 F.2d, page 1 at pages 14-15 (1978). The pagination for in memoriam proceedings can be confusing. At one time, as when Murrah's was conducted, the transcript was numbered with Arabic numbers, as was case material. Thus in 574 F.2d there are two page 7s, one with in memoriam materials, and one with case material. Eventually, West Publishing Company saw the light. It now uses Roman numerals for in memoriam proceedings.

[27] APM to Horace K. Calvert, October 10, 1970, Murrah Papers. Later that year, Murrah spoke before the Joint Honor Societies of Oklahoma Baptist University at the invitation of Boren. David L. Boren to APM, October 12, 1970, Murrah Papers.

[28] Michael Barone and Grant Ujifusa, *The Almanac of American Politics 1994, National Journal* (Washington, D.C.), 1035.

[29] *Daily Oklahoman*, April 28, 1994, 1.

[30] List of charter members of the Touchdown Club, December 9, 1947, Murrah Papers; APM to Orville Wilson, November 26, 1954, Murrah Papers.

[31] APM to H.B. Kniseley, June 7, 1954, Murrah Papers.

[32] APM to Judge John C. Pickett, October 19, 1953, Murrah Papers.

[33] *Oklahoma Daily*, July 18, 1953, 1; *Daily Oklahoman*, July 19, 1953, 1; *Daily Oklahoman*, July 23, 1953, 1A; *Daily Oklahoman*, July 24, 1953, 1A;

Long and Hart, *The Sooner Story*, 85.

[34]APM to Mrs. O.M. Baker, July 23, 1953, Murrah Papers.

Chapter 3:

[1]1APM to Mrs. Robert J. Pickett, July 25, 1974, Murrah Papers.

[2]Records of the Oklahoma Bar Association.

[3]There is irony in Murrah beginning his practice with Smith, for he became one of Smith's strongest political foes (see chapters four and six). Smith's political career was colorful. See Scales and Goble, *Oklahoma Politics*, 173, 180, 194-195, 222-226, 235, 246, 248, 256-257 and 291, and Monroe L. Billington, *Thomas P. Gore: The Blind Senator From Oklahoma* (Lawrence: University of Kansas Press, 1967), 175-177, 180.

[4]Records of the Oklahoma Bar Association.

[5]Seminole County, in the east-central part of the state, "almost exactly coincides with the old Seminole Nation." Angie Debo, *And Still The Waters Run: The Betrayal Of The Five Civilized Tribes* (Princeton: Princeton University Press, 1940), 181. The Seminoles were the smallest of the Five Tribes, and "[n]obody knows much about the history or government of this conservative tribe after its forced removal to the Indian Territory." Angie Debo, *Oklahoma Foot-Loose and Fancy-Free* (Norman: University of Oklahoma Press, 1949). *Ibid.*, 199.

[6]Donald Kennedy, president of Oklahoma Gas and Electric Company, *In Memoriam Proceedings for Judge Alfred P. Murrah, op. cit.*, 8.

[7]Jane Bryan, "The Birth Of A Boom-Town," *American Heritage*, VIII (April 1957), 97-98.

[8]Kenny A. Franks, Paul F. Lambert, and Carl N. Tyson, *Early Oklahoma Oil: A Photographic History, 1859-1936* (College Station: Texas A&M University Press, 1981), 173.

[9]Debo, *Oklahoma Foot-Loose and Fancy-Free*, 199.

[10]*Watson v. Johnson*, No. 13469; *Smith v. Board of County Commissioners*, No. 13470; *McConathy v. Haynes Bros. Drilling Co.*, No. 13898; *Melton v. Barnsdall Oil Co.*, No. 14077; *LaHue v. DeWise*, No. 14132; *Talley v. Douglas*, No. 14221; *Jones v. Sinclair Oil & Gas Co.*, No. 14234; *McConathy v. Haynes Drilling Co.*, No. 14439; *Allen v. Halliburton*, No. 14537; *Lewis v. Bergman & Co.*, No. 14712; *King v. Bergman & Co.*, No. 14713; *Hopper v. Bergman & Co.*, No. 14714. Office of the Court Clerk for Seminole County, Wewoka, Oklahoma.

[11]*State v. Powell* (robbery with firearm), CRF-00-3237; *State v. Keyes* (robbery), CFR-00-3236; *State v. Barnes* (murder), CRF-00-3266. Office of the Court Clerk for Seminole County, Wewoka, Oklahoma.

[12]*Thompson v. Mills*, No. 13621; *Davis v. Brown*, No. 14282. Office of the Court Clerk for Seminole County, Wewoka, Oklahoma.

[13]*Ware v. Lowless*, No. 13821; *Ware v. Brooks*, No. 13823; *Ware v. Howard*, No. 13824. Office of the Court Clerk for Seminole County, Wewoka, Oklahoma.

[14]*Burton v. A.C. Kidd*, No. 13968; *Ware v. Williams*, No. 14647. Office of the Court Clerk for Seminole County, Wewoka, Oklahoma.

[15]*Patterson v. Patterson*, No. 13397; *Cade v. Cade*, No. 13400; *Bartell v. Bartell*, No. 13419; *Craven v. Craven*, No. 13468; *Trice v. Trice*, No. 13520; *Rogers v. Rogers*, No. 13564; *Bartell v. Bartell*, No. 13609; *Mayo v. Mayo*,

No. 13610; *Gyles v. Gyles*, No. 13611; *Thompson v. Thompson*, No. 13620; *Davis v. Davis*, No. 13785; *Winninger v. Winninger*, No. 13786; *Dittmar v. Dittmar*, No. 13822; *Campbell v. Campbell*, No. 13863; *Ozburn v. Ozburn*, No. 13864; *Simmons v. Simmons*, No. 13865; *Van Brunt v. Van Brunt*, No. 13939; *Hendrickson v. Hendrickson*, No. 13969; *Tuttle v. Tuttle*, No. 14091; *Magee v. Magee*, No. 14157; *Spires v. Spires*, No. 14370; *Brown v. Brown*, No. 14371; *Buster v. Buster*, No. 1 4536; *Hauchen v. Hauchen*, No. 14593; *Newman v. Newman*, No. 14746. Office of the Court Clerk for Seminole County, Wewoka, Oklahoma.

[16]*Seminole Morning News*, November 13, 1928, 1.

[17]*State of Oklahoma v. James Rodwick*, No. 3309, Criminal Appearance Docket 5, page 109; Minute Book 11, 91. Office of the Court Clerk for Seminole County, Wewoka, Oklahoma.

[18]*Kansas City Star* (Missouri), February 28, 1937, 1C.

[19]Records of the Oklahoma Bar Association.

[20]*Acker & Wall Operating Co. v. Roy Martin*, No. 14872; *Strosnider v. Baker*, No. 15126; *Seminole Motor Co. v. Smoot*, No. 15202; *Parker v. Murphy*, No. 15308; *Cissna v. The Oklahoma Co.*, No. 15312; *Raymond State Bank of Raymond, Kansas v. Parsons*, No. 15332. Office of the Court Clerk for Seminole County, Wewoka, Oklahoma.

[21]*Myers v. Carter Oil Company*, No. 15133; *Shores v. State Highway Commission*, No. 15955. Office of the Court Clerk for Seminole County, Wewoka, Oklahoma.

[22]*Hurt Tire & Supply Co. v. Electric Super Service Station*, No. 15335; *Hughes, Bozarth & Anderson Co. v. Young & Gurnsey*, No. 15420; *First State Bank v. French Dry Cleaners*, No. 15583; *Seminole Motor Co. v. Robinson*, No. 16169. Office of the Court Clerk for Seminole County, Wewoka, Oklahoma.

[23]*Seminole Motor Co. v. Palmer*, No. 15421; *First State Bank v. Edgerton & Glessco*, No. 16097. Office of the Court Clerk for Seminole County, Wewoka, Oklahoma.

[24]*Siscoe v. Ben Cooper Motor Co.*, No. 14657. Office of the Court Clerk for Seminole County, Wewoka, Oklahoma.

[25]*Davis v. Physicians Health & Acc. Ins. Co.*, No. 15564; *Stuart Oil Co. v. Home Ins. Co.*, No. 15565. Office of the Court Clerk for Seminole County, Wewoka, Oklahoma.

[26]*In Re application of Wall-Acker Operating Co. for an Order & Decree of Dissolution*, No. 15501. Office of the Court Clerk for Seminole County, Wewoka, Oklahoma.

[27]*Logan v. Logan*, No. 14784; *Thomas v. Thomas*, No. 14813; *Hammett v. Hammett*, No. 14896; *Parento v. Parento*, No. 15518; *McCarty v. McCarty*, No. 15617; *Mullen v. Mullen*, No. 15587; *Gibbens v. Gibbens*, No. 16318. Office of the Court Clerk for Seminole County, Wewoka, Oklahoma.

[28]*Hatten v. Johnson Motor Co.*, No. 14681; *Brown v. Atkins*, No. 14795; *Dunham v. Atkins*, No. 14796; *Nealey v. Pickwick Greyhound Lines, Inc.*, No. 15519; *Hackleman v. Lake Wewoka Park Co.*, No. 17348. Office of the Court Clerk for Seminole County, Wewoka, Oklahoma.

[29]APM to John Mabee, August 23, 1956, Murrah Papers.

[30]*Denver Post* (Colorado), August 1, 1954, 2AA.

[31]*Ibid.* On another occasion he recalled, "My first experience with law and law enforcement came twenty years ago when I left the University of Okla-

homa with a diploma in one hand and an extra shirt in the other, to begin the practice of law in the turbulent Oklahoma oil town of Seminole. It was there that I met law enforcement officers whom, I am sorry to say, I could not respect, either as men or officers. It was there, while I slept in my law office over a justice of the peace court that ran day and night, that I saw fee deputies and constables roam the oil fields for victims at the rate of three dollars apiece. It was there that I first felt the pulse beat of humanity in its relationship to law enforcement—it was there that I came to the full realization of the need for more efficiency and respectability in law enforcement." Speech before International Association of Chiefs of Police, New York, October 13, 1948, Murrah Papers.

[32]See Creel, "Socialists in the House: The Oklahoma Experience, Part 2," 260-263.

[33]*Directory of Oklahoma, 1973*, 160. *Daily Oklahoman*, July 25, 1934, 1; *Daily Oklahoman*, November 7, 1934, 9.

[34]*Atlantic Oil Producing Co. v. Malone*, 3 P.2d 874 (Okl. 1931); *Parson-Gibson Buick Corp. v. Fox*, 4 P.2d 38 (Okl. 1931); *Blackstock v. Airington*, 5 P.2d 381 (Okl. 1931); *Pure Oil Co. v. Price*, 6 P.2d 1048 (Okl. 1931; rehearing denied 1932); *City of Norman v. Bowers*, 7 P.2d 482 (Okl. 1932); *Scott & Co. v. Followill*, 7 P.2d 852 (Okl. 1932); *Indian Territory Illuminating Oil Co. v. Pound*, 9 P.2d 417 (Okl. 1932); *Vaughn & Rush v. Stump*, 9 P.2d 764 (Okl. 1932); *Brooks & Dahlgren, Inc. v. Dollar*, 9 P.2d 926 (Okl. 1932); *Magnolia Petroleum Co. v. Nalley*, 10 P.2d 249 (Okl. 1932); *Loffland Bros. Drilling Co. v. State Industrial Commission*, 10 P.2d 1096 (Okl. 1932); *Savery v. Graves Farm Loan Inv. Co.*, 11 P.2d 462 (Okl. 1932); *Wood and Co. v. Maxwell*, 11 P.2d 524 (Okl. 1932); *Pinkston Hardware Co. v. Hart*, 12 P.2d 681 (Okl. 1932); *Mabee Inc. v. Seaberry*, 12 P.2d 912 (Okl. 1932); *Associated Indemnity Corporation v. Holton*, 13 P.2d 130 (Okl. 1932); *Oklahoma Pipe Line Co. v. Farrell*, 15 P.2d 599 (Okl. 1932); *Century Indemnity Co. v. Strength*, 16 P.2d 242 (Okl. 1932); *Maryland Casualty Co. v. Rose*, 20 P.2d 1046 (Okl. 1933); *Taubman Supply Co. v. Nance*, 21 P.2d 20 (Okl. 1933); *Aetna Life Ins. Co. v. Hennington*, 21 P.2d 773 (Okl. 1933); *Gulf States Corp. v. Liston*, 22 P.2d 376 (Okl. 1933); *Independent Oil Well Cementing Co. v. Curtis*, 22 P.2d 1005 (Okl. 1933); *Western Oil Corp. v. Davis*, 23 P.2d 686 (Okl. 1933); *City of Duncan v. Ray*, 23 P.2d 694 (Okl. 1933); *Terminal Oil Mill Co. v. Wilson*, 25 P.2d 294 (Okl. 1933); *Home Indemnity Co. of New York v. Dollar*, 25 P.2d 337 (Okl. 1933); *Nu-Way Laundry v. Wilson*, 25 P.2d 657 (Okl. 1933); *Eason Oil Co. v. Neal*, 26 P.2d 197 (Okl. 1933); *Staas v. Rogers*, 26 P.2d 206 (Okl. 1933); *Dunning Const. Co. v. Franklin*, 26 P.2d 914 (Okl. 1933); *Deep Rock Oil Corp. v. Evans*, 28 P.2d 7 (Okl. 1933); *Southwestern Cotton Oil Co. v. State Industrial Commission*, 29 P.2d 122 (Okl. 1934); *Sterling Milk Products Co. v. Underwood*, 29 P.2d 937 (Okl. 1934); *Tippett & Bond v. Moore*, 31 P.2d 583 (Okl. 1934); *Parrott Motor Co. v. Jolls*, 31 P.2d 925 (Okl. 1934); *Southwestern Cotton Oil Co. v. Hall*, 46 P.2d 455 (Okl. 1935); *Pinkston Hardware Co. v. Hart*, 46 P.2d 501 (Okl. 1935); *Feenberg Pipe & Supply Co. v. Matthews*, 49 P.2d 76 (Okl. 1935); *Phillips Petroleum Co. v. Malcolm*, 53 P.2d 1113 (Okl. 1936); *Earl W. Baker & Co. v. Morris*, 54 P.2d 353 (Okl. 1935; rehearing denied 1936).

[35]*In re Threadgill*, 27 P.2d 601 (Okl. 1933).

[36]*Great Southwestern Life Ins. Co. v. Gibson*, 66 P.2d 500 (Okl. 1937).

[37]*Hatten v. Johnson Motor Co.*, No. 14681. Office of the Court Clerk for

Seminole County, Wewoka, Oklahoma.

[38]*Blackstock v. Airington*, 5 P.2d 381 (Okl. 1931).

[39]APM to John Mabee, *op. cit.*, note 32.

[40]Mileham family history in Murrah Papers.

[41]Interview Mrs. A.P. Murrah, Sr. Mrs. Murrah died August 4, 1994. *Sunday Oklahoman*, August 7, 1994, 30A. Murrah had the bluest of blue eyes, and they literally sparkled. Under his gaze, many a law clerk and lawyer have dissolved into blubbering insensibility.

[42]*Daily Oklahoman*, July 17, 1940, 11.

[43]APM to John McKee and Vance Winningham, August 22, 1970, Murrah Papers.

Chapter 4:

[1]APM to Josh Lee, December 30, 1936, Murrah Papers.

[2]Interview Arthur Ramsey, 1989 Archives Division, Oklahoma Historical Society, Oklahoma City, Oklahoma.

[3]Office Lease between Starrett Oklahoma Corporation and Murrah & Bohanon, July 1, 1935, Murrah Papers.

[4]Act June 16, 1906, 34 Stat. 276.

[5]*Ibid.*

[6]Surrency, "Federal District Court Judges and the History of Their Courts," 40 F.R.D. 139 at 265.

[7]William C. Kellough, "Power and Politics of the Oklahoma Federal Court," *The Chronicles of Oklahoma*, LXV (Summer 1987), 186-187.

[8]*Ibid.*, 184.

[9]*Directory of Oklahoma, 1973*, 309.

[10]See generally Edward E. Dale, *Pioneer Judge: The Life of Robert Lee Williams* (Cedar Rapids: Torch Press, 1958).

[11]Act of September 14, 1922, 42 Stat. 837.

[12]A few years later, Kennamer's older brother Charles was appointed to the federal district court bench in Alabama, thus having the unusual situation of siblings serving as federal judges at the same time. As of this writing, brothers Richard Sheppard Arnold and Morris Sheppard Arnold are not merely both federal judges but also serve on the same court as well, the eighth circuit.

[13]In 1920 the state supreme court consisted of nine justices elected for six-year terms. The terms were staggered on a two-year basis, i.e., each two years three justices were elected. However, four justices were elected in 1920, three for six-year terms and one to fill an unexpired term. The four Republicans elected in 1920 were Kennamer, C.H. Elting, George M. Nicholson and John R. Miller. Republican E.S. Bessey was also elected to the three-judge criminal court of appeals. *Directory of Oklahoma, 1973*, 334-335.

In 1959 the name of the criminal court of appeals, for obvious reasons, was changed to court of criminal appeals. *Oklahoma Session Laws 1959*, chapter 2, 107.

[14]The first Republican to serve on the state supreme court was George S. Ramsey who was appointed to fill a vacancy in 1920. He resigned after serving six months. *Directory of Oklahoma, 1973*, 149.

[15]Kellough, "Power and Politics of the Oklahoma Federal Court," 191.

[16]*Ibid.*

[17]Act of January 10, 1925, 43 Stat. 731.

[18]*Kennamer v. State*, 57 P.2d 666 (1936); *State v. Hurst*, 57 P.2d 666 (1936). See also *Harmon v. State*, 60 P.2d 404 (1936).

[19]*Tulsa Tribune*, September 27, 1944, 1. Murrah wrote Judge Kennamer, "This morning's paper brought the sad news. You have the consolation of knowing that he sleeps in a hero's grave—he paid the supreme sacrifice for the liberty he loved better than life." APM to Franklin E. Kennamer, September 27, 1944, Murrah Papers.

[20]Kellough, "Power and Politics of the Oklahoma Federal Court," 192.

[21]*Ibid.*

[22]Act of June 22, 1936, 49 Stat. 1804.

[23]*Oklahoma News*, November 5, 1936, 5.

[24]Elmer Thomas to Joseph B. Keenan, assistant to the attorney general, September 21, 1936, Elmer Thomas Papers, Box 3, Folder 90, Carl Albert Congressional Research Center, University of Oklahoma.

[25]Elmer Thomas to Mart Brown, November 30, 1936, Box 2, Folder 46, Elmer Thomas Papers.

[26]Billington, *Thomas P. Gore*, 20.

[27]*Ibid.*, 25. Gore was elected to a full term in 1909 rather than in 1908 because the 17th Amendment, providing for the popular election of senators, had not yet become law. Consequently, the election was by legislative vote, and the Oklahoma legislature did not convene until January 1909.

[28]*Directory of Oklahoma 1973*, 323.

[29]*Ibid.*, 332. See Scales and Goble, *Oklahoma Politics*, 97-101; Billington, *Thomas P. Gore*, 120-126.

[30]*Directory of Oklahoma—1973*, 354, 356.

[31]*Ibid.*

[32]*Ibid.*

[33]*Ibid.*, 334.

[34]*Ibid.*, 340.

[35]*Ibid.*, 343.

[36]*Ibid.*, 349.

[37]*Ibid.*, 359.

[38]*Ibid.*, 365.

[39]*Ibid.*

[40]*Ibid.*, 368.

[41]Scales and Goble, *Oklahoma Politics*, 196.

[42]*Ibid.*

[43]*Ibid.*, 195.

[44]Elmer Thomas to R.E. Bowling, December 8, 1936, Box 3, Folder 91, Elmer Thomas Papers. In this letter he wrote, "I would not concede to the appointment of any one to the Federal judgeship who would fail to enforce our prohibition laws so long as they remain on our statutes. Also I would not concede to the appointment of a Judge who was opposed to either the interests of agriculture or the interests of the wage earners."

[45]*Directory of Oklahoma, 1973*, 369.

[46]Scales and Goble, *Oklahoma Politics*, 194.

[47]Schlesinger, *The Politics of Upheaval* (New York: Houghton Mifflin, 1960), 558.

[48]Elmer Thomas to J. F. Kirby, April 14, 1937, Box 3, Folder 95, Elmer Thomas Papers.

[49]*Oklahoma News*, November 5, 1936, 5. As one writer commented in the *Norman Transcript* (November 9, 1936, 5): "Practical politics would require that Thomas, up for re-election two years hence, reach an amicable agreement with Lee on the appointment, in order to have Lee's support in 1938." In the *Oklahoma City Times* (December 11, 1936, 20) was the comment, "[O]bservers expect the senior senator to approve Lee's first choice in the hope of drawing support from the Lee organization in the 1938 campaign."

[50]Theoretically, Thomas was committed to A.G.C. Brier, a prominent Logan County lawyer and former member of the territorial supreme court. Thomas's commitment to Brier was made during the 1926 senate election. Elmer Thomas to Justice Fletcher Riley, May 16, 1936, Box 3, Folder 16, Elmer Thomas Papers. Thomas knew, however, that Brier's age—he was past seventy—would doom him with the justice department, but Thomas was insistent that the doom come from the department, not from him. Elmer Thomas to Justice Fletcher Riley, January 28, 1936, Box 3, Folder 16, Elmer Thomas Papers. That is precisely what happened when the Roosevelt administration announced that it would not nominate any person past 60 years of age for a judgeship (see the *Tulsa World*, December 30, 1936, page 1). The age factor also eliminated E.L. Richardson, a former district judge, state bar president, and prominent Lawton and Oklahoma City attorney. Richardson was close to Thomas and Lee and would have been an ideal compromise candidate, but the inexorable march of time removed him from the judgeship picture.

[51]*Directory of Oklahoma, 1973*, 344.

[52]*Ibid.*, 356.

[53]*Ibid.*, 368.

[54]*House Journal*, Regular Session, Twelfth Legislature, II, 2378-2412, 2721-2723, 2737-2750.

[55]*Daily Oklahoman*, May 15, 1929, 1; May 17, 1929, 1. See also, Creel, "Court In Peril: The Legislative-Judicial Struggle of 1927-1929," *The Chronicles of Oklahoma*, LII (Summer 1974), 220.

[56]Fletcher Riley to Elmer Thomas, January 23, 1935, Box 3, Folder 16, Elmer Thomas Papers. Murrah was infuriated by Riley's efforts to portray himself as an original Lee supporter. He reminded Lee that "Fletcher Riley tried to catch the bandwagon after you led the field by approximately 50,000 votes but at that time the wagon was traveling so fast that Fletcher barely got the caboose." APM to Josh Lee, December 31, 1936, Murrah Papers.

[57]*Norman Transcript*, November 9, 1936, 5. Similarly, *Harlow's Weekly* (December 26, 1936, 1) reported, "Senator-elect Lee is understood to have a commitment to Attorney A.P. Murrah, of Oklahoma City"; the *Oklahoma News* (November 7, 1936, 2) opined that "A.P. Murrah, young Oklahoma City attorney, may be the first choice of Josh Lee, senator-elect, for Oklahoma's new federal judgeship"; and the *Oklahoma City Times* (December 11, 1936, 20) reported, "An indorsement by the Oklahoma City Trades and Labor council brought speculation into the open Friday that A.P. Murrah, one of the 'Rover boys,' is Josh Lee's first choice for federal district judge." "Murrah is understood to be the first choice of Senator Josh Lee," said the *Tulsa World* of December 30, 1936, 1.

Not everyone saw it that way, however. R.M. M'Clintock, political writer for the *Daily Oklahoman* (November 27, 1936, 9), not only asserted that Murrah had little chance, but also misspelled his name, calling him Murragh.

[58]Elmer Thomas to Sam F. Wilkinson, November 30, 1936, Box 3, Folder 91, Elmer Thomas Papers.

[59]*Daily Oklahoman*, February 9, 1937, 5. Numerous articles commented on the appointment: "Senator Josh Lee was understood to be insisting on Mr. Murrah, his campaign manager last summer, in the face of mild opposition from Sen. Elmer Thomas" (*Oklahoma News*, January 8, 1937, 24); "Murrah is credited with backing Lee in the 1934 campaign and with 'shoving' the congressman into the senate race" (*Oklahoma City Times*, December 11, 1936, 20); "A.P. Murrah, Oklahoma City lawyer, and chief sponsor for Josh Lee throughout his remarkable political ascendancy" (*Harlow's Weekly*, November 14, 1936, 10); "It was Murrah who is given credit for inducing Lee to become a candidate for Congress and later for the United States Senate. It was Murrah who headed the close organization that directed the senatorial campaigns" (*ibid.*, February 13, 1937, 9); "Murrah was among the first of those who felt that the former head of the University of Oklahoma's public speaking department could win nomination and election to the United States Senate" (*Daily Oklahoman*, February 12, 1937, 24).

[60]"In fact, Murrah was known to be backing Arnold who defied criticism to stump the state for Lee in the first primary," *Oklahoma City Times*, December 11, 1936, 20.

[61]See note 1 above.

[62]"Justice Riley is here making a fight for the place but until Savage and Murrah are acted upon I doubt if Fletcher can be considered seriously." Elmer Thomas to Judge Thomas H. Doyle, January 11, 1937, Murrah Papers.

[63]APM to Josh Lee, December 31, 1936, Murrah Papers.

[64]*Daily Oklahoman*, January 8, 1937, 18.

[65]Oklahoma City Trades and Labor Council to Elmer Thomas, December 10, 1936, Box 2, Folder 53, Elmer Thomas Papers; C. C. Strode to Elmer Thomas, December 14, 1936, *ibid.*; *Oklahoma City Times*, December 11, 1936, 20.

[66]Petition signed by "chairmen of representative railway organizations" sent under cover letter of Pottawatomie County Democratic Central Committee, December 29, 1936, W.A. Miskell, secretary, Box 2, Folder 67, Elmer Thomas Papers.

[67]Veterans of Industry of America of McCurtain County to Elmer Thomas, January 16, 1937, Box 2, Folder 80, Elmer Thomas Papers. For a recent history of the Veterans of Industry of America, and its founder, Ira Finley, see Patricia E. McGinnis, *Oklahoma's Depression Radicals Ira M. Finley and the Veterans of Industry of America* (New York: Peter Lang Publishing, 1991).

[68]Brotherhood of Railroad Trainmen to Elmer Thomas, December 14, 1936, Box 2, Folder 53, Elmer Thomas Papers.

[69]Elbert L. Costner to Elmer Thomas, December 6, 1936, Box 2, Folder 52, Elmer Thomas Papers.

[70]International Brotherhood of Boiler Makers, Iron Ship Builders and Helpers of America, Lodge Number 293, January 12, 1937, Box 2, Folder 80, Elmer Thomas Papers.

[71]International Brotherhood of Bookbinders, Local 180, January 8, 1937, Box 2, Folder 78, Elmer Thomas Papers.

[72]Telegram from D.W. Banzett to Elmer Thomas, January 18, 1937, Murrah Papers.

[73]Telegram from Earl Witt for Farmers Union to Elmer Thomas, January 14, 1937, Murrah Papers.

[74]*Daily Oklahoman*, January 10, 1937, 4A. See also *ibid.*, January 8, 1937,

18, "alleged wetness."

[75]*Ibid.*, January 10, 1937, 4A.

[76]J.W. Williamson to Elmer Thomas, January 4, 1937, Box 2, Folder 70, Elmer Thomas Papers, University of Oklahoma; Reverend Alfred H. Freeman to Elmer Thomas, date illegible, Box 2, Folder 70, Elmer Thomas Papers; Elizabeth House to Elmer Thomas, January 2, 1937, Box 2, Folder 73, Elmer Thomas Papers; Mrs. E.J. Rost to Elmer Thomas, January 6, 1937, Box 2, Folder 74, Elmer Thomas Papers; Robert L. Saunders to Elmer Thomas, January 8, 1937, Box 2, Folder 77, Elmer Thomas Papers.

[77]S.D. Friedman to Elmer Thomas, January 5, 1936 (misdated), Box 2, Folder 73, Elmer Thomas Papers.

[78]A.D. Erdberg to Elmer Thomas, December 22, 1936, Box 2, Folder 60, Elmer Thomas Papers.

[79]Peter Senkcywski to Elmer Thomas, December 14, 1936, Box 2, Folder 56, Elmer Thomas Papers: "and we know that Fish will discharge his duties in a capable and efficient manner."

[80]Sebe Christian to APM, December 23, 1936, Murrah Papers.

[81]*Ibid.* Warren Kice, an attorney in Pontotoc County, obtained endorsements from the court clerk, mayor of Ada, Ada city commissioner, cashier of the First National Bank, assistant county attorney, editor of the *Ada Evening News*, various attorneys, and the county sheriff. Kice wrote Murrah, "it was a real pleasure for me to obtain these endorsements for you." Warren Kice to APM, January 8, 1937, Murrah Papers.

[82]Guy O. Merchant to Elmer Thomas, December 14, 1936, Box 2, Folder 62, Elmer Thomas Papers; H.L. Blackstock to Elmer Thomas November 24, 1936, Box 2, Folder 46, Elmer Thomas Papers.

[83]E.E. Duncan, executive secretary of Allied Merchants of Oklahoma, to Elmer Thomas, December 5, 1936, Box 2, Folder 52, Elmer Thomas Papers.

[84]Clayton B. Pierce to Elmer Thomas, November 27, 1936, Box 2, Folder 46, Elmer Thomas Papers.

[85]Reginald Williams to Elmer Thomas, December 1, 1936, Box 2, Folder 47, Elmer Thomas Papers; Orval Grim to Elmer Thomas, December 5, 1936, Box 2, Folder 50, Elmer Thomas Papers; D.L. Cook, Jr., to Elmer Thomas, December 5, 1936, Box 2, Folder 50, Elmer Thomas Papers.

[86]George C. Crump to Elmer Thomas, November 27, 1936, Box 2, Folder 46, Elmer Thomas Papers; Claude S. Chambers to Elmer Thomas, November 28, 1936, Box 2, Folder 47, Elmer Thomas Papers.

[87]Thomas H. Doyle to Elmer Thomas, December 10, 1936, Box 2, Folder 46, Elmer Thomas Papers; George H. Giddings, Jr., to Elmer Thomas, November 23, 1936, Box 2, Folder 46, Elmer Thomas Papers.

[88]Clyde Faught to Elmer Thomas, December 10, 1936, Box 2, Folder 53, Elmer Thomas Papers.

[89]Charles Hiner to Elmer Thomas, November 30, 1936, Box 2, Folder 47, Elmer Thomas Papers.

[90]Georgia E. Wells to Elmer Thomas, December 5, 1936, Box 2, Folder 49, Elmer Thomas Papers.

[91]Weldon W. Hall to Elmer Thomas, December 15, 1936, Box 2, Folder 55,

Elmer Thomas Papers. Perhaps the writer was thinking of Herndon's comment that Lincoln's ambition "was a little engine that knew no rest." Quoted in Benjamin P. Thomas, *Abraham Lincoln A Biography* (New York: Alfred A. Knopf, 1980), 161.

[92]E.L. Harvey to Elmer Thomas, December 21, 1936, Box 2, Folder 60, Elmer Thomas Papers; Ben F. Johnson to Elmer Thomas, December 10, 1936, Box 2, Folder 52, Elmer Thomas Papers; S.P. Smith to Elmer Thomas, December 4, 1936, Box 2, Folder 50, Elmer Thomas Papers.

[93]Ruth Hendricks to Elmer Thomas, December 5, 1936, Box 2, Folder 50, Elmer Thomas Papers.

[94]W.S. "Sonny" Rodgers to Elmer Thomas, December 19. 1936, Box 2, Folder 58, Elmer Thomas Papers.

[95]James O. Hood to Elmer Thomas, undated, Box 2, Folder 46, Elmer Thomas Papers.

[96]Elmer Thomas to J.F. Kirby, April 14, 1937, Box 3, Folder 95, Elmer Thomas Papers.

[97]*Oklahoma State Bar Journal*, VII (January 1937), 192.

[98]*Harlow's Weekly*, January 2, 1937, 8.

[99]APM to Josh Lee, December 31, 1936, Murrah Papers. The bar did not speak for all lawyers in the state. One attorney was "quite chagrined about the resolution. Whoever heard of the appointment of a federal judge not being a political appointment? It is considered so in regard to the United States Supreme Court and every other branch of the judicial department. If I were you, I would, in my own mind at least, tell the Bar Association to go to hell, and use my own judgment in recommending a man for this position." Dan Nelson to Josh Lee, January 12, 1936 (*sic*), Murrah Papers.

[100]Elmer Thomas to J.F. Kirby, April 14, 1937, Box 3, Folder 95, Elmer Thomas Papers.

[101]Elmer Thomas to Royce Savage, December 29, 1936, Box 3, Folder 31, Elmer Thomas Papers.

[102]Elmer Thomas to Judge Thomas H. Doyle, January 11, 1937, Murrah Papers.

[103]H.G. McKeever to Attorney General Homer S. Cummings, December 1, 1936, Box 2, Folder 75, Elmer Thomas Papers; H.G. McKeever to Attorney General Homer S. Cummings, December 11, 1936, Box 2, Folder 75, Elmer Thomas Papers.

[104]*Tulsa World*, February 9, 1937, 1.

[105]Memorandum, Daniel E. McGrath to Matthew McGuire, January 11, 1937 and attachment, Subject Files Relating to Judicial Districts—General—Oklahoma, Record Group 60, National Archives, Washington, D.C.

[106]*Ibid.*

[107]*Ibid.*

[108]*Ibid.* Interestingly, some of the opposition letters and telegrams which Thomas received were cast specifically in terms of favoring Savage over Murrah. See Ed B. Moffett to Elmer Thomas, January 6, 1937, Box 3, Folder 32, Elmer Thomas Papers; E.W. Foley to Elmer Thomas, January 6, 1937, Box 3, Folder 32, Elmer Thomas Papers; C.J. Howard to Elmer Thomas, January 6, 1937, Box 3, Folder 32, Elmer Thomas Papers.

[109]*Daily Oklahoman*, January 5, 1937, 2A.

[110]*Ibid.*

[111]"From Washington comes an interesting echo of the meeting between

President Roosevelt and Judge Murrah. Senator Josh Lee had taken his close friend and endorsee to meet the President. After the introduction the President is said to have inquired of Senator Lee: 'He is young enough, but does he have the slant of the average man of the field, factory and street as well as the man in the sky-scraper?' Senator Lee's reply is not recorded, but it is assumed that he outlined the life story of A.P. Murrah—the boy who demanded a chance to go to school; who slept on the floor of his first law office; who never forgot the man who gave him his first job and the good woman who took the place of a mother during the years he mastered common and high school courses." *Harlow's Weekly*, March 13, 1937, 7.

[112]*Tulsa World*, February 4, 1937, 1. As Murrah remembered it, Keenan was supportive of his appointment: "I have known him for many years—in fact he was the Assistant to the Attorney General when I was appointed to the federal bench at the age of thirty-two. He had confidence in me when almost no one else did, and I shall never forget it." APM to Frederick R. Weiner, November 3, 1948, Murrah Papers.

[113]*Oklahoma News*, February 6, 1937, 5. In early January of 1937, Thomas wired Judge Thomas H. Doyle asking if in Doyle's opinion Murrah was "qualified by experience and age to render satisfactory services as federal judge." Elmer Thomas to Judge Thomas H. Doyle, January 4, 1937, Murrah Papers. Doyle's response was a ringing endorsement: "Considering his character as a man, his unquestionable integrity, his ability as a lawyer, and his experience as a practicing attorney before the State and Federal Courts, he is well qualified to fill the duties of the position. Considering his intellectual endowments, and his professional attainments, temperament, disposition and sound judgment he has all the high qualifications that go to make a good judge." Judge Thomas H. Doyle to Elmer Thomas, January 4, 1937, Murrah Papers.

Doyle was one of Oklahoma's leading legal figures, and his opinion likely carried great weight with Thomas. Appointed to the first criminal court of appeals on its creation in 1908, Doyle was elected for six-year terms in 1910, 1916, and 1922. Defeated in the 1928 Hoover landslide, he served on the state industrial commission until he regained his seat on the criminal court of appeals in 1934. Given his extensive workmen's compensation practice, Murrah likely appeared before Doyle many times.

[114]*Congressional Record*, LXXXI, Part 1, 75th Congress, 1st Session, 967. Although Thomas did not meet with justice department officials until February 6, the attorney general's letter to the president recommending Murrah is dated February 5, 1937. Homer Cummings to Franklin Roosevelt, February 5, 1937, Collection OF 208aa, Box 10, Oklahoma 1933-1945, Franklin D. Roosevelt Library, Hyde Park, New York. In the letter, Cummings states that Thomas has endorsed Murrah.

[115]C.R. Reeves to Senator W.A. Borah, February 12, 1937, Box 2, Folder 75, Elmer Thomas Papers; Reeves to Franklin D. Roosevelt, February 13, 1937, Collection 208aa, Box 10, Oklahoma 1933-1945, Franklin D. Roosevelt Library, Hyde Park, New York; *Daily Oklahoman*, February 20, 1937, 1; Elmer Thomas to APM, February 23, 1937, Murrah Papers; Elmer Thomas to APM, February 26, 1937, Murrah Papers.

[116]*Congressional Record*, LXXXI, Part 2, 75th Congress, 1st Session, 1613.

[117]*Oklahoma News*, November 7, 1936, 2.

[118]Elmer Thomas to J.F. Kirby, April 14, 1937, Box 3, Folder 95, Elmer Thomas Papers.

[119]Thomas seems to have been sincerely concerned about Murrah's and Savage's ages. "These applicants are youngsters, not over thirty-three years of age, so I am advised. They are fine young men, but lack experience and I am fearful that the business men of the State would not be satisfied with the selection of a lawyer so young and inexperienced." Elmer Thomas to Sam F. Wilkinson, November 30, 1936, Box 3, Folder 91, Elmer Thomas Papers.

However, what one person perceives as weakness, another may perceive as strength. The chronology is suggestive. The justice department approved Murrah February 3, 1937. On Friday, February 5, Roosevelt announced his "court reform" or "court-packing" proposal for the appointment of an additional federal judge for each federal judge who had served at least ten years and who did not retire within six months of reaching 70 years of age. The president could not appoint more than six additional supreme court justices, nor more than 44 inferior federal court judges. On Monday, February 8th, without notice to Thomas or Lee, Roosevelt sent 32-year-old A.P. Murrah's name to the senate for confirmation as a federal judge. Murrah was the first federal judge nominated by Roosevelt after the February 5th bombshell.

Coincidence? Or did Murrah's youth appeal to Roosevelt in his fight against the nine old men? Alsop and Catledge, *The 168 Days* (New York: Doubleday and Doran, 1937), remains the classic work on the court-packing plan. See also Ariens, "A Thrice-Told Tale, or Felix The Cat,"107 *Harvard Law Review* 620 (January 1994).

Time (March 22, 1937, 4), *Business Week* (February 20, 1937, 16), and *New York Times* (March 13, 1937, 11) all reported Murrah's appointment. *Time, ibid.*, noted that "he promised solemnly to retire at 70."

[120]Dale, *Pioneer Judge*, 331.

[121]Elmer Thomas to Judge Thomas H. Doyle, January 11, 1937, Murrah Papers.

[122]Robert Lee Williams to Elmer Thomas, January 20, 1937, Box 3, Folder 83, Elmer Thomas Papers.

[123]*Ibid.*

[124]*Daily Oklahoman*, February 9, 1937, 5.

Chapter 5:

[1]APM to Elmer Thomas, February 25, 1937, Murrah Papers.

[2]*Tulsa World*, March 5, 1937, 1.

[3]*Tulsa Tribune*, March 5, 1937, 6.

[4]*Tulsa World*, March 5, 1937, 1.

[5]*Daily Oklahoman*, March 13, 1937, 1.

[6]*Ibid.*

[7]*Ibid.*

[8]*Ibid.*

[9]*Daily Oklahoman*, December 22, 1937, 1.

[10]*Oklahoma City Times*, June 4, 1940, 18.

[11]*Daily Oklahoman*, March 12, 1937, 11. Murrah had high opinions of Jewish jurists in general. He wrote Elmer Thomas urging a federal judicial appointment for Saul Yager, a lawyer and former district judge from Tulsa. Murrah observed that "some of our greatest Jurists of the past and today are

Jews, as for example Judge Brandeis and Judge Cardozo and many other Jews now occupying places on the Circuit Court of Appeals." APM to Elmer Thomas, March 31, 1937, Murrah Papers.

[12]APM to Josh Lee, July 22, 1937, Murrah Papers.

[13]APM to Marie Thomas, department of justice, March 9, 1937, Murrah Papers.

[14]The Court of International Trade, formerly the Customs Court, exercises trial jurisdiction, but it has a specialized subject matter cognizance. See generally, Charles Alan Wright, et.al., *Federal Practice and Procedure* (St. Paul: West Publishing, 1969), XVII, Section 4103. Jed Johnson, Sr., a member of congress from Oklahoma 1927-1947, served as a judge of the predecessor Customs Court after leaving congress.

[15]APM to Josh Lee, March 18, 1937, Murrah Papers.

[16]*Ryan-Richards, Inc. v. Whitesides*, 96 F.2d 826 (10th Cir. 1938); *Houser v. Kurn*, 100 F.2d 488 (10th Cir. 1938).

[17]*Hamrick v. Bryan*, No. 1203, 21 F. Supp. 392 (N.D. Okl. 1937); 106 F.2d 245 (10th Cir. 1939).

[18]*Nail v. American Nat. Bank of Bristow*, No. 1100, 21 F. Supp. 385; 22 F.Supp. 977 (N.D. Okl. 1938); 103 F.2d 37 (10th Cir. 1939); *Wells v. Helms*, 105 F.2d 402 (10th Cir. 1939).

[19]*Burton v. Equitable Life Assur. Society*, No. 6251, 21 F.Supp. 62 (W.D. Okl. 1937).

[20]*Petroleum Royalties v. Hartford Accident & Indemnity Co.*, 106 F.2d 440 (10th Cir. 1939); *Monohan v. New York Life Ins. Co.*, Nos. 6386, 6300, 1898, 26 F.Supp. 859 (W.D. Okl. 1939); 108 F.2d 841 (10th Cir. 1939); *Southwestern Brewing Corporation v. United States Fidelity & Guaranty Co.*, 115 F.2d 228 (10th Cir. 1940).

[21]*Phillips Petroleum Co. v. Threlkeld*, 123 F.2d 434 (10th Cir. 1941).

[22]*Simon v. H.F. Wilcox Oil & Gas Co.*, 123 F.2d 25 (10th Cir. 1941); *New York Casualty Co. v. Sinclair Refining Co.*, 108 F.2d 65 (10th Cir. 1939).

[23]*Dunn v. Micco*, 106 F.2d 356 (10th Cir. 1939).

[24]*Mason Corporation v. Halliburton*, No. 4542, 30 F.Supp. 405 (E.D. Okl. 1939); 118 F.2d 729 (10th Cir. 1941); Haynes Stellite Co. v. Osage Metal Co., Inc., 110 F.2d 11 (10th Cir. 1939).

[25]Public Law 718, 52 Stat. 1060.

[26]*Directory of Oklahoma, 1973*, 423.

[27]See Creel, "Socialists in the House: The Oklahoma Experience," Part Two, *op. cit.*

[28]307 U.S. at 275; 59 S.Ct. at 876; 83 L.Ed. at 1287.

[29]*Ibid.*, at 276, 876, 1288.

[30]*Ibid.*, 277, 877.

[31]24 F.Supp. at 623.

[32]*Ibid.*, 624.

[33]*Ibid.*, 631.

[34]*Ibid.*, 636.

[35]Act of March 21, 1937, 50 Stat. 738, codified as 28 U.S.C. § 1341.

[36]21 F.Supp. at 998.

[37]*Ibid.*, 999.

[38]21 F.Supp. at 395.

[39]*Ibid.*

[40]*Ibid.*

[41]*Ibid.*, 399.
[42]APM to W.B. Henderson, June 12, 1973, Murrah Papers.
[43]*Oklahoma State Bar Journal*, VIII, No. 10 (1938), 213.
[44]*Ibid.*
[45]*Ibid.*
[46]*Muskogee Daily Phoenix*, June 30, 1937, 2.
[47]*Ibid.*
[48]*Daily Oklahoman*, March 23, 1937, 1.
[49]*Shawnee Morning News*, January 26, 1938, 1.
[50]"The jury convicted King on one count, and acquitted him on two others. 'Well, Chester, it looks as if we lost the case,' said Attorney Murrah. 'Yes sir,' answered the defendant. 'But we put up a good fight.' 'Yes, sir.' 'You may go now,' said Judge Murrah. The defendant brightened. 'That is, you may go with the sheriff,' added the judge. The defendant did, sadly." *Ibid.*
[51]*Daily Oklahoman*, February 5, 1938, 4. Shortly after "representing" this defendant, Murrah was "in Muskogee, and this one colored boy stood before me and I looked down at his record and saw that it was just about a foot long, and I asked him if he had a lawyer and he said, 'No, no, sir.' He didn't have a lawyer and I knew at a glance that he needed a lawyer and I said 'Well.' I went into great detail to explain his constitutional rights because I thought it was my duty to do so. Of course, he probably knew more about it than I did but I said, 'Now you can represent yourself if you don't have a lawyer and don't want to hire one, but the Court will be glad to appoint one or you can represent yourself or the Court will represent you,' but I said, 'Now, I want to tell you in case you choose the Court I think it is only fair for me to tell you that the Court represented a defendant just the other day over in Oklahoma City charged with the same offense and he got convicted and got two years in the penitentiary,' whereupon this colored boy he looked up to me and he shifted from one side to the other with a big smile on his face and he said 'Well, Your Honor, please, if its all the same with you in a case like that I believe I would like to have a real lawyer.'" "Justice Now Or Never," 10 *Arkansas Law Review* 430 (Summer 1956).
[52]See chapter four.
[53]*Muskogee Times-Democrat*, April 19, 1937, 1.
[54]*Ibid.*
[55]*Muskogee Daily Phoenix*, April 24, 1937, 1.
[56]*Ibid.*
[57]*Clinton Daily News*, February 4, 1938, 1.
[58]*Oklahoma State Bar Journal*, VIII, No. 10 (1938), 211.
[59]*Daily Oklahoman*, October 26, 1937, 2.
[60]*Ibid.*, October 27, 1937, 1.
[61]Dale Stamphill to APM, October 21, 1943, Murrah Papers.
[62]Dale Stamphill to APM, September 1, 1953, Murrah Papers.
[63]APM to W.L. Baker, January 28, 1974, Murrah Papers.
[64]*Oklahoma News*, October 17, 1938, 1.
[65]*Ibid.*
[66]*Daily Oklahoman*, February 10, 1940, 1.
[67]*Ibid.*
[68]*Ibid.*
[69]*Muskogee Times-Democrat*, June 29, 1937, 2.
[70]*Ibid.*

[71]*Ibid.*

[72]W.H. Stephenson to Josh Lee, July 16, 1937, Murrah Papers.

[73]*Ibid.*

[74]Josh Lee to W.H. Stephenson, July 22, 1937, Murrah Papers.

[75]Josh Lee to APM, July 22, 1937, Murrah Papers.

[76]APM to Josh Lee, July 30, 1937, Murrah Papers.

[77]APM to George McElroy (Lee's secretary), May 8, 1937, Murrah Papers.

[78]APM to Josh Lee, January 18, 1940, Murrah Papers; APM to Elmer Thomas, undated, Murrah Papers.

[79]APM to Elmer Thomas, undated, Murrah Papers.

[80]APM to Elmer Thomas, March 17, 1940, Murrah Papers. In this letter, Murrah states that he received Lee's approval of his elevation to the circuit court of appeals on March 4th.

[81]*Ibid.*

[82]APM to Josh Lee, March 18, 1940, Murrah Papers.

[83]APM to Josh Lee, March 28, 1940, Murrah Papers.

[84]APM to Josh Lee, April 4, 1940 (this letter is dated March 4, 1940, but the context makes clear that the date should be April 4, 1940), Murrah Papers.

[85]*Tulsa Tribune*, May 15, 1940, 2; *Daily Oklahoman*, May 18, 1940, 4; *Denver Post*, May 26, 1940, 9. More than 50 years later, a reporter for the *Tulsa Tribune* remembered "there was talk that Lee wanted that appointment for himself" (Joe Howell writing in the *Tulsa Tribune*, February 18, 1991, 3A).

[86]APM to Josh Lee, April 4, 1940 (see note 84 supra), Murrah Papers.

[87]APM to Elmer Thomas, May 11, 1940, Murrah Papers.

[88]See also the *Daily Oklahoman*, May 18, 1940, 4; and *Oklahoma City Times*, May 28, 1940, 11.

[89]APM to Lloyd Benefield, May 27, 1940, Murrah Papers.

[90]*Congressional Record*, LXXXVI, Part 9, 76th Congress, 3rd Session, 9859.

[91]*Ibid.*, part 10, 11227.

[92]APM to Elmer Thomas, May 11, 1940, Murrah Papers.

[93]*Tulsa Tribune*, May 28, 1940, 2.

[94]See note 80. There were Colorado and Wyoming names mentioned to succeed Judge Lewis. In Colorado, James Marsh, Democratic national committeeman, and two justices of the state supreme court, William Lee Knous and Otto Bock, were named as contenders (*Denver Post*, May 22, 1940, 7). In Wyoming, Robert R. Rose, the law partner of Democratic Senator Harry Schwartz, was said to be under consideration (*Denver Post*, May 26, 1940, 9). However, it does not appear there was any serious possibility the appointment would go any place but to Oklahoma.

[95]Judge Bratton was appointed to the circuit court of appeals while serving as United States Senator from New Mexico. He was a strong supporter of the New Deal in the senate.

[96]*Tulsa Tribune*, May 16, 1940, 1; *Daily Oklahoman*, May 18, 1940, 4.

[97]*Congressional Record*, LXXXVI, Part 11, 76th Congress, 3rd Session, 12554 (September 24, 1940).

[98]*Ibid.*, 12778 (September 27, 1940).

[99]As discussed in chapter four, Broaddus was Thomas's candidate to succeed Judge Williams in the eastern district in 1937, but he did not receive the appointment "because of the opposition of my colleague [Lee]" (Elmer

Thomas to Earle Witt, June 17, 1937, Box 3, Folder 96, Elmer Thomas Papers). Thomas was no less supportive of Broaddus in 1940, but the political environment that year was appreciably different from 1937. Thomas had survived the toughest test of his political career, winning reelection in 1938, and was in only the second year of a six-year term. Consequently, he no longer needed to give Lee the deference in judicial appointments which he had extended in 1937. The result was a division of judicial spoils. Lee would make the appointments to the circuit court of appeals and the northern district, and Thomas would make the appointments to the roving position vacated by Murrah, and the newly created western district position. "It looked like a neat package. Lee would get Savage and Murrah; Thomas would get Chandler and Broaddus" (Howell, *op. cit.*; see also *Tulsa Tribune*, May 4, 1961, 31, "Savage and Murrah were Lee appointees. Broaddus and Chandler were named by Thomas."

At least after Murrah's appointment in 1937, Thomas had committed himself "rather positively in favor of Fletcher Riley for the next vacancy on the Circuit Court" (Elmer Thomas to O.J. Logan, April 9, 1937, Box 3, Folder 94, Elmer Thomas Papers). Thomas also thought that Lee regarded Riley "as perhaps the leading jurist of our state"—*ibid.* For whatever reason, Riley does not appear to have played any part in the 1940 judicial chess moves.

Chapter 6:

[1]Act of March 3, 1891, 26 Stat. 826.

[2]Wright, *Federal Practice and Procedure*, XIII, § 3506, p. 21.

[3]Act of June 16, 1906, 34 Stat. 275.

[4]Act of February 28, 1929, 45 Stat. 347. The present tenth circuit is the second tenth circuit in the history of the federal judiciary. The Act of March 3, 1863, 12 Stat. 794, created a circuit of California, Nevada and Oregon, and designated it the Tenth Circuit. This tenth circuit was abolished by the Act of July 23, 1866, 14 Stat. 209. See Surrency, "Federal District Court Judges and the History of Their Courts, 40 F.R.D. 139 at 146.

[5]Act of December 13, 1926, 44 Stat. 919.

[6]Act of July 31, 1946, 60 Stat. 716.

[7]Harold Chase, Samuel Krislov, Keith Boyum and Jerry Clark, *Biographical Dictionary of the Federal Judiciary* (Gale Research Company, 1976), 220; Memorial Service for The Honorable Orie L. Phillips, 516 F.2d, page 5 (1975). See also note 26, chapter two.

[8]Until 1948 the circuit judge of a given circuit who was senior in commission was known, appropriately, as the senior circuit judge for that circuit. In 1948 the senior circuit judge became known as the chief judge of the circuit. Senior circuit judge still has a meaning in federal judicial terminology, however. It refers to a circuit judge who has retired from active service, but who retains his commission and sits as his services are needed.

[9]Chase, Krislov, Boyum and Clark, op. cit., page 29; Proceedings of the Annual Judicial Conference Tenth Circuit In Memoriam Of The Honorable Sam G. Bratton, 36 F.R.D., 5 (1964). See note 26, chapter two. There are advantages to being a United States Senator. Bratton was nominated and confirmed the same day. *Congressional Record*, LXXVII, Part 5, 73rd Congress, 1st Session, 4760.

[10]Chase, Krislov, Boyum and Clark, *op. cit.*, 135; In Memory of The

Honorable Walter A. Huxman, 474 F.2d, 5 (1973). See note 26, chapter two.

[11]*Frankfort Distilleries, Inc. v. The United States*, 144 F.2d 824 (10th Cir. 1944). The issue was the sufficiency of certain indictments in a number of separate cases to charge violations of the Sherman Antitrust Act. The court held the indictments sufficient in some of the cases and insufficient in others. Judge Bratton wrote for the court, and Murrah concurred in his opinion. Judge Phillips concurred in the cases setting aside the charges, and dissented in the cases sustaining them.

The supreme court granted certiorari in the cases setting aside the indictments and reversed, *United States v. Frankfort Distilleries*, 324 U.S. 293, 65 S.Ct. 661, 89 L.Ed. 951 (1945). It denied certiorari in the cases upholding the charges.

[12]Although the seat of the court was in Denver, the judges maintained their residences and chambers in their home states. Thus Judge Bratton continued to live in Albuquerque, Judge Huxman in Topeka, and Murrah in Oklahoma City.

[13]Judge William J. Holloway, Jr., to Von Russell Creel, March 22, 1993; Judge Howard C. Bratton to Von Russell Creel, March 30, 1993; Judge Howard Bratton, Senior United States District Judge for the District of New Mexico, is the son of Judge Sam Bratton.

[14]Under certain conditions, a district judge can sit with the court of appeals, a court of appeals judge can sit on the district court, and a supreme court justice can sit on the court of appeals, or the district court. This is referred to as sitting by designation. As a district judge, Murrah wrote three opinions for the circuit while sitting by designation: *Oklahoma Natural Gas Corp. v. Municipal Gas Co.*, 113 F.2d 308 (10th Cir. 1940); *Citizens State Bank of Barstow, Texas v. Vidal*, 114 F.2d 380 (10th Cir. 1940); and *A.R. Jones Oil & O. Co. v. Commissioner of Internal Revenue*, 114 F.2d 642 (10th Cir. 1940).

It may be that Murrah found the transition from the trial bench to the appellate court difficult to make. Less than six months after his appointment to the circuit court, he wrote:

> Since my appointment to the Circuit Court of Appeals, nothing worth writing about ever happens here. I am locked up in my library about seven hours a day trying to learn to draft an opinion in the Holmes style.
>
> I have failed to attain the rhetorical attributes of a Holmes or a Hughes, but I manage to tell them what I think in words containing not more than two syllables.
>
> I do not enjoy my work on the Circuit Court as much as I did my work on the district bench but everyone said I should not refuse the appointment and I did not.(APM to Joe Dynan, February 11, 1941, Murrah Papers).

Murrah thought regular sittings on the trial bench were beneficial to an appellate judge. Until he became chief judge, he sat in the district court at least thirty days a year. APM to Judge James L. Oakes, October 6, 1972, Murrah Papers.

[15]Wright, *Federal Practice and Procedure*, XVI, section 3940, p. 301.

[16]*Ibid.*

[17]Murrah authored opinions enforcing board orders in *Magnolia Petro-*

leum Co. v. N.L.R.B., 115 F.2d 1007 (10th Cir. 1940); *N.L.R.B. v. Keystone Freight Lines*, 126 F.2d 414 (10th Cir. 1941); *N.L.R.B. v. Continental Oil Co.*, 159 F.2d 326 (10th Cir. 1947); *N.L.R.B. v. Fairmont Creamery Co.*, 169 F.2d 169 (10th Cir. 1948). His opinions denied enforcement in *Boeing Airplane Co. v. N.L.R.B.*, 140 F.2d 423 (10th Cir. 1944); and *N.L.R.B. v. Enid Co-Op. Creamery Ass'n*, 169 F.2d 986 (10th Cir. 1948).

[18]The Emergency Court of Appeals continued in existence for many years after World War II. The final session of the court is reported at 299 F.2d, 1. See note 26, chapter two.

[19]In certain instances, congress has provided that cases commenced in a state court may be removed to the appropriate federal court. See, generally, 28 U.S.C. § 1441 et seq.

[20]Murrah dissented in only four other cases during this time. He parted company with his brethren when they held that the Better Business Bureau was exempt from a tax levied by the Social Security Act as an organization operated exclusively for educational purposes, *Jones v. Better Business Bureau*, 123 F.2d 767 (10th Cir. 1941); that certain bonds were not tax deductible as bad debts in the year the taxpayer claimed, *Green v. Commissioner Of Internal Revenue*, 133 F.2d 76 (10th Cir. 1943) ("In the determination of when value becomes extinct, and hence the debt worthless, courts should not substitute their judgment for the judgment of the investors"—*ibid.*, 78; that Oklahoma could not seize and confiscate a shipment of liquor beginning outside Oklahoma and destined for the Fort Sill Military Reservation, *Johnson v. Yellow Cab Transit Co.*, 137 F.2d 274 (10th Cr. 1943), affirmed 321 U.S. 383, 64 S.Ct. 622, 88 L.Ed. 814 (1944); and that one insurance policy was in effect, and another was not, *Equity Mut. Ins. Co. v. General Casualty Co. of America*, 139 F.2d 723 (10th Cir. 1943).

[21]*Rogers v. United States*, 129 F.2d 843 (10th Cir. 1942); *Scott v. United States*, 145 F.2d 405 (10th Cir. 1944); *Thomas v. United States*, 154 F.2d 365 (10th Cir. 1946); *Young v. United States*, 168 F.2d 242 (10th Cir. 1948); *Briggs v. United States*, 176 F.2d 317 (10th Cir. 1949).

[22]*Haigler v. United States*, 172 F.2d 986 (10th Cir. 1949).

[23]*Pandolfo v. United States*, 128 F.2d 917 (10th Cir. 1942); *Hines v. United States*, 131 F.2d 971 (10th Cir. 1942); *Hawley v. United States*, 133 F.2d 966 (10th Cir. 1943); *Perry v. United States*, 136 F.2d 109 (10th Cir. 1943); *Estep v. United States*, 140 F.2d 40 (10th Cir. 1943).

[24]*Long v. United States*, 160 F.2d 706 (10th Cir. 1947).

[25]*Broadbent v. United States*, 149 F.2d 580 (10th Cir. 1945).

[26]*Tooisgah v. United States*, 137 F.2d 713 (10th Cir. 1943).

[27]*Smith v. United States*, 145 F.2d 643 (10th Cir. 1944).

[28]*Waley v. Johnson*, 316 U.S. 101, 62 S.Ct. 964, 86 L.Ed. 1302 (1942). See also Wright, et.al., *Federal Practice and Procedure,* XVII, sections 4261-4268.

[29]See note 14, *supra*.

[30]When a faculty member at the University of Denver School of law found fault with Avrick, the court "gave him an opportunity to criticize the opinion last summer in conference." APM to Judge Claude McColloch, April 12, 1948, Murrah Papers. "We believe in summary judgments, but we also believe that the practice can be abused. It is important to expedite the disposition of business, but it is more important to secure everyone his full day in court"—*ibid.*

[31]See note 14, *supra.*

[32]Judge Walter Mansfield of the second circuit observed that this language of Murrah "has been repeatedly quoted with approval by the Supreme Court." *McRedmond v. Wilson*, 533 F.2d 757 (2nd Cir. 1976). See also *McNeese v. Board of Education*, 373 U.S. 668, 83 S.Ct. 1433, 10 L.Ed.2d 622 (1963); and *Zwickler v. Koota*, 389 U.S. 241, 88 S.Ct. 391, 19 L.Ed.2d 444 (1967).

[33]One authority refers to "abstention doctrines," rather than "the abstention doctrine," because he has identified at least four different situations in which abstention may be appropriate. Wright. et.al., *Federal Practice Procedure*, XVII, sections 4241-4248.

[34]*W.S. Ranch Co. v. Kaiser Steel Corp.*, 388 F.2d 257 (10th Cir. 1967), was a diversity action in which the primary issue was whether New Mexico law permitted a private entity to condemn private land to secure water for a private business. Abstention was suggested, but a Murrah opinion thought the suggestion unpersuasive. On certiorari, the supreme court held that the importance of water to an arid state such as New Mexico and the novelty of the question warranted the federal court in staying its hand pending resolution of a state proceeding. *Kaiser Steel Corp. v. W.S. Ranch Co.*, 391 U.S. 593, 88 S.Ct. 1753, 20 L.Ed. 835 (1968).

[35]Madison: University of Wisconsin Press (1985).

[36]Alfred Naifeh to Elmer Thomas, January 2, 1937, Box 2, Folder 69, Elmer Thomas Papers.

[37]APM to Robert Naifeh, July 15, 1974, Murrah Papers. After having many law clerks, Murrah concluded that the "best law clerks are those who have a good liberal arts education. It is the men of letters who have distinguished themselves in the law." APM to Judge Irving R. Kaufman, January 15, 1973, Murrah Papers.

[38]APM to William O. Douglas, May 4, 1942, Murrah Papers; APM to William O. Douglas, May 28, 1942, Murrah Papers; APM to Lieutenant E.L. Cherry, May 28, 1942, Murrah Papers; APM to Joe Milam June 27, 1942, Murrah Papers; APM to William O. Douglas, October 15, 1942, Murrah Papers.

[39]APM to William O. Douglas, March 6, 1941, Murrah Papers; William O. Douglas to APM March 13, 1941, Murrah Papers.

[40]*Ibid.*

[41]William O. Douglas to APM, March 13, 1941, Murrah Papers.

[42]APM to William O. Douglas, October 18, 1941, Murrah Papers.

[43]William O. Douglas to APM, May 19, 1942, Murrah Papers.

[44]APM to William O. Douglas, June 2, 1943, Murrah Papers.

[45]APM to William O. Douglas, January 3, 1944, Murrah Papers; APM to William O. Douglas, July 2, 1942, Murrah Papers.

[46]William O. Douglas to APM, June 15, 1953, Murrah Papers.

[47]William O. Douglas to APM, April 20, 1950, Murrah Papers.

[48]APM to William O. Douglas, October 15, 1942, Murrah Papers. James Allred was governor of Texas from 1935-1939, and Murrah met him during that time. Shortly after leaving the governor's office, Allred was appointed United States District Judge for the Southern District of Texas, but his tenure was brief; he resigned to make an unsuccessful race for the United States Senate in 1942. Murrah hoped that Allred would be appointed to the fifth

circuit, but Allred could not overcome the opposition of Senator W. Lee "Pappy" O'Daniel whom he had opposed in the 1942 race. APM to William O. Douglas, *ibid.*, Murrah Papers; James Allred to APM, May 10, 1943, Murrah Papers; APM to James Allred, May 13, 1943, Murrah Papers.

Allred was one of Lyndon Johnson's lawyers during the famous 1948 senate battle with Coke Stevenson. In 1949, his client now in the senate, Allred was named again to the southern district bench where he served until his death in 1959.

Interestingly, Murrah was also a good friend of Dan Moody, the governor of Texas from 1927-1931. Moody was a strong supporter of Stevenson in the 1948 senate race and was one of his lawyers in the subsequent legal battles. See Robert A. Caro, *The Years of Lyndon Johnson: Means of Assent* (New York: Alfred A. Knopf, 1990). Perhaps because of his friendship with Allred, Murrah hoped that Johnson would win the 1941 special senate race in Texas which he lost to Pappy O'Daniel. APM to Mack Taylor, July 17, 1941, Murrah Papers.

49 APM to William O. Douglas, September 27, 1951, Murrah Papers; Wilbur La Roe to William O. Douglas, October 10, 1951, Murrah Papers; William O. Douglas to APM, October 11, 1951, Murrah Papers.

50 APM, to William O. Douglas, January 27, 1944, Murrah Papers.

51 *Ibid.*

52 *Ibid.*

53 APM to Paul Murrah, September 9, 1960, Murrah Papers. Murrah was close to Justice Tom C. Clark as well. Clark and Murrah shared an abiding interest in judicial administration, and they worked together on various projects over the years to improve the administration of justice.

Hugo Black was another supreme court justice for whom Murrah had the greatest respect. Learning that Black had received the Thomas Jefferson Award, Murrah wrote, "I thank God that our great President left behind men of courage and learning like you. While they yet live, the torch of liberty and justice will never go out." APM to Justice Hugo Black, April 17, 1945, Murrah Papers. On Black's death, he commented that Black "not only survived, he prevailed. And the law is better for it." APM to Daniel J. Meador, December 23, 1971, Murrah papers.

In a newspaper story, Murrah praised Black as one who "did more to weld us together as a union than anyone since (John) Marshall" (*Daily Oklahoman*, September 26, 1971, 24). He observed that some of Black's major opinions "went contrary to his own convictions because he believed the Constitution required it." Murrah called Black and John Marshall Harlan "giants in the law"—*ibid.*

Naturally, Murrah followed with great interest appointments to the high court. When Judge Clement Haynsworth was rejected by the senate, he wrote,

> Dear Clement:
>
> It was a damn shame but please don't let it deter you from your course of duty. It will only add to your stature as a judge. You have the confidence and the respect of all those who know you. Let history be your judge. (APM to Judge Clement Haynsworth, November 24, 1969, Murrah Papers.)

And when a nominee was being sought to fill the vacancy created by the resignation of Abe Fortas, Murrah had a conversation with William P. Clements, a power in Republican politics and later the first GOP governor of Texas since Reconstruction (1979-1983 and 1987-1991), in which he suggested a lawyer from Richmond, Virginia, named Lewis F. Powell, Jr. William P. Clements, Jr., to Peter O'Donnell, November 18, 1970, Murrah Papers; William P. Clements, Jr., to APM, December 6, 1971, Murrah Papers. Harry Blackmun, rather than Powell, received the nod. But a short time later, Powell was named to the supreme court as well.

Murrah himself was mentioned for the supreme court. Two Oregon judges, one federal and one state, told him that they had "decided to run you for the Supreme Court. We didn't intend to ask your opinion or anything." Judge Claude McColloch to APM, August 9, 1949, Murrah Papers. The other judge was George Rossman, a justice of the Supreme Court of Oregon. Murrah answered, "you are very kind, and I am sorry to let you down, but honestly I have no ambition in that direction." APM to Judge Claude McColloch, August 16, 1949, Murrah Papers.

John Caskie Collet was a federal judge in Missouri and a close friend of Harry Truman. When Justice Wiley Ruthledge died, he wrote Truman:

> I know you will not have a scarcity of suggestions of names of men to fill his place, and in all probability the man I have in mind will be suggested to you by others. But even so, I want to make sure that he is not overlooked. You know Judge Murrah of Oklahoma City, a member of the Court of Appeals of the Tenth Circuit. He is as fine a gentleman as you can find and has had a magnificent judicial career. He was appointed United states District Judge at the same time that I was appointed. He was then only 31 or 32 years old; and after serving only a few years, two or three, I think, he was appointed to the Court of Appeals and has had a fine record since. And, believe it or not, he has survived the slings and arrows which ordinarily assail a Circuit Judge and has retained his youth and vigor, while adding a great store of wisdom and experience. And also of great importance, his friends are your friends, and his friends are valuable friends. If you haven't definite plans made about Wiley's successor and want to put in two or three days or a week of listening to a recitation of the qualifications of my friend, Murrah, let me know and I will come out and make my speech in person—and, of course, bring with me a ham and fifty bucks. (Judge John Caskie Collet to President Harry S. Truman, September 15, 1949, Murrah Papers.)

[54]Directory of Oklahoma, 1973, 379.

[55]*Ibid.*, 380.

[56]APM to Josh Lee, November 4, 1942, Murrah Papers.

[57]APM to Cecil Murrah, December 1, 1942, Murrah Papers. Murrah had some very strongly held opinions regarding the war and the coming postwar years:

> I am convinced of one thing, if we are to have an equality of opportunity among men, those who fought the war will have to demand it when they return, otherwise they will not get it because there is a little greedy crowd of international gangsters who care nothing about humankind, and are interested only in the material things of life—they want it all for themselves and they are going to have it if we don't

watch them. They killed our great President, the only President that the people have had since Woodrow Wilson, and one of the few that they have ever had, and they will leave the veterans of this war to sell apples on the street if we don't watch them.

No Tommy, all is not lost, but you can't quit fighting when this war is over if we expect to enthrone the principles of humanity instead of the principles of greed and selfishness. It is up to you and men like you—this country will be what you make it, no better and no worse. (APM to Lt. Thomas S. Ray, April 17, 1945, Murrah Papers.)

[58]For example, see APM to Josh Lee, March 4, 1937, Murrah Papers; APM to Josh Lee, March 18, 1937, Murrah Papers; APM to George McElroy, March 25, 1937, Murrah Papers; APM to George McElroy, March 29, 1937, Murrah Papers; APM to Josh Lee, May 19, 1937, Murrah Papers; APM to George McElroy, July 29, 1937, Murrah Papers; APM to Josh Lee, March 26, 1941, Murrah Papers; APM to Josh Lee, April 24, 1941, Murrah Papers; APM to Lloyd Benefield, April 25,1941, Murrah Papers. Actually, Murrah corresponded with Lee about virtually everything. "I am glad to learn that at last you have realized the necessity of the proper care of your teeth. I have suspected for some time that your teeth were giving you a lot of trouble." APM to Josh Lee, May 19, 1937, Murrah Papers.

[59]Draft in Murrah Papers; Josh Lee to APM, March 9, 1942, with revisions, Murrah Papers; APM to Josh Lee, March 10, 1942, Murrah Papers.

[60]APM to Josh Lee, December 30, 1936, Murrah Papers; APM to Josh Lee, December 31, 1936, Murrah Papers.

[61]APM to Josh Lee, March 10, 1942, Murrah Papers.

[62]APM to Josh Lee, August 11, 1941, Murrah Papers. On another occasion, Murrah wrote, "I raised so much hell that the feeling between Josh and me has been strained for some time, although I am still his friend and always will be." APM to Jim Gowdy, October 24, 1944, Murrah Papers.

[63]APM to Judge John Caskie Collet, March 4, 1948, Murrah Papers; Luther Bohanon to Josh Lee, October 4, 1955, "I want you to know that Judge A.P. Murrah is doing a yeoman's job in his efforts to bring about your reappointment." Murrah Papers.

[64]APM to Charles E. Dierker, September 20, 1973, Murrah Papers.

[65]Program on the occasion of the presentation to the State of Oklahoma of the Portrait of Senator Josh Lee, Oklahoma City, Oklahoma Historical Society, January 25, 1962.

[66]*Daily Oklahoman*, January 30, 1967, 1.

[67]*Ibid.*, 2.

[68]*Ibid.*, August 11, 1967, 2; *ibid.*, August 14, 1967, 1.

[69]APM to Judge Huxman, January 5, 1971, Murrah Papers.

[70]Walter A. Huxman to APM, October 2, 1961, Murrah Papers.

[71]APM to Mrs. Frank W. Farmer, November 19, 1974, Murrah Papers.

[72]*Ibid.*

[73]APM to Mrs. Frank W. Farmer, November 29, 1974, Murrah Papers.

[74]Judge Phillips to APM, December 10, 1948, Murrah Papers.

[75]Judge Phillips to Judge Huxman, April 1, 1950, Murrah Papers.

[76]APM to Judge Bratton, February 22, 1956, Murrah Papers.

[77]APM to Judge Huxman, August 25, 1944, Murrah Papers.

[78]APM to Judge Bratton, December 8, 1954, Murrah Papers.

[79]APM to Judge Pickett, February 13, 1961, Murrah Papers.

[80]APM to Loyd Benefield, January 31, 1941, Murrah Papers.

[81]Judge Huxman to APM, April, 27, 1942, Murrah Papers.

[82]APM to Judge Huxman, August 25, 1944, Murrah Papers.

[83]APM to Judge Huxman, October 2, 1957, Murrah Papers.

[84]Judge Huxman to APM, October 8, 1956, Murrah Papers.

[85]Judge Huxman to APM, May 7, 1954, Murrah Papers.

[86]APM to Judge Huxman, April 12, 1963, Murrah Papers. Judge Williams also gave his robe to Murrah. "I've worn Judge Williams' robe for twenty-three years. Every time I put it on I want to cuss the Republicans and raise heck on the bench. Now, with your robe, I ought to be able to demean myself more like a Judge, and do a better job."

[87]Judge Huxman to APM, January 9, 1971, Murrah Papers. Judge Huxman was not at a loss for views regarding the functioning of the court, even after he ceased sitting entirely. Regarding law clerks, he wrote, "I understand that the judges now have so many law clerks, they do not have time to write opinions, they are busy keeping the law clerks busy. I guess they do still take time to read the opinions before they "Sign them."

[88]APM to Judge Huxman, August 10, 1959, Murrah Papers.

Chapter 7:

[1]In 1948 the name of the Circuit Court of Appeals was changed to United States Court of Appeals for the ______________ Circuit. Act of June 25, 1948, 62 Stat. 870.

[2]Act of August 3, 1949, 63 Stat. 493.

[3]*Congressional Record*, XLV, Part 10, 81st Congress, 1st Session, 13234.

[4]*Ibid.*, Part 11, 14387.

[5]Chase, Krislov, Boyum, and Clark, *Op. Cit.*, 221; *The Richard M. Pickett Family and John C. Pickett Memoirs* (privately printed); Special Memorial Service for The Honorable John C. Pickett, 775 F.2d, LXIX.

[6]Pickett wrote:

> After my confirmation by the United States Senate, I attended a meeting of the Nebraska Bar Association at Omaha. Judge Murrah was one of the principal speakers at that meeting and we had an opportunity to get together and become better acquainted. We left the Omaha meeting and went to Lincoln, Nebraska, to attend a football game between the University of Nebraska and the University of Oklahoma. The game was a disaster for Nebraska, but Murrah was happy, and we had a great time. It was quite obvious that he and I were going to get along quite well. This proved to be true in the years that followed, as we always roomed together at court sessions and other meetings. *(Memoirs*, 50.)

[7]Chase, Krislov, Boyum, and Clark, *Op. Cit.,* 165; In Memoriam for The Honorable David T. Lewis, 787 F.2d, LXXXV.

[8]Chase, Krislov, Boyum and Clark, *Op. Cit.,* 30; Testimonial to The Honorable Jean S. Breitenstein, 732 F.2d, CV; Resolution In Memoriam of The Honorable Jean S. Breitenstein, 832 F.2d, LXXV.

On more than one occasion, Murrah and Breitenstein saw the proper resolution of a case differently. Nevertheless, Murrah's respect for

Breitenstein's judicial ability was great:

> It has been a great pleasure and a privilege to be associated with you on the Court of Appeals, but our professional acquaintance spans a period of more than thirty years. Well do I remember your disappointment when as a trial judge sitting in Denver in 1937 I finally refused to direct a verdict or grant a new trial in a jury case in which you so ably represented a corporate defendant. The jury verdict was $2,000 for a claim of many thousands. That was not the last time you have been vexed with me, but there has never been a time when you did not have my abiding respect and confidence. We have never disagreed when I did not have a lingering, tantalizing reservation that you just might be right.
>
> Now that we have achieved senior status, we can look back over the years together with the satisfaction that we have done our best and only wait to be called for further service in the cause of justice. (APM to Judge Breitenstein, December 24, 1970, Murrah Papers.)

[9]Perhaps Murrah was thinking of Holmes's statement in *Compania General de Tabacos de Filipinos v. Collector of Internal Revenue*, 275 U.S. 87 at 100, 48 S.Ct. 100, at 105, 72 L.Ed. 177 at 183 (1927), that "Taxes are what we pay for civilized society." Morton Salt Company had been before the court of appeals previously on appeal from denial of a preliminary injunction. See chapter six.

[10]*New York Times*, February 15, 1945, 1. Subsequently, his sentence was commuted to life imprisonment. *New York Times*, June 24, 1945, 1.

[11]See *Time*, XLV, January 15, 1945, 21, and February 26, 1945, 20; *Newsweek*, XXV, February 26, 1945, 59.

[12]Murrah once left his glasses in Washington, D.C., and they were mailed to him by an attorney he knew in the justice department. His thank-you note stated, "My glasses arrived at a critical time when I was using a pair borrowed from a very wealthy friend of mine. My secretary accused me of looking at the tax cases purely from the taxpayer's viewpoint. When, however, the glasses safely arrived and I discarded the taxpayer's glasses, I immediately began looking at the tax problems objectively and from the standpoint of revenue only." APM to Helen Goodner, October 17, 1950, Murrah Papers. Murrah applied issue preclusion against the government in Commissioner of *Int. Rev. v. Texas v. Empire Pipe Line Co.*, 176 F.2d 523 (10th Cir. 1949), when the same issue had been actually litigated and necessarily decided in prior litigation between the same parties, and the controlling law and the operative facts were unchanged.

[13]After almost two decades as an appellate judge, Murrah wrote Paul regarding dissents:

> So it is in the profession of the law. In every lawsuit, someone wins and someone loses. And right does not prevail every time. Justice is pure only in theory because it is the product of humankind. Sometimes I dissent from my associates because of my conviction of their errors. I even think that justice is perverted sometimes when my brethren do not agree with me. But then when I think upon the nobility of their minds and the pureness of their hearts, it sometimes occurs to me that even I could be wrong and they could be right, and that after all, justice is not measured by inflexible formulas. It is the product of the

strivings of men toward the eternal goal for which they reach but never quite touch. (APM to Paul Murrah, October 13, 1958, Murrah Papers.)

[14]Earlier, the court had reversed Travis's conviction on the ground that it was error to cross-examine his character witnesses concerning Travis's invocation of the 5th Amendment privilege against compulsory self-incrimination—*Travis v. United States*, 247 F.2d 130 (10th Cir. 1957). Murrah agreed with the holding, but he concurred specially on the basis that it was also error to cross-examine the witness regarding Travis's conviction for contempt of court. A conviction for contempt of court did not bear "any relationship whatsoever to his truth and veracity"—*ibid.*, 136.

[15]When New Mexico decided what Murrah could not believe, he held New Mexico's decision did not violate the equal protection clause of the 14th Amendment. See *Schloss v. Matteucci*, 260 F.2d 16 (10th Cir. 1958), this chapter, *supra*.

[16]In other three-judge cases, Murrah wrote opinions (1) holding that under Oklahoma law an employer did not have a Fourteenth Amendment protected property interest in the state's unemployment compensation fund—*Arrow Design and Engineering Company v. Oklahoma Employment Security Commission*, 151 F.Supp. 844 (W.D. Okl. 1956); (2) holding not unconstitutional on its face an Oklahoma statute requiring owners and operators of natural gas wells to make natural gas from the wells available to certain purchasers at a reasonable price in preference to any other use—*Phillips Petroleum Company v. Jones*, 147 F. Supp. 122 (W.D. Okl. 1955); (3) interpreting the power of the Interstate Commerce Commission to regulate contract motor carriers—*Auto Transports v. United States*, 101 F.Supp. 132 (W.D. Okl. 1951); and (4) holding a claim of malapportionment of the Oklahoma legislature in violation of the Fourteenth Amendment a political question and not cognizable in the federal courts—*Radford v. Gary*, 145 F. Supp. 541 (W.D. Okl. 1956) (asked to predict that the school integration cases indicated the supreme court would take a different approach to apportionment matters, Murrah declined the invitation. "[I]t is not the function of this Court to psychoanalyze the justices of the Supreme Court in order to divine the trend of their decisions"—*ibid.*, 554.

[17]C. Herman Pritchett, *The American Constitution* (New York: McGraw-Hill, 1959), 589.

[18]Dissents were penned in *Champlin Refining Company v. United States*, 95 F. Supp. 170 (W.D. Okl. 1950), and *Gulf Oil Corporation v. Corporation Commission of Oklahoma*, 147 F. Supp. 640 (W.D. Okl. 1956). The cases concerned the correct interpretation of the Interstate Commerce Act and abstention.

The Interstate Commerce Commission ordered Champlin Refining Company (1) to file certain reports under Section 20 of the Interstate Commerce Act, and (2) to file and publish rate schedules under Section 6. A three-judge court held that Champlin did not fall within the class of carriers regulated by the pertinent sections, and to apply Section 6 to Champlin would violate the due process clause of the 5th Amendment. Murrah disagreed. He thought that Sections 20 and 6 clearly applied to Champlin and that the regulations did not take property without due process of law. On appeal the supreme court reversed the judgment as to Section 20, and affirmed it as to Section 6—*United States v. Champlin Refining Company*, 341 U.S. 290, 71 S.Ct. 715, 95 L.Ed. 949 (1951). The decision as to Section 6 was based upon interpretation of the statute, not on constitutional grounds.

Gulf Oil Corporation filed suit challenging an order of the Oklahoma Corporation Commission requiring crude oil purchasers to take the full allowable production from wells unless the commission granted permission to take a lesser amount. The district court dismissed the action on the ground that an adequate state remedy was available and that state proceedings might obviate the necessity of deciding difficult federal constitutional questions.

Murrah argued that this was not an appropriate case for applying the abstention doctrine. Plaintiff was challenging the order as a discriminatory burden on interstate commerce, and because of the great national interest implicated by that claim it was not "in the public interest to send the plaintiff without day"—*ibid.*, 647. Turning to the merits, he concluded that the order unduly and impermissibly burdened interstate commerce, thus warranting injunctive relief. On appeal—*Gulf Oil Corporation v. Corporation Commission of the State of Oklahoma*, 354 U.S. 916, 77 S.Ct. 1377, 1 L.Ed.2d 1432 (1957)—the supreme court affirmed summarily. Justices Frankfurter, Douglas and Brennan would have given the case plenary consideration.

Chapter 8:

[1]See chapter six, note 8. Unlike chief justices of the United States, circuit chief judges are not appointed by the president. The president appoints circuit judges who may then become chief judges by meeting the requisite statutory criteria. Not every circuit judge becomes the chief judge of her or his circuit. And a chief judge may cease being chief judge without creating a circuit judgeship vacancy. Thus when Judge Bratton relinquished the chief judgeship, he did not take senior status, and there was no new appointment to be made to the circuit. By contrast, when Judge Phillips ceased being chief judge, he also took senior status. He was succeeded as chief judge by Judge Bratton and as circuit judge by Judge Lewis.

[2]Act of May 19, 1961, 75 Stat. 80.

[3]Chase, Krislov, Boyum, and Clark, 124; 639 F.2d LXXIX; 896 F.2d LXXXIX.

[4]Chase, Krislov, Boyum, and Clark, 248-249; 897 F.2d LXXXV.

[5]Chase, Krislov, Boyum, and Clark, 123; 436 F.2d, p. 5, see chapter two, note 26.

[6]Act of June 18, 1968, 82 Stat. 184.

[7]William J. Holloway, Sr. was lieutenant governor in 1929 and became governor when Henry Johnston was impeached, convicted, and removed. This is why he served two rather than four years as chief executive.

[8]As circuit chief judge, Murrah became a member of the Judicial Conference of the United States. Established by the Act of September 14, 1922, 42 Stat. 838, and originally called the Conference of Senior Circuit Judges, the conference is akin to the board of directors and policy-making arm of the federal judiciary. The membership has varied over the years. When Murrah became a member, the conference consisted of the chief justice of the United States, the chief judges of the regional circuits, the chief judge of the court of claims, and a district judge from each circuit. Murrah had been active in the work of the conference since the early 1940s (see chapter nine), but he was not a member until he assumed the chief judgeship.

Regarding being chief judge, Murrah wrote Huxman:

This is our first day of court and the Chief Judge is exercising his prerogative to sit it out on the first day. That's about the only change that has been made in procedure here during this regime. The Chief Judge is too busy chief judging to worry about little matters such as law suits. Only this morning at the Council meeting, we went down the line to find that I was the only one with a case unwritten. Whereupon, I promptly assigned it to someone else. Now that's what is called good administration. (APM to Judge Huxman, September 9, 1963, Murrah Papers.)

[9]James C. Otis to APM, August 12, 1971, Murrah Papers. The case was *State v. Curtis*, 290 Minn. 429, 190 N.W.2d 631 (Minn. 1971).

[10]Irving Kaufman to APM, December 18, 1963, Murrah Papers.

[11]18 U.S.C. Section 17. And see *United States v. Denny-Shaffer*, 2 F.3d 999 (10th Cir. 1993), at footnote 1 (per Holloway, Circuit Judge).

[12]This issue has resurfaced in the tenth circuit recently—*Harris v. Champion*, 938 F.2d 1062 (10th Cir. 1991); *Harris v. Champion*, 15 F.3d 1538 (10th Cir. 1994).

[13]Although bankruptcy is a matter within the exclusive jurisdiction of the federal courts, many issues are decided by reference to state law.

[14]The meaning of the 7th Amendment for bankruptcy matters has continued to be the subject of supreme court scrutiny—*Granfinanciera, S. A. v. Nordberg*, 492 U.S. 33, 109 S.Ct. 2782, 106 L.Ed.2d 26 (1989). And the circuits have been speaking to the power of bankruptcy judges to conduct jury trials—In re Clay, 35 F.3d 190 (5th Cir. 1994); *Official Committee of Unsecured Creditors v. Schwartzman* (In re Stansbury Poplar Place, Inc.), 13 F.3d 122 (4th Cir. 1993); *Rafoth v. National Union Fire Insurance Co*; (In re Baker & Getty Financial Services Inc., 954 F.2d 1169 (6th Cir. 1992)); *Kaiser Steel Corp. v. Frates* (In re Kaiser Steel Corp., 911 F.2d 380 (10th Cir. 1990)); In *re United Missouri Bank of Kansas City, N.A.*, 901 F.2d 1449 (8th Cir. 1990); In *re Ben Cooper*, Inc., 896 F.2d 1394 (2nd Cir. 1990). And see Kline and Bryant, "Jury Trials in Bankruptcy Cases (or Esoteric Analysis Through a 'Guessing Marathon')," *Consumer Finance Law Quarterly Report 44* (Winter, 1993), 47.

[15]On *voir dire*, the judge, and sometimes the lawyers, question prospective jurors concerning their qualifications to serve.

[16]The supreme court has recently discovered constitutional constraints on the power to make race- and gender-based peremptory challenges—*Batson v. Kentucky*, 476 U.S. 79, 106 S.Ct. 1712, 90 L.Ed.2d 69 (1986); *Powers v. Ohio*, 499 U.S. 400, 111 S.Ct. 1364, 113 L.Ed.2d 411 (1991); *Edmonson v. Leesville Concrete Co.*, 500 U.S. 614, 111 S.Ct. 2077, 114 L.Ed.2d 660 (1991); *Georgia v. McCollum*, 112 S.Ct. 2348, 120 L.Ed.2d 33 (1992); *J.E.B. v. Alabama* ex rel. T.B., 114 S.Ct. 1419, 128 L.Ed.2d 89 (1994).

[17]The Sentencing Reform Act of 1984 created the United States Sentencing Commission as part of the judicial branch of the United States, and charged it with the promulgation of mandatory sentencing guidelines for the federal courts. In addition to limiting the sentencing judge's discretion, the act authorizes appellate review of sentences for being above or below the defined range, or for being an incorrect application of the guidelines. See 18 U.S.C. 3351 et seq., and *Mistretta v. United States*, 488 U.S. 361, 109 S.Ct. 647, 102 L.Ed.2d 714 (1989).

[18]As usual, there were a number of N.L.R.B. cases. Murrah wrote 19 N.L.R.B. opinions as chief judge: *N.L.R.B. v. International Union Of United Brewery, Etc.*, 272 F.2d 817 (10th Cir. 1959) (enforcement denied); *N.L.R.B. v. Central Oklahoma Milk Producers Ass'n.*, 285 F.2d 495 (10th Cir. 1960) (order enforced); *N.L.R.B. v. Brown-Dunkin Company*, 287 F.2d 17 (10th Cir. 1961) (order enforced); *N.L.R.B. v. McFarland*, 306 F.2d 219 (10th Cir. 1962) (order enforced); *N.L.R.B. v. Bear Brand Roofing, Inc.*, 312 F.2d 616 (10th Cir. 1962) (order enforced); *N.L.R.B. v. Southwestern Porcelain Steel Corporation*, 317 F.2d 527 (10th Cir. 1963) (order enforced); *N.L.R.B. v. Bechtel Corporation*, 328 F.2d 28 (10th Cir. 1964) (order enforced in part); *N.L.R.B. v. Ideal Laundry And Dry Cleaning Co.*, 330 F.2d 712 (10th Cir. 1964) (order vacated); *N.L.R.B. v. Groendyke Transport, Inc.*, 372 F.2d 137 (10th Cir. 1967) (remanded for further consideration); *N.L.R.B. v. Ideal Laundry and Dry Cleaning Co.*, 372 F.2d 307 (10th Cir. 1967) (order enforced); *Betts Baking Co. v. N.L.R.B.*, 380 F.2d 199 (10th Cir. 1967) (order enforced); *N.L.R.B. v. Jordan Bus Co.*, 380 F.2d 219 (10th Cir. 1967) (order enforced); *Furr's, Inc. v. N.L.R.B.*, 381 F.2d 562 (10th Cir. 1967) (order enforced); *N.L.R.B. v. United Nuclear Corporation*, 381 F.2d 972 (10th Cir. 1967) (order enforced); *J.C. Penney Co. v. N.L.R.B.*, 384 F.2d 479 (10th Cir. 1967) (order enforced); *N.L.R.B. v. Midwestern Manufacturing Company*, 388 F.2d 251 (10th Cir. 1968) (order enforced in part; denied in part); *N.L.R.B. v. King Radio Corporation, Inc.*, 416 F.2d 569 (10th Cir. 1969) (order enforced in part; denied in part); *N.L.R.B. v. Groendyke Transport, Inc.*, 417 F.2d 33 (10th Cir. 1969) (N.L.R.B.'s petition for enforcement granted, and company's petition for review denied); *N.L.R.B. v. Gold Spot Dairy, Inc.*, 417 F.2d 761 (10th Cir. 1969) (order enforced in part; denied in part). Murrah wrote no F.L.S.A. opinions as chief judge.

[19]*New York Times*, March 19, 1962, 7; *ibid.*, March 20, 1962, 1; *ibid.*, July 12, 1962, 1.

[20]APM to Senator Robert S. Kerr, July 21. 1961, Murrah Papers.

[21]Judge Orie L. Phillips to Bernard G. Segal, chairman American Bar Association committee on the federal judiciary, June 7, 1961, Murrah Papers; copy sent to Deputy Attorney General Byron White, June 7, 1961, Murrah Papers.

[22]Matthew F. McGuire, department of justice, to Elmer Thomas, October 17, 1939, Box l, Folder 76, Elmer Thomas Papers; Elmer Thomas to Stephen S. Chandler, October 18, 1939, Box 3, Folder 96, *ibid.*

[23]*Tulsa Tribune*, February 18, 1991, 3A.

[24]Chase, Krislov, Boyum, and Clark, 46; biographical information sheet, morgue of Oklahoma Publishing Company, Oklahoma City, Oklahoma, 1961.

[25]Act of May 24, 1940, 54 Stat. 219.

[26]*Tulsa Tribune*, February 18, 1991, 3A; Kellough, "Power and Politics of the Oklahoma Federal Court," *op. cit.*, 196.

[27]See *Sunday Oklahoman*, March 16, 1941, 22A; *Daily Oklahoman*, April 3, 1941, 9; *ibid.*, April 4, 1941, 22; *Sunday Oklahoman*, June 1, 1941, 18A; *Daily Oklahoman*, December 9, 1942, 1; *ibid.*, December 12, 1942, 1; *ibid.*, February 2, 1943, 12. When Lee was defeated for a second term in 1942, there was speculation that he might be appointed to the new western district position. *Ibid.*, November 21, 1942, 1.

[28]The morgue records of the Oklahoma Publishing Company contain this information:

From Reynolds-Robinson attention Oklahoma City desk:

Re story on opposition of Senator Langer to Stephens [sic] for western district judge, wired Monday night: off the record, Langer says he is opposing confirmation on grounds of moral turpitude, that Stephens [sic] paid off a woman to the extent of $3,500, when she threatened to bring charges of rape against him. Would be difficult to use in story until he makes it privileged, which he says he will do by filing report in Senate. At any rate, he refused to give out charges for publication.

[29]*Congressional Record*, LXXXIX, Part 3, 78th Congress, 1st Session, 4143-4144, 4148-4149.

[30]APM to Elmer Thomas, July 2, 1940, Murrah Papers.

[31]*Ibid.*

[32]*Ibid.*

[33]APM to Chief Judge John Biggs, December 30, 1955, Murrah Papers.

[34]As late as 1961, Murrah asked Chandler to serve as chairman of the arrangements committee for the annual meeting of the tenth circuit judicial conference. APM to Judge Stephen S. Chandler, January 18, 1961, Murrah Papers.

[35]*Richard M. Pickett Family and John C. Pickett Memoirs* (Privately printed), 63.

[36]*Ibid.*

[37]For the criminal charges, see the *Oklahoma Journal*, August 26, 1965, 1; *Daily Oklahoman*, August 26, 1965, p. 1; *ibid.*, August 29, 1965, 1; *Daily Oklahoman*, October 22, 1965, 1; *Oklahoma City Times*, October 27, 1965, 1; *Oklahoma Journal*, October 28, 1965, 1; *Daily Oklahoman*, November 10, 1965, 1; *Oklahoma City Times*, November 10, 1965, 1; *Daily Oklahoman*, November 11, 1965, 1; *Oklahoma City Times*, November 11, 1965, 1; *ibid.*, 1; *ibid.*, November 27, 1965, 6.

Chandler's arraignments on the information and the indictment were handled somewhat unusually. In one instance, he went before a justice of the peace who was having dinner at the Twin Hills Golf and Country Club—*Oklahoma City Times*, August 27, 1965, 1. In the other, he appeared before a district judge in chambers at 7:15 a.m.—*ibid.*, November 10, 1965, 1.

The district judge was Jo Ann McInnis. McInnis was elected a district judge for Oklahoma and Canadian counties in 1964 to fill a newly created position. Seeking a full term in 1966, she was defeated.

A few months after leaving office, her former husband, also a lawyer, entered her law office, shot and killed her, and then took his own life. *Daily Oklahoman*, June 20, 1966, 1.

In 1963 Chandler was named defendant in a $10 million malicious prosecution, libel, and slander suit. This litigation was finally resolved in Chandler's favor November 30, 1965 on the ground of judicial immunity—*O'Bryan v. Chandler*, 352 F.2d 987 (10th Cir. 1965). And see *O'Bryan v. Chandler*, 249 F. Supp. 5, (W.D. Okl. 1964).

[38]Copies of the order were filed in the court of appeals December 27, 1965, and in the western district December 28, 1965. Judge Chandler was served personally with a copy of the order by a United States marshal.

[39]As history would have it, Chandler was named in 1965 to the American

Bar Association committee on judicial selection, tenure, and compensation. *Oklahoma City Times*, September 24, 1965, 4.

[40]Judge John C. Pickett to APM, February 1966, Murrah Papers, day of month illegible, but from context it is clear that the letter was written subsequent to February 4, 1966. Because of its importance, the Pickett-Murrah correspondence regarding the Chandler matters is printed in full as an appendix.

[41]*Richard M. Pickett Family and John C. Pickett Memoirs*, 63.

[42]In the years following the supreme court's decision, Judge Chandler was a plaintiff and defendant in civil litigation. See the *Daily Oklahoman*, April 21, 1970, 16; *Oklahoma Journal*, June 27, 1978, 7. He said that he would not comply with a directive of the Judicial Conference of the United States; *Oklahoma City Times*, August 7, 1970, 1. He was removed from a case—*ibid.*, January 10, 1978, 2. And he was reversed and writted when he summarily disbarred the United States attorney and several other government lawyers and ordered them to show cause why they should not be held in contempt—*Burkett v. Chandler*, 505 F.2d 217 (10th Cir. 1974; rehearing denied 1975).

Judge Chandler took senior status on October 20, 1975—395 F. Supp. XXI. He died on April 27, 1989, at 89 years of age—709 F. Supp. XXVII.

[43]Congress also had its say in the Chandler controversy. In February of 1966 Chairman Emanuel Celler of the house judiciary committee announced the appointment of an ad hoc special subcommittee to investigate the happenings in the tenth circuit. The members were Jack Brooks (D-Texas), chairman, William St. Onge (D-Connecticut), and Richard Poff (R-Virginia). The report of the subcommittee attributed the council's actions to "personal and political rivalries of longstanding," concluded that the council had acted "completely beyond [its] legal authority" and said that the participants had "brought discredit" upon their courts—Investigation of Judicial Behavior in the Tenth Circuit United States Court of Appeals, 72 (April 30, 1968). Having made these condemnatory pronouncements, the report was never officially filed. The authors wish to thank William R. Burkett of Oklahoma City, who had his own experiences with Judge Chandler (see note 42), for a copy of the report which was not a report.

[44]See appendix A.

[45]APM to Judge Pickett, February 15, 1966, Murrah Papers, reprinted in appendix A.

Chapter 9:

[1]Rule 1, Federal Rules of Civil Procedure.

[2]28 U.S.C. § 2072

[3]Murrah, "Pre-Trial Procedure—Some Practical Considerations," 26 American Bar Association Journal 592 (July 1940).

[4]APM to United States Senator Edward Martin (R-Pa.), October 27, 1949, Murrah Papers; APM to Judge T. Blake Kennedy, December 19, 1949, Murrah Papers; APM to Judge J. Skelly Wright, November 25, 1949, Murrah Papers; Proceedings of the Fiftieth Annual Meeting of the Nebraska State Bar Association (1949), 340; 4 F.R.D. 35; 11 F.R.D. 3; 13 F.R.D. 207; 14 F.R.D. 417; 20 F.R.D. 485; 26 *American Bar Association Journal* 592 (July 1940); 44 *American Bar Association Journal* 39 (January 1958).

[5]The Nims-Murrah correspondence fills a thick file folder in the Murrah Papers. The

earliest letter is dated August 3, 1949, and the last December 20, 1967, a few days before Nims's death on January 1, 1968. See *New York Times*, January 2, 1968, 37.

[6]Harry Nims to APM, February 28, 1951, Murrah Papers.

[7]Christenson, "When Is A Pre-Trial Conference A 'Pre-Trial Conference'?", 23 F.R.D. 129 at 138 (1958).

[8]APM to William O. Douglas, January 3, 1944, Murrah Papers.

[9]Phil C. Neal and Perry Goldberg, "The Electrical Equipment Antitrust Cases: Novel Judicial Administration," 50 *American Bar Association Journal* 621 at 622 (July 1964).

[10]Neal and Goldberg, op. cit., 623; Murrah was the only appellate judge on the subcommittee. The remaining members were trial judges.

[11]Hearings Before The Subcommittee On Improvements In Judicial Machinery Of The Committee On The Judiciary United States Senate Eighty-Ninth Congress Second Session on S. 3815, page 51 et seq., 1966.

[12]8 *Oklahoma State Bar Journal* 208 at 211, January 1938.

[13]*Ibid.*, 213. Murrah believed that certain segments of society, particularly the entertainment industry, were rightfully chargeable with romanticizing criminal conduct.

JUDGE MURRAH HITS
COMIC BOOK CRIME

NEW YORK, Oct. 13—A U.S. circuit judge told the International Association of Chiefs of Police Wednesday that comic strips, radio and motion pictures were "insidious propaganda machines for crime."

Judge Alfred P. Murrah of Oklahoma City told the association's fifty-fifth annual conference:

"Today, while masquerading under the banner of law and order and the slogan of 'crime doesn't pay,' the comic strip, radio and moving picture have made crime pay stupendous dividends to those who dramatize, exploit and sensationalize crime and criminals.

"We all know that the by-product of the so-called comic strip, the crime radio programs and the gangster movies is murder, rape, suicide and sexual atrocities.

"While these insidious propaganda machines for crime prey upon the impressionable minds of our youth, law enforcement officers are out piecing together the shreds of evidence to solve some heinous crime incubated in the mind of the author of the comic strip, a crime program or a gangster movie." *Daily Oklahoman*, October 14, 1948, 16.

[14]8 *Oklahoma State Bar Journal, op. cit.*, 210.

[15]*Ibid.*, 211.

[16]*Ibid.* 212.

[17]Originally, the NCCD was named the National Probation and Parole Association.

[18]National Council on Crime and Delinquency, Model Sentencing Act, page 6 (1963). See also "Dangerous Offenders Called Dilemma," *Oklahoma Journal*, November 11, 1974, 3; "Model Citizen or Dangerous Criminal? Standards Set Up," *Daily Oklahoman*, March 4, 1966, 7. Karl Menninger, *The Crime Of Punishment* (New York: The Viking Press, 1966), p. 69, wrote, "In 1963, after many years of hard work, collectively and individually, a Model Sentencing Act was brought out by the Advisory Council of Judges of the National Council on Crime and Delinquency. In my opinion the members of this council make up an honor roll of leadership and progress." Murrah's name headed the list. In the introduction, Menninger included Murrah as one of the judges to whom he was "indebted for inspiration, information and friendly counsel"—*ibid.*, IX.

[19]*Ibid.*, 12.

[20]The act did provide a sentence of life imprisonment for murder in the first degree. *Ibid.*, 21.

[21]*Ibid.*, 18.

[22]*Ibid.*

[23]*Ibid.*, 23.

[24]"The sentencing system should not impose restrictions—for example, a minimum term—on a parole board. A minimum term prevents a parole board from releasing a defendant who in its judgment is suitable for release before the expiration of the minimum term of eligibility. The Act does not authorize a minimum term." *Ibid.*, 13.

[25]Alfred P. Murrah, "Prison Or Probation—Which And Why?" 47 *The Journal Of Criminal Law, Criminology and Police Science* 451 at 453 (1956). Murrah's enthusiasm for probation was noted in chapter five. He thought it "the greatest step in the civilized administration of justice since the abolishment of the old prison system"—APM to Lt. G.E. Barnhart, May 1, 1944, Murrah Papers. The philosophical predicate from which the advisory council proceeded was articulated in the Judge's Creed adopted in May 1962.

JUDGE'S CREED

We Believe:

1. That no person is predestined to be a criminal and that delinquency and crime are preventable;

2. That prevention of individual crime can best be accomplished by creating equality of opportunity for every child to experience the influences of a good home. The accomplishment of this simple-sounding objective requires direct attack upon the major social problems of America which adversely affect the home and community life—such as broken homes, alcoholism, mental illness, poverty, unemployment, illiteracy, bad housing, and minority discriminations, no matter what group they may affect; that next to the influence of a good home, the influences of education and religion are most important assets in molding character;

3. That a far higher percentage of criminal offenders can be salvaged for useful citizenship than is now being done; that a judge's responsibility in sentencing is to protect the public and to find an effective plan for rehabilitation of the offender; that rehabilitation and correction of an offender is ordinarily the best means of protecting society;

4. That dangerous offenders do exist—including those in organized crime—who must be segregated from society; but that for most offenders treatment in the community by probation supervision, suspended sentence, and fine, is the most economical and the most effective means of rehabilitation; and that where institutionalization of this group is needed, a relatively short term in a proper institution is most effective;

5. That sentencing to achieve these goals must not be motivated by either sentimental leniency or social revenge;

6. That criminal conspiracies and organized crime, as evidenced nationally and locally by wholesale narcotic and gambling operations, promote disrespect for law and corruption of law enforcement, and that a massive attack upon organized crime is an essential to public safety and decency;

7. That America must remain a nation of free men through maintenance of our system of ordered liberty under law; that to this purpose it is essential to preserve the integrity of its judicial system through continued dedication to the principles of freedom and justice by an unshackled Bench and Bar.

[26]National Council on Crime and Delinquency, "Narcotics Law Violations A Policy Statement," (1964, 1971) 18.

[27]*Ibid.*

[28]*Ibid.*

[29]American Bar Association, *Standards Relating To Pretrial Release* (1968), 1. See also "Bail Inequities Stir Call For Reform," *Daily Oklahoman*, March 16, 1969, 13.

[30]*Ibid.*

[31]*Ibid.*

[32]*Ibid.*, 2.

[33]*Ibid.*

[34]*Ibid.*, 36.

[35]*Ibid.*, 6. The committee considered pretrial detention as a separate issue, but made no recommendations to the American Bar Association in that regard. Not everyone found the proposal worthy of appreciation. Oklahoma County District Attorney Curtis Harris termed the approach a "radical change in law enforcement" which "would virtually do away with jails in this country." "Pre-Trial Release Plan Draws Prosecutor's Fire," *Oklahoma City Times*, July 21, 1969, 4.

[36]American Bar Association, *Standards Relating To Discovery And Procedure Before Trial* (1969).

[37]"Trial Reform Move Urged," *Daily Oklahoman*, June 29, 1969, 8A. Murrah's involvement with the works of the American Bar Association were many. Among other things, he served as a member of the house of delegates, as chairman of the committee on institutes of the section of judicial administration, and as chairman of the section of judicial administration.

[38]Public Law 90-219, 81 Stat. 664. The law is codified as 28 U.S.C. Sections 621-629 inclusive.

[39]When Murrah was selected as director, the elected members did not include a bankruptcy judge. This provision did not become part of the law until 1978. Public Law 95-598, 92 Stat. 2665.

[40]*Daily Oklahoman*, September 29, 1969, 1.

[41]*Ibid.*

[42]APM to Louis F. Oberdorfer, department of justice, October 27, 1964; American Bar Association Standing Committee on Professional Ethics to APM, December 11, 1964; Louis F. Oberdorfer, department of justice to APM, December 23, 1964, Murrah Papers.

[43]*Daily Oklahoman*, November 7, 1969, 21.

[44]Judge Walter Gewin to APM, January 22, 1970, Murrah Papers. When Gewin wrote Murrah, the fifth circuit was Florida, Georgia, Alabama, Mississippi, Louisiana, and Texas. In 1980 congress placed Florida, Georgia, and Alabama in a new circuit, the eleventh, while Mississippi, Louisiana, and Texas became the new fifth circuit. Act of October 14, 1980, *Public Law* 96-452, 94 Stat. 1994.

[45]APM to Judge Gewin, February 4, 1970, Murrah Papers.

[46]Judge William A. McRae, Jr., to APM, February 11, 1970, Murrah Papers.

[47]*Ibid.*

[48]APM to Judge McRae, February 13, 1970, Murrah Papers.

[49]Judge Harold R. Tyler, Jr., to Von Russell Creel, December 2, 1992.

[50]Judge Harold R. Tyler, Jr., to Von Russell Creel, December 18, 1992.

[51]*Ibid.*

[52]*Ibid.*

[53]Rumor has it that Murrah played a major role in the adoption in 1969 by the Judicial

Conference of the United States of a policy regarding nonjudicial income and financial disclosure by federal judges. That this was an exceedingly controversial issue is evidenced by the minutes of the judicial conference. The policy was adopted after "discussion of the report which began at 10 a.m. and continued until 3:30 p.m., with a forty-five minute break for lunch." *Report of the Proceedings of the Special Meeting of the Judicial Conference of the United States*, June 10, 1969, 42. It may be that Murrah's support for adoption of the policy accounts for the opposition to his appointment as center director.

[54]Murrah wrote Judge Lewis, the new chief judge: "Dear Chief Judge: I want you to know that I have sent my letter to the President, effective May 1st, and I want to be the first to address you as Chief Judge.

"A three-judge matter arose here today, and I took the liberty of setting it up. Since it is an obscenity case, I put myself on it." APM to Judge David T. Lewis, April 27, 1970, Murrah Papers.

Murrah was at least partially responsible for Lewis being named to the federal bench. "There are few men in my life—I could name them on one hand—who have had as profound an influence on me personally as Al Murrah. I succeeded him as Chief Judge but, of course, there is no way to replace him. If it had not been for Judge Murrah, I would never have been on the Federal Bench.

"When I was a State Trial Judge and then President of the State Trial Judges Association, he accepted my invitation to speak at a luncheon, and afterward, in talking to me, he said, 'I hear that you are going to leave the bench.' I said, 'Yes, I intend to.' He said, 'Well, why?' And I said, 'My family can't live on the salary which is paid Judges in this State.' He said, 'Judge Lewis, do you like being a Judge?' I said, 'Yes, I do.' He said, 'Then don't give it up. If you love to be a Judge, you will probably always be satisfactory. If you love it enough, you might even be better. But if you love it at all, don't give it up.' So I thought about it, and I had a very serious conversation with my wife about it. Because of what he told me that day in Utah, I decided to stay on the bench and fate has led us to the subsequent careers we have had.

"We all love Judge Murrah. We always have. I wish I could replace you, Chief, but I can't." Remarks of Judge David T. Lewis at the Judicial Conference of the Tenth Circuit, Santa Fe, New Mexico, July 25, 1975, Murrah Papers.

[55]Judge Frank J. Murray to APM, March 30, 1970, Murrah Papers.

[56]Judge George B. Harris to APM, January 7, 1971, Murrah Papers.

[57]APM to Chief Justice Warren E. Burger and other members of the board, August 5, 1970, Murrah Papers.

[58]*Ibid.*

[59]*Ibid.*

[60]Judge Edward J. Devitt to APM, August 10, 1970, Murrah Papers.

[61]Warren E. Burger to APM, March 23, 1972, Murrah Papers.

[62]APM to Warren E. Burger, March 29, 1972, Murrah Papers.

[63]Warren E. Burger to APM, April 3, 1972, Murrah Papers.

[64]*Ibid.*

[65]*Ibid.*

[66]*Ibid.*

[67]APM to Warren E. Burger, March 13, 1974, Murrah Papers.

[68]APM to Warren E. Burger, September 1, 1972, Murrah Papers.

[69]*Ibid.*

[70]APM to Warren E. Burger, December 12, 1974, Murrah Papers. The biography was Leonard Baker, *John Marshall: A Life In The Law* (New York: MacMillan, 1974).

[71]APM to Warren E. Burger, October 21, 1974, Murrah Papers.

[72]Warren E. Burger to APM, January 7, 1973, Murrah Papers (handwritten).

[73]Warren E. Burger to APM, July 28, 1975, Murrah Papers.

[74]APM, to Warren E. Burger, September 24, 1975, Murrah Papers.

[75]APM to Warren E. Burger, January 3, 1974, Murrah Papers.

[76]Warren E. Burger to APM, January 7, 1974, Murrah Papers.

[77]Warren E. Burger to APM, December 18, 1973, Murrah Papers.

[78]Federal Judicial Center, Annual Report 1971; *ibid.*, Annual Report 1972; *ibid.*, Annual Report 1973; *ibid.*, Annual Report 1974.

[79]APM to Judge Walter E. Hoffman, September 6, 1974, Murrah Papers. Judge Hoffman succeeded Murrah as center director. Annual *Report of the Proceedings of the Judicial Conference of the United States* (1974), 43.

[80]APM to Judge Edward J. Devitt, September 16, 1958, Murrah Papers.

[81]*Ibid.*

[82]Annual *Report of the Proceedings of the Judicial Conference of the United States* (1961), 101.

[83]Federal Judicial Center, Annual Report (1973), 20-21.

[84]*Sunday Oklahoman*, August 12, 1973, 8 (Orbit Magazine Section). At first, "Members of the conference scoffed at the idea of making school boys of judges. They thought a robe and gavel made a judge, and that was that."

[85]Judge E. Barrett Prettyman, "The Spirit of the Rules," 28 F.R.D. 51.

[86]APM to Judge Irving R. Kaufman, November 12, 1968, Murrah Papers.

[87]APM to Judge Gus J. Solomon, August 29, 1974, Murrah Papers.

[88]*Ibid.*

[89]APM to Judge James M. Carter, April 24, 1973, Murrah Papers. Judge Joe Estes, United States District Judge for the Northern District of Texas, wrote Carter about attending a program with Murrah at which a lawyer remarked that in recent years federal judges had started acting if they owned their cases and that lawyers could not wait and try cases when they wanted any more. Estes continued, "Al,...as only he could do, invited their attention to the fact that when cases were in the lawyer's office, they belonged to the lawyers and their clients, but when they got to the courthouse, they belonged to the public. He can tell you better than I what he said, but I guarantee that he 'got 'em told.'" Judge Joe Estes to Judge James M. Carter, April 19, 1973, Murrah Papers.

[90]APM to Judge Irving R. Kaufman, October 17, 1974, Murrah Papers.

[91]APM to Judge Gus J. Solomon, August 29, 1974, Murrah Papers.

[92]APM to Judge Walter E. Hoffman, December 30, 1974, Murrah Papers.

[93]Arthur Miller, 807 F. Supp. LXXI.

[94]Judge Edward J. Devitt to APM, March 20, 1975, Murrah Papers.

[95]Judge Hugh H. Bownes to APM, October 28, 1970, Murrah Papers.

[96]Judge Arthur J. Stanley, Jr., to APM, February 5, 1975, Murrah Papers.

[97]*Daily Oklahoman*, December 5, 1970, 1.

[98]*Ibid.*

[99]Murrah was in dissent in senior circuit judge cases only four times. Each appeal presented public law issues.

Colorado Pump & Supply Co. v. Feboc, Inc., 472 F.2d 637 (10th Cir. 1973), held that certain territorial restrictions on economic activity were not per se violative of the Sherman Act, but were subject to the rule of reason. Murrah thought the restraints fell squarely within the per se condemnation of the statute, and that the court was making a "shambles" of supreme court antitrust jurisprudence—*ibid.*, 642.

Upper Pecos Association v. Stans, 452 F.2d 1233 (10th Cir. 1971), involved interpretation and application of the National Environmental Policy Act. The court held, and Murrah disagreed, that the Economic Development Administration was not required to consider the environmental consequences of a grant it made for the construction of a road.

United States v. Marshall, 451 F.2d 372 (9th Cir. 1972), was an appeal from convictions on two criminal contempt citations. The convictions were vacated on the ground that the alleged contumacious conduct was not sufficiently detailed in the citations for informed appellate review. As to the first citation, Murrah, "willing to resolve any doubts against the exercise of the summary contempt power"—*ibid.*, 378—agreed, but he vigorously demurred as to the second. Quoting extensively from the record of the proceedings, he concluded that "the true nature and gravity of the conduct can only be understood, appreciated and judged by reference to the record of the entire proceedings. In no other way can an appellate court be fully informed of the nature and extent of the conduct held contumacious. The contempt is embodied in the incorporated record and it was not error to fail to record the whole record in haec verbae in the certificate"—*ibid.*, 380. Regarding Marshall, Murrah wrote, "I dissented with all the fervor at my command. I am at a loss to know how trial judges are expected to administer criminal justice without the power to maintain order and to protect themselves from scurrilous attacks." APM to Judge Adrian A. Spears, October 24, 1974, Murrah Papers.

The law of search and seizure, an area in which Murrah had written so much of significance, occasioned his dissent in *United States v. Davis*, 456 F.2d 1192 (10th Cir. 1972). Illegally detained by state authorities, the appellant confessed to a federal crime. The confession was admitted at his trial for that offense, and Davis was convicted. On appeal, he contended that it was error to admit the confession. The circuit disagreed and affirmed the conviction. If, as the record showed, the confession was given voluntarily, then its admission in evidence was not error even though Davis was being detained without authority of law when he made it. Murrah would have excluded the confession as the offspring of the illegal detention. It was self-evident that the unlawful police action was solely for the purpose of obtaining evidence of the federal crime. Affirming a conviction resting on the fruit of the poisonous tree was a subverting of constitutional imperatives: "For this Court to conclude that Davis' detention was completely unjustified on the one hand, and, at the same time, admit evidence which was the target and goal of that unlawful detention has the effect of 'legitimatizing the conduct which produced the evidence' and making the Court 'party to lawless invasions of the constitutional rights of citizens by permitting unhindered governmental use of the fruit of such invasions.'"—*ibid.*, 1197.

[100]28 U.S.C. section 2255 authorizes the movant to seek vacation of his conviction in the sentencing court. The purpose of the section is to provide a remedy in the sentencing court exactly commensurate with that available by habeas corpus in the district court of the district where the petitioner is confined—*Hill v. United States*, 368 U.S. 424, 82 S.Ct. 468, 7 L.Ed.2d 417 (1962).

[101]Murrah strongly approved of the supreme court's initial school prayer decision—*Engel v. Vitale*, 370 U.S. 421; 82 S.Ct. 124; 8 L.Ed.2d 601 (1962). He even took the somewhat unusual step of making public statements in support of the ruling—Speech before the Oklahoma City Y.W.C.A. (1964), Murrah Papers.

The district judge in this case, Willis W. Ritter, was a person of great intellect. He held an S.J.D. from Harvard, and he had been in the groves of academe, private practice, and government service before his appointment to the bench. See Chase, Krislov, Boyum, and Clark, *op. cit.*, 235.

However, certain aspects of his temperament kept him in hot water with the circuit. See, for example, *United States v. Hatahley*, 257 F.2d 920 (10th Cir. 1958); 273 F.2d 30 (10th Cir. 1959). Indeed, if it had not been for Judge Chandler, Ritter would probably be the most famous—or infamous—district judge in the circuit's history. Judge Pickett, who had to deal with both Chandler and Ritter, made a priceless comment: "He was always very cordial and good company. On the bench, however, he had a reputation of being a tyrant. His twenty-five years as a college professor may have had something to do with this." *The Richard M. Pickett Family and John C. Pickett Memoirs, op. cit.*, 65.

[102]"Oath of Office of United States Judges." 28 U.S.C. section 453. This language has been part of the oath of office for Article III judges since the founding of the Republic. See Section 8 of the Judiciary Act of 1789.

[103]*In re* Washington, 544 F.2d 203 (5th Cir. 1976) (opinion by Judge John R. Brown concurring in dissent at 544 F.2d 213).

Judge Brown was a member of the Cowan court, and he concurred in Murrah's opinion. Further reflection persuaded him that Rule 48 "does not loose the Judge to weigh what the so-called public interest is, or whether it is satisfied." This change of thought did not prevent him from considering Cowan one of Murrah's "major Judicial contributions."

For Murrah, opinion writing was an art form, a creative process: "In writing an opinion, I always find that I have given a little sliver of my life." APM to Gary Pavela, July 8, 1974, Murrah Papers.

Opinion writing was not merely the explaining of a decision. It was an integral part of making the decision: "Your note found me in the midst of an opinion, the answer to which defies me. As you know, little by little, word by word, the answer finally emerges." APM to Gary Pavela, December 20, 1974, Murrah Papers.

"I am to write two opinions, in which I am sure the court will be divided, and to be perfectly frank I am not sure of the answer. As Justice Holmes said, I could write it about as well on one side as the other." APM to Judge Walter A. Huxman, December 28, 1943, Murrah Papers.

And opinion writing was a never-ending quest for the unattainable—perfection: "To be perfectly truthful, I have never written an opinion with which I was completely happy. Making a decision is one thing, and giving the reason therefor is quite another." APM to Judge Claude McColloch, April 12, 1948, Murrah Papers.

Over the years Murrah developed a well-defined way of writing opinions. Dissents, concurrences and some opinions for the court were written without participation of the law clerk. In other opinions for the court, the law clerk, after oral argument, would take the briefs and prepare an opinion from "This appeal challenges..." to "Therefore, the judgment is ...." Murrah and the clerk would then sit across from one another at the conference table with briefs, records, reports, and a dictionary. They would go over each phrase, sentence, paragraph, and page revising, reorganizing, and rewriting. Sometimes pages would be done in a brief time. On other occasions, hours would be spent writing one sentence. What was amazing was that when the finished product was ready to submit to other members of the panel, it was pure Murrah from beginning to end—pure Murrah in style, in analysis and in result.

Murrah constantly emphasized to his clerk that they were not deciding cases in the days of Jarndyce and Jarndyce. The litigants were entitled to a decision before they expired from old age. Research carefully and think thoughtfully, but then there is a time when one must take pen in hand and put one little word after another.

Chapter 10:

[1]The inscription read "George Washington Murrah 1866-1920/Honorable Memory Is A Just Reward For A Life Of Industry And Fidelity." APM to Roberts Marble Works, Ballground, Georgia, May 13, 1940, Murrah Papers.

[2]"I think it certainly gives a side of national and international affairs which you don't get elsewhere, and if you don't get both sides, you are apt to get warped when our nerves are on edge." APM to Cecil Murrah, January 19, 1945, Murrah Papers.

[3]Cecil Murrah to APM, July 13, 1945, Murrah Papers.

[4]APM to George Murrah, September 30, 1954; APM to George Murrah, July 20, 1964, Murrah Papers.

[5]APM to George Murrah, September 30, 1954, Murrah Papers.

[6]*Ibid.*

[7]*Ibid.*

[8]APM to Calvin Brock, January 11, 1971, Murrah Papers.

[9]John P. Frank has had an outstanding career as an academician, legal historian, and practicing attorney. He is senior partner in one of Arizona's largest firms.

[10]APM to John Frank, September 8, 1966, Murrah Papers.

[11]APM to Maxine McClintock, January 14, 1974, Murrah Papers.

[12]APM to Ann Murrah, July 5, 1946, Murrah Papers.

[13]APM to Paul Murrah. October 22, 1954, Murrah Papers.

[14]APM to Paul Murrah, June 27, 1945, Murrah Papers.

[15]APM to Judge John Caskie Collet, June 12, 1953, Murrah Papers.

[16]APM to Paul Murrah, September 22, 1953, Murrah Papers.

[17]APM to Paul Murrah, July 27, 1955, Murrah Papers.

[18]Regarding the place of physics in the great scheme of things, Murrah wrote:

> Now son, don't worry a minute about your low grade in physics—you never intended to be a physicist in the first place. That is a field for people who don't have sense enough to do anything else, those who prefer to deal with inanimate things. The Murrahs like people, they like the warmth of friendship, of conversation and the inspiration that comes from association. Some people have an aptitude for science, and they are not fit for anything else. I never expected you to be a physicist or even a scientist, in fact I hoped that you would not. I do think, however, that you should master the course before you finally leave it, just to say that you never left a job undone. (APM to Paul Murrah, February 11, 1952, Murrah Papers.)

[19]"Frankly, I am not certain whether you really want to be a lawyer, and surely hope you will make sure about it before you 'beam' your academic education in that direction. The most unhappy person in the world is the misfit, socially or in business." APM to Paul Murrah, April 15, 1952, Murrah Papers.

[20]*Ibid.*

[21]APM to Paul Murrah, April 3, 1957, Murrah Papers. Paul did. He served as Editor-in-Chief of the *Oklahoma Law Review*, and graduated Order of the Coif.

[22]APM to Ann Murrah, March 2, 1953, Murrah Papers.

[23]*University of Colorado Bulletin*, 1951 Summer Quarter, School of Law. Murrah not only taught at the University of Colorado that summer, he also learned. The course which met before Murrah's and in the same classroom was trusts, taught by Professor Austin Wakeman Scott, Sr. Scott was a leading American authority on the subject, and many days Murrah would sit in the class and listen to Scott before he taught his own course.

[24]The Harper trustee fee did not start until 1959.

[25]APM to Judge Carl Hatch, February 9, 1953, Murrah Papers.

[26]APM to Paul Murrah, October 13, 1958, Murrah Papers.

[27]Interview with Alonzo Jernigan, March 30, 1992.

[28]*Ibid.*

[29]*Ibid.* "I would say he lived a Christian life during the week. He wasn't no two face. One face only. Lotta folks get up in the world like that and put the foot on the little man's head. Judge Murrah didn't do it."

Jernigan was respectful of but not intimidated by the federal judiciary. One clerk remembers Jernigan coming into his office, standing by the window for a few moments, and then asking, "Richard, what are we going to do about these federal judges letting all these criminals out of jail?" That was, of course, the last question in the world the clerk wanted to answer. Richard E. Coulson to Von Russell Creel, December 9, 1994.

[30]APM to Paul Murrah, February 17, 1959, Murrah Papers.

[31]APM to Sue Murrah, February 15, 1960, Murrah Papers.

[32]APM to Ann Murrah, undated, Murrah Papers.

[33]APM to J.D. Lasater, December 18, 1945, Murrah Papers.

[34]APM to Paul Murrah, November 1, 1971, Murrah Papers.

[35]Letter from Ann Murrah to authors.

[36]APM to Paul Murrah, July 8, 1947, Murrah Papers.

[37]Letter from Ann Murrah to authors.

[38]*Ibid.*

[39]*Ibid.*

[40]*Ibid.* Ann turned to poetry to express her feelings about her mother and father:

HER HIGHNESS

She was born the third of May
The piano she likes to play
Her humor is always gay

She is the prettiest thing you ever did see
She is the baby of her family

She always wears a smile
They say she was a beautiful child

She was a school teacher
In her face there is beauty in every feature
And she is kind to every single creature

She never complains a word
And delights at a pretty bird

She was a Red Cross Staff Aid
Two holes in one she has made
Her eyes are a hazel shade

Of Girl Scouts she was Commissioner
And she appreciates the air conditioner

For years she has exercised at Beulah Noyes
In all things she does she has charm and poise
Bet she was admired by all the boys

She plays the violin too
Her favorite colors are yellow and blue

There isn't anything she can't knit or sew
She belongs to P. E. 0.
And is a very good model in a style show

She never thinks of her self and is so gracious and sweet

Her spaghetti supreme is quite a treat

She loves all animals—Maybe dogs the best
Her hands are never at rest
At O.U. she wore the Alpha Gam crest

She likes to bask in the sun
And thinks gin rummy is fun

The wind she doesn't like
But likes to ride a bike
Go skating or take a hike

Good apple butter and strawberry preserves she can fix
And in bridge she knows all the tricks

Her measurements never change
And she looks good at the driving range

Housework she's not crazy about
In the Art Center she has worked a great amount
Her love for flowers there is no doubt

She was a Rotary Ann
And a member of the DAR clan

She is always so busy
But never gets in a tizzy
Her activities would make you dizzy

She enjoys dancing and playing Mah Jong
And likes to whistle a song

She is known as "Babe" by all her friends
Many parties she attends

Her portrait an artist must paint
Would surely be of Agnes the Saint.

YOUR HONOR

He is a rather tall, slim feller
And a wonderful story teller

He likes his face slightly tan
He is known throughout the land
And everyone thinks he's grand

He remembers peoples' faces
He has tried a lot of cases
And has cattle in three different places

He enjoys fishing and hunting game
And is in the Oklahoma Hall of Fame
He has a most famous name

He spells his name M-U-R (a couple of times) A-H
And carries an attache case

Many call him Fish
But ice cream is his favorite dish

He is kinda like a traveling preacher
And for years has been a Sunday school teacher

He will talk for two hours plus
He used to say to us
"Clean your plate," "Take your vitamin pill"
"Babe, if you don't spank them I will"

All this is good advice
And he's really very nice

He has big, blue eyes
And his legs are on the long size
But only Odessa can select his ties

He is really quite a tease
But can't remember his keys

He was the Beaux Arts King
And used to wear a big black ring
I wonder what happened to the thing

In his clothes he takes pride
He walks with an enthusiastic stride
And prefers food that isn't fried

He had golden hair when a lad
And likes to ask "Well are ya mad?"
Many rose bushes he has had

He is very good lookin
But is particular about the cookin
And there is no award he hasn't tooken

He is in the chief Judge's seat
It has been said he has small feet
And about politics he is discreet

He married my mother
Sure glad he finally caught her
Because I like being the Judge's Daughter

He often says "You wanna fight?"
This man I love with all my might
And a poem I did write
Tho it is a wee bit trite.

[41]Letter from Sue Murrah Wadley to authors, March 25, 1993. Charles Baker remembers Murrah "telling me on one occasion that he had no plans to leave his children any substantial inheritance beyond a good education and an unblemished family name." Charles Baker to Von Russell Creel, March 8, 1994.

[42]Paul Murrah to APM, October 25, 1971, Murrah Papers.

[43]APM to Hugh B. Woodward, June 17, 1954, Murrah Papers.

[44]APM to Chief Justice Arthur Vanderbilt, April 28, 1952, Murrah Papers.

[45]*Amarillo Daily News*, October 18, 1957, 39.

[46]APM to Paul Murrah, November 21, 1952, Murrah Papers.

[47]APM to R.G. Miller, August 20, 1952, Murrah Papers.

[48]APM to James Hamill, April 22, 1946, Murrah Papers.
[49]E.K. Gaylord to APM, January 3, 1955, Murrah Papers.
[50]Rabbi Israel Chodos to APM, February 18, 1955, Murrah Papers.
[51]*A History Crown Heights United Methodist Church 1929-1979*, 4.
[52]APM to Mrs. Lee K. Emenhiser, June 15, 1953, Murrah Papers.
[53]APM to Paul Murrah, April 19, 1954, Murrah Papers.
[54]APM to Standley Murrah, November 6, 1972, Murrah Papers.
[55]Charles Johnson to APM, July 20, 1972, Murrah Papers.
[56]APM to Ann Murrah Shaw, undated, Murrah Papers.
[57]APM to Johnston Murray, August 23, 1973, Murrah Papers.
[58]APM to Mrs. W.N. Rucker, August 31, 1953, Murrah Papers. One thing that Murrah could not bring himself to do, however, was take the pulpit, for "that is the highest and most exalted place on Earth." APM to Reverend Ben S. Sturdivant, undated but responding to letter dated April 20, 1954, Murrah Papers.
[59]*Daily Oklahoman*, February 10, 1957, 10A.
[60]*Ibid.*, March, 1957, 5.
[61]*Ibid.*
[62]APM to Paul Murrah, March 9, 1955, Murrah Papers.
[63]APM to L.I. Murphree, March 25, 1970, Murrah Papers.
[64]APM to B.S. Harvey, May 29, 1941, Murrah Papers.
[65]APM to Civil Service Commission Board of Appeals, February 14, 1975, Murrah Papers.
[66]APM to Donna Wilson, October 1, 1972, Murrah Papers.
[67]William J. Robinson to APM, January 22, 1974, Murrah Papers.
[68]APM to Donald P. MacDonald, August 8, 1972; APM to Joseph J. McCain, Jr., May 4, 1970; "Dear 'Lawyer': Thank you very much. Thank you very much indeed." Murrah Papers.
[69]Guglielmo Provenzano to APM, February 3, 1942, Murrah Papers.
[70]APM to Guglielmo Provenzano, March 3, 1942, Murrah Papers.
[71]Parsons v. State, 271 S.W.2d 643 (Tex. Cr. 1953).
[72]Mary Jean Parsons to APM, September 9, 1956, Murrah Papers.
[73]*Ibid.*
[74]APM to Mary Jean Parsons, September 12, 1956, Murrah Papers.
[75]Frank Hunt to APM, November 21, 1943, Murrah Papers.
[76]APM to Frank Hunt, December 2, 1943, Murrah Papers.

Chapter 11:

[1]*Ecclesiastes*, Chapter 3, Verses 1 and 2.
[2]*Oklahoma City Advertiser* (Oklahoma City), March 19, 1954, 1.
[3]John F. Cailloux to APM, February 27, 1953, Murrah Papers.
[4]APM to John F. Cailloux, March 2, 1953, Murrah Papers.
[5]"Is Life Worth Living?", *op. cit.*, note 2.
[6]*Ibid.*
[7]*Ibid.*
[8]*Daily Oklahoman*, May 15, 1972, 21.
[9]Letter to the *Oklahoma City Times*, April 12, 1944, Murrah Papers.
[10]*Ibid.*
[11]*Ibid.*
[12]Murrah wrote Danforth that reading his book "kindled new fires and opened new vistas. It gave me renewed energy and vigor for the problems that

lie ahead." APM to William H. Danforth, November 17, 1954, Murrah Papers.

[13]APM to Guy H. James, October 18, 1956, Murrah Papers. "If it does you and Paul half as much good as it did for me, I shall be very happy indeed."

[14]Remarks of Professor Daniel G. Gibbens, In Memoriam Proceedings for Judge Alfred P. Murrah, 574 F.2d, 1 at 14-15. See also note 26, chapter 2.

[15]See chapter four.

[16]*Oklahoma State Bar Journal*, VIII, Number 10 (January 1938), 209.

[17]The information concerning Murrah's health in his last years was supplied by Mrs. Betty Pate, his secretary during that time. Betty Pate to Von Russell Creel.

[18]Judge James M. Carter to APM, May 8, 1974, Murrah Papers.

[19]APM to Judge James M. Carter, May 14, 1974, Murrah Papers.

[20]APM to Chief Judge David T. Lewis, September 8, 1975, Murrah Papers. Murrah's relationship with the law and judging was a love affair which grew in passion and intensity each passing day: "Unless you are dedicated to the law and willing to give it all you have, you can't make a lawyer. After nearly fifty years of the law, it is as new and challenging to me as the first day I entered law school. I worked Saturday until four o'clock and enjoyed every minute of it." APM to Kem Benefield. December 23, 1974, Murrah Papers.

[21]Executive Order, November 1, 1975, Office of the Secretary of State, Oklahoma City, Oklahoma.

[22]Sermon text, Murrah Papers.

[23]*Ibid.*

[24]*New York Times*, November 1, 1975, 32.

[25]*Tuttle Times*, November 13, 1975, 1. The Tuttle story was written by Mrs. Irma Gannaway, wife of the pharmacy owner (see chapter one) and the lady who had given Murrah the book of poetry by Josh Lee (see chapter four).

[26]*Ibid.*

[27]574 F.2d, 1 at 18. See chapter 2, note 26. Shortly before his death, Murrah's family presented his portrait to his court in a ceremony at which Justice White was the principal speaker—Transcript of Presentation of Portrait of Judge A.P. Murrah to the United States Court of Appeals for the Tenth Circuit, Murrah Papers. The portrait hangs in the court of appeals courtroom in the federal courthouse in Oklahoma City. In 1945 a different portrait of Murrah was painted by Dr. Joseph Sigall, an internationally known artist whose works included kings and presidents. Famous in life, Sigall was famous in death as well, for his passing was shrouded in controversy—*Tulsa Tribune*, September 18, 1953, l; *Tulsa World*, November 5, 1953, 1. There is a mystery concerning this Murrah portrait for no one seems to know where it is.

[28]Quoted in sermon text, *op. cit.*, note 20.

[29]Commencement address, Central State University, May 14, 1972, reprinted in the *Daily Oklahoman*, May 15, 1972, 21.

[30]*Ibid.*

[31]*Daily Oklahoman*, November 3, 1975, 8.

[32]Judge Theodore Roosevelt Dalton to APM, July 5, 1974, Murrah Papers.

[33]Justice Paul Reardon to the *Oklahoma City Times*, November 25, 1975, 24.

[34]"Is life worth living?" *Oklahoma City Advertiser*, note 2.

Appendix Notes:

[1]Murrah called Pickett "Calhoun."

[2]Judge Jean S. Breitenstein.

[3]Odessa James was Murrah's secretary.

[4]Alonzo Jernigan was Murrah's law librarian. See also chapter ten.

[5]Commencement address, John Marshall High School, Oklahoma City, Oklahoma, June 1, 1961.

[6]Delivered before the Judge Advocate General's School, Charlottesville, Virginia, August 1, 1972.

[7]Commencement address, William Mitchell College of Law, June 14, 1965. This speech was Murrah's most frequently delivered address.

[8]Delivered before the Washington County Bar Association, Bartlesville, Oklahoma, November 11, 1965.

[9]James K. Logan was dean of the University of Kansas Law School. A former law clerk for Judge Huxman, he was appointed to the tenth circuit in 1977.

[10]In a speech at the University of Miami Law School, Murrah told his audience, "My ancestors sleep in a rebel's grave. They died for slavery as a way of life. Thank God they died in vain." "By What Authority," Law Day University of Miami Law School, May 1, 1969.

[11]Anthony Lewis, *Gideon's Trumpet* (Random House, 1964).

[12]Abe Fortas.

[13]Alpheus Thomas Mason, *Harlan Fiske Stone: Pillar of the Law* (The Viking Press, 1956).

INDEX